THE RELIGIOUS DIMENSION

New Directions in Quantitative Research

THE RELIGIOUS DIMENSION

New Directions in Quantitative Research

Edited by

ROBERT WUTHNOW

Department of Sociology
Princeton University
Princeton, New Jersey

ACADEMIC PRESS   New York   San Francisco   London
A Subsidiary of Harcourt Brace Jovanovich, Publishers

ACADEMIC PRESS, INC.
111 Fifth Avenue, New York, New York 10003

United Kingdom Edition published by
ACADEMIC PRESS, INC. (LONDON) LTD.
24/28 Oval Road, London NW1   7DX

Library of Congress Cataloging in Publication Data

Main entry under title:

The Religious dimension.

    Includes bibliographies and index.
    1. Religion and sociology——Addresses, essays,
lectures. I. Wuthnow, Robert.
BL60.R44   301.5'8   79–6948
ISBN 0–12–766050–X

PRINTED IN THE UNITED STATES OF AMERICA

79 80 81 82   9 8 7 6 5 4 3 2 1

Contents

Chapter 6

Status Inconsistency and Religious Commitment   **135**

M. S. SASAKI

Chapter 7

The Religious Factor and Delinquency: Another Look at the Hellfire Hypotheses   **157**

GARY F. JENSEN and MAYNARD L. ERICKSON

Chapter 8

Religious Commitment, Affiliation, and Marriage Dissolution   **179**

JAMES McCARTHY

Chapter 9

Religious Affiliation and Socioeconomic Achievement   **199**

JAMES A. RICCIO

Part III

NEW DIRECTIONS IN RESEARCH ON RELIGION AND SOCIAL CHANGE

Chapter 10

The Blending of Catholic Reproductive Behavior   231

CHARLES F. WESTOFF

Chapter 11

Social Change and Commitment to the Work Ethic   241

LARRY BLACKWOOD

Chapter 12

The Effects of Residential Migration on Church Attendance in the United States   257

ROBERT WUTHNOW and KEVIN CHRISTIANO

Chapter 16

Spirituals, Jazz, Blues, and Soul Music: The Role of Elaborated and Restricted Codes in the Maintenance of Social Solidarity

333

ALBERT BERGESEN

Chapter 17

Rational Exchange and Individualism: Revival Religion in the U.S., 1870–1890

351

GEORGE M. THOMAS

Index

List of Contributors

Numbers in parentheses indicate the pages on which the authors' contributions begin.

Albert Bergesen (277, 333), Department of Sociology, University of Arizona, Tucson, Arizona 85721

Larry Blackwood* (241), Department of Agricultural Economics, University of Arizona, Tucson, Arizona 85721

Kevin Christiano (257), Department of Sociology, Princeton University, Princeton, New Jersey 08540

Maynard L. Erickson (157), Department of Sociology, University of Arizona, Tucson, Arizona 85721

Charles Y. Glock (47, 69), Department of Sociology, University of California, Berkeley, Berkeley, California 94720

Andrew M. Greeley (113), Department of Sociology, University of Arizona, Tucson, Arizona 85721

Phillip E. Hammond (311), Department of Religious Studies, University of California, Santa Barbara, Santa Barbara, California 93106

Gary F. Jensen (157), Department of Sociology, University of Arizona, Tucson, Arizona 85721

James McCarthy (179), Office of Population Research, Princeton University, Princeton, New Jersey 08540

Thomas Piazza (69), Survey Research Center, University of California, Berkeley, Berkeley, California 94720

* Present address: 3237 E. 72nd Avenue, Anchorage, Alaska 99507.

xi

James A. Riccio (199), Department of Sociology, Princeton University, Princeton, New Jersey 08540

Wade Clark Roof (17), Department of Sociology, University of Massachusetts, Amherst, Massachusetts 01002

M. S. Sasaki (135), Department of Sociology, The University of Michigan, Ann Arbor, Michigan 48109

John H. Simpson (299), Department of Sociology, Erindale College, University of Toronto, Mississauga, Ontario L5L 1C6 Canada

George M. Thomas (351), Department of Sociology, Stanford University, Stanford, California 94305

Mark Warr (277), Department of Sociology, University of Arizona, Tucson, Arizona 85721

Michael R. Welch (93), Department of Sociology, Florida Atlantic University, Boca Raton, Florida 33431

Charles F. Westoff (231), Office of Population Research, Princeton University, Princeton, New Jersey 08540

Kirk R. Williams (311), Department of Sociology, Memphis State University, Memphis, Tennessee 38152

Robert Wuthnow (1, 47, 257), Department of Sociology, Princeton University, Princeton, New Jersey 08540

Preface

The chapters in this volume, none of which have been previously published, reflect the growing interest in applying systematic, quantitative research techniques to the study of modern religion. As this interest has grown, primarily over the past decade, several new directions have come increasingly to the forefront as foci of research. These include: (1) the search for more sophisticated measures of religious commitment and its alternatives, (2) more rigorous investigations of the social correlates of religious commitment, (3) efforts to explore the relationship between trends in religious commitment and trends in other social configurations, and (4) the application of quantitative methods to historical and comparative studies of religion. The chapters collectively represent an effort to extend the research that has been developing along each of these lines by summarizing and critiquing areas of research where a considerable body of literature has already been produced, by replicating and extending earlier research contributions, and by bringing quantitative data to bear on problems that have previously been unexplored in this manner.

In the sociology of religion, as in the social sciences more generally, the past decade has witnessed a tremendous expansion of activity. If the 1960s can be characterized as a period of exploration in which many of the ground-breaking studies using quantitative methods and large bodies of data were initiated, the 1970s will probably be remembered as a period of intensification in which quantitative research became firmly institutionalized, the number of practitioners expanded, and the volume of research mushroomed. It is too early to determine what the most significant contributions of this research will be. But, in general terms, it is clear that progress has been made in the conceptualization of empirically researchable problems and in the development and application of statistical techniques to those problems. Some progress has also been made in bridging the (still considerable) gap that has existed between theoretical and empirical approaches to the study of religion.

Both the magnitude of research that has been conducted over the past decade and the fact that much of this research has of necessity been exploratory and has focused on widely disparate substantive problems has made it difficult to obtain a clear sense of what the most productive lines of inquiry in the quantitative study of religion have been or what they will be in the future. Still, it behooves practitioners working in subfields of inquiry to periodically take stock of what is happening and to propose some orienting simplifications as guides for further research, even if these simplifications are met with more disagreement than agreement. It was in that spirit that the present volume was initiated.

The purpose of the volume is to provide for the interested layman as well as for the professional student of religion a picture of the "state of the art" in the quantitative study of religion as it exists at the end of the 1970s, not in the usual sense of a literature survey or compendium of research findings but as a sampling of the kinds of work currently being pursued. The chapters in combination illustrate both the problems to which quantitative methods are being applied and the methods and concepts being used to address these problems.

In addition to being an attempt to provide an overview of the quantitative study of religion, and perhaps more importantly, this volume is intended as a guide and stimulus for further research. The "new directions" around which the book is organized will quickly be recognized as not having been discovered by the present contributors or the editor. They are developments that have grown gradually as foci of interest and they are ones that seem likely to continue as fruitful avenues of research. In commissioning chapters for this volume, the primary consideration was that they should address or illustrate problems of this nature that seemed to hold promise for future research. By collecting a number of such studies together in a single volume, it was hoped that these directions for further investigation would be highlighted and sharpened in addition to the specific contributions of the individual chapters.

I particularly wish to express my gratitude to the contributors for their patience with my editorial suggestions and for far improving on the norms of quality and punctuality about which editors so frequently complain. I also wish to thank those persons on the staff at Academic Press, who provided unfailing encouragement and many useful suggestions during the course of preparing the volume. It was through some early conversations with them that the ideas for this volume first began to take form.

The absence of a dedication page is not an oversight, but the result of some frustration with the standard form. A volume celebrating "new directions" should somehow commemorate all those who have paved the way. We have chosen to let bibliography and citation be our commemoration.

Introduction

ROBERT WUTHNOW

Research on religion using quantitative data and methods can be found prior to World War II and even before the turn of the present century. But it has been only since the late 1950s and early 1960s that work of this sort has multiplied to a significant degree. Gerhard Lenski's *The Religious Factor,* which is now regarded as a pioneering work in the quantitative study of religion, was first published in 1961. Thus, when we speak of quantitative religious research, we are speaking of a relatively recent academic development.

The research conducted in the late 1950s and 1960s contributed importantly to the understanding of contemporary religion. We can briefly catalog some of the contributions of this research:

1. It demonstrated that meaningful information on religious beliefs and practices could be obtained in quantitatively analyzable form, and it developed refined concepts and measurements of such information.
2. It produced a descriptive social profile of American religion in terms of denomination, social class, race, age, and other conventional social classifications.

The Religious Dimension:
New Directions in Quantitative Research

3. It analyzed the relationship between religious commitment and a variety of other attitudes and activities, including political orientation, prejudice, morality, secular values, child rearing habits, and personal life style.
4. It provided empirical tests for a number of long-standing theories in the sociology of religion, such as theories about the relationship between Protestantism and worldly success, the role of economic forces in church–sect distinctions, and the effects of conservative religion on politics.
5. It afforded some quantitative comparisons of cross-cultural differences in religion.
6. It led to the establishment of several journals and professional societies concerned with promoting the systematic investigation of religious phenomena.

In the past decade we have witnessed a continuation and expansion of the quantitative religious research that was begun in the 1960s. As greater numbers of students have embarked on careers in the social sciences in general, the number of researchers interested in the quantitative study of religion has also increased. This interest has also been stimulated by an unrest in American values that erupted during the late 1960s and fostered widespread experimentation with new religious movements. And the churches have continued actively to sponsor empirical research to assess the beliefs and practices of their members.

Despite certain continuities, however, the research conducted in recent years can be differentiated from that done in the 1960s. It is convenient and perhaps not too simplistic to think of the period since, about 1970 as a watershed in the quantitative study of religion.

One of the important differences between earlier and more recent quantitative research has to do with the concept of religion itself. Whereas research done in the 1960s concentrated primarily on institutionalized expressions of religion (e.g., religious preference, church attendance, doctrinal orthodoxy, biblical knowledge), the research of the 1970s has been more responsive to broader conceptualizations of religion. Increasingly, attention has been paid to ultimate concerns, questions of meaning and purpose, and to the idea of studying both private and noninstitutional ways of coping with these questions and concerns. In part, this reorientation has come about because in the course of earlier research it was discovered that sizable segments of the population were, by conventional definitions, without religious commitment. New concepts of religion in the theoretical literature—"invisible religion," "civil religion," "sacred canopies," and so forth—also contributed to this reorientation, as did the growth of nontraditional religious movements. The net result of these developments is that one of the most active directions of empirical research in recent years has been toward the measurement and comparison of alternative conceptualizations of religious commitment.

A second direction currently discernible in the study of religion involves the emergence of what might be described as a "second-generation" literature aimed at replicating and refining the results of earlier studies. Efforts have been made to reexamine many of the relationships between religion and other social factors that were tentatively established by the empirical studies done in the 1960s, such as those between religion and prejudice, age, social class, socioeconomic achievement, degree of political conservatism, delinquency, and anomie. These efforts have been facilitated by the accumulation of large-scale data-sets and by the increasing inclusion of religious questions in these data-sets. Replication and analytic refinement have also benefited from the availability of more sophisticated statistical procedures. Much of the research published in the 1960s was based either on the inspection of percentage tables or on the use of simple correlation coefficients. In the past few years, a number of more refined analytic techniques have been invented or adapted for use in the social sciences, some of which are especially suited to the kinds of data with which researchers interested in religion typically work. These techniques have afforded greater statistical precision in drawing inferences and have made possible the analysis of more complex systems of variables. The application of these techniques to the growing body of quantitative data has begun to produce a number of modifications in the conclusions of earlier research.

Another direction that recent research has begun to take is toward an investigation of religious change and the relationship between religion and other forms of social change. This work has been made possible largely through the growing availability of cross-sectional surveys conducted at periodic intervals on comparable samples and by soliciting responses to comparable questions. Examples include Gallup poll data on church attendance, the Michigan Election Studies, which contain basic questions about religious affiliation and church attendance as well as numerous political opinion items, the Detroit Area Surveys, which have replicated some of Lenski's early questions on religion, and, more recently, the National Opinion Research Center (NORC) General Social Surveys, which have been conducted annually since 1972 and have included several comparably worded questions about religious commitment. These and similar sets of data have proved to be of considerable value in the study of religion, since they afford evidence on current trends in religious commitment, about which there has been much speculation. They also afford a basis for making limited inferences about the causal connections between changes in religion and changes in other social conditions assumed to be affected by religion. The increasing availability of data replicating earlier surveys promises to make these kinds of analyses of continuing interest to students of contemporary religion.

Finally, there also appears to be a trend toward a more extensive application of quantitative methods to comparative and historical studies of religion. This kind of researh continues to remain underdeveloped in comparison with the large body of research conducted each year on aspects of contemporary religion within the United States. It is a particularly promising area of research, however, since more and more quantitative comparative and historical data are becoming available. Some of this material, such as that contained in the Human Relations Area Files, has long been availabe and only awaits further exploitation by students of religion. To this material has now been added a considerable amount of survey data collected in Europe, Canada, Japan, and parts of the Third World. These foreign data are particularly valuable for determining the general applicability of theories about the social sources and consequences of religious commitment. The growing availability of quantitative historical data has also afforded new tests of theories that have ordinarily been applied only to contemporary cases. Some of this historical material, such as the U.S. Censuses of Religious Bodies, which were conducted decennially between 1906 and 1936, is now readily available in computerized form. Data from nineteenth-century U.S. censuses that included questions about religious affiliations also become, as they are made public, of great potential value, since the original census sheets contain information at the level of individual cases. In addition to these sources, the work of historians in recent years, especially on the religious histories of England and France, is opening a number of new possibilities for systematic quantitative analysis.

This book represents a sampling of the research that is being done along these new lines in the quantitative study of religion. The aim of the book is to present some of the results and, thereby, to provide empirical models that will, it is hoped, encourage further inquiry along these lines. The book is directed chiefly at two audiences: professional researchers engaged in the study of religion, and the broader contingent of students, social scientists, clergy, and lay persons interested in keeping abreast of research developments in modern religion. For the former, we hope that the chapters in this volume will illustrate some fruitful methodological approaches and some useful substantive results that may contribute to further advances in the quantitative study of religion. For the latter, we have attempted to include studies of both theoretical and practical importance covering a wide variety of topics concerning the nature of contemporary religion and its social correlates. The present volume does not, however, aim to provide either a comprehensive summary of recent religious research or a systematic sampling of all the kinds of research currently being conducted in this area (for example, we have intentionally excluded studies of religious organizations, since to do justice to such studies would require a large volume in itself). What we have tried to include here are studies, all previously unpublished, that represent some of the best work currently being done along each of the new lines of inquiry just outlined.

Three kinds of studies were commissioned for this volume. The majority are attempts to break new ground in the quantitative study of religion by developing and empirically testing new concepts and hypotheses, by applying previously untested theories to the interpretation of empirical data, or, in several instances, by examining data with an eye toward suggesting new hypotheses and directions for further research. The second category of studies consists of efforts to replicate and extend previous research through the use of more extensive data or more refined methods of analysis. Several of these chapters illustrate new statistical techniques that the authors have developed or adapted especially for the problem at hand. These techniques appear to have broad implications for similar kinds of research problems. Finally, several chapters were commissioned to explore areas where there has already been a great deal of quantitative research done. The task assigned to these chapters was not to present new findings but to review the existing literature critically and to suggest the most fruitful strategies for further research.

The chapters are organized into four sections corresponding roughly to the four lines of inquiry already discussed. Part I concerns problems arising from the measurement of religious commitment. These are problems that have received considerable attention in previous research. Most of this attention has been devoted to the measurement of institutionalized religious commitment, particularly to the problems of identifying dimensions of religious commitment and of developing indicators of these dimensions. Progress has been made by previous research, but (as the critical review in Chapter 1 indicates) much of the work in this area has failed because of inadequate attention to the theoretical uses of the indicators of religious commitment. Problems of measurement have also become more complex as broader definitions of religion have been made by empirical research. In Chapter 1, Wade Clark Roof reviews the main indicators of religious commitment, evaluates their strengths and weaknesses, and indicates some of the considerations that should be emphasized in further work. Chapters 2 and 3, by Charles Y. Glock and his associates, represent two empirical attempts to develop measures of religious commitment that may contribute predictive power beyond that of more familiar indicators. The former chapter focuses on those people who have traditionally been classified as "low" on measures of religious commitment and illustrates the differences in values and attitudes that may exist between the nominally religious and the nonreligious, and between those in these categories and persons experimenting with alternative religions. The latter chapter focuses on a more traditional item of religious commitment—beliefs about God—and illustrates the differences, particularly in political views, that may be associated with alternative images of God. The concern in all of these chapters is with individual religiosity. In contrast, Chapter 4 focuses on the relatively neglected problems of measuring variations at the level of religious groups. Taking Bryan Wilson's typology of religious sects as a theoretical starting point, Michael R. Welch uses multidimensional scaling to develop a highly promising method of quantitatively classifying religious groups. He also discusses some of the uses to which this method might be put in testing some widely held notions about the development of religious sects.

The chapters in Part II are concerned with the social correlates of religious commitment. The correlates with which these chapters are concerned have all been the subject of previous speculation and research and seem likely to remain of interest either as possible sources or as possible consequences of religious commitment. These chapters update this research by using the latest data and methods available. In Chapter 5 Andrew M. Greeley, to determine the role of ethnicity in influencing religious commitment, brings data from national samples to bear on the speculation surrounding the new wave of ethnic identification. The findings indicate that more attention should probably be devoted to ethnicity than has typically been the case in religious research. The effects of ethnicity appear, however, to be more pronounced in certain religious groups than in others. M. S. Sasaki, in Chapter 6, examines another of the social conditions that has often been discussed as a factor influencing styles and degrees of religious commitment. With the exception of Demerath's well-known study, little quantitative evidence has existed on the relationship between religious commitment and status inconsistency. Sasaki offers a thorough analysis of these relationships, using a variety of religious items from three recent studies of the national population. He also presents a new method of measuring and analyzing status inconsistency that solves many of the problems that have plagued previous studies. His results overturn many of our well-worn conceptions about the effects of status inconsistency on religious commitment. In addition, he provides some interesting results pertaining to contemporary religious developments, such as "born again" experiences and beliefs in faith healing.

The remaining chapters in Part II deal with social phenomena that have generally been regarded as consequences of religious commitment. Delinquent behavior among adolescents is one phenomenon that has been thought to be influenced by the presence or absence of religious commitment. In Chapter 7, Gary F. Jensen and Maynard L. Erickson present data on this relationship from a new study that affords a look both at kinds of delinquent activities and at religious contexts not previously studied. They also reanalyze data from one of the best-known studies of delinquency and religious commitment and point out flaws in the original analysis. Divorce, or marriage dissolution more generally, is another social phenomenon that has been shown to be significantly affected by variations in religious commitment. Like delinquency, it has been a topic of special interest in recent years as divorce rates have climbed to record highs. The correlative decline in church attendance and other indicators of religious commitment has led to speculation about possible causal connections. Most of the research to date, however, has been limited either by inadequate data on marital histories or by inadequate analytic techniques. In Chapter 8, James McCarthy develops a new method based on demographic life-table techniques for estimating probabilities of marriage dissolution and uses this method to analyze data from a recent national survey containing detailed marriage-history questions. His analysis yields, for the first time, estimates of the likelihood of marriage dissolution within American religious groups for particular durations of marriage. A comparison of cohorts also provides some clues about trends in the relationship between religion and marital dissolution. In the final chapter in Part II, James Riccio reviews the extensive literature that has developed concerning the effects of religion on socioeconomic achievement and indicates some of the new directions that research on this relationship might fruitfully take. His review provides both a convenient summary of the research and a pointed critique of its weaknesses.

Part III consists of chapters that assess the relationship between religion and social change. Although the approaches taken in the chapters differ widely, they cover some of the more interesting social changes that have occurred in recent years and suggest a number of theoretical and empirical leads for more research. In Chapter 10, Charles F. Westoff summarizes the evidence on religious differences in fertility rates, contraceptive behavior, and attitudes toward abortion that he and his colleagues at the Office of Population Research have collected over the past 25 years. In Chapter 11, Larry Blackwood examines the changes that have taken place in the Detroit area in the work ethic since Lenski first studied these attitudes in 1958. Blackwood illustrates the effectiveness of using log-linear models and logit regression techniques for the analysis of complex contingency tables involving data collected at more than one time. Like Westoff, he finds that religious variables that once produced significant differences may no longer serve as important explanatory variables. Wuthnow and Christiano explore, in Chapter 12, the relationship between changes in residence and religious commitment. The evidence presented suggests that widespread residential mobility—from one community to another, to the suburbs, and to the West and South—may have important adverse effects on church attendance. In the final chapter in this section, Albert Bergesen and Mark Warr discuss the relationship between religion and political change. They develop an innovative theoretical approach that they then use to account for the moral consequences that followed the Watergate disclosures and that culminated in the election of Jimmy Carter to the Presidency.

Part IV is devoted to studies involving either comparative or historical analyses. All of these studies deal with religion at the aggregate, rather than individual, level. They illustrate that important theoretical properties, which have generally been neglected in studies of individual religiosity, can be observed at the group level. John H. Simpson's study in Chapter 14 builds on Swanson's (1960) work dealing with the relationship between authority structures and religious beliefs in primitive societies. In replicating Swanson's research, he finds that certain characteristics of primitive economies also correlate significantly with the presence of "high gods." This finding has important theoretical implications, since it suggests that religious beliefs may be affected by the kinds of initiative individuals are expected to exert in different societies. In Chapter 15, Phillip E. Hammond and Kirk R. Williams develop an innovative theoretical scheme for making cross-national comparisons of alternative "moral climates." They then devise empirical indicators that afford classifications of moral climates on the basis of available economic and political data. These indicators, it turns out, produce a number of interesting results that lead to several general hypotheses about the relationship between modernization and the character of moral obligations. The remaining two chapters are historical rather than cross-cultural. Bergesen's analysis of the history of black music in Chapter 16 draws theoretical parallels between religious rituals and language (including music) and uses these parallels to interpret the relationship between variations in black music and the social structure of black Americans. This chapter provides both a valuable summary of Basil Bernstein's theoretical work on symbolic codes and a rare exploration of the sociology of religious music. Finally, Chapter 17 presents a quantitative analysis of the social history of revival religion in late nineteenth-century America. Using census data and a careful application of lagged dependent-variable regression-analysis, George M. Thomas tests and extends some widely held views of the relationship between industrialization and religious evolution. His analysis demonstrates the care that must be exerted in attempting to make generalizations about these relationships.

As mentioned earlier, the chapters in this volume represent some of the more interesting and promising directions that quantitative research on religion has been taking in recent years. And although they also point to some common substantive conclusions, the overriding consideration in the commissioning of these chapters was the eliciting of methodologically and theoretically innovative techniques that would advance research in the quantitative study of religion. Accordingly, it seems useful to summarize in advance some of the particular research needs and opportunities to which these chapters point.

One such need is that of replication and empirical refinement. Because quantitative research on religion is a relatively recent development, and one that has been poorly funded in comparison with other research areas that have enjoyed the benefits of government support, quantitation results have been generated in a piecemeal fashion, often from studies designed primarily for other purposes or from studies involving inadequate designs (as Riccio's review in Chapter 9 and similar reviews published elsewhere have documented). In consequence, there is a considerable need for research that summarizes existing literature, reexamines the findings of previous research in light of the more sophisticated analytic techniques that are now available, and perhaps presents new findings based on more recent or more comprehensive data. The opportunities for such replications are abundant, since many large-scale data-sets containing religious items are now available for secondary analysis.

Perhaps the most telling fact that illustrates the need for further replications and empirical refinements is that little is actually known about some of the more common aspects of religious commitment in American society, such as church attendance or religious affiliation. It would, for example, prove extremely difficult to summarize with any degree of confidence the relationship between church attendance and even the most elementary social variables, such as age, income, marital status, or urbanization. It is ironic that we have often explored the more esoteric varieties of religion—or its surrogates—while neglecting some of the more obvious features of religion about which there are considerable data available for analysis.

The point becomes painfully obvious when religious research is compared with demography. Had demographers abandoned the study of fertility after a few early exploratory studies and moved on to consider the "functional alternatives" by which people reproduce themselves (e.g., work, art, sports), demography would scarcely have progressed toward becoming an exact science in the way that it has. The analogy, of course, should not be overdrawn. Religious research has been greatly enriched by studies taking a broader approach to the subject. The point is only that the painstaking work needed to pin down basic correlates of traditional religious commitment should not be neglected.

A second need pointed to by a number of the chapters in this volume is for more careful contextual specification of the relationship between religion and other variables. The theories that have implicitly guided much of the research on religion, perhaps because that research has focused so heavily on individual religiosity, have been largely social-psychological. That is, they have tended to emphasize cognitive factors (such as the conflict between faith and reason), emotive factors (such as deprivation-induced needs), or values (such as the relationship between religious and political values), without giving much attention to the contexts in which these factors might or might not be operative. Yet, empirical studies have failed to indicate that any of the social-psychological correlates of religious commitment are so general as to apply in all situations. As Jensen and Erickson show in Chapter 7, for example, the relationship between religious commitment and delinquency differs with denomination and with town size. Or, to give some other examples, studies conducted among college students frequently find results that differ from studies among adults; studies of church members often show different relations than studies of the general population; and the same holds true for blacks versus whites and for the South versus the North. What these differences (e.g., races, church membership, education, geography) suggest is the importance of taking social context into account in theories about religious commitment. The indication is that some contexts trigger particular social-psychological effects, whereas other contexts inhibit these effects. Rather than ignoring these differences or simply attributing them to sampling biases, as has often been done in past research, considerable progress could be made toward developing better theories of religious commitment if these differences were systematically examined and interpreted as meaningful contextual information. In future research we hope that more attention will be paid to the interactions among complexes of variables that would indicate contextual specifications. Again, it is fortunate that some of the newer analytic techniques, particularly log-linear analysis and logit regression, are especially suited to the exploration of such interactive effects.

A third kind of research need involves expansion of the study of religious commitment to include correlates that have as yet been little explored. One of the surprising facts associated with some of the chapters in this volume is that, even though they sometimes deal with rather familiar topics (status inconsistency, divorce, and migration, for example), they are still among the few empirical studies that have been done on these topics. There have been a few topics that have been explored extensively with respect to religious commitment, such as prejudice, political conservatism, sexual morality, and achievement values. There are many other phenomena that theory would lead us to expect to be significantly associated with religious commitment, and one of the new directions of research in the past few years has been to explore some of these phenomena. But many—such as drug use, alcoholism, happiness, the quality of life, altruism, moral reasoning, sex roles, and attitudes toward foreign policy—have only begun to be examined.

As an example of how "thin" the coverage of the relationship of religion with other variables has been, we might consider the status of research on the relationship of religion to family. The family is probably the institution that we would expect to be most closely associated with religion. Both are a source of basic values and both function primarily within the private sphere. Churches have traditionally encouraged loyalty to the family, and the family has been a major pedagogic symbol in religious belief. Both have also been subject to many of the changes in values and life styles that have taken place over the past decade (as Westoff's and McCarthy's chapters illustrate). Thus, it would appear to be both theoretically and practically interesting to know what is happening to the relationship between these two institutions. At least five topics seem to be of particular importance: (*a*) the relationship between religion and changing standards of sexual conduct; (*b*) the relationship between religion and changing views toward fertility and contraception; (*c*) the relationship between religion and changing rates of marital stability; (*d*) the relationship between religion and changing sex roles; and (*e*) the relationship between religion and changing child-rearing values. Yet, with the exception of some of the work done by Greeley, Westoff, and several others, one can search the literature almost in vain for sound quantitative evidence on these relationships. What is particularly surprising is that much of the data that would shed light on these relationships is readily available for analysis.

Another area of both need and opportunity in the quantitative study of religion stems from the recent interest (alluded to earlier) in formulating alternative conceptions of religion and in exploring alternative varieties of religious expression. Although traditional religious institutions are likely to remain central to the understanding of American religion, private and experimental forms of religion may come to play an increasingly important role alongside these traditional forms. Religious experience, meditation, participation in new religious movements, mysticism, syncretic conceptions of meaning and purpose—all merit much more extensive examination.

As yet, theoretical discussion and ethnographic inquiry have outpaced quantitative research into the less-institutionalized varieties of religion. However, as Roof discusses in Chapter 1, some promising leads have been made in this direction. Much of this work is rooted in conceptions of symbol systems, such as those articulated by Bellah, Berger, Langer, and others. Ideas about "meaning" and the construction of reality are central to these conceptions.

There is another, relatively neglected, theoretical approach that might be pursued. That approach is one that stresses the moral and ethical dimensions of religious consciousness. The chapters by Hammond and Williams and by Bergesen in this volume come closest to taking this approach in that they are concerned with moral climates and problems of moral order. The theoretical roots of this approach lie less in phenomenology than in the Parsonian tradition of concern with social norms. Clifford Geertz's stress on religion as ethos offers one such starting point. However, the development of specific concepts and hypotheses still remains largely to be worked out. Research on the practical norms and ethical criteria that translate religious beliefs into everyday behavior would appear, furthermore, to provide an important counterweight to the current interest that has been focused heavily on ultimate concerns and broad (almost metaphysical) systems of meaning or belief. For example, even within the domain of traditional religion, far more research has been done on conformity to formal doctrines and creeds than on the actual rules of conduct that church members strive to follow in their daily lives. Fortunately, some of the ethnographic work that has been done on new religious movements has begun to provide some comparative evidence on these aspects of daily conduct in different religious contexts.

Research on religious organizations—and on religion at the aggregate social level more generally—is another area of particular need and opportunity. The importance of organizational factors has been clearly recognized in recent ethnographic studies of new religious movements. These factors are also important in shaping the character of religious commitment in conventional churches and have become the subject of much attention among church planners and pastors. However, as yet only a few applications of quantitative research techniques have been made to the study of religious organizations. Most research remains at the level of individual beliefs and activities. There are two strategies that might usefully be employed to examine religious organizations. One would involve collecting data from individuals within organizations, and sampling with sufficient density to afford measurements of contextual properties and of interaction. The current resurgence of interest in network analysis among sociologists seems especially suited to the study of interaction among members of religious groups. The other approach would involve collecting data at the organizational level itself, as Welch illustrates in Chapter 4. Measures of size, authority structure, worship styles, formal beliefs, and so forth could be collected, as Welch has done for historic sects, and their relationships quantitatively analyzed.

The final area of research need and opportunity that deserves some mention lies in the application of quantitative techniques to comparative and historical data. As mentioned earlier, a growing amount of such data is becoming available. Some of it, as Thomas' chapter on nineteenth-century revival religion illustrates, is amenable to systematic analysis, since it involves large numbers of cases. In other cases, the data are less ample but, as in Bergesen's treatment of black music, can still be used to test certain theoretical inferences. There is no question that the collection and analysis of cross-cultural or historical data are time-consuming. The reason that it is so important that such analyses be conducted, however, is that many of our most important theories—such as those having to do with secularization, church–sect development, religious evolution, institutional differentation, or civil religion—imply evidence of social change and require large-scale comparisons to be made among different societies. If knowledge about the macroscopic dimensions of religion is to progress, we must pursue comparative and historical research.

Much of what has just been said will, of course, come as no surprise to researchers familiar with the literature in these areas. By underscoring these needs and opportunities, it is to be hoped that others will be encouraged to pursue research along some of these lines.

One final introductory note also needs to be added. It would be irresponsible not to acknowledge the current deep rift between those students of religion engaged primarily in quantitative research and those who favor ethnographic, phenomenological, or humanistic approaches. The exclusive emphasis in this volume upon the former does not mean that the editor or the contributors regard quantitative research as the only useful approach to the study of religion. The truth is, as many of the remarks in the following chapters attest, that both quantitative and nonquantitative research are needed and productive. Also, interaction between practitioners of the two traditions needs to be encouraged. The present chapters illustrate the kinds of advances that are currently being made through quantitative research. But the limitations of quantitative research are also evident—perhaps especially so to those who have worked with it for very long.

Part I

NEW DIRECTIONS IN THE
MEASUREMENT OF RELIGIOUS
COMMITMENT

Chapter 1

Concepts and Indicators of Religious Commitment: A Critical Review

WADE CLARK ROOF

I. Introduction

Few topics in the empirical study of religion have received as much attention in the past 20 years as has the conceptualization and measurement of
religious commitment. During the 1960s, a pace-setting decade in this area, a
framework of analysis was established and an agenda of issues for investigations was provided. In the 1970s, research proliferated with revisions and
refinements, new approaches and techniques. Fortunately, there are signs that
the field is achieving, a greater maturity, both conceptually and
methodologically. In this chapter, I review these developments, with attention
both to continuities and to changes in this field of research.

A decade ago the very nature of religious commitment was widely
debated—whether religion is a discrete, unitary phenomenon or a complex,
multidimensional matter with diverse and possibly unrelated elements.
Reviewing the field at the time, James E. Dittes (1969) foresaw the emergence

The Religious Dimension:
New Directions in Quantitative Research

of a new climate of scholarly opinion characterized not by doctrinaire or simplistic approaches to measurement issues, but by a maturing and genuinely synthetic perspective. In the 1970s, this synthesis of views became even clearer. Old debates about multidimensionality have subsided somewhat as researchers have come to recognize the many diverse forms of religious commitment. There is an awareness that decisions about the meaning and measurement of religion depend, also, on the theoretical frameworks that researchers employ and the kinds of questions they seek to answer. Increasingly, it is agreed that the phenomenon is so complex and convoluted that not only multiple dimensions but also multiple approaches are required for analysis.

Three questions are important for grasping the present condition of the field:

1. What are the current approaches to conceptualizing and measuring religious commitment?
2. What criteria have evolved for assessing the approaches and findings?
3. What future directions for research seem most promising?

But, before addressing these questions, we need to establish the boundaries of our review and to examine briefly the intellectual foundations of the research traditions.

Scope of the Review

Of concern here is religious commitment (or "religious involvement," "religiosity," or "religiousness," as it is variously called) as a characteristic of individuals. Without engaging in debate over what may or may not be included under the rubric "religion," it is useful for our purposes to adopt a fairly broad approach. Hence, religious commitment will refer to *an individual's beliefs and behavior in relation to the supernatural and/or high-intensity values.* The object of orientation—the supernatural or ultimate values—is purposely left open. Thus defined, religious commitment encompasses both institutionalized and noninstitutionalized forms of belief and behavior, and church as well as non-church-oriented meaning systems.

Intellectual Traditions

A broad focus is also adopted with respect to analytic frameworks for explaining religious commitment, both as a personal–subjective and as a social-collective phenomenon. Considerable attention has been given to each of these, and our understanding of religion today is enriched from the insights of both approaches. Although, as Dittes (1969) points out, personal versus institutional modes of commitment are a source of continuing tension in Western Judeo-Christian culture, the two still serve as complementary perspectives on the individual and his or her religion.

Social-Collective

More than anyone else, Emile Durkheim was responsible for defining the major elements in the social–collective approach to religion. In his now classic study of religion, *The Elementary Forms of the Religious Life* (1947), Durkheim drew a distinction between *beliefs* and *rites* relative to sacred things and suggested that both serve to unite religious followers into a moral *community* or church. Distinguishing among these three characteristics, he combined both cultural and social organizational components into a definition to show that religion is an "eminently collective" phenomenon. Durkheim argued that in the most elementary forms of religion these components overlap; but in a more complex, modern society, he expected the cultural and organizational aspects to separate. He expected that modernization would lead to greater "religious individualism" or a rise in privatized religious forms largely independent of communal structures.

Durkheim's work was of generative significance for developing multidimensional approaches to religion. Wach (1944) drew from it in his comparative studies, suggesting that worldwide expressions of religious experience fall under three headings: *theoretical* (belief), *practical* (ritual), and *sociological* (fellowship). In the United States, a Durkheimian perspective on religious forms and functions was of central importance to many studies in the 1950s and 1960s. It is reflected in Herberg's (1955) essay on America's trifaith communities—Protestants, Catholics, and Jews—and his assumption that religious identities are formed and sustained by the religious community, apart from an individual's actual affiliation with, or participation in, a distinct religious congregation. Religious community and religious congregation are, or may be, functionally differentiated in contemporary society—a fact demonstrated empirically by Lenski. In *The Religious Factor* (1961), Lenski showed that it is useful to distinguish between *associational* and *communal* types of religious group involvement. Associational involvement refers to an individual's participation in institutional or congregational activities; by contrast, communal involvement entails primary-group interaction at the broader level of family and friends, among those who share a common religious and cultural heritage. His was the first major empirical work to employ multiple measures of religiosity of this kind and to underscore the significance of the many social and cultural forms of religion in a modern, pluralistic society. Other, contemporary work also reflects a strong concern with the social–collective bonds of religion (e.g., Carrier, 1965; Fichter, 1951).

Personal-Subjective

In the same years, psychologists of religion were making strides in exploring empirically many of the inferences drawn from the substantive works of such earlier writers as William James and Rudolf Otto. Especially influential was the work of Allport, who led the way in elaborating the implications of the orientations, or subjective approaches, individuals bring to personal faith. In 1950, Allport distinguished between *institutionalized* and *interiorized* types of religion, attempting to show how prejudice and other negative social outlooks were often associated with the manifest and conformist qualities of the former but not with the deeper, more universalistic and ethical meanings of the latter. Later he shifted terminology to *extrinsic* versus *intrinsic* (1959) stressing more the differences in individual personality styles and motivational characteristics. The distinction emphasized the importance of ultimate versus instrumental religion in a person's motivational system. Extrinsic belief stresses the external, self-serving, and utilitarian "uses" of faith, but intrinsic belief subordinates self and personal motives to the fundamental teachings and moral precepts of the faith. As Allport conceived the two, they were not separate and distinct orientations, but rather alternative ends of the same motivational continuum.

Allport's work gained early empirical support, especially his efforts at unraveling the psychological and religious correlates of prejudice, intolerance, and ethnocentrism (cf. Spilka, 1958; Whitam, 1961; Wilson, 1960). Over the years, his basic insights have been expanded to include a belief–disbelief continuum and general proreligious attitudes (Allport, 1966; Allport and Ross, 1967; Brown, 1964; Feagin, 1964); also, the concepts have become more sharply defined and better operationalized (see Hoge, 1972; Hunt and King, 1971). A related distinction is that offered by Allen and Spilka (1967), who employ the terms *consensual* and *committed* in place of extrinsic and intrinsic. This pair of concepts focuses somewhat greater attention on the cultural values and experiences that help to shape cognitive orientations and personal belief systems. Emphases upon the concrete, the tangible, and the conventional, plus a high valuation of conformity are traits of consensual religion. By contrast, a more abstract, open, and flexible, set of beliefs is characteristic of committed religion. The distinction is helpful to researchers, drawing attention to the cultural underpinnings of belief systems and shedding light upon the numerous personality, value, and cognitive traits that contribute to the formulation and maintenance of such systems (for reviews of this literature, see Dittes, 1969, 1971; Spilka, 1971).

II. Approaches to Religious Commitment

Turning to current research, we review "church-type" religious commitment, which has been the predominant concern, and examine more recent efforts at measuring nonchurch religious forms.

"Church-Type" Religious Commitment

Two empirical studies important in the development of multidimensional research were Lenski's and Fukuyama's. Employing both social–collective and personal–subjective approaches, Lenski (1961) identified four "dimensions": two types of religious group involvement, *associational* versus *communal*, and two types of religious orientation, *doctrinal orthodoxy* and *devotionalism*. His Detroit data revealed very weak relationships between the two types of group involvement and between the two religious orientations. On the basis of these data, he concluded that these were "separate and independent" aspects of religion. In the same year, Fukuyama (1961) published the results of an exploratory study in which he examined alternative ways in which people are religious. With measures for *cognitive* (knowledge), *cultic* (ritual), *creedal* (belief), and *devotional* (experience) dimensions, he showed that these were related differently to one another and varied in relation to basic social and demographic correlates such as sex, age, education, and social class.

The inspiration behind Fukuyama's study, and much of the research since, is attributable to Charles Y. Glock. In an early essay (1954) and a later publication (1959), Glock delineated the dimensions of commitment in order to increase understanding of American religion in the fifties and sixties. More elaborate statements were put forth by Glock in 1962 and by Glock and Stark in 1965. Five core dimensions, which all religions presumably share, were described: the *ideological,* the *ritualisitic,* the *experiential,* the *intellectual,* and the *consequential.* The approach focused generally upon the various ways in which people are religious and drew from intuitive understanding of how religious expressions manifest themselves in everyday life. The primary concern was, to isolate the internal components of these core dimensions and, secondarily, to explore the patterns of interrelations among them. Later, following Fukuyama's lead, Stark and Glock chose not to include the consequential as a substantive dimension per se; other researchers influenced by their work have, however, been reluctant to eliminate it.

Empirically, Stark and Glock examined, in addition to their four core dimensions, two relational measures (communal involvement and congregational friendships), adapted primarily from Lenski's work, and two secondary measures of belief (particularism and ethicalism). Particularism—a measure of the extent to which people believe that theirs is the one true faith—bears some cognitive resemblance to the narrow, rigid traits identified earlier with consensual belief. Ethicalism represents nearly the opposite: a type of commitment, among those who have rejected orthodox supernaturalism, to "doing good" and "loving thy neighbor" on a person-to-person basis. From their study of Northern California church members, they concluded (1968: 176–182):

1. The dimensions are independent of each other (the highest correlation between any two dimensions was .57).
2. Orthodoxy is the best single predictor of the other dimensions of commitment.
3. Ethicalism is the poorest predictor, since it was virtually unrelated to any of the other dimensions.

4. Intercorrelations among the dimensions are slightly greater among Protestants than among Roman Catholics.

Subsequent researchers have not always followed Glock's advice about giving primary attention to the internal components of religious dimensions. Typically, researchers have been more concerned with the empirical interrelations among dimensions than with exploring the content and meaning of the dimensions themselves. Most attention has centered on the first two, and most basic, of Stark and Glock's conclusions: the general assumption of multidimensionality and centrality of beliefs in religious commitment. These issues remain controversial, and, although no full resolution has been reached, some progress has been achieved. To elucidate the extent of this progress, we examine two on-going research operations that have dealt with these issues over the past decade: one identified with the work of Gordon F. DeJong and Joseph E. Faulkner, and a second with that of Morton B. King and Richard A. Hunt.

Faulkner and DeJong

Beginning in 1966, Faulkner and DeJong sought to develop measures of religiosity for each of Glock's five core dimensions (see Table 1.1). Most concerned to test empirically the multidimensional hypothesis, they constructed Guttman scales for each of the separate dimensions and examined the interrelations among the 5-D scales using a Pennsylvania State University student sample. Empirically, their scales met the Guttman scaling criteria, suggesting that each was a separate and distinct aspect of religiosity. Moreover, correlations among the dimensions varied, ranging from .36 to .58, lending support to the view that "religious involvement is characterized by several dimensions—some of which are more closely related than others [Faulkner and DeJong, 1966:252]." Although the dimensions were all positively interrelated, given the diversity in degree of association among them, the findings were interpreted as evidence of multidimensionality. Other researchers with similar findings offer essentially the same interpretation in support of multidimensional commitment (Campbell and Fukuyama, 1970; Lehman and Shriver, 1968).

Still others, with much the same kind of evidence, have seriously questioned the claims of multidimensionality. Weigert and Thomas (1969) argue that, in terms of content validity, many of the 5-D scale items used by Faulkner and DeJong are not distinctly differentiated, despite the fact that as separate scales they each meet minimum standards of scalability. Gibbs and Crader (1970) point to the moderately large correlations among dimensions and to the lack of an adequate criterion for making a judgment about whether the results support uni- or multidimensional claims. Of the criticisms raised, those of Richard Clayton are probably the most severe. In 1971, Clayton demonstrated that the

TABLE 1.1   Faulkner and DeJong's Dimensions and Scale Items

Ideological

a. The world will come to an end according to God's will.
b. The deity is a Divine God, creator of the universe, who knows my innermost thoughts and feelings, and to whom one day I shall be accountable.
c. God's forgiveness comes only after repentance.
d. God acts and continues to act in the history of mankind.
e. The Bible is God's word, and all it says is true.

Intellectual

a. The story of creation as recorded in Genesis is literally true.
b. I believe the report of miracles in the Bible; this is, they occurred through a setting aside of natural laws by a higher power.
c. Religious truth is higher than any other form of truth.
d. Name at least three of the Gospels.

Ritualism

a. It is impossible for an individual to develop a well-rounded religious life apart from the institutional church.
b. I spend more than one hour a week reading the Bible.
c. I have attended at least three of the past four Sabbath worship services.
d. Prayer is a regular part of my behavior.
e. A marriage ceremony should be performed only by a religious official.

Experiential

a. My religious commitment gives to my life a purpose it would not otherwise have.
b. I frequently or occasionally feel close to the Divine.
c. Religion offers me a sense of security in the face of death that would not otherwise be possible.
d. Religion provides me with an interpretation of this existence that could not be discovered by reason alone.
e. Faith, meaning putting full confidence in the things we hope for and being certain of things we cannot see, is essential to one's religious life.

Consequences

a. Nonessential businesses should not be open on the Sabbath.
b. Sexual intercourse before marriage is wrong.
c. It is better to vote for a political candidate who is affiliated with a religious organization.
d. Cheating on your income tax is wrong.

Source: Adapted from Faulkner and DeJong (1966).

so-called separate and distinct 5-D scales themselves actually constitute a "composite" Guttman scale. That is, he found in a study of southern students that the separate scale scores when treated as items of a larger complex more than adequately met Guttman criteria of unidimensionality. From this he concluded that the scales were probably components of a single-dimensional phenomenon, and not separate and alternative aspects of religiosity as generally assumed. More recently, Clayton and Gladden (1974) have suggested that the 5-D scales, except possibly for the consequential scale, measure different aspects of ideological, or belief, commitment. On the basis of a factor analysis of two sets of southern student data gathered in 1967 and 1970, they find that ideological commitment accounts for as much as 78 and 83% of the common variance in the two studies, respectively. Additional evidence of the interdependence of the scales followed from a second-order factor extraction, in which one general factor—the ideological—emerged from each of the data sets.

Clayton and Gladden's results are provocative and challenging, if nothing else, because they force the question of the centrality of belief and the extent to which other expressions of religion flow from it. They write that:

> In effect we would argue that the crucial task in the study of religiosity is, first, to pinpoint the belief system (Ideology) with which a subject identifies or toward which he reacts. His or her religiosity (Ideological Commitment) is determined by the degree of acceptance or nonacceptance of the traditional—and/or nontradi-tional—beliefs indigenous to the Ideology and the salience of those beliefs to his or her world view. The strength of the respondent's religiosity (Ideological Commit-ment) is or can be expressed in *one* or *more* of the directions in which commitment strength flows [1974:142].

That belief may be of greater centrality than originally thought is, in fact, acknowledged by Faulkner and DeJong themselves. In their latest study, De-Jong, Faulkner, and Warland (1976) uncover evidence in college student samples from both Penn State and a West German university confirming the dominance of the ideological factor over all others. Thirty-eight items on religious commitment were included, and in both instances these clustered into six factors in an initial oblique rotation (belief, knowledge, social conse-quences, moral consequences, religious practices, and religious experience). Yet, in a second-order analysis, three of these—belief, experience, and prac-tices—also formed a more generalized, single dimension. Because religious knowledge and social consequences were not reducible to the more generalized dimension, the authors stand by their argument about multidimensionality. Generally, however, they conclude that religiosity may be defined and measured *either in a generalized fashion or in a more precise, dimensional manner, depending on the level of abstraction and degree of specificity desired.* Whether this is a satisfactory resolution of the matter remains to be seen; but, quite clearly, there has emerged from the debate a more balanced perspective on the multidimensionality question.

King-Hunt

Proceeding along somewhat different lines, Morton King and Richard Hunt have engaged in what is unquestionably the most comprehensive, sustained ef-fort to date to test the multidimensionality hypothesis. Beginning with a pilot study of Methodists in Texas, followed by a larger study of Disciples,

Lutherans, Methodists, and Presbyterians in metropolitan Dallas and Ft. Worth, and, more recently, with a nationwide study of United Presbyterians, they have sought to unravel the structure of religious commitment in exploratory, empirical fashion. Reported findings are not always consistent, but generally their results show a considerable degree of similarity over the period in which the investigations occurred. Major findings and developments in interpretation are described by King (1967) and by King and Hunt (1969, 1972a, 1972b, 1975).

Unlike Faulkner and DeJong, Clayton, and others who have relied upon student data, King and Hunt base their work on church members from several of the large Protestant denominations. Also, rather than seeking simply to test Glock's typology, they have incorporated, as well, other concepts and measures, such as those of Allport, Fichter, and Lenski. Consequently, their findings reflect more of an "inside" view within mainline Protestantism and thereby yield a more differentiated set of dimensions for describing individual religiosity. Both their use of church members as a data source and their examination of a greater number of items for measuring commitment serve to increase the likelihood of varied, and more subtle, responses.

Although the number of dimensions and the labels given to them have varied somewhat over the years, the 13 dimensions shown in Table 1.2 have

TABLE 1.2   Thirteen King-Hunt Scales and Items

Basic religious scales

Creedal assent
   I believe in God as a Heavenly Father who watches over me and to whom I am accountable.
   I believe that the Word of God is revealed in the Scriptures.
   I believe that Christ is a living reality.
   I believe that God revealed Himself to man in Jesus Christ.
   I believe in salvation as release from sin and freedom for new life with God.
   I believe in eternal life.

Devotionalism
   How often do you pray privately in places other than at church?
   How often do you ask God to forgive your sins?
   When you have decisions to make in your everyday life, how often do you try to find out what God wants you to do?
   Private prayer is one of the most important and satisfying aspects of my religious experience.
   I frequently feel very close to God in prayer, during public worship, or at important moments in my life.

Church attendance
   If not prevented by unavoidable circumstances, I attend church: (More than once a week— Twice a year or less).
   During the last year, how many Sundays per month on the average have you gone to a worship service? (None/Three or more).

(continued)

TABLE 1.2, cont.

Basic religious scales

How often have you taken Holy Communion (The Lord's Supper, the Eucharist) during the past year?

Organizational activity

How would you rate your activity in your congregation? (Very active—Inactive).

How often do you spend evenings at church meetings or in church work?

Church activities (meetings, committee work, etc.) are a major source of satisfaction in my life.

List the church offices, committees, or jobs of any kind in which you served during the past twelve months (Coded: None—Four or more).

I keep pretty well informed about my congregation and have some influence on its decisions.

I enjoy working in the activities of the Church.

Financial support

Last year, approximately what percentage of your income was contributed to the Church (1% or less—10% or more).

During the last year, how often have you made contributions to the Church IN ADDITION TO the general budget and Sunday School? (Regularly—Never).

During the last year, what was the average MONTHLY contribution of your family to your local congregation? (Under $5—$50 or more).

In proportion to your income, do you consider that your contributions to the Church are: (Generous—Small).

I make financial contributions to the Church: (In regular, planned amounts—Seldom or never).

Orientation to growth and striving

How often do you read the Bible?

How often do you read literature about your faith (or church)? (Frequently—Never).

The amount of time I spend trying to grow in understanding of my faith is: (Very much— Little or none).

When you have decisions to make in your everyday life, how often do you try to find out what God wants you to do?

I try hard to grow in understanding of what it means to live as a child of God.

I try hard to carry my religion over into all my other dealings in life.

Composite religious scales

Salience: Behavior

How often in the past year have you shared with another church member the problems and joys of trying to live a life of faith in God?

How often do you talk about religion with your friends, neighbors, or fellow workers?

How often have you personally tried to convert someone to faith in God?

How often do you read the Bible?

When faced with decisions regarding social problems how often do you seek guidance from statements and publications provided by the Church?

How often do you talk with the pastor (or other official) about some part of the worship service: for example, the sermon, scripture, choice of hymns, etc.?

During the last year, how often have you visited someone in need, besides your own relatives?

(continued)

TABLE 1.2, cont.

Salience: Cognition

Religion is especially important to me because it answers many questions about the meaning of life.

I try hard to grow in understanding of what it means to live as a child of God.

My religious beliefs are what really lie behind my whole approach to life.

I frequently feel very close to God in prayer, during public worship, or at important moments in my daily life.

I often experience the joy and peace which come from knowing I am a forgiven sinner.

When you have decisions to make in your everyday life, how often do you try to find out what God wants you to do?

I believe in God as a Heavenly Father who watches over me and to whom I am accountable.

I try hard to carry my religion over into all my other dealings in life.

The active regulars

If not prevented by unavoidable circumstances, I attend church: (More than once a week— Twice a year or less).

How would you rate your activity in your congregation? (Very active—Inactive)

How often have you taken Holy Communion (The Lord's Supper, The Eucharist) during the past year?

During the last year, how many Sundays per month on the average have you gone to a worship service? (None—Three or more)

How often do you spend evenings at church meetings or in church work?

Church activities (meetings, committee work, etc.) are a major source of satisfaction in my life.

During the last year, how often have you made contributions to the Church IN ADDITION TO general budget and Sunday School? (Regularly—Never)

I make financial contributions to the Church: (In regular, planned amounts—Seldom or never)

Last year, approximately what percentage of your income was contributed to the Church? (1% or less—10% or more)

Religious despair

My personal existence often seems meaningless and without purpose.

My life is often empty, filled with despair.

I have about given up trying to understand "worship" or get much out of it.

I often wish I had never been born.

I find myself believing in God some of the time, but not at other times.

Most of the time my life seems to be out of my control.

The Communion Service (Lord's Supper, Eucharist) often has little meaning to me.

Cognitive style variables

Intolerance of ambiguity

You can classify almost all people as either honest or crooked.

There are two kinds of women: the pure and the bad.

There are two kinds of people in the world: the weak and the strong.

A person is either a 100% American or he isn't.

(continued)

TABLE 1.2, cont.

Cognitive style variables

A person either knows the answer to a question or he doesn't.
There is only one right way to do anything.
It doesn't take very long to find out if you can trust a person.

Purpose in life: Positive
Facing my daily tasks is usually a source of pleasure and satisfaction to me.
My life is full of joy and satisfaction.
I have discovered satisfying goals and a clear purpose in life.
I usually find life new and exciting.
If I should die today, I would feel that my life has been worthwhile.
Purpose in life: Negative
My life is often empty, filled with despair.
My personal existence often seems meaningless and without purpose.
I often wish I had never been born.
Most of the time my life seems to be out of control.

Source: Adapted from King and Hunt (1975).

emerged in several repeated factor-analyses. Most of the six basic scales correspond fairly closely to, or can be derived from, Glock's belief, experiential, and ritual dimensions. Thus, they bear a good deal of resemblance to those described by other researchers. However, the remaining two sets of King and Hunt's dimensions are quite different. Composite religious scales incorporate orientations and/or generalized responses that cut across the others: the salience of religion for everyday behavior and in thought and feelings; congregational faithfulness in terms of involvement and support ("Active Regulars"); and psychological and religious depression, or despair. Likewise, the cognitive styles identify dimensions of personality that may have bearing on the character of religious commitment: ability to cope with mental ambiguity, and purposeness, or sense of order and meaning in life. Similar factor structures are found for both the Texas and the nationwide samples, and efforts to date at obtaining higher-order factor solutions have failed to produce results that are significantly different.

Intercorrelations among the 13 dimensions for the nationwide Presbyterian sample reveal: (*a*) that relationships among scales of belief and attitude and among those of participation are stronger than across the two types; and (*b*) that measures of belief and experience are more strongly related to intolerance of ambiguity than are those of participation. Clustering of the scales in this manner is theoretically meaningful, because it suggests that among the basic, or core, dimensions two subsets may be identified along the lines established in earlier religious research, one pertaining to the personal-meaning aspect and the other to the social-belonging aspect. These two subsets and their differing social and psychological correlates, as was pointed out earlier, are central to the study of individual religiosity. Not only do King and Hunt empirically identify these clusters, but over the years they have explored their relationship to such factors as tolerance, cognitive simplicity, intrinsic and extrinsic orientations, and numerous social background characteristics.

In sum, King and Hunt find greater support for multidimensionality from their study of church members than do Faulkner and DeJong, Clayton, and others. Both their repeated replications and more subtle delineations of dimensions attest to this claim. Perhaps most importantly, their work sensitizes researchers to other kinds of criteria that have a bearing on the number and meaning of dimensions—that is, the choice of population studied and theoretical significance of the dimensional structures. As we shall describe in more detail later, considerations such as these are of considerable importance in resolving basic questions concerning multidimensionality.

Civil Religious Commitment

Another aspect of traditional religion, one attracting growing interest on the part of empirical researchers, is the American civil religion. By civil religion, of course, is meant—following Rousseau—the "civil profession of faith . . . without which a man cannot be a good citizen or a faithful subject [Whitney, 1968:373]." In the American context, the notion of a national faith, or a "religion of democracy," is elaborated in the writings of such figures as Warner (1961), Herberg (1955), Hammond (1963), Cherry (1971), and Bellah (1967). In particular, Bellah argues that there exists in the United States, alongside of and somewhat differentiated from the religious institutions, an elaborate civil religion that is a vital element of American culture. Commenting on the substance of this faith, he describes it as:

> Certain common elements of religious orientation that the great majority of Americans share. These . . . provide a religious dimension for the whole fabric of American life, including the political sphere. This public religious dimension is expressed in a set of beliefs, symbols, and rituals that I am calling the American civil religion [1967:3].

The ritual locus of this faith is in public political events, not in the churches, temples, and synagogues; it is manifest in national crises, holidays, presidential inaugurations, and in "a heritage of moral and religious experience. [1967:197]."

Bellah speaks of civil faith as a "dimension" of American religion, yet only recently have there been empirical attempts to establish it as a dimension of religions commitment. Perhaps the most direct attempt at this is by Wimberley *et al.* (1976), whose research title aptly poses the fundamental question—"The

Civil Religious Dimension: Is It There?'' Actually, two issues are addressed in their research: Is there a civil religious factor separate from other types of church religion? And, if so, what are its relationships to the core dimensions of belief, behavior, and experience? In attempting to shed some light on these matters, the authors included a set of civil religious items (see Table 1.3) along with more conventional, church-type measures in a follow-up study of participants in a Billy Graham crusade and subjected the entire set of items to factor analysis.

From this emerged four factors in an oblique solution. Six of the civil religious items loaded heavily on the first factor—"civil religion"; only the items on God's chosen nation and Christian patriotism failed to load strongly on this, or any other, factor. A second factor centered upon religious belief, with high loadings for items describing life after death, existence of the Devil, Biblical authenticity, and the like. Factor three was religious behavior (church attendance and church leadership positions), and factor four was labeled religious experience (private prayer, guidance in everyday matters, and awareness of God's presence). Given that three of the four subsets of items describe core dimensions in Glock's typology, the emergence of these discrete dimensions is not so very surprising. Of greater interest is that, in a second-order analysis, only two factors surfaced: "church religion," on which the behavior, belief, and experience scales load; and "civil religion," on which items of this kind loaded strongly, and experience and belief to a lesser extent. The first of the higher-order factors draws mainly upon the behavior and belief aspects, indicative of a generalized dimension of church religion. By contrast, civil religion stands apart from the other and is especially independent of behavioral, or ritual, forms of church religion.

Empirical research on American civil religion is in its formative stages and is, obviously, still very exploratory. The possibility of a civil religious dimension somewhat apart from the other religious forms calls for further investigations into its component parts and a more thorough analysis of its interrelationships

TABLE 1.3 Civil Religion Items in the Wimberley *et al.* Study

---

1. We should respect the president's authority since his authority is from God.
2. National leaders should not only affirm their belief in God but also their belief in Jesus Christ as Savior and Lord.
3. Good Christians aren't necessarily good patriots.
4. God can be known through the experience of the American people.
5. The founding fathers created a blessed and unique republic when they gave us the Constitution.
6. If the American government does not support religion, it cannot uphold morality.
7. It is a mistake to think that America is God's chosen nation today.
8. To me, the flag of the United States is sacred.

Source: Wimberley *et al.* (1976).

with church-type religiosity. Perhaps civil religious subdimensions exist, and, if so, the notion of civil religion must be broken down, conceptually elaborated, and empirically refined—in much the same way as have church-type dimensions. As broadly based a cultural phenomenon as it is in American society, amazingly little is known about the parameters of civil religion and the extent to which it overlaps, or is separate from, traditional church and synagogue life. Far more investigation is called for before we can justifiably speak of a "civil religious dimension" in quite the way we do with other dimensions, but clearly work is underway toward accomplishing this.

Ultimate Concerns

A quite different research strand of religious commitment centers upon people's ultimate concerns, or on what is called by some "invisible religion." Concerned that the study of religion not be limited simply to institutional religious forms, scholars such as Luckmann (1967) and Yinger (1969, 1970, 1977) have encouraged greater study of the basic, presumably universal, substructures of concern that give rise to religious expressions. They propose a functional approach to religion, focusing upon life's persisting dilemmas and upon how people's beliefs and practices—conventionally religious or otherwise—enable them to cope with these dilemmas. Approached in this way, the crucial question is not "How *religious* is a person?" according to some preconceived, culturally specific standards, but rather "*How* is the person religious?" keeping in mind institutionalized as well as more emergent, highly privatized religious meaning systems.

Yinger, like Geertz (1966), Berger (1967), and others, takes the position that religious belief systems are shaped in great part by the experiences of suffering, injustice, and meaninglessness. In various writings (1969, 1970, 1977), he has called for greater attention to generalized measures that get at "awareness of, and interest in the continuing, recurrent, *permanent* problems of human existence [1970:33]." His measures are deliberately nondoctrinal, with items designed to tap cross-cultural expressions of concern over life's persistent problems plus the conviction that, despite their universal quality, such concerns can be dealt with by means of specific types of beliefs and behaviors. These "invisible religious" items are shown in Table 1.4.

Using student data gathered in eight countries, including a large sample of undergraduates from 10 midwestern colleges in the U.S., Yinger found that nearly three-fourths of all responses expressed "ultimate" religious concerns (1977). The mean percentage doing so across four of his aggregated samples ranged from 71 to 78, indicative of the conviction that, behind the difficulties of life, order and meaning can be discerned. Not only did those adhering to a major world religion assent to these affirmations, but also, in about equal pro-

TABLE 1.4 Yinger's Nondoctrinal Items

1. Suffering, injustice, and finally death are the lot of man, but they need not be negative experiences; their significance and effects can be shaped by our beliefs.
2. In face of the almost continuous conflict and violence in life, I cannot see how men are going to learn to live in mutual respect and peace with one another.
3. Somehow, I cannot get very interested in the talk about "the basic human condition" and "man's ultimate problems."
4. Man's most difficult and destructive experiences are often the sources of increased understanding and powers of endurance.
5. Despite the often chaotic conditions of human life, I believe there is order and pattern to existence that someday we'll come to understand.
6. There are many aspects of the beliefs and practices of the world's religions with which I do not agree; nevertheless, I consider them to be valuable to deal with man's situation.
7. Efforts to deal with the human situation by religious means, whatever the content of the beliefs and practices, seems to be misplaced, a waste of time and resources.

Source: Yinger (1969).

portions, did those who professed no religious identity. In further analysis of the correlates of nondoctrinal religion, sex and social class were found to be unrelated, and citizenship, age, education, and religious identity were only weakly related. Lack of strong social correlates implies, of course, the widespread existence of these basic concerns across heterogeneous groups of respondents.

Other researchers have been concerned about the validity and reliability of Yinger's items and have sought to determine if, indeed, the items all tap similar concerns. Nelson and associates (1976) subjected the seven items to a factor analysis and concluded that (*a*) the items do *not* form a unidimensional scale; and (*b*) the items are themselves moderately related to traditional religious forms and, thus, perhaps are not as invisible as claimed. With a sample of southern university students, they uncovered two factors—one they called "Acceptance of Belief and Order" and a second they called "Value of Suffering"—both of which were positively correlated with institutional, church-type beliefs and practices. Similarly, Roof and associates (1977), using a student sample from the Northeast, found little internal consistency among the items and obtained evidence to suggest that three factors may be present: "Value of Religious Efforts," "Value of Difficult Experience," and "Belief in Order and Pattern." All three were related to several measures of Judeo-Christian religion, including belief in God, attendance at worship services, prayer, Bible reading, meditation, and self-rated religiosity. In yet another study, Machalek and Martin (1976) find considerable support for the existence of privatized expressions of religiosity outside the institutionalized religious context but do not offer any summary measures describing how people's ultimate concerns vary in relation to traditional, institutionalized religious forms.

In sum, studies underscore the claims of Yinger about the empirical existence of privatized, "invisible" religious structures but suggest that, as in the case of church religion, they may not be unidimensional in content. More research is necessary, using data from sources other than students, to establish more firmly the subdimensional structures of such commitment and to determine the relationship between these and church-type beliefs and practices. As with civil religion, ultimacy is a particularly important aspect of religiosity in need of far more attention than it has yet received at the hands of empirical researchers. In the years ahead, there should be further advances in this research and very likely a replay of many of the issues and controversies that have surfaced in other realms of religious measurement.

Alternative Meaning Systems

A fourth, and emerging, approach in religious measurement to be reviewed here is that of alternative meaning systems. Building on the theoretical work especially of Berger (1967), Geertz (1966), and Bellah (1970), a number of researchers have sought to examine empirically not only people's expressions of ultimate concern but also the symbolic constructions used in defining and ordering reality. The central question, or starting point, for this work is: How do people interpret experiences and events in their lives that call for some kind of judgment about the nature of reality? Presumably, people deal with such experiences and events by making assumptions about the forces that govern life and by adopting a mode of explanation consistent with these assumptions. Such explanations may or may not be associated with conventional religion, depending on the characterization of the reality structures.

Wuthnow's research (1976) is the most systematic of this kind to date. In his study of recent religious change in America, he postulates four types of meaning systems distinguished from one another by what they identify as the primary force governing life: theism, individualism, social science, and mysticism. These meaning systems encompass differing notions of the causal mechanisms in reality and differing symbolic conceptions of how and why the world is as it is (see Table 1.5 for types and item components). Using these, he argues that some fundamental shifts are occurring in the way people make sense of their lives. Traditional theistic and individualistic conceptions, fused together historically in American culture, appear to be declining, whereas social-scientific and mystical meaning systems have become more widespread. Likewise, Glock and Piazza (1978) point to the same trends in the structuring of reality, noting that the distribution of meaning systems varies considerably along the lines of age, education, and religious background.

Another example of pioneering research in this mode is seen in McCready and Greeley's work (1976), which approaches the question of meaning in

TABLE 1.5 Wuthnow's Types of Meaning Systems and Item Components

Theism
 Suffering—devil
 Suffering—disobey God
 Influenced by God
 Believe in God
 Creation
 Afterlife
 Poverty—God

Individualism
 Suffering—naturally selfish
 Suffering—own fault
 Influenced—by willpower
 No succeed—own fault
 Work hard—do anything
 Fail—blame self
 Poor—don't work

Social science
 Evolution
 Influenced by childhood
 Ideas depend on income
 Poor—American way
 Learn from psychology
 Poor—power structure
 Influenced by power structure
 Influenced by way raised
 Suffering—social setup
 Suffering—power structure

Mysticism
 Experienced the sacred
 Experienced nature
 Experienced harmony
 Learn from the arts
 Influenced by new insights
 Learn from the woods
 Live in fantasy world
 Suffering—no inner peace

Source: Wuthnow (1976).

terms of how people respond to the presence of good and evil in the world. They assume five basic responses: religious optimism, secular optimism, hopefulness, pessimism, and diffusion. Among Americans, they find in their survey analysis that approximately one-fourth are pessimists, one-fifth each are religious optimists and hopeful, and less than one-fifth each are secular optimists or diffused.

In all these instances, it is the approach to religiosity and the alternative

meaning systems that are uncovered that are important. By attempting to con-
ceptualize and measure the sacred worlds in which people live, the approach
treats as worthy of investigation the larger question of religious reality construction itself and raises issues not usually dealt with by more conventional
religious measures. As with the "invisible" religion approach, such an approach aids in capturing the meaning systems of those in the population who
are not oriented to church-type beliefs and values. For this reason it lends itself
to new and imaginative uses not bounded by institutional religious forms, and
no doubt it will become increasingly important as a measurement approach in
the future.

III. Criteria for Assessing Religious Measurement

Despite the growing interest in religious measurement in recent years, the
critical question concerns its overall significance and development as a field of
inquiry. Do we know more about the structures of religious commitment today
than we did a decade or so ago? Quite clearly we do know more, but probably
the greatest advances lie in our better understanding of the criteria by which to
evaluate what we know. In this section, we review some of the major criteria
for assessing religious measures: conceptual, theoretical, and empirical.

Conceptual Considerations

This tradition of research has been, and continues to be, plagued by alternative and inconsistent conceptual schemes, often making it difficult to
replicate findings from one study to another. All too often in religious
research, investigators proceed in an *ad hoc* fashion, looking at any and all
"dimensions" that are presumed to exist without serious concern for their
theoretical meanings, logical interrelations, or substantive significance. This
results in a good deal of confusion over whether dimensions are of central or
only of peripheral significance, and exactly how the many dimensions add up
to a comprehensive conception of religion. And the lack of a good analytic
scheme often results in a potpourri of empirical findings, difficult to interpret
in any meaningful sense.

Efforts are underway at establishing a clearer conceptual framework for the
analysis of religion. Himmelfarb (1975), examining the various synthesis
typologies and schemes, suggests that there are really only two basic types of
religious orientation: *behavioral* versus *ideational*, or religion "acted out" versus religion internalized in beliefs and attitudes. By cross-classifying these basic
types with the objects of religious orientation (i.e., supernatural, communal,
cultural, and interpersonal objects), he is able to extract various logical modes

of religious involvement similar to, if not identical with, many of the empirical dimensions already discussed. In his own analysis of Jewish data, he obtained support for this parsimonious scheme; and comparable patterns are evident in King and Hunt's research as well as in Nudelman's analysis of Glock and Stark's data (1971). Dimensions concerned with belief, feelings, and experience tend to cluster together, as do those involving ritual participation, communalism, and social involvement. The first pertains to "meaning" in religion, the second to "belonging".

These two foci of religious commitment are fundamental to the study of Western religious forms and offer a framework for interpreting empirically derived dimensions of commitment. Such a framework helps in organizing the fit of specific modes of religiosity into a broader pattern and directs attention to the most basic, most general aspects of religion. Not all empirical dimensions are reducible, perhaps, but most can probably be subsumed under these rubrics. Much would seem to be gained by adhering, where possible, to general rather than overly specific dimensions, that is, to those generic components that hold across religious traditions and across populations. Empirically, these are more likely to emerge in any given study, and, analytically, they offer a great deal more in the way of providing useful and meaningful building blocks for interpretation.

Theoretical Considerations

Theoretical considerations play so important a part, both in the selection and in the evaluation of religious measures, that they deserve further comment. In some instances a complex, multidimensional approach to religion is unnecessary and may even confuse rather than clarify issues. One thinks, for example, of research in the Weberian "Protestant ethic" tradition wherein the primary theoretical consideration is the role of religious ideology and where other aspects of religiosity are of little relevance to the substantive questions addressed. Yet, in other instances, precise dimensional variations are very pertinent to theories as, for example, with deprivation explanations of religion—where possibly the behavioral and ideational aspects relate differently to social class and, thus, have a direct bearing on the argument itself.

In the final analysis, any scheme of religious measures must be judged by its capacity for answering worthwhile questions. Religiosity may be defined and/or measured as either a highly generalized or as a very precise and diversely structured phenomenon, depending on the uses to which it is put. Which is "correct" varies with the kinds of questions asked and the level of analysis involved. Dittes (1969:606) adopts much the same position when he writes that "theoretical considerations argue strongly for a complex multitude of variables within the domain of religion and make the use of 'religion' as a single variable appear as conceptual or operational laziness and naivete; but . . . there is some empirical warrant for treating religion as a single variable, especially when it is appropriate to regard it as an object of general cultural perception." So does Spilka (1971:508), who speaks of a "criterion problem" in religious research, pointing out the necessity for establishing theoretical guidelines for choosing between these two approaches.

From a theoretical standpoint, a more generalized approach would seem appropriate (*a*) where cultural attitudes toward religion, or religious institutions, are of primary interest (see Gray, 1970, as well as the older studies by Chave, 1939, and Thurstone and Chave, 1929); (*b*) where religiosity is examined as part of a larger set of cultural values and norms (see Allport, Vernon, and Lindzey, 1960; Hunt, 1968); (*c*) where church-type religiosity is examined in relation to civil religion, "invisible" religion, or alternative religious meaning systems; and (*d*) wherever religion is one of several competing explanations for some "dependent" variable, and thus necessarily treated as a single factor. On the other hand, more specific, multidimensional conceptualizations are preferable (*a*) for describing alternative styles of commitment *within* a religious institution; (*b*) for breaking down interrelations among the cognitive, affective, and behavioral components of religion; and (*c*) for exploring the determinants, correlates, and consequences of the various aspects of religious commitment. The choice between the two—generality versus specificity—is not between right or wrong approaches or even necessarily between crude and more sophisticated types of analysis. Rather, it is a matter of explanatory purpose and level of analysis, resolvable only in terms of the broader questions to which the research is addressed.

Data Base Considerations

Empirically, there are two important considerations in the way the data base, or population studied, and the measures and procedures used for analysis bear upon the findings of any given study. Researchers are generally becoming more aware of the fact that in order to develop and test theories of religious commitment it is essential to postulate what Hubert M. Blalock, Jr. (1968) describes as an "auxilliarly theory," or set of assumptions about how sampling and measurement factors affect substantive results. Theoretical and methodological considerations mesh together in research, such that it is crucial to look for ways in which each bears upon the other when one is engaged in efforts at empirical verification.

Increasingly, it is recognized that the populations studied influence both the number of dimensions found and their relative significance. General population samples are more likely to yield a single, general religious factor, as the examples of Clayton and De Jong *et al.* illustrate. Because the samples are representative of the culture at large and heterogeneous with respect to religious commitments, they offer an "outside" view—often a general pro-religious response that is "best interpreted as representing favorableness of attitudes toward religious institutions, forms, personnel, and official doctrine [Dittes, 1971:93]." But, with church member samples, there is more of an "inside" view, characterized by finer distinctions and a more diversely structured pattern of religious styles. King and Hunt's research provides a good example of how this latter type of sample produces more subtle, sophisticated religious responses. Quite clearly, the best case for multidimensionality is made by examining those who are most committed to the beliefs, practices, and values involved.

The data source often results in subtle consequences for religious research, since many underlying social and psychological traits may vary along with religious attributes. For example, Filsinger (1978) has shown rather convincingly that the factor structures of religiosity differ for three empirically derived types of religious individuals in a sample of German students. The types identified were: *the socially-oriented humanists, the traditionally religious,* and *the nonreligious.* Among the traditionally religous, he found somewhat stronger intercorrelations among the several religious dimensions, indicative of an underlying religious response; but with the other two the patterns were more erratic. As he points out, something like this may help to explain discrepancies in the findings of Clayton and Gladden and of De Jong *et al.* Given that the former rely upon data from a small, liberal arts college in the South, it is possible their sample consists of more traditionally religious individuals whose faith possesses a definite and coherent logic. But in the latter study, involving a more religiously heterogeneous student population in a large, Eastern state university, perhaps there is less theological congruence, and hence its greater support for a multidimensional factor solution.

Denominational subcultures yield differing dimensional structures arising from variations in religious and cultural traditions (cf. Cline and Richards, 1965; Keene, 1967a, 67b; Nudelman, 1971; O'Connell, 1975; Tapp, 1971). To date, there has been very little systematic exploration of interfaith comparisons of religious styles. But the explorations we have, indicate that significant differences exist. In one such study, Klemmack and Cardwell (1973) report differing dimensional patterns for Protestants and Catholics, noting that Protestants are more inclined to think in terms of how their beliefs affect behavior, whereas Catholics tend to consider beliefs more in relation to ritual obligations. Depending upon a religious group's heritage—theological as well as cultural—there are variations in interpretations of ritual requirements, centrality of beliefs, and personal and social ethics. Especially along liberal-conservative lines, there tends to be considerable subculture variation.

Measurement Considerations

Finally, there is today, a growing awareness of the measurement problems in this research. One of these problems concerns the items used to measure religiosity. A close check of the items reveals that questions and statements put to respondents, even those often intended for measuring the same dimension, tap alternative and possibly distinct aspects of the mode of commitment involved. Verbit (1970) identifies four aspects of religiosity that, though different, often get lumped together in composite measures: *content, frequency, intensity,* and *centrality.* Content refers to the substantive characteristics of religion; frequency taps the amount of involvement; intensity measures determination or consistency in commitment; and centrality has to do with the importance attributed to a given act, belief, or feeling within the total religious system. Mixing these differing aspects and item formats is rather common in religious research, yet it raises serious questions about construct validity for the indices and perpetuates a good deal of confusion as to what is really measured in the name of religion.

Furthermore, the greater the diversity of item-types, the greater the chances that multiple dimensions will be uncovered in an empirical study. On the surface, multiple measures would appear to be obviously advantageous. Yet this is not always the case. Gorsuch and McFarland (1972) convincingly demonstrate that in some instances single-item scales may be equally satisfactory as multiple-item scales. Their research suggests that a single item probably measures intrinsic religious commitment as well but that multiple items are better at tapping traditional, orthodox beliefs; both types of measures appear to predict ethical attitudes (e.g., prejudice, business immorality) about equally well. Large numbers of items, even with high internal consistencies, may not necessarily result in greater validity; and, even if so, the slight increase in precision often fails to justify the greater costs to the research. Essentially, the point is that decisions about measurement cannot be made in the abstract but must take into consideration such factors as the differing approaches to religion, the relative validity of alternative measures, and the research costs.

More evident today, also, are the limitations of factor analysis. As a procedure for extracting factors from data, it can be quite useful in exploratory analysis. Factors produced by this method, however, are often sensitive both to the population examined and to the number and composition of items included in the analysis. It is also the case that, even though factors are usually determined according to criteria of statistical independence, there are alternative rotation methods for exploring the factor space, primitive and higher-order analyses, and varying degrees of rigor are enforced in making judgments about factor structures. The results of any given analysis must, therefore, be scrutinized carefully to establish comparability from one research study to another. As procedures have proliferated, researchers have come to be more and more concerned about how captive their findings and interpretations are to the methods they employ.

IV. Conclusions

That religion is multifaceted is taken for granted today, and the question is no longer uni- versus multidimensional approaches but rather the conditions under which a particular analytic approach is appropriate. Religious measures, as with much social scientific measurement, are developed for varying purposes and are used in many contexts. Awareness of this has led to a more self-consciously critical and constructive phase of intellectual development. Trends in this direction will likely continue in the 1980s as the scientific study of religion builds upon the work of previous decades.

Two directions for future research are crucial in following Glock's earlier advice to pursue investigations at both the intra- and the interdimensional levels. With the first—*within* dimensions—there is still a need for exploring subdimensional components of the core dimensions (i.e., belief, participation, and experience). In the realm of belief, especially, researchers have relied heavily on traditional orthodox doctrines as a baseline for describing the content of theistic conceptions. Broughton's (1975) work demonstrates what we all know but have not fully heeded—that the beliefs of church people are much more diverse and varied than the measures we use for characterizing them. Several attempts have been made to "get at" these subtleties (e.g., Davidson's (1975) "vertical" versus "horizontal" beliefs and Hunt's (1972) "literal" versus "mythological" types of commitment). Additional research is needed for exploring the belief systems of church members, and even more called for grasping the so-called "invisible" or alternative meaning systems of the populace at large. In view of the limitations and biases built into the use of conventional belief measures, this would seem to rank high on an agenda of research priorities in the decade ahead.

With the second—*between* dimensions—the need is for less exploration and description and more theoretical analysis. Already, some efforts are underway to incorporate dimensional schemes into theoretical paradigms, as in Lazerwitz's (1973) research linking religious behavior and beliefs to childhood religious socialization, in Finney's (1978) model of religious belief and practice as a consequence of religious group involvement, and in my own work (Roof, 1978) on local community "plausibility structures" for traditional church religion. These all share a concern to move beyond simply describing religious factors, in search of an explanatory scheme spelling out as much as possible logical and causal connections among dimensions. In all three instances, the "belonging" and "meaning" clusters of dimensions turn out to be instructive and a quite versatile basis for substantive theory construction. There are other theoretical points of departure, both sociological and psychological, that should prove to be enlightening as well. As a strategy for research, there is probably more to be gained from developing theoretical models utilizing the basic, or core, dimensions that are generalizable across populations than from endless efforts at uncovering new, or even refining old, dimensions. To be sure, refinements are still needed and desirable, but the real test for multidimensional measures is, in some final sense, their usefulness in an explanatory framework. How well the dimensions help in understanding the role of religion in social and cultural context or in elucidating the intricate relations between religion and personality—these are the tests of their lasting value insofar as the scientific study of religion is concerned.

References

Allen, Russell O., and Bernard Spilka
  1967   "Committed and consensual religion: A specification of religion–prejudice relationships." *Journal for the Scientific Study of Religion* 6:191–206.

Allport, Gordon W.
  1950   *The Individual and His Religion*. New York: MacMillan.
  1959   "Religion and prejudice." *The Crane Review* 2:1–10.
  1966   "The religious context of prejudice." *Journal for the Scientific Study of Religion* 5:447–457.

Allport, Gordon W., and J. M. Ross
  1967   "Personal religious orientation and prejudice." *Journal of Personality and Social Psychology* 5:432–433.

Allport, Gordon W., P. E. Vernon, and G. Lindzey
  1960   *The Study of Values*. Boston: Houghton Mifflin.

Bellah, Robert
  1967   "Civil religion in America." *Daedalus* 96:1–21.
  1970   *Beyond Belief*. New York: Harper and Row.

Berger, Peter
  1967   *The Sacred Canopy: Elements of a Sociological Theory of Religion*. Garden City, New York: Doubleday.

Blalock, Hubert M.
  1968   "The measurement problem: A gap between the languages of theory and research." Chapter 1 in H. M. Blalock and Ann B. Blalock (Eds.), *Methodology in Social Research*. New York: McGraw-Hill.

Broughton, Walter
  1975   "Theistic conceptions in American Protestantism." *Journal for the Scientific Study of Religion* 14:331–344.

Brown, L. B.
  1964   "Classification of religious orientation." *Journal for the Scientific Study of Religion* 4:91–99.

Campbell, Thomas and Yoshio Fukuyama
1970 *The Fragmented Laymen*. Philadelphia: Pilgrim Press.
Carrier, Herve
1965 *The Sociology of Religious Belonging*. New York: Herder and Herder.
Chave, E. J.
1939 *Measure Religion: Fifty-two Experimental Forms*. University of Chicago Press.
Cherry, Conrad
1971 *God's New Israel: Religious Interpretations of American Destiny*. Englewood Cliffs, New Jersey: Prentice-Hall.
Clayton, Richard R.
1971 "5-D or 1?" *Journal for the Scientific Study of Religion* 10:37-40.
Clayton, Richard R., and James W. Gladden
1974 "The five dimensions of religiosity: Toward demythologizing a sacred artifact." *Journal for the Scientific Study of Religion* 13:135-143.
Cline V. B., and J. M. Richards
1965 "A factor analytic study of religious beliefs and behaivor." *Journal of Personality and Social Psychology* 1:596-78.
Davidson, James
1975 "Glock's model of religious commitment: Assessing some different approaches and results." *Review of Religions Research* 16:83-93.
DeJong, Gordon, Joseph Faulkner, and Rex Warland
1976 "Dimensions of religiosity reconsidered: Evidence from a cross-cultural study." *Social Forces* 54:866-89.
Dittes, James E.
1969 "Psychology of religion." Pp. 602-659 in Gardner Lindsey and Elliot Aronson (Eds.), *The Handbook of Social Psychology*. Reading, Massachusetts: Addison-Wesley.
1971 "Two issues in measuring religion." Pp. 79-106 in M. P. Strommen (Ed.), *Research on Religious Development*. New York: Hawthorne.
Durkheim, Emile
1947 *The Elementary Forms of the Religious Life*. New York: The Free Press.
Faulkner, Joseph E., and Gordon F. DeJong
1966 "Religiosity in 5-D: An empirical analysis." *Social Forces* 45:246-254.
Feagin, Joe R.
1964 "Prejudice and religious types: A focus study of Southern Fundamentalists." *Journal for the Scientific Study of Religion* 4:3-13.
Fichter, Joseph H.
1951 *Dynamics of a City Church*. Chicago: University of Chicago Press.
Filsinger, Erik E.
1978 "A confirmatory factor analysis of religiosity comparing three cluster analysis-derived types of religious individuals." Unpublished paper, Arizona State University.
Finney, John M.
1978 "A theory of religious commitment." Sociological Analysis 39:19-35.
Fukuyama, Yoshio
1961 "The major dimensions of church membership." *Review of Religious Research* 2:154-161.
Geertz, Clifford
1966 "Religion as a cultural system." Pp. 1-46 in M. Banton (Ed.), *Anthropological Approaches to the Study of Religion*. New York: Praeger.

Gibbs, James O., and Kelly W. Crader
  1970 "A criticism of two recent attempts to scale Glock and Stark's dimensions of religiosity." *Sociological Analysis* 31:107–114.

Glock, Charles Y.
  1954 "Toward a typology of religious orientation." New York: Bureau of Applied Social Research, Columbia University.
  1959 "The sociology of religion." Pp. 153–177 in Robert Merton, Leonard Broom, and Leonard Cottrell (Eds.), *Sociology Today*. New York: Basic Books.
  1962 "On the study of religious commitment." *Research Supplement to Religious Education* 57:98–110.

Glock, Charles Y., and Thomas Piazza
  1978 "Exploring reality structures." *Society* 15:60–65.

Glock, Charles Y., and Rodney Stark
  1965 *Religion and Society in Tension*. Chicago: Rand McNally.

Gorsuch, Richard L., and Sam G. McFarland
  1972 "Single vs. multiple-item scales for measuring religious commitment." *Journal for the Scientific Study of Religion* 11:53–64.

Gray, David B.
  1970 "Measuring attitudes toward the Church." *Journal for the Scientific Study of Religion* 9:293–297.

Hammond, Phillip E.
  1963 "Religion and the 'informing' of culture." *Journal for the Scientific Study of Religion* 3:97–106.

Herberg, Will
  1955 *Protestant-Catholic-Jew*. Garden City, New York: Doubleday.

Himmelfarb, Harold
  1975 "Measuring religious involvement." *Social Forces* 53:606–18.

Hoge, Dean R.
  1972 "A validated intrinsic religious motivation scale." *Journal for the Scientific Study of Religion* 11:369–376.

Hunt, Richard A.
  1968 "The interpretation of the religious scale on the Allport–Vernon–Lindzey study of values." *Journal for the Scientific Study of Religion* 7:65–77.
  1972 "Mythological–symbolic religious commitment: The LAM scales." *Journal for the Scientific Study of Religion* 11:42–52.

Hunt, Richard A., and Morton King
  1971 "The intrinsic–extrinsic concept: A review and evaluation." *Journal for the Scientific Study of Religion* 10:33–356.

Keene, James
  1967a "Baha'i world faith: A redefinition of religion." *Journal for the Scientific Study of Religion* 6:221–235.
  1967b "Religious behavior and neuroticism, spontaneity, and worldmindedness." *Sociometry* 30:137–157.

King, Morton
  1967 "Measuring the religious variable: Nine proposed dimensions." *Journal for the Scientific Study of Religion* 6:173–185.

King, Morton, and Richard Hunt
  1969 "Measuring the religious variable: Amended findings." *Journal for the Scientific Study of Religion* 8:321–323.

1972a *Measuring Religious Dimensions: Studies in Congregational Involvement.* Dallas: Southern Methodist University.

1972b "Measuring the religious variable: Replication." *Journal for the Scientific Study of Religion* 11:240–251.

1975 "Measuring the religious variable: National replication." *Journal for the Scientific Study of Religion* 14:13–22.

Klemmach, D. L., and J. D. Cardwell
1973 "Interfaith comparison of multidimensional measures of religiosity." *Pacific Sociological Review* 16:495–507.

Lazerwitz, Bernard
1973 "Religious identification and its ethnic correlates: A multivariate model." *Social Forces* 52:204–222.

Lehman, Edward C. Jr., and Donald W. Shriver, Jr.
1968 "Academic discipline as predictive of faculty religiosity." *Social Forces* 47:171–182.

Lenski, Gerhard E.
1961 *The Religious Factor.* Garden City, New York:Doubleday.

Luckmann, Thomas
1967 *The Invisible Religion: The Transformation of Symbols in Industrial Society.* New York: Macmillan.

Machalek, Richard, and Michael Martin
1976 " 'Invisible' religions: Some preliminary evidence." *Journal for the Scientific Study of Religion* 15:311–321.

McCready, William C., and Andrew M. Greeley
1976 *The Ultimate Values of the American Population.* Beverly Hills: Sage.

Nelson, Hart M., Robert F. Everett, Paul Douglas Mader, and Warren C. Hamby
1976 "A test of Yinger's measure of non-doctrinal religion: Implications for invisible religion as a belief system." *Journal for the Scientific Study of Religion* 15:263–267.

Nudelman, A. E.
1971 "Dimensions of religiosity." *Review of Religious Research* 13:42–56.

O'Connell, Brian J.
1975 "Dimensions of religiosity among Catholics." *Review of Religious Research* 16: 198–207.

Roof, Wade Clark
1978 *Community and Commitment: Religious Plausibility in a Liberal Protestant Church.* New York: Elsevier.

Roof, Wade Clark, Christopher K. Hadaway, Myrna L. Hewitt, Douglas McGaw, and Richard Morse
1977 "Yinger's measure of non-doctrinal religion: A Northeastern test." *Journal for the Scientific Study of Religion* 16:403–408.

Spilka, Bernard
1958 "Some personality correlates of interiorized and institutionalized religious beliefs." *Psychological Newsletter* 9:103–107.

1971 "Research on religious beliefs: A critical review." Pp. 510–520 in M. P. Strommen (Ed.), *Research on Religious Development.* New York: Hawthorne.

Stark, Rodney, and Charles Y. Glock
1968 *American Piety: The Nature of Religious Commitment.* Berkeley: University of California Press.

Tapp, Robert B.
    1971   "Dimensions of religiosity in a post-traditional group." *Journal for the Scientific Study of Religion* 10:41–47.

Thurstone, L. L., and E. J. Chave
    1929   *The Measurement of Attitude.* Chicago: University of Chicago Press.

Verbit, Mervin
    1970   "The components and dimensions of religious behavior: Toward a reconceptionaliza-tion of religiosity." Pp. 24–38 in Phillip Hammond and Benton Johnson (Eds.), *American Mosaic: Social Patterns of Religion in the United States.* New York: Random House.

Wach, Joachim
    1944   *Sociology of Religion.* Chicago: University of Chicago Press.

Warner, W. Lloyd
    1961   *Family of God: A Symbolic Study of Christian Life in America.* New Haven: Yale University Press.

Weigert, Andrew, and Darwin Thomas
    1969   "Religiosity in 5-D: A critical note." *Social Forces* 48:260–263.

Whitam, F. L.
    1961   "Sub-dimensions of religiosity and race prejudice." *Review of Religious Research* 3:166–174.

Whitney, John R.
    1968   "Commentary on civil religion in America." Pp. 365–381 in Donald R. Cutler (Ed.), *The Religious Situation: 1968.* Boston: Beacon Press.

Wilson, W. C.
    1960   "Extrinsic religious values and prejudice." *Journal of Abnormal and Social Psychology* 60:286–288.

Wimberley, Ronald, Donald Clelland, Thomas Hood, and C. M. Lipsey
    1976   "The civil religious dimension: Is it there?" *Social Forces* 54:890–900.

Wuthnow, Robert
    1976   *The Consciousness Reformation.* Berkeley: University of California Press.

Yinger, Milton J.
    1969   "A structural examination of religion." *Journal for the Scientific Study of Religion* 8:88–99.
    1970   *The Scientific Study of Religion.* New York: Macmillan.
    1977   "A comparative study of the substructures of religion." *Journal for the Scientific Study of Religion* 16:67–86.

Chapter 2

Departures from Conventional Religion: The Nominally Religious, the Nonreligious, and the Alternatively Religious

CHARLES Y. GLOCK and ROBERT WUTHNOW

I. Introduction

In the past decade dozens of new religious groups have appeared, some of them attracting followers numbering in the hundreds of thousands. Many of these movements, inspired by Eastern philosophies, clearly fall outside the traditional orientations. Alongside heightened religious experimentation and revitalization, there are also signs of religious defection, of people abandoning religion altogether in favor of some secular philosophy or trying to live their lives without a religious or philosophical foundation. At the same time, it is clear that many people remain committed to traditional faiths.

This curious mixture of religious loyalty, experimentation, and defection is widely recognized by students of religion, but it is more speculated about than studied. By and large, there has been little systematic research directed to exploring alternative styles of religious commitment. As a consequence, very little is known systematically about how many are still committed to conventional religion, about the extent and character of the appeal of alternative

The Religious Dimension:
New Directions in Quantitative Research

religions and alternatives to religion, or about how many are indeed content to live their lives without a religious referent at all.

Using a variety of religious measures, some of which were specifically designed to go beyond the standard measures of traditional religion that have been much used in the past, we have drawn on data collected as part of the Berkeley Religious Consciousness project in order to afford, first of all, a descriptive portrait of the state of the religious dimension in the minds of the population of the San Francisco Bay Area. Second, we have engaged in some exploration of the difference it makes for people to be conventionally religious or to have departed from conventional religion in various ways.

The San Francisco Bay Area, it will be recognized, is not representative of America or of any other community. It is, however, among American communities that have been bellwethers of change in society. Many of the new religious movements that have surfaced in the United States in recent years had their start there. And it was, and continues to be, a place for more general countercultural innovation as well. As such, the Bay Area affords a valuable laboratory in which to compare a variety of religious styles not comparable in many other parts of the country.

Our more general inquiries into contemporary religious consciousness led us to pursue ethnographic studies of particular religious and quasi-religious movements in the Bay Area with the aid of a 1000-interview survey of the Bay Area population. In the survey, conducted in 1973, the under-30 age group in the population was oversampled to enable more in-depth analysis of this age group than is possible in the usual cross-sectional survey. However, the sample was drawn so that the results could be weighted as representative of the entire population.

It is widely believed, although again little studied, that youth in America have departed considerably from their elders in their religious orientations. To find out how true this is for the Bay Area, a descriptive portrait is constructed to compare the younger (under 30) and the older (30 and over) parts of the sample population. We begin our portrait with a consideration of the contemporary status of traditional religion in the Bay Area.

II. A Religious Portrait of the Bay Area Population

Traditional Religion

When we ask people in the Bay Area to identify themselves religiously, we find that the majority, both young people and their elders, still prefer a conventional religious identification, that is, Protestant, Roman Catholic, Jewish, Eastern Orthodox, or Mormon. Among youth, the majority is a bare 52%; among ''matures,'' it is a substantial 76%.

Youth and matures in the Bay Area are, however, considerably less likely to identify with conventional religion than their counterparts in the national population. In fact, a recent Gallup poll of the nation's youth—age's 18–24—found that as high a percentage of this age group (76%) identified themselves by traditional categories as did persons 30 years of age and over in the Bay Area.

Thirty-six percent of youth in the Bay Area disavow any connection with formal religion: Seventeen percent say they have no religious beliefs, 13% report themselves to be agnostic or atheist, and 6% define themselves as humanist. Eighteen percent of matures gave one or another of these three responses.

Not a large proportion of youth or matures (only 3% of each group) identify with non-Western religions—Buddhism, Hinduism, Islam, or Mysticism—and, in the Bay Area, a good proportion of these are likely to be Asian–Americans.

The remaining 9% of youth checked their religious preference as "Other." (Less than half as many matures—3%—did so.) It is evident from the responses of those defined as "Other" that this group is made up primarily of persons who do not want to identify themselves with traditional religion, but who, at the same time, want to say that they still think of themselves as somehow religious. By far the most frequent "other" response was "my own."

These results can be interpreted as the reader wishes—either that "fully" 52% of youth still identify with traditional religion or that "only" 52% do so—the interpretation is in the eyes of the beholder. Judging from what youth report to be the religion of their parents, however, the change is clearly away from conventional religion. Eighty five percent of mothers and 74% of fathers are reported to have been traditionally religious. (The figures for all matures are slightly higher—91% and 84%, respectively).

That defection from conventional religion is the order of the day is also indicated by what younger and older San Franciscans report about their religious practices. Although 65% of youth say that they attended church or synagogue weekly when they were growing up, only 34% say they take part in the activities of a church or synagogue now, and considerably fewer (15%), report doing so on a weekly basis. Among matures, 41% say they (ever) go to church or synagogue now; 22% say they go weekly; 72% said they went weekly when they were growing up.

Commitment to conventional religion was also assessed by asking respondents about their beliefs about God. One out of two youths claims to believe in God or to lean toward believing in God, about the same proportion who identify with conventional religions. The remainder is not made up entirely of strict nonbelievers, however. Just over a fifth of youth say they are atheistic (6%) or agnostic (14%) or that they lean toward not believing in God

(4%). A slightly smaller proportion (19%) say that they feel uncomfortable about the word "God" but do believe in something "more" or "beyond." Thus, 7 out of 10 youths are inclined to believe in some conception of the supernatural.

Matures are more inclined than youth to accept a traditional view of God. Seventy-seven percent either believe definitely or lean toward believing. Matures are also somewhat less inclined than youth to have abandoned belief in God. Fourteen percent (in comparison with 24%) say they are atheistic: or agnostic, or lean toward not believing in God. The unorthodox view also gets less support from matures than from youth; 8% say they are uncomfortable about the word "God" but do believe in something "more" or "beyond." Altogether, however, 86% of matures believe in some concept of the supernatural.

Attitudes toward the possibility of life after death afford another assessment of how much commitment there is to conventional religion and how much to other views. Here traditional views gain considerably less acceptance. Only 20% of youth are firm in their belief that there is life after death—16% believing there is life after death, with rewards for some and punishment for others, 4% saying that there is life after death, but without punishment. The respective figures for matures are 20% and 4%.

The reticence of subjects in both samples to accept traditional views of life after death is matched by a nearly equal reticence to deny the possibility of life beyond death: Only 14% of youth and 20% of matures score as firm disbelievers. More than half of both samples—61% of youth and 51% of matures—express uncertainty, saying either that they are just unsure whether or not there is a life after death (23% and 15%, respectively) or that they think there must be something beyond death but have no idea what it might be like (38% and 36%, respectively).

Reflecting the apparently growing impact of Eastern religion on Western thought, 5% of both youth and matures say that reincarnation comes closest to expressing their view of what happens to people when they die.

Overall, it is evident that traditional religion remains the principal reference point from which the majority of youth and matures judge their own religiosity. Among youth, however, the majority is a bare one, and the implications for religious practice suggest that commitment to traditional religion, where it prevails in these samples, is more nominal than vigorous and vital. Still, traditional religious categories continue to have an appeal for substantial numbers in this highly cosmopolitan and sophisticated metropolis.

Judging from the results of parents' religious preferences, the appeal of traditional religion is on the wane. It is impossible from these data, however, to predict the pace and to ascertain whether the direction is irreversible. The data do suggest that disenchantment with conventional religion will not necessarily be associated with an abandonment of religion itself. Although there are substantial minorities who appear to have defected from religion altogether, there are also significant signs that a religious ethos will prevail even as commitment to conventional religion declines further.

New Religions

"New" religious and quasi-religious movements are very apparent in the Bay Area. Our studies showed more than a hundred such movements that have been started since the middle sixties. A rich fare of alternative religions and alternatives to religion is not necessarily unique to the Bay Area, of course. Along with the rest of California, the Bay Area has long led the rest of the nation in affording a wide spectrum of countertraditional religions.

Part of our survey was devoted to assessing familiarity with, involvement in, and evaluation of the more visible and successful of the new movements. The movements asked about included four offshoots of Eastern religion (Transcendental Meditation, Hare Krishna, Zen Buddhism, and Yoga groups), four groups having Christian roots (Children of God, Campus Crusade for Christ, Christian World Liberation Front, Jews for Jesus), and two groups of Western origin, although outside of the Christian tradition (Scientology and Satanism). We also asked about familiarity with groups that speak in tongues.

Among youth, as can be seen from the upper part of Table 2.1, 14–65% have heard of these groups, with the Christian World Liberation Front (CWLF), a Berkeley-based offshoot of the Jesus movement, being at the low end of the range and Yoga at the upper end. Matures are less likely than youth to have heard of any of these groups; the range is from 10% (CWLF) to 40% (Yoga).

Not surprisingly, far fewer people in the Bay Area have taken part in these groups than have heard of them. The groups that have attracted the most participants are Yoga (14% of youth and 5% of matures) and Transcendental Meditation (9% of youth and 3% of matures). Tongue-speaking groups, which are likely to have a Christian base, come next in order of participants, 8% of youth and 5% of matures. Of the other Christian-based movements, Campus Crusade for Christ has attracted the most participants (4% among youth and 3% among matures). In all instances, young people are more likely to have participated than their elders.

The survey is flawed in that it did not discriminate as to degree of participation, and it is probable that some respondents claimed participation on the basis of the most casual exposure to a group. Otherwise, some groups would have huge numbers. Even so, it is evident that some of these movements are attracting the interest of substantial numbers of people, if not substantial proportions of the population.

TABLE 2.1 Response to "New" Religions among Bay Area Youth and Their Elders[a]

	Eastern religion				Christian					Other	
	Transcendental Meditation	Hare Krishna	Zen	Yoga	Children of God	Campus Crusade for Christ	Christian World Liberation Front	Jews for Jesus	Tongue Speaking Groups	Scientology	Satanism
Percentage who have heard of movement											
Youth	45%	47%	34%	65%	19%	23%	14%	27%	29%	32%	53%
Mature	26%	35%	29%	40%	13%	18%	10%	19%	25%	19%	29%
Ratio of knowledgeable youth to matures	1.73	1.34	1.17	1.63	1.46	1.28	1.40	1.42	1.16	1.68	1.83
Percentage who have participated in movement											
Youth	9%	2%	5%	14%	1%	4%	2%	1%	8%	2%	2%
Mature	3%	1%	1%	5%	1%	3%	*	1%	5%	*	*
Of those knowledgeable, ratio of those attracted to those turned off by a movement											
Youth	3.56	.29	3.32	5.66	1.48	.82	1.93	.80	1.00	.57	.19
Mature	2.86	.31	3.91	3.44	1.82	2.44	1.87	1.68	.51	.79	.11

[a] Asterisk indicates less than .5%.

Our study was also designed to see whether these groups were arousing positive feelings, negative feelings, or indifference among the general population. Toward each of these groups, many of those who had only heard of them have had no reaction, with matures on the average (43%) being more indifferent than youth (39%). Among those with an opinion (see lower part of Table 2.1), the groups achieving the most positive responses are those inspired by Eastern religion. Yoga, for example, is mentioned favorably about 6 times as often as unfavorably by youth; among matures, the ratio is 3.4 to 1. Transcendental Meditation and Zen also generate a very favorable response. Hare Krishna does not fare well and, among both age groups, receives a net unfavorable evaluation. For the most part, Christian-based movements receive somewhat more positive than negative reactions, especially among matures, but not nearly as strongly as do the Eastern groups. Groups speaking in tongues get a neutral score from youth—they are judged favorably as often as unfavorably. Among matures, however, negative opinion outweighs positive reaction by a substantial margin. Scientology gets a mildly unfavorable net reaction and Satanism a highly unfavorable net reaction among both age groups. It should be mentioned that there is a highly visible Satanism church in the Bay Area.

Overall, these results indicate that these new religions, expecially those rooted in Eastern religion, have become known to a substantial proportion of the Bay Area population. Actual participation is considerably less, although movements that can attract 5% or more of the population can scarcely be dismissed out of hand. The extent to which Eastern groups have aroused a favorable response is striking. It is evident that there is considerably greater interest in and empathy for Eastern religious practices than is represented by the 3% or so found earlier to identify themselves naturally with Eastern religions. That youth are more often attracted to new religions than matures was perhaps to be expected. Unfortunately, we cannot judge from these cross-sectional data whether the difference is a permanent, generational one or an artifact of comparing two groups at different points in the life cycle.

It might be debatable as to whether or not the occult falls within the domain of religious phenomenon. In a study of how people respond to alternative religious forms, however, it did not seem inappropriate to inquire about reactions to what may loosely be termed occult beliefs and practices, such as spiritualism, astrology, and extrasensory perception.

Subscription to spiritualistic beliefs was not assessed in any comprehensive way in the interview. Respondents were asked, however, to respond to the claim of some spiritualists that it is possible to communicate with the dead. More youth are convinced that such communication is not possible (33%) than are sure that it is (8%). Most take middle positions, with 26% saying that it is probable and 33% responding that it is probably not. As many matures as youth (8%) are convinced that communication with the dead is possible. A considerably larger proportion of matures (56%) than youth (33%), however, deny the possibility entirely.

Astrology, like spiritualism, is something that few are willing to deny completely. Only 24% of youth say they are firm disbelievers in the claim that the stars, the planets, and our birthdays influence our destiny in life. There are more firm disbelievers (34%) among matures. On the other hand, relatively few in either age group seem to be firmly convinced about astrology. Only 8% of youth and 11% of matures identify themselves as firm believers. The majority in both samples (68% and 55%, respectively) say they are doubtful.

That astrology attracts little serious involvement even though it clearly elicits much less serious interest and speculation is also shown by what people claim to know about it and how interested they are in their horoscopes. Among youth, 4%, and among matures, 2%, claim to know a good deal about astrology. But, 35% of youth claim to know at least a fair amount of astrology, a higher proportion than for matures (21%). Similarly, a small minority claim to be quite interested in their horoscopes, 9% and 10% in the two samples.

Despite the fact that not many people seem to be seriously caught up in astrology, it is important to recognize that astrology is salient for most people, at least minimally. For example, only 4% of youth and 7% of matures say they do not know what a horoscope is. It is more significant, perhaps, that 98% of youth and 86% of matures are able to identify their astrological signs.

Parapsychological phenomena, like spiritualism and astrology, are not considered religious phenomena in the minds of most people. Many people also prefer to distinguish them from other phenomena that are ordinarily classed as occult. However they may be classified, there is, nevertheless, an extraordinary degree of openness on the part of most people to parapsychological phenomena. The overwhelming majority (96% of youth and 87% of matures) are familiar with ESP, and, among those who have heard of it, 91% of youth and 87% of matures think it *probably* exists. Among youth, nearly two-fifths (39%) are *sure* it exists. The equivalent figure for matures is almost as high (36%). At the other extreme, only 1% of youth and 3% of all Bay Area respondents are sure ESP does not exist.

Not only is there widespread belief in the existence of ESP, but surprising proportions—50% of youth and 45% of matures—report they have had ESP experiences. These respondents were then also asked to describe their experience or, if more than one, their most profound experience. Forty-four percent of these descriptions concerned telepathic experiences, 42% precognition, 2% clairvoyance, 1% psychokinesis, 1% experiences of leaving the body, 3% apparitions, with the remainder not being classifiable. The largest subgroup of experience involved simply thinking the same thought at the same time as somebody else (26%). These usually tended to be described as relatively superficial coincidences. Other subgroups of experiences that were reported most often were premonitions of danger, tragedy, or illness (9%); awareness at a distance of deaths, danger, or illness (9%); simple déjà vu feelings (9%); and precognitions about minor personal events (8%).

For those reporting telepathic experiences, the kind of person with whom they had had the experience was also recorded. Most commonly, the person was identified as a friend (37%); spouses, parents, and children were mentioned equally (11% each). For those reporting precognitive experiences, an attempt was made to discover the mode of the precognition. Vague feelings was the most frequent response (34%), followed by dreams (31%).

Judging from the way they described their experiences, most respondents did not view them as being of profound importance in their lives. Experiences were virtually never viewed as having any religious significance, for example. Nevertheless, in their remarks, many people conveyed a desire to *believe* that they had had a personal encounter with ESP. Indeed, it is striking that both more youth and more matures are sure, or lean toward believing, that ESP exists than that God exists.

Religious Questions

Thus far, the results indicate that even if traditional religion is in decline, there is still a considerable degree of interest in what might be described as alternatives to conventional religion, namely, in new religious movements and in occult phenomena. Moreover, this interest in alternatives is as great and more often greater among youth than among matures. Clearly, matures, more often than youth, choose a conventionally religious response. When the choice is between admitting the possiblity of a religious dimension, however defined, or denying it entirely, however, it is the matures rather than youth who more often choose the nonreligious response.

The continuing saliency of the religious dimension for the majority of people is also demonstrated by responses to questions about interest in "ultimate concerns" of life. For example, 71% of youth and 70% of matures say they sometimes think about the purpose of life; 31% and 29%, respectively, say they do this often. Similarly, 70% of youth say that they sometimes think about the question "How did I come to be the way I am?" and 61% of matures do so. Although matures are more inclined than youth to think sometimes about "the existence of God" (77% as compared with 64%), the question does have saliency for a majority of youth. Even such a fundamental question as how the world came into being continues to bother a majority— 56% of youth and 57% of matures think about this sometimes or often. The age-old problem of why there is suffering in the world is also thought about widely, by 79% and 85% of the two samples. And the question as to whether there is life after death is still a matter of concern for most people.

The average amount of interest expressed in these questions shows that 28% of youth often think about questions such as these, 38% think about them sometimes, 18% have thought about them in the past but do not now, and 16% never think about them. Among matures, these proportions are 31%, 37%, 12%, and 20%, respectively. Many of the more "ultimate" questions are reported to be thought about as often as such things as money matters, events in the news, and health.

Religious Experience

The final area in which an attempt was made to assess the religious dimension had to do with its experiential side. Once again, the results reveal a widespread sensitivity to and interest in religious phenomena, albeit not as conventionally expressed. When asked, for example, whether they had ever had the feeling that they were in close contact with something holy or sacred, 52% of youth and 49% of matures said they had not. About half of these in both age groups, however, said they would like to have such an experience. Of the 48% of youth who had had such an experience, moreover, almost half said it had had a lasting influence on their lives. For matures, three out of five reported the experience as having been a lasting one.

Much larger proportions of youth (83%) and matures (81%) report having experienced the beauty of nature in a deeply moving way. Considerably fewer—37% of youth and 41% of matures—report having had the feeling that they were in harmony with the universe, an experience associated more with Eastern religious thought. Among those who have had no such experience, about three out of five of each age group would like to have one.

Taken in sum, the foregoing affords no easy conclusions about the course of religion in contemporary society. More and more, people may be coming to regard conventional religion with skepticism or disinterest. There is little in this evidence, however, to suggest that religious sentiments are dying out. On the contrary, although taking different forms, religious sentiments remain pervasive throughout the age spectrum in this sophisticated American community.

At the same time, it is clear that many persons, especially youth, are content to dissociate themselves from any formal identification with religion and that for many who continue such identification their religious commitments occupy only a peripheral place in their lives. Nevertheless, the religious dimension remains, by and large, extraordinarily salient. And, as the new interest in the occult, in parapsychology, and in Asian religions testifies, there are religious sentiments to be appealed to.

III. The Broader Meaning of Religious Orientations

Defection from conventional religion and experimentation with alternative religion may be epiphenomena having little or nothing to do with other major currents in the society. Or they may be signs of something more profound and far-reaching than simply religious change. Which of these alternatives comes closer to representing the true situation cannot be answered systematically, even for the San Francisco Bay Area, with data such as ours, collected at one point in time. By virtue of there being enough defectors and experimenters in the sample to allow for statistical treatment, however, the data do afford a rare opportunity to explore the meaning of such defection and experimentation. Such exploration cannot answer questions about the rate of change or about the causal processes. Still, in the absence of national social indicators to measure change in the religious dimension in a comprehensive way, such exploration recommends itself as a means to generate clues about what may be taking place.

An exploration of religious loyalty, defection, and experimentation requires some means to classify the alternatives. For present purposes, we sought to select relatively ''pure'' examples of the three types from the sample. To score as religiously loyal, by which we mean conventionally religious, respondents had to do at least two of the following three things: identify themselves with a religion in the Judeao–Christian heritage, express themselves as firmly believing in life after death, and engage in religious activity in church or synagogue at least once a week.

To score as nonreligious, by which we mean defection from all religion, respondents had to say they had never had an experience of the sacred and would not want to. In addition, they had to do at least two of the following three things: identify themselves religiously as without religious belief, as atheist, or as agnostic; say they were atheist or agnostic when asked about their belief in God; and reject outright the possibility of life after death.

Respondents who scored as conventionally religious or as nonreligious by the aforementioned criteria were automatically ruled out of consideration for being judged as alternatively religious. This type was chosen from the remainder, using the criteria that the respondent express discomfort with the word ''God'' but profess a belief in something ''more'' or ''beyond'' and identify themselves religiously as humanist, mystical, or other.

Of the 1000 respondents (using the weighted sample), 523 were assigned, following these procedures: 337 to the category conventionally religious, 108 to the category nonreligious, and 78 to the category alternatively religious. Of the remaining 477 respondents, 46 were eliminated because of incomplete data, leaving 431 whom we have labeled as ''nominally religious.'' Their inconsistent responses reveal them to be in some state of limbo about their religious orientation, but still not wanting to abandon religion entirely.

This rather judgmental mode of classification did not produce quite the degree of purity in the three primary types that ideally we would have liked. Comparing the three primary types with the residual group on a variety of religious variables not used to classify them, however, their response is as their mode of classification would predict. Thus, for example, on a question as to whether they think suffering comes about because people do not believe in God, 76% of the conventionally religious said they think so, compared with 17% of the areligious and 23% of the alternatively religious. The nominally religious fall between the extremes; 48% feel that suffering is a result of God's not being obeyed. As can be seen in Table 2.2, the same pattern emerges from answers to other questions affording a choice as to identification with conventional religion: By and large, the conventionally religious do, and the nonreligious and alternatively religious do not.

The typology is predictive not only of responses about commitment to conventional religion, but also of responses about openness to alternative

TABLE 2.2 Saliency of Conventional Religious Symbolism by Religious Orientation[a]

Percentage who say:	Religious orientation			
	Conventional	Nominal	None	Alternative
Suffering is merely a result of God not being obeyed.	76%	48%	17%	23%
God created the first man and woman.	89%	57%	10%	12%
Great importance in life to follow God's will.	76%	30%	1%	7%
Great importance in life to take part in church.	48%	7%	*	4%
(N)	(337)	(431)	(108)	(78)

[a] Asterisk indicates less than 1%.

TABLE 2.3 Openness to "New" Religions by Religious Orientation

Ratio of favorable to unfavorable responses to:	Religious orientation			
	Conventional	Nominal	None	Alternative
Yoga	2.4	4.6	2.8	37.1
Zen Buddhism	1.4	4.9	1.9	12.6
Transcendental Meditation	1.9	5.6	1.8	3.5
Hare Krishna	.2	.4	.1	.4
Percentage who practice meditation using definite techniques	7%	6%	3%	14%
(N)	(337)	(431)	(108)	(78)

religions. On such questions, as can be seen in Table 2.3, the alternatively religious are the most open to the alternatives. Now, however, the nonreligious, rather than resembling the alternatively religious as they did on questions asking about conventional religion, respond as the conventionally religious do.

When it comes to the "ultimate concerns" of life, the strength of the predictive power of the different orientations depends on whether or not the concern is one to which conventional religion has given attention. Thus, the conventionally religious are considerably more apt than the other groups to be concerned about the existence of God; only a small proportion of the nonreligious find this question salient. A similar pattern prevails with respect to what happens after death. On questions not so closely identified with traditional religion, such as "the purpose of life," "finding happiness in life," "why there is suffering in the world," "why you are the way you are," and "how the world came into being," the conventionally religious and the alternatively religious are about equally likely to express concern. Fewer of the nonreligious express interest in such questions, although the differences are not very great, as can be seen in Table 2.4.

In sum, then, the four orientations differ less in how salient their members consider ultimate questions of life to be than in how much credence they give to the possibility of religious answers to such questions and to different kinds of religious answers. The nonreligious see no possibility of religious answers being supplied by conventional or alternative religions. The alternatively religious are about as inclined as the nonreligious to give up on conventional religious answers, but, unlike the nonreligious, they acknowledge that there *are* religious answers. For the conventionally religious, what the Judaeo–Christian tradition supplies by way of answers suffices. The nominally religious fall mostly between the other three types. They are less skeptical of conventional religion than the nonreligious and alternatively religious, more open to a nonreligious perspective than are the conventionally and alternatively

TABLE 2.4   Interest in Ultimate Questions of Life by Religious Orientation

Percentage who say they think some or a lot about:	Religious orientation			
	Conventional	Nominal	None	Alternative
The existence of God.	92%	77%	23%	54%
What happens after death.	73%	53%	33%	61%
Purpose of life.	67%	66%	63%	76%
Why there is suffering in the world.	86%	81%	81%	82%
How you come to be the way you are.	67%	59%	61%	82%
How world come into being.	62%	57%	50%	57%
(N)	(337)	(431)	(108	(78)

religious, and more attracted to alternative religion than are the nonreligious or the conventionally religious.

Since the religious history of respondents is not known in detail, it cannot be said for sure which of these religious orientations is ascendent and which descendent. Judging from reported parental religion, the primary change is in the direction of defection from rather than recruitment to conventional religion, with the defection being largely toward becoming nominally religious rather than toward being not religious or alternatively religious. There are certainly more nonreligious and alternatively religious persons among respondents than among their parents, but because parents' religion was not asked about in sufficient detail, it is impossible to say how much movement there is or to judge whether the direction is more to nonreligion or to alternative religion.

What difference does religious orientation make to other kinds of attitudes and values? The usual assumption is that to be religiously conventional is to be conventional in other ways as well. Which comes first—conventional religion or other conventionalities—is not always clear. The common experience has been to find that the two go together. What is not so self-evident, mostly because not enough people with alternative religious commitments have heretofore been available to study as a type, is what it means to be alternatively religious. Whether to expect the alternatively religious to be more like the nonreligious or more like the conventionally religious in life-style and social outlook has not been explored, by and large, or even speculated about.

The data allow exploration of the connections between religious orientations and four other spheres of life: personal morality, political outlook, material comfort, and life-style. We shall begin the exploration by comparing the conventionally religious with the nonreligious. Then, bearing in mind their similarities and dissimilarities, we shall turn to the alternatively religious to see which, if either, of the other groups they resemble. Finally, we shall consider where the nominally religious fit into the picture.

The Conventionally Religious and Nonreligious

It has just been remarked that to be conventionally religious is to be conventional in other ways as well. By analogy, this would mean that to be nonreligious is to be unconventional. As it seems with all generalizations, there is some truth and some untruth in this one. The conventionally religious do turn out to be more conventional than the nonreligious in some realms of life other than the religious one. There are realms, however, where the nonreligious show equal or even greater proclivities for the conventional.

The two orientations are most sharply divided on canons of personal morality, the conventionally religious, as one would expect, being the more committed to mores that were dominant in America's past. The differences are revealed with respect to how much importance in life is attached to living up to strict moral standards. More than three and a half times as many of the conventionally religious (53%) as of the nonreligious (15%) consider this to be of great importance. They are also revealed in the extent to which changes in moral conventions of society are sanctioned. Whereas only 30% of the conventionally religious, for example, approve of an unmarried couple living together, 76% of the nonreligious do so. Twenty-three percent of the nonreligious would oppose more freedom for homosexuals, whereas the figure for the conventionally religious is 61%.

When it comes to behaving in a way that would violate conventional morality, the two groups are not so sharply divided, although it is the conventionally religious who are more often more conventionally moral. Thus, whereas 59% of the conventionally religious would definitely not be willing to say they were sick when they were not, in order to get an extra day off, only 41% of the nonreligious would be unwilling to do so. Similarly, 85% of the conventionally religious say they would definitely not buy a radio or TV from someone who had stolen it and was selling cheap, whereas the nonreligious figure is 61%.

These differences are not a function of the nonreligious being younger on the average than the conventionally religious. Age makes a difference, of course, but so does religious orientation. On the question of buying a stolen radio or TV, for example, 72% of the conventionally religious youth say they would not consider doing so, but only 48% of nonreligious youth would not consider doing so. In general, the differences between religious orientations are sharper for youth than for matures, but differences are in the same direction as indicated by the total figures.

The conventionally religious are also more prone to be conservative in their political outlook and in their attitudes on political issues, the differences being in the same range as on questions of personal morality. The nonreligious, for example, are three times as likely as the conventionally religious to consider themselves liberal or to the left of the politically liberal, 40% as compared with 13%. On questions about giving police more power, legalizing marijuana, or admiring someone who is trying to keep Communism from spreading in the United States, the nonreligious are about half as likely to give a conservative response as are the conventionally religious.

A realm of the conventional that has not been explored in previous research on the correlates of conventional religiosity has to do with what may be called the creature comforts of conventional life. Here it is not as self-evident as it was with regard to personal morality and politics as to what the two orientations ought to imply. Viewed from the perspective that religion traditionally has sought to emphasize the spiritual over the material in life, the results might be expected to indicate a greater disposition of the nonreligious toward creature comforts, since their religious outlook affords no antimaterialistic constraints. On the other hand, from what we have just learned about their political outlook, the nonreligious, more than the conventionally religious, have political reasons for opposing materialism.

By and large, the two outlooks nearly cancel each other out, although there is a slight tendency in the direction of the greater inclination of the nonreligious to attach importance to the material aspects of life. This tendency does not extend to job security, to which essentially the same proportions (45% and 46%) of the two orientations attach importance. Such things as having a high-paying job, a beautiful home, a new car, and other nice things or of becoming famous are by slight margins, however, more often judged to be of great importance by the nonreligious. Twenty-four percent of the nonreligious, for example, attach great importance to having a good job, whereas only 16% of the conventionally religious do so.

These results suggest that, despite their ideological differences with the conventionally religious, the nonreligious may be no more willing, when the chips are down, to break sharply with the conventional if this means sacrificing material comforts. The results are only faintly suggestive of this possibility, of course, but the idea gains additional credence when the two groups are compared with respect to their openness to alternative life-styles. The nonreligious are somewhat more open to such alternatives, but not nearly as much as the wide divergence in political and moral outlook would predict. For example, 93% of the conventionally religious are "turned off" by the prospect of living in a commune, but almost as many (88%) of the nonreligious feel this way. The quantitative differences between the two groups are similarly small with respect to trying organic foods or herbs and are nonexistent on such matters as believing it important to be aware of your body or to live close to nature. The only *sharp* difference in life-style between the 2 groups is that the nonreligious are almost five times as likely (38%) as are the conventionally religious (8%) to smoke marijuana (pot).

The Alternatively Religious

By and large, to be alternatively religious represents a sharper and more pervasive break with the conventional than does being nonreligious. The differences between the conventionally and alternatively religious on canons of personal morality are in every instance greater than between the conventionally religious and the nonreligious. The same applies to political outlook and political attitudes. Thus, for example, whereas 30% of the conventionally religious and 76% of the nonreligious countenance unmarried couples living together, 91% of the alternatively religious do. On political outlook, it will be recalled, 13% of the conventionally religious and 40% of the nonreligious identify themselves as liberal or left of liberal. For the alternatively religious, the figure is 56%. The differences are not limited to these items. Whatever item is used to compare the orientations on matters of personal morality or political attitude, the alternatively religious are the most in disagreement with conventional norms.

Unlike the nonreligious, the alternatively religious break with the conventionally religious in other realms of life. Thus, the alternatively religious in all comparisons are the least likely of the three orientations to attach great importance to the "creature comfort" items. Seven percent of the alternatively religious, for example, assign great importance to having a high-paying job, whereas 24% and 16%, respectively, of the nonreligious and the conventionally religious do so. Similarly, whereas about 45% of both the conventionally religious and the nonreligious are concerned about job security, only 26% of the alternatively religious are.

Openness to alternative life-styles is also more characteristic of the alternatively religious than of either of the other two groups, which, it will be recalled, resemble each other in this respect. Fifty-nine percent of the alternatively religious, for example, deem it of great importance to live close to nature, and 44% think it important to be aware of your body. Among the conventionally religious, the comparable figures, respectively, are 32% and 23%, and, among the nonreligious, they are 33% and 24%. As for pot smoking, in which more of the nonreligious than the conventionally religious were found to indulge, the alternatively religious are even more likely to do so. The figures are 8%, 38%, and 54%.

These results, once again, are not an artifact of group age. When examined controlling for age, the results are always in the same direction. Among both youth and matures, the alternatively religious are more sharply and pervasively in conflict with the conventionally religious on all of the issues examined than are the nonreligious.

The Nominally Religious

The nominally religious fall between the conventionally religious and the nonreligious in personal morality and political outlook. As can be seen in Tables 2.5 and 2.6, they are always less disposed to give a conservative response than are the conventionally religious, but more likely to do so than the nonreligious (and, of course, the alternatively religious). In most instances, they more closely resemble the conventionally religious than the nonreligious, although, if there is any movement, presumably it is away from the stances of the conventionally religious. What we cannot tell with these data on personal morality and political outlook is whether the nominally religious are more

TABLE 2.5 Personal Morality by Religious Orientation

Percentage who:	Religious orientation			
	Conventional	Nominal	None	Alternative
Say it is of great importance in life to live up to strict moral standards.	53%	31%	15%	15%
Disapprove of unmarried couples living together.	60%	29%	18%	7%
Disapprove of more freedom for homosexuals.	61%	40%	23%	14%
Are unwilling to say they are sick in order to get an extra day off.	59%	51%	41%	38%
Are unwilling to buy a stolen radio or TV.	85%	75%	61%	58%
(N)	(337)	(431)	(108)	(78)

TABLE 2.6 Political Outlook and Attitudes by Religious Orientation

Percentage who:	Religious orientation			
	Conventional	Nominal	None	Alternative
Identify themselves as liberal or left of liberal in politics.	13%	22%	40%	56%
Admire someone who was trying to stop Communism from spreading in the U.S.	65%	62%	39%	19%
Favor legalizing marijuana.	23%	37%	64%	88%
Favor giving police more power.	48%	39%	28%	17%
Favor new laws or taxes making it impossible for anyone to become extremely wealthy.	36%	36%	43%	61%
(N)	(337)	(431)	(108)	(78)

likely to end up in the camp of the nonreligious or of the alternatively religious or to remain close to where they are.

Arguing against their ending up in the alternatively religious camp are the figures bearing on commitment to creature comforts. Here, as can be seen in Table 2.7, the nominally religious resemble the nonreligious and not the alternatively religious. The nominally religious are also more like the nonreligious in their openness to the possibility of living in a commune, to trying organic foods and herbs, and to smoking pot. (See Table 2.8.)

These suggestions that the nominally religious, if they move at all, are more likely to end up in the nonreligious than in the alternatively religious camp are in some contradiction, of course, with earlier evidence revealing the nominally religious to be much more attracted to the so-called new religions than either

TABLE 2.7 Interest in Material Comforts by Religious Orientation

Percentage who assign great importance in life to:	Religious orientation			
	Conventional	Nominal	None	Alternative
Having job security.	46%	46%	46%	26%
Having a high-paying job.	16%	25%	24%	7%
Having a beautiful home and car.	12%	17%	19%	9%
Being famous.	4%	9%	4%	6%
(N)	(337)	(431)	(108)	(78)

TABLE 2.8 Openness to Alternative Life-Styles by Religious Orientation

Percentage who:	Religious orientation			
	Conventional	Nominal	None	Alternative
Would not consider living in a commune.	93%	88%	88%	60%
Have tried organic foods.	48%	50%	58%	87%
Use organic foods regularly.	9%	11%	4%	21%
Would try out some herbs to make them feel better.	39%	40%	41%	70%
Smoke pot.	8%	19%	38%	54%
Percentage who assign great importance in life to:				
Living close to nature.	32%	39%	33%	59%
Being aware of one's body.	23%	30%	24%	44%
Spending a lot of time getting to know your inner self.	27%	33%	27%	59%
(N)	(337)	(431)	(108)	(78)

the conventionally religious or the nonreligious. That the issue is far from settled is also indicated by the additional evidence, reported in Table 2.8, that the nominally religious are also more likely than the conventionally religious and nonreligious to assign great importance to living close to nature, learning to be aware of your body, and spending a lot of time getting to know your inner self, aspects of life that the alternatively religious are especially prone to treasure.

IV. Conclusions

The portrait of the broader meaning of the four types of religious orientation that has emerged is one of relative rather than absolute differences.

Clearly, there are other factors, aside from the religious one, that signal how people are going to live and to respond to events. Still, as the foregoing testifies, religious orientation is not without effect; it constitutes an influence and, in some respects, a significant one, in shaping and reflecting the lives of individuals and the character of society.

Consequently, it is of no small moment that the American religious land-scape is in the process of change. What form that process takes will shape not only the future character of religious life in America but also the character of social life as well.

The scenario for the future of religion, implicit in much social science writing on the subject, is that religion has no future; the future of religion is nonreligion. Perhaps this is not what is intended when social scientists talk about secularization and about how the secularization process seems to be an inexorable one. Yet, as the evidence of a decline of conventional religion in American society has mounted, the most common assumption among social scientists has been that defection from conventional religion means defection from religion altogether.

The San Francisco Bay Area data do not rule out such a possible scenario. It is evident that people are being recruited, or at least socialized to, being nonreligious and are, apparently, living quite comfortably with being so. Their numbers are not large, but, judging from the appeal of nonreligion to youth and to the educated, there is potential for growth if the trend toward more education continues and if the trend is a generational one rather than simply an artifact of the life cycle.

The kind of society that would accompany the ascendence of nonreligion is only hinted at in our explorations. The data suggest that it would be marked by changing standards of personal morality and by a political shift to the left. Any drastic change in social arrangements, however, is likely to be inhibited by a reluctance on the part of those without religion to change their style of life, including the material advantages that it now enables them to enjoy.

The data testify more to the possibility than to the probability that nonreligion will ever become dominant. The pervasiveness of a religious ethos, of a longing for religious answers, gives pause to the assumption that a major-ity of Americans will ever, or at least in the foreseeable future, be content with a world without religion. However, the prospects are not great, judging from these data, that the religion that will prevail will be religion as Americans have traditionally known it, although that possibility should not be ruled out prematurely. This is not because there are signs in these data that conventional religion is enjoying a revival. It seems reasonably clear that this is not the case. Still, given the tenacity of commitment to conventional religion on the part of a still large proportion of the Bay Area population, plus other evidence that the commitment is even more widespread in other areas of the country, it seems wise to be cautious about predicting the early or even the eventual demise of conventional religion. The possibility also cannot be ruled out that, in the competition for those now searching for new religious answers, some new vision of traditional faith may be the successful competitor. It is also possible that conventional religion can make some successful accommodation with the growing interest in alternative religion. Their appeal, the data suggest, derives largely from their emphasis on religious experience. The experiential component, except at the fringes of conventional religion, has played "second fiddle" to religious belief and practice for a long time. The time may be ripe for trying to change its status, and, if this is a direction in which conventional religion should move, and there are already signs that it is doing so, as witness the emergence of the Catholic Charismatic Renewal, the prospects for revival may be far greater than the present data suggest.

Compared with other religious orientations, conventional religion is at present more inhibiting than encouraging of social change. Were it to return to dominance in its present form, its return would undoubtedly be accompanied by a reaction against the present direction of social, moral, and political change. The chances are, however, that, to produce a major revival of conventional religion, any new interpretation or new emphasis would have to break with the past, not only spiritually, but socially and politically as well.

The newest, probably the most exciting, and certainly the most intriguing prospect set forth by the data is for a future characterized by a growing diffusion of religion that gains its inspiration from other than Western religious thought. This is a prospect not much contemplated in previous speculation about the future of religion in America. It may be premature to contemplate it now. As was remarked earlier, alternative religion is no stranger to the Bay Area. Its present size and variety seem greater than in the past. This is at least the impression conveyed from reading about the past and talking to oldtimers who lived through the last surge of alternative religion in the 1930s, but this may be more a function of a larger current population than of substantially greater popular interest. Still, with as many as 8% of the population already involved with alternative religion, as the data suggest, and with several times that proportion expressing disenchantment with conventional religion, the prospects for alternative religion seem as great if not greater than those for nonreligion or conventional religion, at least in its present configuration.

Currently, the alternative religious scene is a pluralistic one, and in our studies we found no one version of it giving promise of becoming dominant. It is conceivable, though doubtful, that the "mass base" to become a significant force in American religious future can be achieved if alternative religion maintains its current pluralistic cast. Alternative religion, were it to become ascendent, would bring with it, if the present data are any indication, not only a sharp break with America's religious past but pervasive change in life-style, in moral standards, and in social and political arrangements as well.

The key to America's future religious course probably rests with those whom we have classified as nominally religious. They are now the largest group in the Bay Area and, we suspect, in the nation as a whole. The direction they take, consequently, is likely to determine which of various possible scenarios for the future of religion works out. What the data mostly reveal about the nominally religious, however, is their enigmatic character. None of the options is ruled out. Their nominalism could conceivably be transformed into nonreligion. It has potential for being challenged by alternative religion, for remaining where it is, or, even, given the proper circumstances, for being rewon by conventional religion.

Chapter 3

Images of God and Their Social Meanings

THOMAS PIAZZA and CHARLES Y. GLOCK

I. Introduction

Since the early years of the Gallup Poll, a cross-section of Americans has periodically been asked "Do you believe in God?" Every time the question has been asked, the proportion answering "yes" has been at least 90%. In 1944, for example, 96% said they believed in God; in 1975, 94% expressed such belief.[1] Although the proportion of believers varies somewhat with respect to geographical region, age, and level of education, the fact remains that an overwhelming proportion of Americans profess a belief in God.

In spite of this apparent near-unanimity, however, it is clear that people do not all mean the same thing when they acknowledge a belief in God. Not only do people differ considerably in the strength of their belief, but their conceptions of what God is like also vary. In sum, most Americans believe in *a* God, but this does not necessarily imply that they have the same thing in mind.

---

[1] The 1944 figure is from Gallup (1972:473). For 1975, see Gallup (1976:14).

The Religious Dimension:
New Directions in Quantitative Research

That believers vary in their images of God has long been known, but, to our knowledge, there has been little effort to describe this variation or to explore its significance. For the most part, researchers have been satisified to distinguish believers from non believers, further dividing believers into Protestant, Catholic, and Jewish (Caplovitz and Sherrow, 1977). Where greater refinement has been sought, believers have been distinguished according to the *strength* of their belief, but not according to the *content* of their belief in God. In this chapter we will focus on the differences among believers in the content of their belief, that is, on the variation in how God is conceptualized. What we propose to do is, first of all, to divide those who believe in God into different groups, depending on their images of God. Then we will explore what those different images seem to imply for the social attitudes of those who hold the images. The data we will use to study these issues are from a 1973 attitude survey of a sample of the adult population of the San Francisco Bay Area.[2] Although these data were collected originally for another purpose, questions were included that make it possible to distinguish among different types of believers in God and to explore the social meaning of different types of belief.

II. Measuring Images of God

The basic question about belief in God asked in the 1973 survey had respondents choose, from among a battery of alternatives, the statement that

TABLE 3.1 Belief-in-God Statements and Their Support

Statements	Percentage choosing	(N)
1. I don't believe in God.	5	(34)
2. I don't think it is possible for me to know whether there is a God.	11	(69)
3. I am uncertain but lean toward not believing.	3	(16)
4. I am uncertain but lean toward believing.	16	(101)
5. I definitely believe in God.	55	(359)
6. I am uncomfortable about the word "God" but I do believe in some kind of transcendent force or energy.	8	(52)
7. None of above; no answer.	2	(15)
	100%	(646)

---

[2] The survey was a mail-back questionnaire titled "Intergroup Relations in America Today." It was conducted by the Survey Research Center at the University of California, Berkeley. The completed number of questionnaires was 646, and the response rate was 65%. Case weights were used to standarize the sample to 1970 Census figures for age, education, sex, and race in the Bay area.

came closest to expressing their belief. The statements, and the proportion of respondents choosing each, are reported in Table 3.1.

As can be seen, only 5% say unequivocally that they do *not* believe in God (statement 1). The other 95%, however, are far from unanimous about what they do believe. As with other samples, a majority—55%—say that they "definitely" believe in God (statement 5). Another 8% choose a statement (6) expressing discomfort about the word "God" but professing belief in some kind of transcendent force or energy. The remaining 30% choose statements that reflect either some degree of uncertainty about their belief (3 and 4) or agnosticism (2).

It is clear from Table 3.1 that substantial variation in belief about God is masked when people are asked simply whether or not they believe in God, as has been the practice in most national polls. Asked in that way, the vast majority of these respondents would probably have preferred to say that they believe, rather than not believe. Yet, when presented with the range of options shown in Table 3.1, only a bare majority—55%—say that they "definitely" believe in God.

But what do people mean when they report that they "definitely" believe in God? It could be that they all mean the same thing. More likely, they have somewhat different things in mind. Were a new inquiry into these matters to be started, it would obviously be desirable to conduct in-depth interviews with a sample of firm believers in order to sort out the different images of God that lurk behind the simple acknowlegment of belief. The present data fall short of that ideal, but additional questions about their conception of God were asked of "definite" believers. These questions allow us to distinguish further among believers according to whether or not God is conceived as being influential in their personal lives and according to whether or not social arrangements are seen as having been ordained by God.

Relevant to the first distinction was a question asking respondents to report the extent to which their lives were personally influenced by "God or some other supernatural force." The possible response categories were "determines my life almost entirely," "has a strong influence," "has a small influence," and "has no influence at all." On the basis of responses to this question, those who "definitely" believe in God were divided into two groups: those who responded that God has a determining or strong influence on their lives and those who reported that God has no influence or only a small influence on their lives.[3] Seventy-nine pecent of firm believers fall into the first group, 21% into the second.

---

[3] The responses were collapsed as described both for conceptual reasons and because an inspection of uncollapsed results indicated that this was the most appropriate cutting point for dichotomizing this variable. This same comment applies to the item discussed in the next paragraph.

The second item used to distinguish among firm believers was a question about "why there are still so many poor people in America." One explanation presented was that "God gave people different abilities so that the work of the world will get done." Respondents could agree strongly, agree somewhat, disagree somewhat, or disagree strongly. Firm believers who agreed (strongly or somewhat) with that explanation were put into one group; those who said they disagreed were put into another. Fifty-four percent of believers fell into the first group, 46% into the second.

The effect of using these two questions jointly to distinguish among those who "definitely" believe in God is shown in Table 3.2. Forty-three percent of the believers say that God influences both themselves and the social order. This image of God, as active at both the personal and the social levels, is one that is often associated with fundamentalist Christianity. At the other extreme are 10% who, although they are firm believers in God, do not conceive of God as either a personal influence in their lives or as exercising social influence; for them, God exists but is somewhat remote.

Of the remaining believers, 36% affirm God's influence on their own lives but do not see social conditions, such as poverty, as having been ordained by God. For this group, God is a referent who affords guidance in life but is not a determinant of the conditions of life. The final group of believers are the 11% who see God as determining social arrangements but not as having a personal influence in their lives. This image of God as personally distant but still regulating the social order seems potentially an alienating one, bordering on fatalism.

These distinctions among types of belief in God seem logical enough and are interesting from a theoretical point of view.[4] The crucial question, still to be answered, is whether or not and, if so, how these images of God relate to the way people live their lives and respond to their social worlds. Unless

TABLE 3.2   Distribution of Definite Believers in God according to Whether God Is Seen as Personally and/or Socially Influential (in Percentages)[a]

God ordains social life	God influences own life		Total
	Yes	No	
Yes	43	11	54
No	36	10	46
Total	79	21	100

[a] $N = 359$.

[4] Dividing the firm believers into four categories based only on responses to two questions is somewhat crude methodologically. However, the resulting categorization has some conceptual justification. It would be possible in further research to adopt more refined modes of classification.

believers with different images respond in distinctive and interpretable ways to other questions of interest, the typology will not be particularly useful to the analysis and understanding of the relationship between religion and society. This issue is confronted in the remainder of this chapter. The relationship between these images of God and other aspects of religious belief and practice are examined first. Then we will explore the relationship between these images and respondents' political orientation and attitudes on selected social issues.

III. Religious Beliefs and Practices

If the classification of "definite believers" into four image-of-God categories is valid, there should be observable differences between these categories with regard to religious belief and practice. At the very least, there should be a substantial difference between those believers who see God as influencing both their own lives and the social order, and those believers who do not conceive of God as influencing either sphere. It is to be expected that the former group will be quite religious in a traditional sense; the latter group, which views God as remote, should not be found to be very religious.

The information available on the religious beliefs and practices of each image-of-God type is summarized in Table 3.3. Data are given on each of the four types and, for purposes of comparison, on those who believe in some transcendent force (statement 6 in Table 3.1) and on those who are either agnostics or atheists (statements 1 and 2 in Table 3.1).[5] The results are presented in this and subsequent tables, using a statistic designed to assess the extent to which different images of God predispose those who hold them to overselect or underselect a particular response category, in comparison to the average of all respondents.[6] To understand the nature of this "over–under" statistic, one will notice that in the first row of Table 3.3 the proportion of the total sample who believe that there is life after death with rewards and punishments is 18%. One should note also in the first row the "over–under" statistic of 1.06 for those whose image of God is personal–social. The 1.06 means that those holding this image of God are 106% more likely to believe that there are rewards and punishments after death than is the average respondent. (The corresponding cell percentage of 37 is 106% higher than 18.) A positive over-

---

[5] The response patterns for atheists and agnostics were sufficiently similar to warrant combining them into a single category.

[6] If the observed cell percentage is 0 and the expected (overall) percentage is E, the formula for the statistic is $(0 - E)/E$. The negative limit of the statistic is -1 (no cases in the corresponding cell.) Although there is no positive limit, statistics in these tables rarely exceed $+1$ (cell percentage double the overall percentage).

TABLE 3.3 Subscription to Traditional Religious Beliefs and Practices by Images of God (Over–Under Scores)

	Image of God				Comparison		Total percentage
	Personal social	Personal only	Social only	Remote	"Force"	Agnostic–atheist	
Conservative belief							
There is a life after death with rewards for some people and punishment for others.	1.06	1.11	-.13	-.80	-1.00	-.92	18
Darwin's theory of evolution saying that human beings evolved from lower forms of animal life is untrue.	.92	.52	.44	-.45	-.93	-.86	35
Religious practice							
Go to church weekly	.79	.78	.57	-.44	-.72	-.89	27
Pray daily	.65	.78	.42	-.37	-.72	-.88	37
Other							
Believe that God participates in history	.39	.26	.28	-.33	-.30	-.66	69
Find spiritual experiences helpful in life	.36	.26	-.07	-.16	.11	-.48	68
(Lowest *N*)	(125)	(109)	(25)	(18)	(31)	(64)	(489)

under statistic means that a particular response category has been overselected by an image-of-God type as compared with the sample as a whole; a negative statistic means that the response category has been underselected by the image-of-God type as compared with the sample as a whole. The higher or lower the over–under statistic, the greater the degree of over- or underselection.

The first indicator of religiosity included in Table 3.3 is the view that there is life after death with "rewards for some and punishment for others."[7] There are substantial differences in the degree to which this statement is accepted by the different image-of-God types. As might be expected, this traditional view of life after death is rejected overwhelmingly by the agnostics–atheists; their over–under score is − .92. It is also rejected by all those who acknowledge the existence of a supernatural force but are uncomfortable with the word "God."

Among firm believers in God, those for whom God is remote (perceived as both personally and socially noninfluential) are the most likely to reject the concept of rewards and punishments after death; their score of − .80 is close to the − .92 of the agnostics–atheists. Those who conceive of God as only a social force also underselect the traditional concept of an afterlife, although considerably less so than those whose image is remote. Most likely to affirm the existence of rewards and punishments after death are those for whom there is a personal component to their belief in God, whether the social component is present or not.

Examination of the other items summarized in Table 3.3 reveals that, with some slight variation, the pattern of association just noted, between images of God and belief in an afterlife, holds for the associations between images of God and other indicators of traditional religious belief and practice as well. Those who see God as influential in their own lives are consistently the most likely to accept traditional beliefs and to engage in traditional religious practices. Whether or not they also conceive of God as influencing the social order is not usually of importance.

At the other extreme, among firm believers, are those who view God as remote. They are less religious on all indicators than the average respondent. Those who see God as behind the present social order but who do not think that God influences their own lives tend to fall, statistically, between those for whom God is personally influential and those for whom God is remote.

One interesting, although not surprising, divergence from the general pattern is reflected in the responses of those who believe in a transcendent force. This group is relatively unlikely to go to church, to pray often, or to hold conservative views on life after death and on creation. Nevertheless, they are more

---

[7] Most of our respondents believe in some form of life after death, but they tend to prefer a more vague description. The most popular statement (chosen by 38%) was "I believe there must be something beyond death, but I have no idea what it may be like."

likely than the average to say that spiritual experience can help them understand their lives. This group, in these and other regards, as will be seen, is similar to those referred to as "alternately religious" in the preceding chapter of this book.

Let us summarize the discussion to this point. We have divided the "definite" believers in God into four groups, based on their different images of God. Comparison of the four groups has revealed that the classification into image-of-God types is not simply arbitrary but reflects genuine differences between the types in their acceptance of traditional religious beliefs and practices. The question now to be addressed is whether or not the images are also related to respondents' political orientation and to attitudes on social issues.

IV. Political Orientation and Social Attitudes

The research that has been done on the relationship between belief in God and political orientation (on American samples) has usually concluded that believers tend to be more conservative than nonbelievers. However, not all measures of religion or religiosity have always been found to be related to political conservatism. Indeed, as Wuthnow (1973) has pointed out, the empirical evidence on the association between religion and politics is somewhat contradictory, and the conditions under which religious commitment is associated with conservative politics have yet to be sorted out fully and clearly.

The present exploratory study is certainly not going to resolve this wideranging problem. We might contribute, however, to reformulating the question. If different images of God are consistently related to different political and social policy positions, this would suggest that belief in God is not the key variable, since all respondents in our image-of-God categories say that they "definitely" believe in God. Such a finding would further suggest that the *kind* of God in which one believes is more relevant to political and social positions than the mere fact of belief. Let us examine the data with this issue in mind.

Table 3.4 shows the relative disposition of the different image-of-God types to describe their general political position as liberal, middle of the road, or conservative.[8] The figures, once again, are over–under scores and are to be interpreted as indicating the degree to which a particular political orientation is over- or underselected by each image-of-God type, as compared with the sample as a whole.

---

[8] Response categories provided for respondents to identify themselves as radical, liberal, conservative, strongly conservative, and middle of the road. For present purposes, radical and liberal respondents have been grouped under the label "liberal"; conservative and strongly conservative respondents have been combined to form the conservative cateogry.

TABLE 3.4 Political Position by Images of God (Over–Under Scores)

	Image of God				Comparison		
	Personal social	Personal only	Social only	Remote	"Force"	Agnostic–atheist	Total percentage
Political position							
Liberal	−.53	.21	−.42	−.12	.68	.26	39
Middle of road	.03	−.04	−.38	.42	−.41	.20	33
Conservative	.71	−.25	1.04	−.34	−.47	−.60	28
(N)	(130)	(98)	(30)	(32)	(49)	(80)	(551)

The most liberal respondents are those who believe in a transcendent force; the next most liberal are the agnostics–atheists. Also more liberal than average, however, are those who say that God influences their own lives but not the social order. This group, it will be recalled, was found previously to be relatively traditional in religious belief and practice. Their religious conservatism does not, apparently, carry over to political conservatism.

In contrast, the most conservative respondents are those who say that God has ordained the social order. Such an image of God could logically be associated with rather conservative political values, and this was, indeed, found to be the case. Those who see God as controlling the social order are relatively conservative, regardless of whether or not they say that God is influential in their personal lives. It is not enough, however, to reject God as controlling social life in order to be a liberal. Those who conceive of God as remote reject that image, but they are less likely to be liberal than those who also say that God has influenced their own lives.

As will be noted below, the four groups of believers differ somewhat from one another and from the two "nonbeliever" types in such background factors as sex, age, and education. When these variables are introduced as controls, however, the associations just reported between image-of-God types and political orientation are largely maintained.[9] Image of God is related to political orientation independent of the effects of age, sex, and level of education.

These results allow us to specify the relation between religion and political orientation in a way not found in previous research: Being religiously conservative is associated with being politically conservative under the special circumstance that God is conceived of as exercising control over the social order. If God is not seen in this way, and if God is viewed as being influential in one's life, a conservative religious orientation and a liberal political one appear compatible. Indeed, such a view of God is more associated with a liberal political outlook than is a view that pictures God as remote from the affairs of this world, even though the latter view is associated with a less traditional religious outlook than the former. In sum, these results suggest a need to distinguish between types of belief, if the relationship between religion and politics is to be fully understood.

Although the results previously noted are quite interesting, they are based on the responses to a single question on political self-identification. We also wanted to determine whether or not these same results would emerge if other

---

[9] The procedure used was an analysis of covariance, with years of age, years of education, and sex as the covariates. Our purpose was, first of all, to evaluate the significance level of the net effect of the image-of-God classification on the various political and social issues. Second, we inspected the multiple-classification-analysis tables of unadjusted and adjusted effects to ensure that the patterns noted in the text were not altered by controlling for the demographic variables.

measures of political outlook were used. We, therefore, compared the responses of the image-of-God types on a number of questions on specific social issues. We will report first on the responses to questions concerning the role of women. Then we will explore the respondents' positions on racial policies.

Women's Role in Society

The feminist literature is virtually unanimous in maintaining that religion has played an important part in legitimizing discrimination against women. If such is the case, it should follow that all believers would be found to hold more traditional views about women's roles than nonbelievers. What such a sweeping indictment of religion does not make clear, however, is how various groups of believers might differ from one another.

The survey included several questions relevant to respondents' attitudes about the role of women in modern society. One question had to do with the traditional view that women have a special, innate ability to care for children. Respondents were asked if they agreed or disagreed with the statement that "when it comes to caring for babies and small children, men *by nature* are less patient and giving than women." A second question, addressed to the acceptability of women participating in political life, asked respondents how comfortable they would feel about having a woman as President. A third question dealt with the tactics most appropriate for advancing women's rights. Respondents were to choose between the statement that "the only way women will gain their civil rights is by constant protest and pressure" and the statement that "women would be better off, and the cause of equal rights for women would be advanced, if they were less pushy about it."

The responses to these questions on women's roles are summarized in Table 3.5. The last column of that table shows the percentage of those responding who gave the profeminist response to these questions; the feminist position was supported by one-third to one-half of the respondents. For each image-of-God type, over–under scores are presented to show how each type differs from the average respondent in their answers to these questions.

The most compelling characteristic of Table 3.5 is the sharp contrast between the responses of the "force" and "none" categories, on the one hand, and of all four groups of "definite" believers, on the other. The former two groups are substantially more likely than the latter groups to give a profeminist response to these questions. The contention that persons committed to traditional religious belief are less likely than others to support the women's movement receives considerable support from these data.

Nevertheless, the four "definite" believer groups are not equally conservative on this issue. One should compare in particular the first two groups in

TABLE 3.5 Support for Feminist Positions on Women's Role by Images of God (Over–Under Scores)

Feminist Positions	Image of God				Comparison		Total percentage
	Personal social	Personal only	Social only	Remote	"Force"	Agnostic–atheist	
Feminist Positions							
Rejection of the view that when it comes to caring for babies and small children, men *by nature* are less patient and giving than women.	−.34	−.04	−.07	−.11	.74	.33	34
Being comfortable with a woman as President of the United States	−.26	−.05	−.60	−.31	.68	.31	45
The only way women will gain their civil rights is by constant protest and pressure.	−.46	.01	−.25	−.10	.32	.36	42
(Lowest N)	(140)	(121)	(35)	(29)	(48)	(84)	(598)

Table 3.5, both of which say that God is an important influence in their lives and both of which are committed to traditional religious belief and practice. The first group, which sees God as also controlling the social order, is relatively antifeminist in responding to these questions. The second group, which rejects the idea that the social order is ordained by God, responds to these questions in ways very close to the average respondent in the sample as a whole. Although not as liberal as the nonbelievers, this second group is slightly more liberal than the "remote" group, which is not deeply committed to traditional religion at all. It appears, then, that although religious belief in general is associated with conservative attitudes about women's role in society, a certain kind of religion, represented here by the personalist image-of-God type, can partially offset these tendencies.

These image-of-God differences do not disappear when age, education, and sex are controlled. It is worth mentioning, in particular, that although women generally are more likely to support the feminist position on these questions, the most liberal groups in Table 3.5 are those which, as shall be seen, do not have proportionately more women than the sample as a whole. Moreover, the differences between image-of-God groups are just as pronounced when the sex of the respondent is controlled as when both sexes are combined. The image-of-God typology has an impact of its own on attitudes toward women, when common demographic variables are controlled. Let us turn now to see if there is also an association between image of God and attitudes on another social issue—namely, racial policy.

Racial Policy

Racist policies and attitudes in America have sometimes been justified by reference to traditional religious beliefs. The idea that God specifically created different races, for example, has been used to defend discrimination against blacks. On the other hand, it is clear that many elements of traditional belief, such as the injunction to love one's neighbor, are directly opposed to racial intolerance and bigotry. We are faced, therefore, with conflicting expectations about what relationship we should find between religious belief and liberal racial policies. What we do expect to find, however, is that those believers who perceive God as ordaining the social order will show little enthusiasm for policies designed to help blacks.

Several questions included in the survey allow the matter to be explored. One question asked respondents whether, generally speaking, they favored or opposed school integration. Another question asked how actively respondents thought the federal government ought to "press business to have a fair proportion of blacks in all kinds of jobs." The response categories to this question included two calling for the government to pressure business, either by fines or by withholding government contracts; the other alternatives were to let businesses decide for themselves on this matter, with the government role limited to expressing, at most, its support for employing blacks. Finally, a third question asked (white) respondents how they would feel if they "had a child who wanted to marry a black person who had a good education and a good job." They could, on the one hand, approve or at least not care either way; on the other side, the answer categories allowed respondents to object, to disapprove in silence, or to say they did not know.

The responses to these questions, for white respondents only, are summarized in Table 3.6. The last column of the table shows the percentage of whites in the sample who favor the liberal position on these questions. They range from 24% who would approve or not care if their child wanted to marry a black to 77% who say they favor school integration. Over–under scores are given for each image-of-God type in order to facilitate comparison of their responses with the overall percentages.

There are several aspects of Table 3.6 to be commented upon. First of all, the agnostic–atheist group is not particularly liberal when it comes to racial policy. Although they are substantially more likely than the average respondent to accept their own child's marrying a black, they differ little from the average when it comes to favoring school integration or putting pressure on businesses. Apparently, a *lack* of religious belief, although associated with less overt racial prejudice, does not guarantee support for efforts to overcome black–white social inequality.

A second noteworthy characteristic of Table 3.6 is that those believers whose image of God is personalist stand out. Whereas the other three image-of-God groups are more conservative than average on all of the questions of race, those who say that God has influenced their lives (but not the social order) are more liberal than average in their responses to all three questions. Furthermore, on two of the three questions, the responses of this personalist image-of-God group are more liberal than the agnostics–atheists.

The responses to these questions on racial policy follow the same general pattern found previously for the questions on political orientation and on the role of women. The most conservative respondents are those believers who conceive of God as standing behind the present social order. At the liberal extreme are those who say that they are uncomfortable with the word "God" but who believe in some kind of transcendent force or energy. These results are more or less in line with what would be expected if conservatism in religion were unambiguously associated with conservatism in politics and on social issues.

This expected association between religious and political conservatism has been contradicted consistently, however, by those whose image of God is personalist. As was seen in Table 3.3, this group of believers, who say that God

TABLE 3.6 Support for Liberal Racial Policies by Image of God (Over-Under Scores)[a]

	Image of God				Comparison		Total percentage
	Personal social	Personal only	Social only	Remote	"Force"	Agnostic– atheist	
Liberal racial policies							
Favor school integration	−.11	.15	−.15	−.18	.13	.03	77
Favor government pressure on businesses to have a fair proportion of blacks in all kinds of jobs	−.16	.32	−.82	−.03	.52	−.02	33
Approve or would not care if child married a black person	−.72	.11	−.76	−.54	1.40	.74	24
(Lowest N)	(105)	(81)	(20)	(28)	(42)	(69)	(455)

[a] Only white respondents are included in this table.

has strongly influenced their lives but who do not conceive of God as behind the social order, is relatively traditional on religious matters. Yet, on political and social issues they must be rated as relatively liberal, or at least as not conservative.[10] What is responsible for this liberalizing tendency?

One important factor, certainly, is the group's rejection of the idea that the social order is ordained by God. But this rejection cannot be the whole explanation of the group's distinctiveness, since believers whose image of God is remote also reject that idea but are consistently less liberal than the personalist group. Nor is it enough to focus on the fact that this group personally experiences God's influence. Those with a personalist–social image also affirm that influence, but they are consistently conservative.

Unfortunately, with the present data it is not possible to pinpoint how this one group of believers manages at once to be both religiously conservative and politically rather liberal. There is some additional evidence, however, that provides some insight into the kind of people they are.

V. Personal Helpfulness

Certain questions in the survey asked respondents how they personally would respond to someone in distress. A hypothetical situation was described, and they were then asked what they would do. Two of these situations and their answer categories were as follows:

A co-worker and close friend of yours has been in an accident and is laid up for a long time in bed. He lives off his insurance and savings but finally these run out. He calls you up and asks for a loan of money each week until he gets well. The loan he asks for is in an amount you could afford although it will mean pinching pennies. What do you think you would do in this situation?

> Suggest that he try to get a loan from a bank
> Lend him the money but ask for interest
> Lend him the money without interest
> Truly don't know

Imagine that you are boarding a bus and you overhear the driver say to the person ahead of you, "Sorry, I don't carry any change; unless you have a quarter, you'll have to get off." In such a situation, what do you think you would do?

> Give the person a quarter
> Offer to change a dollar for the person

---

[10] The assertion that even religiously conservative members of the personalist image-of-God group are relatively liberal on political and social issues goes beyond the evidence presented in Tables 3.3 and 3.6. Tables showing the *joint* effects of image-of-God and of religious conservatism on these social policy issues do in fact support this assertion, but we omit their presentation for the sake of brevity.

Probably do nothing
Truly don't know

Table 3.7, using over–under scores, shows the relative degree to which each image-of-God type chose the most helpful response category in answering these two questions.

The most helpful respondents in both situations are those who hold the personalist image of God. The second most helpful group is the one whose members believe in a transcendent force. The other groups are less helpful, although the pattern of relative helpfulness is different for them in the two situations.

These responses to the questions on personal helpfulness suggest that the relative liberalism of those with the personalist image of God may be partially rooted in a willingness to help others. Their belief in a God who strongly influences their lives may encourage them to reflect on the ethical demands of religion. Since this group does not believe that God has ordained the present social order, their desire to do God's will can be freely channeled into helping others, whether on a one-to-one basis or by supporting social programs to help the disadvantaged. Further research would be required to establish that this in fact is what is happening. Nevertheless, it does indicate one possible way in which conservatism on religious matters can lead to, or at least coexist with, a relative liberalism on social issues.

VI. Background Characteristics

In the foregoing analysis, a constant check was made to ensure that the pattern of relationships presented was maintained when differences in the age, sex, and educational backgrounds of the different image-of-God groups were taken into account. This condition, as has already been noted, was met for all of the results discussed here. Thus, the principal differences found between the image-of-God groups were not simply the result of the groups' coming from different backgrounds. Image of God appears to have an effect that is independent of at least these basic demographic variables.

The different groups, nevertheless, do differ somewhat in background, and in this section some of the major differences are reported. To begin, Table 3.8 shows, for each image-of-God group, the average age, the average number of years of education, the proportion of men, and the proportion of minority background.

Those who reject a "definite" belief in God are younger, on the average, than the believers, with those in the "force" group being somewhat younger than the agnostics–atheists. Among believers, the oldest are those who believe that God is behind the social order. Believers who reject that concept are

TABLE 3.7 Personal Helpfulness by Images of God (Over–Under Scores)

	Image of God				Comparison		Total percentage
	Personal social	Personal only	Social only	Remote	"Force"	Agnostic–atheist	
Loan money to co-worker without interest	.03	.21	−.44	−.24	.13	.03	44
Give bus fare to stranger	−.17	.33	−.14	.01	.25	.10	30
(Lowest N)	(140)	(115)	(34)	(33)	(37)	(82)	(571)

TABLE 3.8 Demographic Characteristics of Image-of-God Types

	Image of God				Comparison		
	Personal social	Personal only	Social only	Remote	"Force"	Agnostic–atheist	Total
Average age in years	48	42	50	42	37	40	42
Average number of years of education	12	12	11	12	14	13	12
Percentage male	39	53	14	34	47	58	47
Percentage member of a minority group	21	28	42	14	7	14	21
(Lowest N)	(154)	(129)	(40)	(36)	(52)	(88)	(642)

substantially younger. Given that these data are cross-sectional, it is not possible to establish whether these differences represent life-cycle effects or generational change. We suspect that the latter is principally the case and that acceptance of the belief that God ordains social arrangements is in decline. Nevertheless, as noted later, there continue to be good reasons for certain persons to view social conditions as being in accord with God's plan.

The image-of-God types differ only slightly among themselves in average education. Those who conceive of God as responsible for the social order (only) are the least educated. The members of the "force" group are slightly better educated, on the average, than the agnostics–atheists, and both of these have a year or two more of education than those who definitely believe in God.

The groups differ considerably more from one another both in sexual composition and in ethnic background. Those who see God as influencing the social order, but not their own lives, are especially distinctive. This group is composed disproportionately of women and of minority-group members. On the average, they are also, as already noted, the oldest and least educated. Furthermore, it is worthy of mention that this group scores higher than any other on a scale of anomie. The image of God held by these persons may reflect their resignation or sense of helplessness in the face of very unfavorable odds for dealing successfully with American society. Believing that God is behind the social order may be a way for them to make sense of and to deal with a problematic and hostile environment.

Religious Preference

A final background characteristic examined was the denominational affiliation of each image-of-God type. A reasonable presumption is that a person's image of God will be related to his or her religious denomination, since it is widely thought that different denominations project somewhat different conceptions of what God is like. Earlier in this chapter, it was mentioned that an image of God as being both socially and personally influential is one that is usually associated with fundamentalist Christianity. That assumption is what we are primarily interested in examining now. It is also to be expected that the agnostics–atheists will be underrepresented among the religiously affiliated, as will those who believe in a transcendent force.

These speculations can only be tested in a tentative way with these data, since, except for the Roman Catholics, there are very few cases in any single denomination. Still, because the matter is of some interest, the relative recruitment of the different image-of-God types from major Protestant denominations and from the Roman Catholic Church is presented in Table 3.9.

The data in the first two rows of Table 3.9 show the degree of over- or underselection of each image of God by those in the most conservative Protes-

TABLE 3.9 Membership in Selected Religious Denominations by Images of God (Over-Under Scores)

	Image of God				Comparison		Total percentage
	Personal social	Personal only	Social only	Remote	"Force"	Agnostic–atheist	
Conservative Protestants							
Sects	1.05	1.53	−1.00	−1.00	−1.00	−1.00	3.8
Southern Baptists	.59	1.65	.05	−.16	−1.00	−1.00	3.7
Moderate Protestants							
American Baptists	1.45	−.76	−.40	.64	−1.00	−.43	4.2
Methodists	.08	−.46	1.33	2.67	−.37	−.75	5.2
Liberal Protestants							
United Presbyterians	.11	.63	−1.00	.11	.22	−1.00	2.7
Episcopalians	.10	−.19	.57	−.48	.76	−.62	2.1
Roman Catholics	.44	.14	.34	.70	−.95	−.71	24.3
Others							54.0
(N)	(155)	(111)	(38)	(35)	(50)	(87)	(614)

tant denominations. As can be seen, none of those who say they belong to a sect (such as the many small Pentecostal groups) or to the Southern Baptists are classified in the "force" or agnostics–atheists categories. They are heavily concentrated in the first two image-of-God types, that is, among those who say God is a strong influence on their lives. Between the first two types, however, they have a relative preference for the second, more liberal, type, one that does not see God as behind the social order.

It is to be noted, however, that, if respondents who belong to minority groups are removed from Table 3.9, the results are somewhat different. Among white members of sects, the relative preference for the first type is larger than for the second (1.46 versus 1.14); among white Southern Baptists, the relative preference is equal (both 1.13). These results for whites alone are more in line with the assumption that fundamentalist Christians would tend to have an image of God as determining the social order. Nevertheless, the data suggest that the strength of that tendency should not be overestimated.

Support for the "personalist–social" image of God also comes from the American Baptists and, to a lesser degree, from the Roman Catholics. The Methodists in the sample favor the "social" and "remote" images, which could be considered middle-of-the-road. Finally, Episcopalians are the most likely of the major denominations to have an image of God as a transcendent force. Although these results seem to make sense in general, the reader is reminded that the results are based on very few members of each denomination and that it would be unwise to generalize these relationships unduly.

VII. Conclusion

The purpose of this chapter has been to explore possible differences within a group of persons who are commonly lumped together—namely, those who say that they "definitely believe in God." This chapter has shown that substantial variation is hidden behind that common affirmation of belief. As a result, unless this variation is taken into account, it is not a simple matter to examine the implications of belief in God for other realms of life.

Most contemporary research on the social meanings of religious belief has been content to divide believers by major denominational groups (Protestant, Catholic, Jewish) and/or by degree of religiosity or strength of commitment. A principal result of the present inquiry has been to show that, among believers, it could be quite important to consider differences in the kind of God in which they believe. By focusing on their different images of God, we have seen that believers who are relatively traditional in religious matters do not always tend to be conservative in political and social matters. More importantly, some insight has been gained into the conditions under which traditional religious commitment is likely to be associated with political conservatism.

The results of this study suggest that one element behind the frequently found association between traditional religion and conservative politics is the image of a God who ordains the present social order. Armed with this image, believers derive from their faith an essentially conservative social message— that such things as the organization of social life reflect God's will and are not to be tampered with. The results also show, however, that not all persons who are traditional in religious belief and practice have such an image of God. Believers who do not conceive of God as regulating the social order, but who do see God as influencing their own lives, can be relatively liberal on political and social issues.

It is evident that much research will be required to gain a better qualitative understanding of different ways of imagining God and of how those images are linked to attitudes and behaviors in other spheres of life. We hope, however, that this chapter has shown the potential fruitfulness of such a line of inquiry. In attempting to understand the relationship between religious belief and social life, the type of God in which people believe may be one of the most important things to study.

References

Caplovitz, David, and Fred Sherrow
    1977   *The Religious Drop-Outs.* Beverly Hills, California: Sage.

Gallup, George H.
    1972   *The Gallup Poll: Public Opinion 1935-1971.* New York: Random House.
    1976   *The Gallup Opinion Index,* Report No. 130.

Wuthnow, Robert
    1973   "Religious commitment and conservatism: In search of an elusive relationship." Pp. 117–132 in Charles Y. Glock (ed.), *Religion in Sociological Perspective.* Belmont, California: Wadsworth.

Chapter 4

Quantitative Approaches to Sect Classification and the Study of Sect Development[1]

MICHAEL R. WELCH

I. Introduction

With Troeltsch's (1931) formulation of the church–sect dichotomy, a line of research developed—under the rather broad heading of church–sect theory—that has been of central importance to the sociology of religion. As Wilson (1974:605–606) notes, the major contributions of this body of insights can be sorted into two basic categories:

> One set of studies has worked to refine the overall typology of religious institutions, often with an attempt to relate the types of institutions [and the changes they undergo] to other social factors. . . . The other group of studies has been primarily directed to the refinement of the concept of 'sect' as a concept. The chief means has been the elaboration of typologies of sectarianism. A frequent approach to this matter has been through straightforward classification of sectarian groups.

[1] Work was begun on this project while the author was supported by an NIMH traineeship in the Department of Sociology, Univeristy of North Carolina at Chapel Hill. I wish to thank David Heise and Gerhard Lenski for the valuable suggestions they provided during early stages of work on this project. In addition, I also wish to thank the Society for the Scientific Study of Religion for allowing me to reproduce material that had appeared in the Journal for the Scientific Study of Religion.

The Religious Dimension:
New Directions in Quantitative Research

Within these two categories, the largest amount of research has been of the former, rather than the latter, type. However, despite this collective scholarly investment of time and energy, it is the contention of some (Eister, 1967; Goode, 1967; Greeley, 1972:78) that the results of this labor have failed to meet expectations and have been disproportionately small in relation to the effort expended. Some scholars (Demerath, 1967:82–83; Goode, 1967:77; Johnson, 1971:137) have gone so far, in fact, as to call for an abandonment of church–sect typologizing, a request that has been generally ignored.

Perhaps one reason such impatience with the seemingly interminable proliferation of religious typologies has arisen is that so little has been done to test the utility of the conceptual schemes that now exist. The church–sect area is replete with conceptual guideposts, but we have yet to determine clearly which ones lead us up theoretical cul-de-sacs. As I have indicated elsewhere (Welch, 1977:549), it would probably be more profitable to turn attention to the development of quantitative strategies that will produce relatively unambiguous empirical determinations about the descriptive and explanatory utility of the concepts we presently possess.

II. Refining the Concept of Sect: Sect Classification Revisited and Revised

Work on sect classification—the second category of church–sect research Wilson describes—cannot be exempted from past criticism, for little progress has been made beyond the typologies of religious sects formulated by Clark (1949), McComas (1912), and Wilson (1961, 1967, 1969, 1970).[2] McComas (1912), for example, offered one of the earliest sect classification schemes, one that categorized sects into three types based on individual members' motivations for participating in group activities. This trinitarian categorization consisted of three sect classes: the intellectual sect (one in which intellectual stimulation and the quest for knowledge of the universe and/or oneself is a major motive for membership), the feeling sect (one in which members are actively seeking at least one form of Maslovian peak experience, i.e., the conversion experience), and the action sect (one in which members are attracted by the translation of the social gospel into tangible reformist programs). Clark (1949) focused less exclusively on member psychology and more on organizational characteristics (specifically, doctrinal patterns and the general nature of sectarian belief systems) than McComas but also failed, nonetheless, to pro-

---

[2] Yinger's (1970:273–279) typology could also be included among this group; however, because of its highly derivative character (i.e., it is based, in large part, on Clark's and Wilson's descriptions), it will not be discussed in detail.

duce a highly systematic sect classification. Like Niebuhr (1929) before him, Clark's delineation of sect types arises from a rich description of the distinctive features of various sects; however, like Niebuhr also, Clark has not identified explicitly the underlying dimensions on which sect types are arrayed. Indeed, for Clark (1949:21), aside from describing the details of sect existence, the possibility of a more systematic definitional or classification scheme seems remote. Thus, Clark is content to lay out a seven-category typology for which, he admits, "the lines of demarcation [between types] cannot be strictly drawn [p. 21]": pessimistic or adventist sects, perfectionist or subjectivist sects, charismatic or pentecostal sects, communistic sects, legalistic or objectivist sects, egocentric or New Thought sects, and, finally, esoteric or mystic sects. Wilson's work (particularly 1961, 1967, 1969, 1970) on religious sects is much more detailed than the work of his predecessors, and the sect typology (1969:364–376) he has constructed reflects this. Drawing upon a variety of historical cases and applying an implicity inductive approach, Wilson identifies seven types of sects based on their "response to the world" (1969:363): conversionist, introversionist, manipulationist, reformist, revolutionary, thaumaturgical, and utopian. One major contribution of this typology is Wilson's formulation of a general dimension along which religious sects can be ordered, that is, by their response to the world. This dimension reflects most directly the sect's ideational stance and, more implicitly, the organizational characteristics of the sect that shape, and are shaped by, doctrinal prescriptions.

Much of the most recent work on religious sects (Beckford, 1975; Wallis, 1975, 1977; Whitworth, 1975) exhibits the same descriptive orientation and historical case-study approach employed in these earlier studies described before, providing subtle variations to existing themes. One recent study, though, has focused directly on the problem of sect classification, and it represents a significant departure from preceding approaches.

Following the strategy described by Winter (1977:110), Welch (1977) has attempted to identify and operationalize the classificatory basis of the most sophisticated existing sect typology (Wilson, 1969) and to represent empirically the underlying dimensions along which different classes of sects vary. As Winter (1977:110) and Eister (1967:86) before him note, this decomposition of typological categories into component dimensions offers a flexible yet rigorous method for studying diverse religious organizations, for it allows one to examine quantitatively the empirical relationships between sectarian attributes rather than simply assuming the existence of such links—a shortcoming for which past church–sect studies have been criticized.[3]

---

[3] This empirical dimensionalizing approach to sect classification also offers other advantages compared to earlier approaches. First, representational inaccuracies in existing classification

A Quantitative, Multidimensional Approach
to Sect Classification

Although my recent work on Wilson's sect typology (Welch, 1977) is the
only study to have employed multidimensional scaling techniques specifically
for sect classification purposes, quantitative scaling procedures have been used
previously to examine the similarity of major religious organizations. Nosanchuck (1968), Rokeach (1960), Russell (1975), and Schroeder and Obenhaus
(1964), for example, have employed nonmetric multidimensional scaling
(MDS) to classify Christian churches and denominations. All used the
judgments of individuals to scale the perceived similarity of institutional belief
systems.[4] None of these studies, however, attempted to scale objectively determined organizational or doctrinal characteristics of religious groups. Unlike
Nosanchuck (1968) and the others (Rokeach, 1960; Russell, 1975; Schroeder
and Obenhaus, 1964), I scaled organizational and ideational attributes of
American sects to examine the fit between Wilson's conceptualizations and a
representation of the empirical similarities of sects. In addition, I hoped to be
able to identify basic dimensions underlying sect structure and development,
as well as ''actual characteristics which differentiate classes of religious sects
from each other [Welch, 1977:126].'' A brief discussion of the methodology
and findings of this study will be presented later.

To adequately examine the empirical accuracy of Wilson's (1969) sect
typology, data were gathered on 21 American sects (see Welch, 1977:127 for a
list of sample units). These sects were chosen to represent most types (i.e., conversionist, introversionist, manipulationist, reformist, and thaumaturgical)
described by Wilson (1969). Indicators of sect and doctrinal and organizational
properties were selected to tap the major dimension Wilson (1969:363) iden-

---

schemes can be identified clearly by comparing proposed types to the observed characteristics of
sects. Refinement of these typologies can then follow, without discarding the useful distinctions a
given classification makes—a prudently selective strategy for modification. Second, the identification of the basic dimensions of religious groups—specifically sects—makes it possible to study
covariation of environmental conditions impacting on the organization and the appearance of certain organizational characteristics. This breakthrough allows us to avoid the lamentable aspects of
previous church–sect theorizing Greeley (1972:78) rightfully derides (i.e., the presentation of
often untestable, quasi-hypotheses) and to begin testing real hypotheses about, for example,
organizational transformation. This preceding advantage ties in to a third and final benefit derived
from the dimensionalizing approach, the ability to place theorizing about religious groups into the
broader context of general organizational theory. Determination of the component dimensions of
religious organizations facilitates conceptual cross-fertilization between the areas of formal
organization and the sociology of religion—a development that can only redound to the benefit of
both (Benson and Dorsett, 1971:138; Winter, 1977:110).

[4] Laumann (1969) and Mueller (1971) have also used nonmetric MDS to study interdenominational friendship patterns and interdenominational mobility, but these studies have less relevance
for church–sect research.

tifies as underlying sect variation—response to the world. Doctrinal indicators used in the study represented sectarian themes defining members' orientation and activity in the world; organizational indicators represented the extensiveness and elaboration of the sect's bureaucratic structure and secular activities, mechanisms through which the sect's doctrinal injunctions are enacted. One hundred and seven indicators fulfilling these criteria were identified in the descriptions of sects provided by Clark (1949), Mead (1964), and Rosten (1955). (See Welch, 1977:140–141 for a complete listing of indicators.) Determinations about whether a sect displayed a given indicator were made systematically, with a variety of sources (e.g., Clark, 1949; Mead, 1964; and Rosten, 1955 were used, as were historical treatises, sect newsletters, sect yearbooks, and annual reports issued by sects) being consulted. Despite the complexity of this coding procedure, it nevertheless produced a relatively high level of intercoder reliability. (For a detailed description of coding procedures used in this study, see Welch, 1975:11–13.)

Once all codes for sect characteristics had been determined, a between-sects similarities matrix (Green and Carmone, 1970:42–45, 56–57) was created, in which coefficients represented the degree of similarity existing between all pairs of sects in the sample, based on their differential possession of specified attributes, that is, the doctrinal and organizational indicators.[5] This sect similarities matrix was then used as input for a nonmetric MDS program (Young, 1973).

Nonmetric MDS is an especially suitable analytical procedure for scaling similarity matrices, such as the one I have described previously, for two

---

[5] Measures of sect similarity were derived through the use of a taxonomic coefficients program. In effect, the program creates a 2 × 2 table for all pairs of sects included in an initial profile matrix (in this case, the Sect × Indicators coding sheet) and calculates coefficients expressing the degree of similarity between all pairs of units (sects) represented in the rows of the matrix. (Documentation for this program, Taxonomic Coefficients, may be obtained from Kenneth Hardy, Director of the Statistical Laboratory, Institute for Research in Social Science, University of North Carolina, Chapel Hill, North Carolina 27514.)

Kulcynski's coefficient (SK$_2$) (Sokal and Sneath, 1963:128–138) was selected as the most appropriate measure of sect similarity:

$$SK_2 = \frac{1}{2}\left[\frac{a}{a+c} + \frac{a}{a+b}\right]$$

where
  a = number of indicators displayed by both sect A and sect B;
  b = number of indicators displayed by sect B but not by sect A;
  c = number of indicators displayed by sect A but not by sect B.
The beneficial mathematical properties of this coefficient derive from its exclusion of negative matches (number of indicators displayed by neither sect A nor sect B) from the similarity equation.

reasons. First, it allows one to generate an interval scaling of units (sects, in this case) from merely ordinal-level data (Shepard *et al.*, 1972; Young 1970, 1973). (Given the simple presence–absence format on which the similarity measures used in my study were based, this initial reason was crucial in selecting an appropriate analytic technique.) Second, it offers an interpretable geometric representation of the empirical similarity between the units being studied (i.e., how they cluster), as well as a dimensional grid for identifying the latent structure of the data and determining precisely how similar units are on a particular dimension (Green and Carmone, 1970:42–70; Rabinowitz, 1975; Romney *et al.*, 1972).

The mathematical objective of nonmetric MDS is to match an input matrix of similarities (or dissimilarities) to an interpoint distance matrix, a matrix that maps the distances between the units being scaled in a given *n*-dimensional space. These interpoint distances are measured by standard distance functions, such as the Euclidian metric (the metric used in my study).[6] To perform the matching operation just described, a matrix of disparities (cf. Jones, 1974:4–8; Young, 1973:5) is first fitted to the distance matrix through a least-squares transformation, under the condition that cell entries in the disparities matrix must remain monotonically related to cell entries in the original similarities matrix. The acceptability of the various *n*-dimensional representations of data points produced by the preceding procedure is reflected in an estimate of the degree of fit between the interpoint distances and the disparities. This fit is normally represented by one of Kruskal's stress coefficients (Young, 1973:101).

The nonmetric scaling procedure I used yielded an interesting and highly interpretable two-dimensional configuration of sects, with a low stress value ($<$ .13). This configuration is represented in Figure 4.1.

As can be seen from Figure 4.1, the two dimensions structuring this configuration were identified as organizational precariousness and secular retreatism–secular activism, dimensions that had been discussed previously in the church–sect literature (cf. Benson and Hassinger, 1972; Coleman, 1968;

---

[6] The Euclidian distance metric is represented by the following formula:

$$d_{ij} = \sum_{k=1}^{r}\left[(x_{ij} - x_{jk})^2\right]^{1/2}$$

where

i = score on dimension i and

j = score on dimension j.

This metric has the highly desirable property of rotational invariance: Configurations of data points can be rotated around the origin without any change in interpoint distances (Green and Carmone, 1970:26).

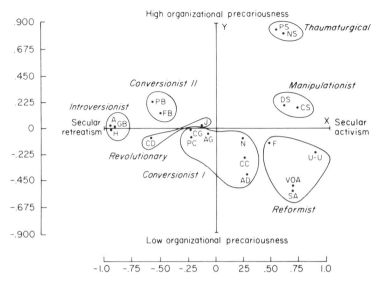

Figure 4.1. Dimensions of religious sectarian response to the world. (Clusters are drawn to represent groupings of sects inferred from Wilson's typology. The Conversionist II cluster has been drawn differently to facilitate interpretation and approximate sect loadings have been provided.) (Exact sect loadings may be obtained from the author.)

Demerath and Thiessen, 1966; Wilson, 1967, 1969, 1970) but had never been substantiated empirically. In addition to the discovery of this latent structure of sect groupings, the analysis identified 27 organizational or doctrinal features that differentiated sect classes from one another (see Welch, 1977:131 for a listing of these differentiae). Finally, and perhaps the most important finding of all, the clustering of sects illustrated in Figure 4.1 demonstrated very clearly the classificatory strengths and shortcomings of Wilson's (1969) original sect typology. In particular, it is apparent the original typology subsumes under some categories, that is, the conversionist, reformist, and revolutionist types, sects that are empirically dissimilar, thus limiting the discriminatory power of the typology as a whole (Welch, 1977:133–134).

These findings—especially the last—underscore some of the limitations (cf. Winter, 1977:108–110) of traditional approaches to sect classification. Although many of the earlier typologies such as Wilson's (1969) have proved fecund ground for insights into sect structure and dynamics, few reflect the diversity of organizational adaptations represented empirically in the sectarian milieu. Fewer still are useful for studying the actual transformations religious organizations undergo (e.g., the adoption of formal selection and training procedures for clergy, the adoption of mass media techniques for proselytizing and recruitment, etc.), transformations that hold a central place in church–sect theory.

III. The Analysis of Sect Development: Some Proposals for the Study of Religious Organizational Change

Even more than church–sect typologizing, the hypothesized transformation of religious sects into denominations has been a central issue in the sociology of religion (cf. Winter, 1977:153–173). The observations of some of the earliest researchers (Boisen, 1940; Eister, 1949; Niebuhr, 1929; Pope, 1942; Troeltsch, 1931) working in the church–sect area emphasized this issue in particular, and their work generally seemed to support "Wesley's law" (i.e., the growth of a religious organization—specifically, its bureaucratic structure and secular sphere of influence—is attended by a corresponding dilution of doctrinal purity and increased pressures toward ideological inclusiveness as opposed to exclusivity). More recent research (Brewer, 1952; Clear, 1961; Harrison, 1959; Isichei, 1964; Muelder, 1957; O'Dea, 1954; Pfautz, 1956; Redekop, 1974; Robertson, 1967; Warburton, 1967; Whitley, 1955; Wilson, 1969; Young, 1960) on sect development has continued to reiterate many of the themes first discussed by Niebuhr, Pope, Troeltsch, and the others, elaborating and expanding their work in useful ways, but still no attempts have been made to test the empirical accuracy of descriptions of organizational change. It is precisely these empirical investigations, however, that are deemed necessary to raise church–sect research from "mere" typologizing to actual hypothesis-testing (Eister, 1967:87; Greeley, 1972:77; Winter, 1977:153). This type of criticism, of course, does not imply the body of insights on religious organizational change is historically inaccurate or misleading; rather, we simply do not know, for it has not yet been put to any empirically rigorous test. Such recognition is not really surprising, though, when one realizes few methods for systematically studying sect change have been available, apart from the standard, descriptive case-study approach. This lack of an effective set of techniques for studying sect change may have been an obstacle to past research, but it is an obstacle that can be overcome. Using nonmetric MDS, we can now identify the latent structure of religious sectarian space, locate a given group on a specific dimension, and represent its degree of divergence from other groups on the same dimension. Moreover, once the basic dimensions have been discovered, we can perform a type of longitudinal analysis that compares the dimensional positioning of an organization at different periods in its history—precisely the type of analysis needed to test various hypotheses about sect development processes.

For example, one might wish to determine whether sects undergo temporal transformations in their basic patterns of response to the world while still retaining their sectarian character. This really amounts to asking whether a specific sect (or group of sects) passes from one type (Wilson, 1969) or sect class (Welch, 1977) to another during its (their) history. Such a change may represent only an intermediate stage in the transition from sect to denomination, or it may be the only transformation the organization ever experiences, but, whatever the pattern, such metamorphoses can be studied systematically. First, to study patterns of sect development quantitatively, one must begin by gathering data on specific target features of a sect's organization and doctrine (see Welch, 1977:140–141, for a list of such features) as they are displayed by the group at different points in its history. Once this has been done, one then creates a sect profile matrix (Welch, 1977:128–129) in which the features are coded dichotomously (i.e., present = 1, absent = 0) for all sects being studied. (Remember, this sample of sects will contain as many subsamples as there are time points for which you have collected data. Thus, each of these subsamples is homogeneous with regard to the temporal characterizations of the component sects. The larger sample, then, is a "Pooled" sample of temporally stratified subsamples.) As I noted in my earlier article (Welch, 1977:124), similarity coefficients (Sokal and Sneath, 1963:128–138) can be computed from the sect profile matrix to provide estimates of sect comparability based on differential possession of the specific target features. The resulting set of coefficients can then be arranged in a similarity supermatrix (Young, 1973:126–127) containing data partitions (submatrices) such as those illustrated in the hypothetical matrix presented in Figure 4.2.

As can be seen from inspection, this matrix provides sets of coefficients that can be interpreted in at least two interesting ways. First, coefficients from submatrices located along the main diagonal could be thought of as representing the similarity between pairs of sects at a single point in time (e.g., 1950). These measures of association have been denoted as "intraperiod coefficients." Off-diagonal submatrices contain coefficients measuring the similarity among members of a single sect class or among members of different classes at different chronological points (e.g., 1950 and 1960, 1950 and 1970, 1960 and 1970). I have labeled these similarity measures as "interperiod coefficients."

To test for sect change across the historical periods sampled, the entire supermatrix can be scaled using nonmetric MDS (Rabinowitz, 1975; Young, 1973). The configurations of sects, thus, would be located in a "transhistorical" space, and any organizational shifts should appear quite clearly (see Figure 4.3).

In Figure 4.3, for example, the change in the positions of sects C and E that occurred between 1950 (points C_1 and E_1) and 1970 (points C_3 and E_3) indicate the two groups have experienced very different patterns of development. Sect C, it appears, has developed and stabilized its organizational base (note the shift from higher to lower magnitudes of organizational precariousness) and has become—perhaps as a result of the former process—slightly less retreatist in orientation. (This pattern probably summarizes the type of changes many

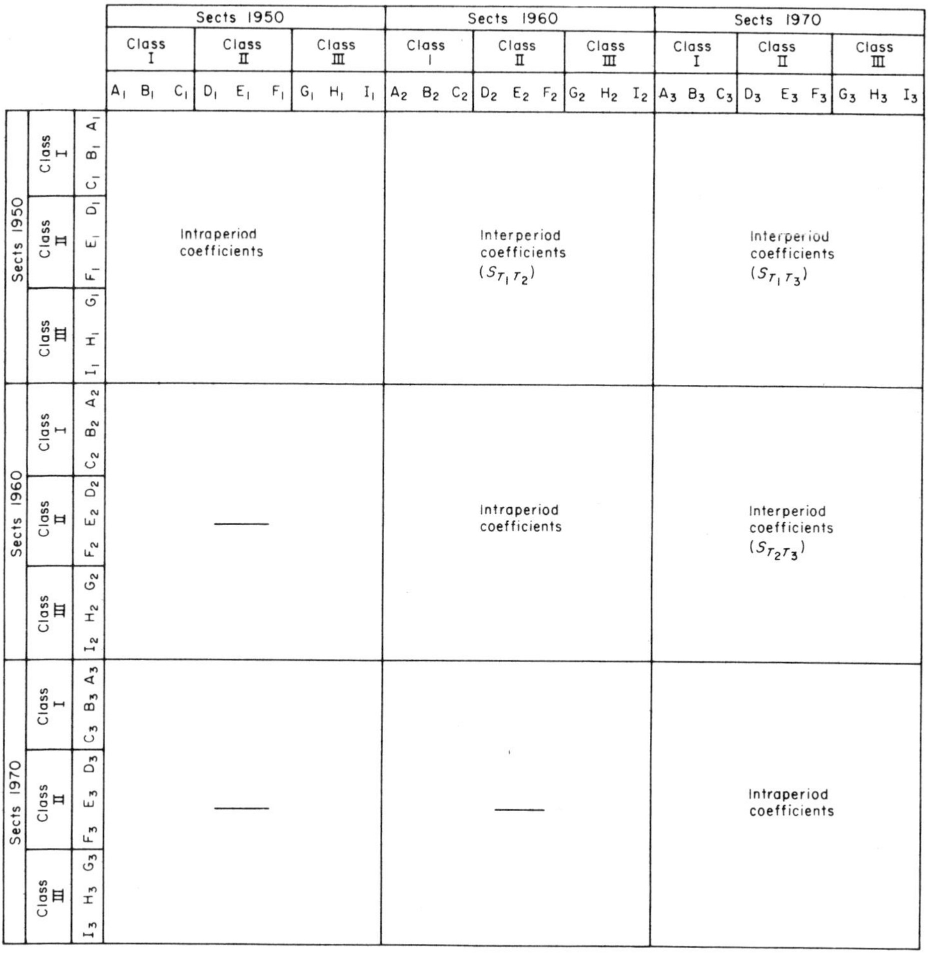

		Sects 1950			Sects 1960			Sects 1970		
		Class I	Class II	Class III	Class I	Class II	Class III	Class I	Class II	Class III
		A_1 B_1 C_1	D_1 E_1 F_1	G_1 H_1 I_1	A_2 B_2 C_2	D_2 E_2 F_2	G_2 H_2 I_2	A_3 B_3 C_3	D_3 E_3 F_3	G_3 H_3 I_3
Sects 1950	Class I A_1 B_1 C_1 / Class II D_1 E_1 F_1 / Class III G_1 H_1 I_1	Intraperiod coefficients			Interperiod coefficients $(S_{T_1 T_2})$			Interperiod coefficients $(S_{T_1 T_3})$		
Sects 1960	Class I A_2 B_2 C_2 / Class II D_2 E_2 F_2 / Class III G_2 H_2 I_2	——			Intraperiod coefficients			Interperiod coefficients $(S_{T_2 T_3})$		
Sects 1970	Class I A_3 B_3 C_3 / Class II D_3 E_3 F_3 / Class III G_3 H_3 I_3	——			——			Intraperiod coefficients		

Figure 4.2 Example of a hypothetical transhistorical supermatrix reflecting intersect similarities at three time points (T_1 = 1950; T_2 = 1960; T_3 = 1970).

conservative Protestant sects have undergone in America.) Sect E, on the other hand, seems to have become less organizationally stable (the change from relatively low organizational precariousness to a higher level) while making a major shift in secular orientation from retreatism to active participation in the secular world. (This pattern may represent what happens when theologically conservative sects "demythologize" doctrine, usually through the appearance of a new charismatic leader whose revelations contradict existing authorities. Such events normally result in a schism, with organizational resources being diverted to the contending factions.)

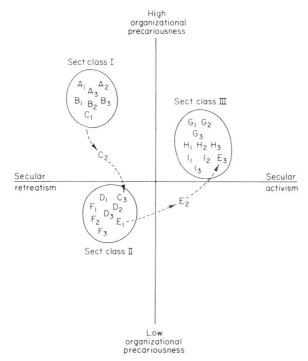

Figure 4.3. Hypothetical two-dimensional configuration (using Welch's dimensions) representing sect class change (for sects C and E) over twenty years. (Subscripts denote group coordinates at the following time points: 1 = 1950, 2 = 1960, 3 = 1970.)

Denominationalization processes can be studied, also, by simply extending the procedures described previously. The only significant alteration performed on the original sect profile matrix would be to add a set of previously identified religious denominations to the samples of sects, including, of course, the appropriate codings on the organizational and doctrinal features for each of these denominations at all of the selected time-points. Similarity coefficients are calculated for each pair of sects and denominations, as well as for all mixed pairs (sect–denomination). These coefficients are again entered in a super-matrix similar to that shown in Figure 4.2, the only difference being the inclusion of *n*-additional partitions of the submatrices representing relationships among the set of denominations and among the set of denominations and the various sects. This mixed unit, transhistorical supermatrix can also be submitted to a nonmetric MDS to produce geometric configurations resembling those in Figure 4.3. For any given sect, then, the historical transition to denominational status can be plotted (see Figure 4.4 for an example showing a hypothetical course of such change).

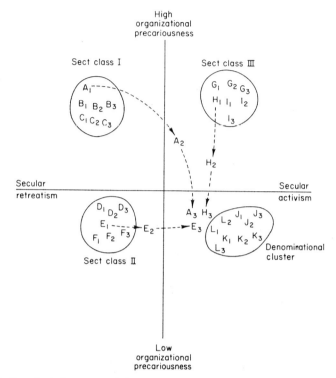

Figure 4.4 Hypothetical patterns of denominationalization: "Routes" of sect transformation over time. (Subscripts denote group coordinates at the following time points: 1 = 1950, 2 = 1960, 3 = 1970.)

As one can easily see, the heuristic advantages of this approach to sect development are considerable. Instead of merely discussing the character of sect transformations in an often discursive way, one is able, simultaneously, to summarize changes in a parisimonious geometric form, identify the fundamental dimensions along which these changes occur, and quantify the magnitude of the transformations with reasonable precision. Rarely can any purely descriptive case-study be carried out as systematically, nor can any such study claim much success in achieving these last two goals, especially. This procedure will allow us to test some of the legitimate sect development hypotheses—such as Wilson's (1967:44–45) contention that conversionist sects will be more likely to achieve denominational status than other types of sects—and thus promote the growth of an empirically validated theory of change in religious organizations. Again, this hypothesis-testing strategy seems to answer the call of critics (Eister, 1967; Greeley, 1972:77–79; Winter, 1977:109–110, 153–165) of past church–sect research, who have suggested researchers should move beyond categorization into the realm of theory-building and theory-testing.

Although elegant and highly systematic, the proposed approaches I have outlined for investigating change in religious organizations suffer from three basic problems. First, getting enough time points and choosing time-sampling intervals may prove problematic. If an unfortuitous interval is selected, imme-nent changes may be missed or antecedent changes overlooked, leading one to conclude, erroneously, that the group being observed has undergone little or no change. Another related problem is the accessibility of coding sources. In particular, considering the literature on American religious groups, it is clear that the more time points one includes, the lower the probability that enough early sources can be located to provide codings for most groups. One standard coding source (Mead's *Handbook of Denominations of the United States*) has editions extending back into the 1950s, but finding other, earlier supplemen-tary sources will probably be quite difficult. Finally, there is the question of which features should be selected for coding and scaling. This is a most critical decision, for, as with factor analysis, it is the character of these indicators and their interrelationships that eventually determine the kind of dimensions that will emerge from subsequent analyses. If one chooses only a few indicators, one is susceptible to charges of bias, and any dimensions that are identified may be challenged as lacking comprehensiveness. As a potential solution to this problem, one might adopt a practice analogous to that used by Cattell and others for identifying the factor structure of human personality: Indicators might be selected to represent all possible domains relating to sect structure and process and used to scale multiple subsamples of diverse religious groups. If similar dimensions emerged in each analysis, one could be somewhat confi-dent that these dimensions correspond to actual latent properties of religious organizations. (For the ancillary problem of labeling the obtained dimensions, no infallible method yet exists. On this issue, one can only choose among the existing alternatives suggested by Green and Carmone, 1970:130).

At present, I can offer no assurances that all of these problems can be solved; however, I am able to point to other research (Welch, 1977) that has overcome some of them and suggest this research as a starting point for future quantitative studies in the church–sect area.

References

Beckford, James A.
  1975 "Two contrasting types of sectarian organizations." In Roy Wallis (ed.), *Sectarianism*. New York: Wiley.

Benson, J. Kenneth, and James H. Dorsett
  1971 "Toward a theory of religious organization," *Journal for the Scientific Study of Religion* 10:130–151.

Benson, J. Kenneth, and Edward W. Hassinger
  1972 "Organizational set and resources as determinants of formalization in religious organizations." *Review of Religious Research* 14:30–36.

Brewer, Earl
  1952 "Sect and Church in Methodism." *Social Forces* 30:400–408.

Boisen, Anton T.
  1940 "Divided Protestantism in a midwest county: A study in the natural history of organized religion." *Journal of Religion* 20:359–381.

Clark, Elmer T.
  1949 *The Small Sects in America*. Nashville: Abingdon.

Clear, Val
  1961 "The Church of God: A study in social adaptation." *Review of Religious Research* 2:129–133.

Coleman, John A.
  1968 "Church–sect typology and organizational precariousness." *Sociological Analysis* 48:574–579.

Demerath, Nicholas J. III
  1967 "In a sow's ear: A reply to Goode." *Journal for the Scientific Study of Religion* 6:77–84.

Demerath, Nicholas J. III, and Victor Thiessen
  1966 "On spitting against the wind: Organizational precariousness and American irreligion." *American Journal of Sociology* 71:674–687.

Eister, Allan W.
  1949 "The Oxford Movement: A typological analysis." *Sociology and Social Research* 34:116–124.
  1967 "Toward a radical critique of church–sect typologizing: Comments and some critical observations on the church–sect dimension." *Journal for the Scientific Study of Religion* 6:85–90.

Goode, Erich
  1967 "Some critical observations on the church–sect dimension." *Journal for the Scientific Study of Religion* 6:69–77.

Greeley, Andrew M.
  1972 *The Denominational Society*. Glenview, Illinois: Scott, Foresman.

Green, Paul E., and Frank J. Carmone
  1970 *Multidimensional Scaling and Related Techniques in Marketing Analysis*. Boston: Allyn and Bacon.

Harrison, Paul M.
  1959 *Authority and Power in the Free Church Tradition*. Princeton: Princeton University Press.

Isichei, Elizabeth Allo
  1964 "From sect to denomination among English Quakers." *British Journal of Sociology* 15:207–222.

Johnson, Benton
  1971 "Church and sect revisited." *Journal for the Scientific Study of Religion* 10:124–137.

Jones, Bryan D.
   1974 "Some considerations in the use of nonmetric multidimensional scaling." *Political Methodology* 1:1–30.
Laumann, Edward O.
   1969 "The social structure of religious and ethnoreligious groups in a metropolitan community." *American Sociological Review* 34:182–197
McComas, Henry C.
   1912 *The Psychology of Religious Sects.* New York: Fleming H. Revell.
Mead, Frank S.
   1964 *Handbook of Denominations of the United States* (4th Ed.). Nashville: Abingdon.
Muelder, Walter
   1957 "From sect to church." In J. Milton Yinger (ed.), *Religion, Society and the Individual.* New York: Macmillan.
Mueller, Samuel A.
   1971 "Dimensions of interdenominational mobility in the United States." *Journal for the Scientific Study of Religion* 10:76–84.
Niebuhr, H. Richard
   1929 *The Social Sources of Denominationalism.* New York: Holt, Rinehart and Winston.
Nosanchuck, T. A.
   1968 "Dimensions of Canadian religions: A preliminary study." *Journal for the Scientific Study of Religion* 7:109–110.
O'Dea, Thomas
   1954 "Mormonism and the avoidance of sectarian stagnation: A study of church, sect and incipient nationality." *American Journal of Sociology* 60:285–293.
Pfautz, Harold W.
   1956 "Christian Science: A case study of the social psychological aspect of secularization." *Social Forces* 34:246–251.
Pope, Liston
   1942 *Millhands and Preachers.* New Haven: Yale University Press.
Rabinowitz, George
   1975 "An introduction to nonmetric multidimensional scaling." *American Journal of Political Science* 19:343–390.
Redekop, Calvin
   1974 "A new look at sect development." *Journal for the Scientific Study of Religion* 13:345–352.
Robertson, Roland
   1967 "The Salvation Army: The persistence of sectarianism." In Byran R. Wilson (ed.), *Patterns of Secatarianism.* London: Heinemann.
Romney, A. Kimball, Roger N. Shepard, and Sara Beth Nerlove (Eds.)
   1972 *Multidimensional Scaling, Vol. II.* New York: Seminar Press.
Rokeach, Milton
   1960 *The Open and Closed Mind.* New York: Basic Books.
Rosten, Leo (Ed.)
   1955 *Guide to the Religions of America.* New York: Simon and Schuster.
Russell, Gordon W.
   1975 "The view of religions from religious and non-religious perspectives." *Journal for the Scientific Study of Religion* 14:129–138.

108 | *Michael R. Welch*

Schroeder, W. Widick, and Victor Obenhaus
    1964   *Religion in American Culture.* New York: The Free Press.
Shepard, Roger N., A. Kimball Romney, and Sara Beth Nerlove (Eds.)
    1972   *Multidimensional Scaling, Vol. I.* New York: Seminar Press.
Sokal, R. R., and P. H. Sneath
    1963   *Principles of Numerical Taxonomy.* San Francisco: W. H. Freeman.
Troeltsch, Ernst
    1931   *The Social Teachings of the Christian Churches* (translation by Olive Wyon). New
           York: Macmillan.
Wallis, Roy
    1975   *Sectarianism: Analyses of Religious and Non-Religious Sects.* London: Peter Owen.
    1977   *The Road to Total Freedom.* New York: Columbia University Press.
Warburton, T. Rennie
    1967   "Organization and change in a British holiness movement." In Bryan
           R. Wilson (ed.), *Patterns of Sectarianism.* London: Heinemann.
Welch, Michael R.
    1974   "Multidimensional scaling as a sect classification device: A preliminary
           investigation." Unpublished Masters Thesis, University of North Carolina, Chapel
           Hill, North Carolina.
    1976   Review of Roy Wallis, *Sectarianism. Social Forces* 55:548-549.
    1977   "Analyzing religious sects: An empirical examination of Wilson's sect
           typology." *Journal for the Scientific Study of Religion* 16:125-141.
Whitley, Oliver R.
    1955   "The sect to denomination process in an American religious movement:
           The Disciples of Christ." *Southwestern Social Science Quarterly* 36:275-282.
Whitworth, John McKelvie
    1975   "Communitarian groups and the world." In Roy Wallis (ed.), *Sectarianism.*
           New York: Wiley.
Wilson, Bryan R.
    1961   *Sects and Society.* London: Heinemann.
    1967a "An analysis of sect development." In Bryan Wilson (ed.), *Patterns of
           Sectarianism.* London: Heinemann.
    1967b "The Exclusive Brethren: A case study in the evolution of a sectarian ideology."
           In Bryan R. Wilson (ed.), *Patterns of Sectarianism.* London: Heinemann.
    1969   "A typology of sects." In Roland Robertson (ed.), *Sociology of Religion.*
           Baltimore: Penguin.
    1970   *Religious Sects.* New York: McGraw-Hill.
Wilson, John F.
    1974   "The historical study of marginal American religious movements." In Irving I.
           Zaretsky and Mark P. Leone (Eds.), *Religious Movements in Contemporary
           America.* Princeton: Princeton University Press.
Winter, J. Alan
    1977   *Continuities in the Sociology of Religion: Creed, Congregation, and Community.*
           New York: Harper and Row.
Yinger, J. Milton
    1970   *The Scientific Study of Religion.* New York: Macmillan.
Young, Forest W.
    1970   "Nonmetric multidimensional scaling: Recovery of metric information." *Psycho-
           metrika* 35:455-473.

1973   "Conjoint scaling." Department of Psychology, University of North Carolina, Chapel Hill, North Carolina.

Young, Frank W.
    1960   "Adaptation and pattern integration of a California sect." *Review of Religious Research* 1:137–150.

Part II

NEW DIRECTIONS IN RESEARCH
ON THE CORRELATES OF
RELIGIOUS COMMITMENT

Chapter 5

Ethnic Variations in Religious Commitment

ANDREW M. GREELEY

I. Introduction

Ethnicity, as the notion is used in much contemporary social science research on the topic, is a "pipeline" variable, one that acts as a conduit for the influence of other unidentified variables. Ethnicity no more "causes" attitudes and behaviors than a heating pipe "causes" the heat that emerges from a radiator. So, when the researcher has discovered an ethnic correlation, he is in roughly the same position as a man who has decided to investigate the heat in his room. He knows the immediate source of the effect witnessed, but he does not know the origin of the forces causing the effect. As the heat researcher must look for the furnace, so the ethnic researcher must search out the subcultural dynamics that have produced the ethnic diversity he has uncovered.

Such a researcher is caught in an awkward problem. He must, first of all, against the reigning assimilationist bias in social science, demonstrate that there is ethnic diversity. Then, having demonstrated its existence, he must make it in effect "go away" so that he can pinpoint the factors at work within the various ethnic subcultures creating the diversity. Otherwise, he runs the risk of being charged with "racism," because he seems to be implying some kind of genetically programmed variety.

The present writer and his colleagues at the National Opinion Research Center (NORC) have successfully performed this exercise on the subject of alcohol problem behavior, first demonstrating wide diversity among five American ethnic groups (English, Irish, Swedish, Italian, and Jewish) and then, through an explanatory model, reducing that variety to a virtual unity. We should always be so lucky. (The reader will be happy to know that it is not necessary to fall back on a genetic explanation for Irish drinking problems. A genetic origin of Irish weakness for "the creature," however, does not seem to be as reprehensible to many scholars as genetic explanations applied to problems of other groups.)

The assumption underlying NORC research on ethnicity (Greeley, 1974) is that American ethnic subcultures are a blend of Old World cultures, American culture at time of arrival of the ethnic group, and subsequent collective experiences within American society. It has been demonstrated (McCready, 1975) that one can make fairly reliable predictions and comparisons among American ethnic groups purely on the basis of a knowledge of the Old World culture. Of course, all the ethnic subcultures represent ways of participating in a common American culture. Indeed, the orientation of the ethnic subcultures from the second generation on, insofar as they are self-conscious at all, is toward their new society. Ethnicity is a way of being an American, and the hyphenated American is an equals sign and not a slash.

The available data enable us to do no more than attempt a sketchy description of the religious variety among the principal American ethnic groups. Whereas some analysis will be attempted in this chapter, it will not be possible to repeat the success achieved in our alcohol research, if only because no agency that funds religious research has either the motivation or the resources that were available to the National Institute on Alcohol Abuse and Alcoholism (NIAAA). We can establish the fact of ethnic religious diversity, particularly among Catholic groups; we are in no position yet to essay an explanation. So much the better for ambitious and imaginative scholars who wish to push further down the path of exploration of American cultural diversity.

Our initial investigation in this chapter is further hampered by the disparity of our three data sources. The first, an NORC General Social Survey of over 9000 cases, provides large numbers of respondents but very few religious questions. The second data set, the Basic Belief file, assembled in a 1973 NORC study (McCready, 1976), has a great many detailed religious questions but insufficient cases to justify much confidence in religioethnic cross tabulations. Finally, the NORC parochial-school studies, which make both longitudinal and intergenerational analysis possible, are limited to Catholic ethnic groups

(Greeley, McCready, McCourt, 1976; Greeley and Rossi, 1966). Our investigation, then, is severely limited both by conceptual weaknesses and by inadequate data. Still, one must begin.

II. Ethnicity and Religious Affiliation

There have been six NORC General Social Surveys. All of them asked present religious and denominational affiliation; four also asked original religious and denominational affiliation. In Table 5.1, there is listed the present and past religious affiliation of all ethnic groups with more than 100 members in the composite NORC General Social Survey file. The majority of English, German, and Irish respondents are either Protestant or former Protestants, as are the majority of Dutch, Scottish, and American Indian respondents. The majority of Russian respondents are Jewish, and the majority of Polish, Italian, and Mexican respondents are Catholic. None of these religious affiliations is particularly surprising given what we know about the country of origin (and the fact that past research has demonstrated that there are more Irish Protestants in the United States than Irish Catholics). Only the predominance of French Protestants over French Catholics is surprising, suggesting, perhaps, a Huguenot component of American life, though the small number of cases makes speculation on that point dubious.

Since the categories in Table 5.1 do not contain enough cases to generate confidence in findings, a religioethnic typology has been developed at NORC

TABLE 5.1 Ethnic Background and Religious Affiliation for Groups with More Than Fifty Cases—NORC General Social Survey

	Total	Protestant	Former Protestant	Catholic	Former Catholic	Jewish	Former Jewish
Africa	374	87.2	6.7	5.1	1.1	.0	.0
England	865	83.9	9.5	4.5	2.0	.1	.1
France	143	47.6	5.6	32.9	14.0	.0	.0
Germany	1148	69.9	7.8	17.2	3.8	1.2	.2
Ireland	672	55.2	6.4	33.6	4.8	.0	.0
Italy	363	8.0	1.1	80.2	10.7	.0	.0
Mexico	139	4.3	1.4	82.0	12.2	.0	.0
Netherlands	111	83.8	5.4	7.2	3.6	.0	.0
Norway	113	83.2	12.4	4.4	.0	.0	.0
Poland	192	6.3	.5	71.4	8.3	12.2	1.6
Russia	107	9.3	.9	14.0	3.7	60.7	11.2
Scotland	202	84.7	10.4	4.0	1.0	.0	.0
Sweden	110	83.6	9.1	4.5	2.7	.0	.0
Other	372	53.2	4.8	32.5	5.1	3.8	.5
American Indian	184	78.8	7.6	9.2	3.8	.0	.5

(Table 5.2) in which all groups having more than 300 members in the six General Social Surveys are represented (with the addition of 127 French Catholics and 221 Jews). Each national origin group consists of the following nationalities: British—England and Wales, Scotland, Canada (non-French); Scandinavia—Denmark, Finland, Norway, Sweden; German—Germany, Austria, Switzerland, Netherlands, Belgium (Protestants only); Irish—Ireland; Slavic—Poland, Czechoslovakia, Hungary, Rumania, Yugoslavia, Lithuania, U.S.S.R.; Italian—Italy; French—France, French Canada, Belgium (Catholics only); Hispanics—all of Latin America including the Hispanic West Indies, Spain, Portugal, the Philippines. Black respondents were coded "black" regardless of national origin or religious preference; Hispanics were coded "Hispanic" regardless of race or religious preference. The category "all else" represents all nonblack, non-Hispanic individuals who either have no religious preference or a religious preference other than Christianity or Judaism. Italian Catholics are the largest of the Catholic ethnic groups, with Irish, German, Slavic, and Hispanic components of the Catholic population all approximately equal in size. The residual "Other Protestant" category is the largest Protestant group, whereas the British and German Protestants both have over 1100 respondents.

Baptists and Methodists account for about one-quarter of the British Protestant population (Table 5.3), Lutherans for half of the Scandinavians and more than one-quarter of the Germans, and Baptists and Methodists for more than half of the Irish Protestants and of the "Other Protestants." It must be kept in mind when reading the subsequent tables that British, Irish, and "Other Prot-

TABLE 5.2 Religio-Ethnic Typology

	Number	Total percentage
Protestants		
British	1128	12.4
Scandinavian	363	4.0
German	1198	13.1
Irish	474	5.2
Other	1698	18.6
Catholics		
Irish	315	3.5
German	331	3.6
Slavic	339	3.7
Italian	362	4.0
French	127	1.4
Other	486	5.3
Jews	221	2.4
Blacks	1077	11.8
Hispanics	332	3.6
All Else	644	7.1

TABLE 5.3 Denomination Affiliation for Protestant Ethnics

	Number	Baptist	Methodist	Lutheran	Presbyterian	Episcopalian	Other	No denomination
British	1127	23.5	26.7	5.9	11.1	8.3	17.9	6.6
Scandinavian	361	8.3	12.7	53.5	5.3	2.8	11.6	5.8
German	1198	16.7	18.8	28.1	8.3	3.3	19.7	5.1
Irish	474	33.5	20.5	4.2	9.3	3.6	22.6	6.3
Other	1695	34.8	19.1	7.8	7.7	3.8	21.7	5.2
Total	4855	32.4	19.6	12.9	7.4	4.1	18.6	4.9

TABLE 5.4 Religious Identification Rates[a] for Protestant Ethnic Groups

	English	German	Other
Baptist	70 (215)	76 (153)	80 (519)
Methodist	68 (273)	65 (175)	66 (279)
Lutheran	75 (40)	82 (273)	77 (80)
Presbyterian	66 (104)	70 (66)	64 (102)
Episcopalian	75 (64)	—	75 (42)

[a] Proportion of those who were born in the denomination who remain in it (of those whose original and present religion is Protestant)

estants'' are at least one-quarter Baptist and that other groups like the Episcopalians and Presbyterians account for only 19% of the English Protestants and 13% of the Irish Protestants.

Among those Americans who were born Protestant and remain Protestant, the Baptists and the Lutherans are those most likely to remain in the denomination to which they belonged when they were 16 years old (the time at which the "original religion" NORC question is pointed). In each of the three ethnic groups, the Baptists, the Lutherans, and the Episcopalians (among the English) and the Other have managed to hold three-quarters of their members. The Methodists and the Presbyterians seem able to hold only about two-thirds of their members. Denominational affiliation, in other words, seems to be more important than ethnic background for Protestants. Ethnicity, as we shall see repeatedly in this chapter, seems to be important as a predictor of religious behavior only among the non-Protestant segments of the population.

Finally, approximately three-fifths of American blacks are Baptists (Table 5.5), and more than three-quarters of American Hispanics are Catholic. The Other Protestants (in this case, most likely, fundamentalists) are the second largest Hispanic group—8%—while 13% of blacks are Methodist, 10% Other Protestant, and 8% Catholic. Unfortunately, the size of our data base does not permit further analysis of the denominational differences among blacks and Hispanics.

III. Ethnicity and Religious Commitments

Slightly under half of the American population goes to church at least two or three times a month (Table 5.6). Among the more devout Catholic groups—the Irish, Germans, Slavs, and the French—the proportion is approx-

TABLE 5.5   Religious and Denomination Affiliation for Blacks and Hispanics

	Blacks	Hispanics
Baptist	59	3
Methodist	13	3
Lutheran	—	1
Presbyterian	1	—
Episcopalian	2	—
Other Protestant	10	8
Protestant, no denomination	1	2
Catholic	8	78
Jewish	0	1
Other	1	1
None	5	5

imately three-fifths, whereas Italian and Hispanic Catholics are little different from the national average. By contrast, only one-tenth of American Jews attend religious services several times a month or more. Thus, the principal ethnic difference among Americans in attending religious services is between Jew and Gentile, with the nonLatin Catholic groups still being somewhat more devout than Latin Catholics and American Protestants.

In all but three of the groups (Scandinavians, Other Protestants, and Jews) there is a statistically significant relationship between age and church atten-

TABLE 5.6   Church Attendance by Religio-Ethnic Typology[a] (Two or Three Times a Month or More)

	All	Under 30	Over 30	College	Not college
Protestant					
British	46	42	48	—	—
Scandinavian	44	—	—	—	—
German	46	35	48	—	—
Irish	47	29	50	—	—
Other	40	—	—	47	37
Catholic					
Irish	60	48	65	—	—
German	63	41	71	—	—
Slavic	60	54	62	—	—
Italian	45	33	50	—	—
French	61	37	72	—	—
Hispanic	48	36	56	—	—
Black	46	38	59	—	—
Jewish	10	—	—	—	—
All	45	—	—	—	—

[a] Only statistically significant differences are shown.

dance, with those under 30 less likely to go to church two or three times a month. The sharpest decline is among Irish Protestants and German and French Catholics. Irish and Slavic Catholics continue to be more devout than their Latin counterparts and Protestant young people. Whether this decline among young people in virtually all ethnic groups is part of a long-range trend or is a phenomenon restricted to a particular generation of young people is a matter for some debate. The best evidence presented on the matter thus far is Wuthnow's *Recent Pattern of Secularization* (1976), which indicates there is a generational rather than a life-cycle, or long-term, secular effect among young people. However, if secularization is a function of greater educational achievement, there is little evidence of secularization in Table 5.6, since only among Other Protestants is there a statistically significant difference in church attendance between college attenders and college nonattenders, and it goes opposite the direction the secularization hypothesis would lead us to expect. It is precisely the college-educated Other Protestant who is the more likely to go to church. Similarly, the absence of a positive impact of college attendance on any of the groups calls into question the social class theory of religious behavior in American society (Greeley, 1978).

The impact of lower levels of religious devotion among young people, then, does not seem to be the result of their having had greater education, and it affects most of the ethnic groups, although British Protestants, German Protestants, Irish Catholics, and Slavic Catholics are less likely to be affected by it.

Most Americans believe in life after death (Table 5.7). The proportion has

TABLE 5.7 Belief in Life after Death by Religio–Ethnic Typology[a] (Proportion Yes)

	All	Under 30	Over 30	College	Not college
Protestant					
British	84	—	—	—	—
Scandinavian	83	—	—	—	—
German	85	—	—	90	83
Irish	89	—	—	—	—
Other	81	—	—	—	—
Catholic					
Irish	74	—	—	85	68
German	85	—	—	95	80
Slavic	65	—	—	81	58
Italian	75	—	—	—	—
French	77	—	—	100	73
Hispanic	66	—	—	94	59
Black	73	57	80	84	71
Jewish	22	—	—	—	—
All	76	—	—	—	—

[a] Only statistically significant differences are shown.

not changed notably since the question was first asked in the 1930s (Greeley, 1978). Between three-quarters and seven-eights of most Gentile American religioethnic groups believe in survival; only Slavic and Hispanic Catholics fall to the two-thirds level. On the other hand, only little more than one-fifth of Jewish Americans believe in life after death. Nor does there seem any likelihood of a decline in conviction of survival with time. Only among blacks is there a statistically significant difference between those under 30 and those over 30 in belief of survival. College attendance has a positive influence on belief in life after death for a number of groups, particularly Catholics—perhaps because the college attenders are more likely to have attended Catholic primary and/or secondary schools (Greeley, McCready, and McCourt, 1976). Protestant ethnic groups are somewhat more likely to believe in life after death than Catholics and substantially more likely than Jews, but, just as the basic division in American church attendance is between Jew and Gentile, so the most important difference in belief in life after death is that between Jew and Gentile. This difference is likely to persist relatively unaffected by age and education.

Catholic are more likely to enter religiously mixed marriages than Protestants and Jews, but there are few differences in the mixed marriage rates within the denominational divisions (Table 5.8). Irish Catholics have the highest intermarriage rate in the country, and, among those under 30, two-fifths of the Irish are in religiously mixed marriages (defined as marriages in which the present religious affiliation of the spouse is not the same as the

TABLE 5.8 Mixed Marriage Rates by Religio-Ethnic Typology—Respondent's Spouse with Different Religious Affiliation[a] (in Percentages)

	All	Under 30	Over 30	College	Not college
Protestant					
British	10	17	9	—	—
Scandinavian	17	—	—	—	—
German	11	18	9	—	—
Irish	10	—	—	—	—
Other	11	—	—	—	—
Catholic					
Irish	27	40	23	—	—
German	21	—	—	—	—
Slavic	19	39	16	—	—
Italian	20	—	—	—	—
Hispanic	22	—	—	—	—
Black	13	—	—	—	—
Jewish	21	—	—	—	—
All	13	—	—	—	—

[a] Only statistically significant differences are shown.

religious affiliation of the respondent—Greeley, 1978). Mixed marriages are twice as likely among British Protestants, German Protestants, Irish Catholics, and Slavic Catholics under 30 than they are among those over 30. However, in no other ethnic group does youthfulness lead to more mixed marriages, and in no ethnic group is there a correlation between college attendance and religious mixed marriages.

To summarize the data from the NORC General Social Surveys, ethnicity seems less important than religious affiliation as a predictor of church attendance, belief in life after death, and religiously mixed marriages. On these three measures, Protestants are more religious than Catholics, and both groups are more religious than Jews on life after death and church attendance measures. There are virtually no important differences among Protestant ethnic groups. The German Catholics are the most likely to go to church, the most likely to believe in life after death, and have very low mixed-marriage rates. The Irish and the Slavs trail behind in religious loyalty, and the Italians and the Hispanics are the least devout, though still far more so than Jews. Most of the differences among the Catholic groups are not large, although 18 points separate German and Italian Catholics in church attendance, 20 points the Germans and the Slavs in belief in life after death, and 8 points the Irish and the Slavs in intermarriage rates.

The NORC Ultimate Belief Survey provides much richer data on religious behavior, though, unfortunately, the number of repsondents is much smaller. Hence, the findings in Tables 5.9–5.12 must be viewed with considerable restraint. There is no possibility of analyzing effects of age and education on religious behavior.

More than half of the American population prays every day (Table 5.9)—from a high of 76% among Polish Catholics to a low 10% among Jews. Sixty-six percent of Irish Protestants and 65% of Other Protestants pray daily, as do 58% of German Catholics, 57% of German Protestants, and 55% of Irish Catholics. Most of the religioethnic groups, it will be observed, cluster in their rates of daily prayer between 50 and 60%, with only Poles (76%), blacks (68%), Irish, and other Protestants above that range, and with only the Jews (10%) below it. The Jew–Gentile distinction continues to be the major one in predicting religiousness.

There are some differences among American ethnic groups that should not follow denominational lines. In the ultimate value study, NORC developed a scale for measuring religion as world view that relied on Clifford Geertz's defintion of religion as a cultural system and on Paul Ricoeur's paradigm of the symbolism of evil. There are basically three different ways to respond to evil—to deny it (the optimist's way), to concede its final power over good (the pessimist's way), or to acknowledge evil but to see good as somewhat stronger

TABLE 5.9 Frequency of Prayer
(Percentage Daily)

Protestant	
British	51 (173)
German	57 (131)
Scandinavian	56 (48)
Irish	66 (72)
Other	65 (88)
Catholic	
Irish	55 (48)
German	58 (50)
Italian	53 (52)
Slavic	76 (43)
Hispanic	52 (33)
Jewish	10 (30)
Black	68 (180)

(the way of hopefulness).[1] The majority of Americans of all religioethnic groups fall in the "optimist" category (Table 5.10); however, Irish Catholics and Scandinavian Protestants are notably more likely than the national average to be high on hopefulness and low on pessimism, whereas the Jews and the Italians are both higher on pessimism than on hopefulness. Thus, when the focus is shifted from the traditional measures of religious devotion such as church attendance, prayer, and belief in life after death to newer methods that try to gauge fundamental world view, ethnic subcultural differences begin to be important. Italians are more like Jews in basic world view than like their Irish compatriots, and the Irish, in their turn, are more like the Swedes than like their German or Slavic coreligionists, and the Swedes have more in common with the Hispanics (who are also relatively high on hope and low on pessimism) than they do with "Other Protestants. Subculture, it would seem, is much more likely to affect basic world view than it is to affect measures of religious devotion.

The high level of Hispanic hopefulness does not, however, seem related to great confidence in religious "truths" (Table 5.11). The respondents in the NORC Basic Belief Study were asked if they believed in life after death, if they

---

[1] The six vignettes that were used to tap these dimensions are presented in the Appendix to this chapter.

TABLE 5.10 "Hopefulness" and "Angry Pessimism" by Typology

	Percentage hopeful	Percentage angry pessimist
Protestant		
British	29	13
German	29	10
Scandinavian	34	6
Irish	23	3
Other	22	13
Catholic		
Irish	35	9
German	20	12
Italian	15	25
Slavic	26	12
Hispanic	30	3
Jewish	17	31
Black	15	8
All	23	14

could find meaning in life, if they believed prayers were heard, that the world is not governed by chance, and that God's love is behind everthing that happens. They were then asked how certain they were of each of these beliefs. A religious conviction scale was constructed based on the number of times a respondent said he was certain, with 1 being a "certain" answer and with 0 for "not certain" or rejection of the belief. Jews were almost one standard deviation below the mean score of the American population, and all the Protestant groups were above the mean, with the Other Protestants one-quarter of a deviation above it. Northern European Catholics clustered around the mean, Irish Catholics 6 points above it, Polish Catholics 11 points above it, and German Catholics 5 points below it. Both the Latin groups—Hispanic and Italian Catholics—were two-fifths of a standard deviation below the mean, not as lacking in confidence as Jews but not as confident of religious "truth" as their fellow Catholics or Protestants.

Irish Protestants are the most likely to report mystical experience in response to the question "Have you ever felt as though you were very close to a powerful, spiritual force that seemed to lift you out of yourself?" (Greeley, 1975). All the Protestant groups were more likely to report such experiences than any of the Catholic groups. Jews, too, were more likely to report such experiences than Catholics, but only by two points (30 versus 28%—the Irish Catholic rate, the most mystical of the Catholic groups). In both Protestant and Catholic denominations, it is the Irish (allegedly a fey and elfin people) who are the most likely to report ecstatic interludes (Table 5.12).

In summary, then, on most measures in both the General Social Survey and the NORC Basic Belief Survey, Protestants are more devout than Catholics,

TABLE 5.11   Rank Order of Ethnic Groups on Certainty
of Religious Conviction Scale[a] (Z-Score)

Other Protestant	.27
British Protestant	.17
Scandinavian Protestant	.15
Slavic Catholic	.11
Irish Protestant	.11
Irish Catholic	.06
Black	.03
German Protestant	.01
German Catholic	− .05
Hispanic Catholic	− .39
Italian Catholic	− .41
Jewish	− .84

[a] A scale composed of answers to the following questions:
   (1) Do you believe in life after death? (If yes) How certain are you? (very certain, pretty certain, not too certain)
   (2) Do you believe that you can find meaning in life?
   (3) Do you believe that prayers are heard?
   (4) Do you believe that the world is not governed by chance?
   (5) Do you believe that God's love is behind everything that happens?
   (Percentage very certain: (1) 32%, (2) 39%, (3) 56%, (4) 29%, (5) 38%)

and Catholics are more devout than Jews. There is little in the way of difference among Protestant ethnic groups save for the higher scores on hopefulness for the Scandinavians. Northern European Catholics are in most respects more religious than southern European Catholics. Among northern Europeans, Germans are more likely to believe in life after death, slightly more likely to go to church, and somewhat more likely to believe in life after death than the Irish but are less likely to enter religiously mixed marriages. The Irish, on the other hand, are more likely than all the other Catholic groups to be hopeful and to have mystical interludes. The most notable payoff, then, in attempting to analyze and explain religious devotional differences among ethnic groups, seems to be in the study of diversity among the Catholics, and particularly their differences in basic world view.

The Basic Belief study also enables us to return to the positive correlation between college attendance and belief in life after death among Catholics (Table 5.13). Whereas there is not a sufficient number of respondents in the Basic Belief study to look at each ethnic group, one still finds that, when all

TABLE 5.12 Proportion Experience a Mystical Interlude Ever and Often

	Ever	Often
Protestant		
British	45	8
German	39	8
Scandinavian	33	2
Irish	50	4
Other	38	1
Catholic		
Irish	28	2
German	17	4
Italian	24	0
Slavic	17	3
Hispanic	15	0
Jewish	26	0
Black	30	12
All	37	5

the Catholics are aggregated, those who have attended college are 19 points more likely (72% versus 53%) to believe in life after death than those who did not attend college. But the difference is entirely specified by Catholic school attendance. Eight percent of the college attenders who went to Catholic elementary schools believe in life after death, whereas only 55% of the college attenders who did not go to Catholic schools believe in life after death—not different significantly from those who did not attend college. The question arises, of course, as to whether this is a Catholic school effect or an effect of religious devotion that predisposes people to attend Catholic schools. Without entering into a discussion of this subject, it is sufficient to say this in both Greeley and Rossi's (1966) *The Education of Catholic Americans* and Greeley, McCready, and McCourt's (1976) *Catholic Schools in a Declining Church* the impact of Catholic school did not seem to be appreciably diminished by holding parental religiousness constant. So, the probability is that, in Table 5.13, one does indeed see a Catholic school effect, especially since it is very likely that a substantial proportion of those who attended Catholic elementary

TABLE 5.13 Belief in Life after Death among Catholics, by Education

	College[a]	Not college
All Catholic	72* (93)	53 (257)
Attended Catholic elementary school	80* (61)	55 (133)
Did not attend Catholic elementary school	55 (29)	50 (118)

[a] Asterisk indicates significantly different from those who did not attend college.

schools and later attended colleges attended Catholic colleges. We know from previous NORC research that it is at the college level that the decisive religious behavioral effects seem to be obtained. (No question was asked in the Basic Belief study about attendance at denominational colleges.)

The data sets available to us enable us to make two attempts to go beyond description of ethnic difference to analysis. We were able to ask whether there are differences in socialization models at work for the different Catholic ethnic groups and whether the same explanation for the decline in religiousness that has occurred in the years since the Second Vatican Council applies to all the Catholic groups.

The religious socialization model developed by William McCready (1971) explains a very high proportion of the variance in religious behavior of Americans—frequently over half the variance. The most important influence on religious behavior of an American adult is the person's spouse, and the second is the person's father.

Interestingly enough, the importance of the religiousness of the spouse varies greatly among American Catholic ethnic groups (Table 5.14). The standardized relationship between spouse's religiousness (with mother's and father's religiousness, education, and sex held constant) and CATHOLOCITY (a scale that measures mass attendance, communion reception, various kinds of organizational and devotional activities and contributions) is almost .5 for the Irish (explaining one-quarter of the variance), .3 for the Germans and Italians (explaining 9% of the variance), and .2 for the Poles (explaining 4% of the variance). In the family life of Irish Catholics, then, the influence of the spouse is enormously more important than it is in the families of other Catholic ethnic groups. (Exactly the opposite is true, incidentally, of alcohol consumption—the spouse has no influence on the average in the Irish family, but substantial influence in other families.)

In three of the groups, there is also a statistically significant standardized correlation between CATHOLICITY and father's religiousness—though the correlation is twice as high for the Irish and the Poles as it is for the Italians. But, in the remaining German group, the beta for mother's religiousness is significant, whereas for father's religiousness it is not. Fathers, in other words, influence the religiousness of their offspring to some extent if they are Italian,

TABLE 5.14 Standardized Coefficients between Religiousness of Role Opposites and Own Religiousness (CATHOLICITY Factor) for Selected American Ethnic Groups (Betas)

	Irish	German	Italian	Polish
Mother	—	.25	—	—
Father	.33	—	.13	.26
Spouse	.48	.30	.28	.19

but considerably if they are Irish and Polish; mothers do not influence their offspring in those ethnic groups. Among Germans, however, it is the mother who has the influence, not the father. Finally, whereas the spouse is by far the most influential religiousness factor for the Irish, Germans, and Italians, the father is more important than among Poles.

Even though there are no differences between men and women in the importance of the spouse's religious influence in the Catholic population as a whole, the picture is considerably more complex when one looks at the various ethnic groups. The spouse has virtually no religious influence on Italian males, but substantial influence on Italian females, whereas Polish men have more influence on their wives than do Polish wives on their husbands. Mothers influence Irish and German men and German and Italian women. Fathers do not influence German men and women and Italian women (Table 5.15). Note that Poles are influenced only by fathers and that the father's support is more important than the spouse's for both sexes, but particularly for women. Italians are influenced by opposite sex parents, the Germans by their mothers, the Irish by their fathers (though Irish men less so than Irish women, in part, perhaps, because the former are also influenced by their mothers).

Before beginning the research reported in *Catholic Schools in a Declining Church,* the present author and his colleagues assumed, as did many others, that the decline in Catholic religiousness that came after the Second Vatican Council was, in fact, a result of the council. (Post hoc ergo propter hoc arguments usually turn out to be valid.) In fact, support for the Vatican Council correlated positively with religious devotion, and "secularization" hypotheses failed to explain the differences. Thus, we were forced to consider the possibility that it was neither the revolution of the Second Vatican Council nor long-term historical changes that accounted for the decline in Catholic religiousness but, rather, the birth-control encyclical of Pope Paul (*Humanae Vitae*) that reaffirmed, despite overwhelming Catholic expectations to the con-

TABLE 5.15 Standardized Coefficients between Religiousness of Role Opposites and Own Religiousness for Men and Women by Sex for Selected American Ethnic Groups (Betas)

	Irish	German	Italian	Polish
Men				
Mother	.16	.12	—	—
Father	.15	—	.36	.30
Spouse	.41	.43	—	.27
Women				
Mother	—	.19	.19	—
Father	.40	—	—	.49
Spouse	.50	.45	.48	.15

trary, the traditional birth-control teaching. The combination of changing Catholic attitudes both on birth control and on papal authority did, in fact, account for *all* of the decline measured between 1963 and 1974. A number of critics complained that the birth-control encylical explanation was too simple (forgetting, perhaps, how important human behavior involving birth control is), despite the evidence from church attendance studies by Gallup (1969) showing that Catholic church attendance did not decline after the council but declined precipitously the year after the encylical and the Princeton fertility studies (Westoff and Bumpass, 1973), which showed that most Catholic women made up their minds that the birth-control pill was moral before the pope's decision was issued, so that the pope spoke after the fact of moral choice and not before it. The critics argued that there had to be some long-term secularization variable at work or, perhaps, merely a sexual revolution. However, although reanalysis of the data did indeed uncover a sexual revolution among American Catholics that may be a part of some long-range "secular" change of attitudes, only one component of the change, shifting attitudes on birth control, accounts for the change in relgious devotion among Catholics. Alone or together, the other variables neither add not detract from the powerful explanatory power of shifting attitudes on birth control.[2]

Each of the four major Catholic ethnic groups (Hispanic Catholics are excluded from this analysis because the skewed distribution of Spanish respondents raises questions in the writer's mind about the utility of NORC's Spanish-speaking subsample) has experienced a sharp decline in church attendance—21% for the Irish, 16% for the Germans, 21% for the Poles, and 22% for the Italians (Table 5.16). The proportion of the decline for the Italians, however, is even sharper because they were somewhat less likely to attend weekly mass than the other three groups to begin with.

There has also been a sharp decline in support for the Church's birth control teaching (48% for the Irish, 41% for the Germans, 41% for the Poles, and 27% for the Italians). Since Italian Catholics, however, were less likely to ac-

TABLE 5.16 Changes in Church Attendance between 1963 and 1974 among Certain Catholic Ethnic Groups (Percentage Weekly or More Often)

	Irish	German	Polish	Italian
1963	77	79	74	66
1974	56	63	53	44
Change	21	16	21	22

[2] Proportion believing that more than two children was the ideal family size, proportion saying that it was wrong to have intercourse for pleasure alone, and proportion saying that one should have as many children as possible and that God would provide—all of which declined by more than 30%.

TABLE 5.17 Birth Control Attitude Changes for Catholic Ethnic Groups (Percentage Accepting Official Teaching)

	Irish	German	Polish	Italian
1963	63	59	52	37
1974	15	14	11	10
Difference	48	45	41	27
	(444)	(510)	(245)	(522)

cept the Church's teaching on birth control in 1963, the net result of the decline is that the other groups have, for all practical purposes, caught up (Table 5.17). Thus, 63% of the Irish Catholics accepted the birth control teaching in 1963, as did 37% of the Italians; in 1974, 15% of the Irish and 10% of the Italians accept the official teaching.

Using the "*d*-systems" model developed in *Catholic Schools in a Declining Church* (Figure 5.1), one may ask to what extent a combination of changing attitudes on birth control and changing attitudes on the authority of the pope (as a successor to Peter) as head of the Church can account for the difference between 1963 and 1974 in each of the ethnic groups in their weekly church attendance. For the Irish and the Poles (Table 5.18), *all* of the decline in church attendance can be accounted for by changes in papal authority and birth control attitudes. For the Germans, not only can the 16-point change be accounted for, it is also "overaccounted for" by a factor of 6 points. The negative relationship betweeen time and mass attendance, in other words,

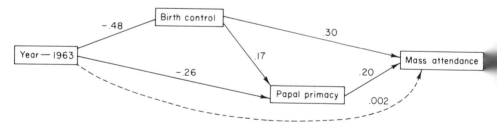

Figure 5.1 "D-System" model for change in church attendance among Irish Catholics.

Time and birth control	$(-.48)(.30)$ =	$-.144$
Time and papal authority	$(-.26)(.20)$ =	$-.052$
Time and both variables (interaction)	$(-.48)(.17)(.20)$ =	$.016$

Total
  Simple D = $-.212$
  Net D   = $-.210$
  D = .21 $-.002$

TABLE 5.18   Explanation of Change in Proportion of Weekly Mass Attendance by Birth Control Encyclical Model

	Irish	German	Polish	Italian
Difference	.22	.16	.21	.22
Birth control	.14	.16	.15	.07
Papal authority	.05	.04	.05	.04
Both	.02	.02	.01	.01
Total explained	.21	.22	.21	.12
Unexplained	00	-.06	00	.10

becomes positive in the German–American model, whereas it is reduced to 0 in the Irish and Polish model.

However, the *Humanae Vitae* model does not account for all the change in church attendance among Italian Catholics. Together, birth control and papal authority account for only 12 of the 22% decline, leaving almost half of the decline unaccounted for. The Italians were less devout to begin with and less likely to accept the Church's birth-control teaching; the change in their attitudes toward birth control is less likely to account for their being even less devout in comparison with the other groups than they were 10 years ago. One must conclude, therefore, that there is a special dynamic at work among Italian Americans not at work among other Catholic groups. For Italians, in other words, there seem to be different mechanisms at work both in religious socialization and in religious social change.

IV. Toward the Future

From the preliminary analysis presented in this chapter, two interesting questions for further study in the ethnicity of religious behavior appear: the difference between Jews and Gentiles and the difference among certain Catholic groups—Latin Catholic versus northern European Catholics in some matters, and Irish Catholics versus everyone else on other matters. The most fruitful areas for further research seem to involve basic belief systems (or world views), religious socialization, and religious change—in the latter two, Italian Catholics would appear to represent an ethnic variance in religious adherence that requires further investigation.

Appendix
Basic Belief Scales

The questions to measure ultimate values were developed by William Mc-Cready. They are:

Now I am going to describe some situations to you. These are things that happen to people sometimes, and I want you to *imagine* that they are happening to you. Please tell me which response on the card comes closest to your own feelings.

24. You have just visited your doctor and he has told you that you have less than a year to live. He has also told you that your disease is incurable. Which of the following statements comes closest to expressing your reaction?

    a) It will all work out for the best somehow..1
    b) No one should question the goodness of God's decision about death..............2
    c) There is nothing I can do about it so I will continue as before 3
    d) I am angry and bitter at this twist of fate.......................................4
    e) I have had a full life and am thankful for that 5
    f) Death is painful, but it is not the end of me....................................6
    g) I cannot answer this question...7
    h) None of the above 8

25. Your son is very likely to be drafted and will be going into a dangerous combat area soon. Which of the following statements reflect your reaction?

    a) Somehow it will all work out 1
    b) If God wants it to happen it must be all right...................................2
    c) This happens to lots of people, you learn to accept it 3
    d) The lottery system is unjust since it does not take individual situations
       into consideration 4
    e) He has been a good son and we are thankful for that 5
    f) It is terrible, but God may provide some opportunity for him to grow and ex-
       pand his life 6
    g) I cannot answer this question...7
    h) None of the above 8

26. You and your husband or wife have been expecting word of a promotion for several weeks. One day it comes through. Which of the following best reflects your reaction to this good news?

    a) Good things usually happen to those who wait their turn 1
    b) God had been good to me and my family..2
    c) These things can go either way; this time it was good...........................3
    d) This is a surprise and I am going to enjoy it 4
    e) I am grateful to my boss for the promotion....................................5
    f) This is a good thing, but my religion tells me life would have been OK with-
       out the promotion 6
    g) I cannot answer this question...7
    h) None of the above 8

27. Imagine that one of your parents is dying a slow and painful death and try to figure out for yourself if there is anything that will enable you to understand the meaning of such a tragedy. Which, if any, of the following statements best expresses your state of mind in this situation?

    a) They are in pain now, but they will be peaceful soon 1
    b) Everything that happens is God's will and cannot be bad 2

    c) There is nothing to do but wait for the end 3

    d) This waiting is inhuman for them; I hope it ends soon 4

    e) We can at least be thankful for the good life we have had together 5

    f) This is tragic, but death is not the ultimate end for us 6

    g) I cannot answer this question 7

    h) None of the above 8

28. Imagine that you have just had a child and that the doctor has informed you that it will be mentally retarded. Which of the following responses comes closest to your own feelings about this situation?

    a) We will try to take care of this child, but it may have to be put in an institution; either way it will all work out 1

    b) God had his own reasons for sending this child to us 2

    c) We must learn to accept this situation 3

    d) I love the baby, but why me? 4

    e) I'm just plain glad to have the child here 5

    f) God has sent us a heavy cross to bear and a special child to love 6

    g) I cannot answer this question 7

    h) None of the above 8

29. Almost every year hurricanes level homes, flood towns, destroy property, and take human lives. How can we make any sense out of such disasters which happen, apparently, by chance? Which of the following statements best describes your answer?

    a) We can never really understand these things, but they usually have some unexpected good effect 1

    b) We cannot know the reasons, but God knows them 2

    c) We cannot know why these occur, and we have to learn to live with that fact 3

    d) The government is responsible for seeing that these disasters do as little harm as possible 4

    e) I am grateful that I don't live in a hurricane area 5

    f) I am not able to explain why these things happen, but I still believe in God's love 6

    g) I cannot answer this question 7

    h) None of the above 8

    The first response (*a*) to each question represents secular optimism; the sixth (*f*) hopefulness; fourth (*d*) anger, fifth (*e*) gratitude. The third response (*c*) represents resignation and loads negatively on the religious optimism and hopefulness scales.

    The agnosticism scale is made up of the following questionnaire items: "Sometimes I am not sure there is any purpose in my life," "I am not sure what I believe," "There may be a God and there may not be." The survival scale is made up of the following items: "Death may contain a pleasant surprise for us,'' ''Whatever happens after death, the person that I am now will not exist any more'' (negative loading). Both scales were created by factor analysis.

References

Gallup
  1969 *Gallup Poll Reports, 1936-1968.* Princeton, New Jersey: American Institute for Public Opinion.
Greeley, Andrew M.
  1974 *Ethnicity in the United States: A Preliminary Reconnaissance.* New York: John Wiley & Sons.
  1975 *The Sociology of the Paranormal: A Reconnaissance.* Beverly Hills, California: Sage Press.
  1978 *Crisis in the Church: A Study of American Religious Evangelization.* Chicago: Thomas More Press (forthcoming).
Greeley, Andrew M., William C. McCready, and Kathleen McCourt
  1976 *Catholic Schools in a Declining Church.* Kansas City: Sheed & Ward.
Greeley, Andrew M., and Peter H. Rossi
  1966 *The Education of Catholic Americans.* Chicago: Aldine.
McCready, William C.
  1971 *Faith of Our Fathers: A Study of the Process of Religious Secularization.* Doctoral dissertation, University of Illinois Circle Campus.
  1975 ''The Transmission of Cultural Heritages.'' In Nathan Glazer and Daniel P. Moynihan (ed.), *Ethnicity: Theory and Experience.* Cambridge: Harvard University Press.
  1976 (with Andrew M. Greeley). *The Ultimate Values of the American Population.* Beverly Hills, California: Sage Press.
Westoff, C. F., and Larry Bumpass
  1973 ''Revolution in birth control practices of United States Roman Catholics.'' *Science* 179(January 5):41-44.
Wuthnow, Robert
  1976 ''Recent pattern of secularization: A problem of generations?'' *American Sociological Review* 41: 850-867.

Chapter 6

Status Inconsistency and Religious Commitment[1]

M. S. SASAKI

I. Introduction

In 1954, Gerhard Lenski initiated the contemporary interest in status inconsistency (also termed "status crystallization"). His observations of modern industrial society led him to pose the following questions:

> Considering the diversity of resources which affect the distribution of rewards in modern industrial societies, the question inevitably arises as to how they are interrelated. This, in turn gives rise to questions of how discrepancies in an individual's statuses affect his actions, and how his actions affect the society of which he is a part [1954:408].

Since Lenski's introduction of the contemparary concept of status crystallization (cf. Hornung, 1972), over 60 authors have attempted to evaluate the legitimacy of the relationship between status inconsistency and its effects

[1] Computer funds for this analysis were provided by both Princeton University and the University of Michigan.

The Religious Dimension:
New Directions in Quantitative Research

(political liberalism, social isolation, psychosomatic symptoms, prejudice, and religious commitment). As a result of this research, the concept of status inconsistency, its theory, theoretical assumptions, and related methods, have all been severely criticized. Indeed, empirical findings have yielded a variety of conclusions, few demonstrating any substantial agreement.

II. Status Inconsistency and Religious Commitment

Compared with other effects of status inconsistency, the effect of status inconsistency on religious commitment has been relatively little explored. The single exception is Demerath (1965), who has stated: "Without suggesting that religion must be considered per force and for its own sake, several considerations recommended an inspection of its link with discrepancy [pp. 128–129]." He continues, "the status discrepant may put inordinate emphasis on his role in the family, the academic community, or, indeed, religion [p. 136]." Religious organizations, he points out, represent relatively non-economic and non-status-oriented institutions.

Demerath partitioned religious commitment into two aspects: churchlike religiosity and sectlike religiosity. He distinguished these two aspects as follows:

> A central idea behind the distinction is that the church may be seen as more or less unconventional by its parishioners. To the church type the religious experience is valuable in its reinforcement of secular values. To the sect type, religion is important as an alternative orientation. Accordingly, sect type and church type emphasize different aspects of the religious program and are committed in qualitatively different ways [1965:137].

Demerath speculated that sectlike religiosity is related to low status and high discrepancy. Conversely, high status and low discrepancy parishioners should be more churchlike in their commitment.

Demerath found that high discrepant Protestants are, indeed, more involved in sectlike religiosity. In further testing, he controlled several variables—denomination, age, sex, subjective class, vertical status, and different combinations of discrepancy—and found that "Of all the various measures of religious commitment, high discrepancy is meaningfully related only to church attendance when other factors are controlled [1965:173]." Moreover, he found that high discrepancy does lead to high church attendance when the discrepancy involves high occupational prestige but low education. On the other hand, discrepancy characterized as high education and lower occupational prestige does not lead to greater church attendance.

Demerath further noted that Sunday services are more compatible with sectlike religiosity than either parish activities or outside affiliations. He concludes: "In any event, and for whatever reason, church attendance is the only measure of religiosity that remains meaningfully associated with discrepancy [1965:155]."

As with other status inconsistency research, however, Demerath's findings must be seriously questioned in light of methodological refinements that have been made since the middle 1960s.

III. Methodological Approach

Methodologically, there have been two different approaches to the study of status inconsistency. The first approach, Lenski's method—which compares percentage sums of consistency and inconsistency—provides no estimation of statistical interaction. Demerath, in his study of religiousness and status inconsistency (1965), also offers a model for generating expected cell values, but here, too, problems of significance testing remain unresolved.

The multiple regression approach, which was also originally suggested by Lenski (1964), does, on the other hand, overcome this limitation. This technique attempts to assess not only the traditional additive effects of variables but also the interaction effects. Olsen and Tully comment:

> This technique differentiates between additive and interaction models, enabling us to separate (a) the effects of interaction between status variables on the dependent political variables, from (b) the straightforward additive effects of these status variables taken separately. The technique also allows us to determine the proportion of total variation in each dependent variable explained by status inconsistency [1972:564].

However, it has been argued that these multiple regression techniques may not necessarily show when the effects are actually due to status inconsistency. Indeed, because of identification and multicollinearity problems (Althauser, 1971; Blalock, 1963, 1965, 1966a,b, 1967a,b,c; Gordon, 1968; Southwood, 1978), it may be impossible to assess the origins of such effects.

A. An Improved Technique for Status Inconsistency Analysis

According to Blalock (1965, 1966a,b, 1967a,b; also cf. Taylor, 1973), a status inconsistency model can be expressed as:

$$Y = a_1 X_1 + a_2 X_2 + a_3(X_1, X_2) + e,$$

where X_1 and X_2 are two different statuses and (X_1, X_2) denotes "some operation" upon X_1 and X_2 and takes the place of an interaction variable (Taylor, 1973).

Taylor (1973) expanded Blalock's model by using nonredundant binary vectors for interaction terms. Hornung (1977) used an approach similar to Taylor's in his analysis of status inconsistency and psychological stress. But, whereas Taylor's approach can avoid the identification problem, it still does not solve the multicollinearity, or some other, problems.

The first of these other problems concerns the number of ranks within a dimension. Doreian and Stockman (1969) have pointed out that two assumptions are traditionally involved here: (*a*) that a dimension only includes a specific number of ranks; and (*b*) that every dimension should contain the same arbitrary number of ranks. A consequence may be a more or less arbitrary assignment of occupations to ranks. As well, respondents' perceptions of occupational status may be wholly different from those of the theorist. The same issues apply to arbitrary income ranks. Doreian and Stockman (1969) suggest using real income instead of breaking income down into arbitrary ranges.

Another problem concerns the actual classification of status consistents and inconsistents. A number of studies have produced very high incidences of status inconsistents; some over 50%! Treiman referred to a study by Nam and Towers in which they found that "over two-thirds of heads of families in the United States [were] status discrepant [Treiman, 1966:653]." Clearly, an incidence as high as 50% indicates methodological or other problems, for we cannot say that over 50% of this population is in a state assumed to be pathological.

Finally, Bauman (1968) has focused his attention on a methodological shortcoming of Lenski's classification system for status consistency versus inconsistency. For instance, he points out that, given discrete ranges for classification, one individual might be placed on the very lowest end of the range on one dimension and on the very highest end of a different range on another dimension, thus leading to the conclusion that this individual is status inconsistent. On the other hand, an individual could be placed at the very lowest point on one range within a dimension and at the highest point in the same range for another dimension. Bauman emphasizes that "the latter consistent person may have a higher degree of status inconsistency than the individual identified as possessing inconsistent status [1968:50]." Therefore, the classification system must be closely examined to avoid such occurrences.

The indication from the preceding discussion is that a new measurement technique for status inconsistency is still needed.

Smith and Sasaki (1979) have developed a numerical method to reduce high correlations between additive and interaction terms. With this technique, we can use multiple regression analysis without worrying about the identification, multicollinearity, or other problems mentioned above. Thus, this technique is well suited for the assessment of status inconsistency effects.

Status inconsistency analysis has also traditionally failed to consider seriously the social norm and its role in status inconsistency measurement. It is particularly appropriate that the degree of status inconsistency be measured as a departure from the norm (Kasl, 1976). Although it is indeed difficult to measure norms, for convenience they can be conceptualized as the "central tendency," which can be expressed by the median.

In previous analyses, the degree of inconsistency has been classified as low, medium, or high, based on the degree of discrepancy among two or three different statuses. However, we can reformulate this concept by referring to status inconsistency based on departures from the central tendency *in opposite directions*. Thus, statistically significant departures in opposite direction from the medians can be regarded as "salient" status inconsistencies, whereas those on the same side of the medians can be regarded as "nonsalient." Figure 6.1 offers a graphic explanation of salient and nonsalient status inconsistencies. The inconsistency between two statuses is in the same direction in Figures 6.1C and 6.1D and is regarded as nonsalient. Cases 1A and 1B depict the salient inconsistencies between statuses.

This new conceptualization of the measurement of status inconsistency helps to reduce the large proportion of status inconsistents often found in a given population—a serious problem discussed previously.

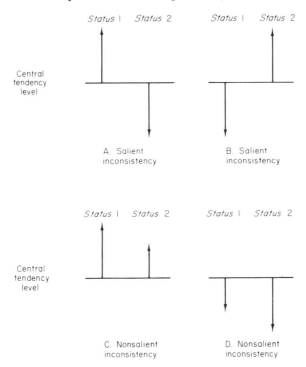

Figure 6.1 Salient and non salient status inconsistencies.

To formulate the above mathematically, we can write:

$$Y = a_1X_1 + a_2X_2 + a_3X_3 + a_4 (X_1-\alpha_1) (X_2-\alpha_2)$$
$$+ a_5 (X_1-\alpha_1) (X_3-\alpha_3) + a_6 (X_2-\alpha_2) (X_3-\alpha_3) + e,$$

where α_1, α_2, and α_3 are medians of X_1, X_2, and X_3, respectively, and X_1, X_2, and X_3 are occupation, income, and education, respectively.

From this equation, we can see that the interaction terms have both status consistency and status inconsistency effects. For example, if we look at the first interaction term, $a_4 (X_1-\alpha_2) (X_2-\alpha_2)$, and coefficient a_4 is positive and statistically significant, we interpret this as a case in which consistency (which has a positive relation to Y, the dependent variable) and inconsistency (which has a negative relation to Y, the dependent variable), or either one, has a positive or negative relationship to a dependent variable. If a_4 is negative and statistically significant, all signs of relationships should be reversed. Therefore, we have to partition the interaction terms into consistency and inconsistency cases and then eliminate the consistency cases because our purpose is to identify the relationship between status inconsistency and the dependent variable.

Let us not forget, however, that the primary purpose of status inconsistency analysis is to determine whether or not a specific type of status inconsistency (e.g., low education–higher occupational prestige) is related to the dependent variables. Hence, the next step is to partition the interaction terms for the inconsistency cases into six different interaction terms for six different types of status inconsistency. The equation can now be written:

$$Y = a_1X_1 + a_2X_2 + a_3X_3 + a_4X_4 + a_5X_5 + a_6X_6$$
$$+ a_7X_7 + a_8X_8 + a_9X_9 + e,$$

where X_1, X_2 and X_3 are different statuses

$$X_4 = (X_1-\alpha_1) (X_2-\alpha_2) \text{ if } X_1 > \alpha_1 \ X_2 < \alpha_2$$
$$X_5 = (X_1-\alpha_1) (X_2-\alpha_2) \text{ if } X_1 < \alpha_1 \ X_2 > \alpha_2$$
$$X_6 = (X_1-\alpha_2) (X_3-\alpha_3) \text{ if } X_1 > \alpha_2 \ X_3 < \alpha_3$$
$$X_7 = (X_1-\alpha_2) (X_3-\alpha_3) \text{ if } X_1 < \alpha_2 \ X_3 > \alpha_3$$
$$X_8 = (X_2-\alpha_2) (X_3-\alpha_3) \text{ if } X_2 > \alpha_2 \ X_3 < \alpha_3$$
$$X_9 = (X_2-\alpha_2) (X_3-\alpha_3) \text{ if } X_2 < \alpha_2 \ X_3 > \alpha_3.$$

If the conditions of one of the variables X_4–X_9 is not met, then that variable is set equal to zero.

One point about the interpretation of the effects of the discrepancies must be emphasized. Because a salient discrepancy has a negative sign, positive regression coefficients for a discrepancy mean that that discrepancy has a *negative* effect on the dependent variable: the greater the discrepancy (the more negative the value of X), the lower the expected value of the dependent variable is (a negative X times a positive coefficient). Conversely, a negative regression coefficient for discrepancy means the discrepancy has a positive effect: the greater the discrepancy, the higher is the expected value of the dependent variable.

IV. Data

Data for this analysis were taken from three sources: the 1972 Center for Political Studies (CPS) National Election Study, the Cumulative (1972–1977) General Social Surveys conducted by the National Opinion Research Center, and a Gallup poll conducted in 1976 on religious studies. All three studies involved questions regarding either churchlike or sectlike religiosity. More specifically, the Gallup poll contained sectlike religiosity questions. The 1972 CPS Election Study and the Cumulative General Social Surveys both contained churchlike and sectlike religiosity questions. For all three surveys, only those respondents who were employed fulltime were utilized in the present analysis. As with Demerath and most other status inconsistency analysts, income, education, and occupational prestige have been utilized as the status categories for this study.

V. Analysis

Like Hornung's (1977) status inconsistency analysis, three different regression models were established for the present analysis: Model 1, linear additive regression; Model 2, curvilinear regression with additive and interaction terms; and Model 3, curvilinear regression with interaction terms only. These can be written as follows:

Model 1 $Y = a_1X_1 + a_2X_2 + a_3X_3 + e$

Model 2 $Y = a_1X_1 + a_2X_2 + a_3X_3 + a_4X_4 + a_5X_5 + a_6X_6$
$\qquad\qquad + a_7X_7 + a_8X_8 + a_9X_9 + e$

Model 3 $Y = a_4X_4 + a_5X_5 + a_6X_6 + a_7X_7 + a_8X_8 + a_9X_9$
$\qquad\qquad + e,$

where X_4, X_5, X_6, X_7, X_8, and X_9 are different types of status inconsistency and X_1, X_2, and X_3 are different statuses.

By utilizing and comparing the results of these three different models, the objectives of this study can be stated as follows: (*a*) in Model 1, to determine whether or not the three status components per se can adequately account for variations in religious commitment and to examine the statistical significance of all relationships; (*b*) in Model 2, to determine whether or not including status inconsistency effects in Model 1 can increase significantly the total variation in religious commitment and to examine the statistical significance of all relationships of the three statuses and status inconsistencies to religious commitment; and (*c*) in Model 3, to determine whether status inconsistency per se or status per se (in Model 1) can better account for variation in religious commitment and, if status inconsistency per se can, then to examine the statistical significance of all relationships.

The results from all three data sources are summarized in Tables 6.2–6.7. Only those items with statistically significant (.05 level) multiple correlation R^2 (using Model 2) are shown in the tables and discussed in the following pages. A summary of the notation used in the tables and discussions is presented in Table 6.1.

Table 6.2 indicates that Model 1 explains only a modest percentage of the variation in the four different dependent variables. So far as each status is concerned, education is negatively related to MISFORTUNE = GOD PUNISHMENT and positively related to GOOD AMERICANS BELIEVE IN GOD and AFTERLIFE BELIEF. Occupational prestige is negatively related to PRAY FREQUENTLY and MISFORTUNE = GOD PUNISHMENT and positively related to GOOD AMERICANS BELIEVE IN GOD. Income is negatively related to PRAY FREQUENTLY and positively related to GOOD AMERICANS BELIEVE IN GOD. Thus, the findings are not entirely consistent, but they suggest that social status is associated with religious commitment in these data, albeit in different ways. In particular, it appears that the idea of Americans believing in God is in general a middle-class belief, whereas praying and attributing misfortune to God appear to be lower-class expressions of religious commitment.

Model 2 finds status inconsistency adding only a slight percentage to the variation in the dependent variables. Among the four religious commitment items, only MISFORTUNE = GOD PUNISHMENT has status inconsistency effects. Besides occupational prestige, the inconsistency defined by low education–higher income (X_7) has a significant relationship to MISFORTUNE = GOD PUNISHMENT. In other words, people with lower occupational prestige and/or people who have status inconsistency between low education and higher income believe somewhat more than average that God sends misfortunes as punishment for sins.

Model 3 finds that status inconsistency components have impact only on MISFORTUNE = GOD PUNISHMENT. However, comparing Models 1 and 3, we can see that the three status components still have greater inpact on this item than the status inconsistency components.

From Table 6.2 we can conclude that even if each status is somewhat related to the various religious commitment items and only one type of status inconsistency is related to one religious commitment item, the explanatory powers

TABLE 6.1 Summary of Notation

Questions and Abbreviated Identifiers	
CPS National Election Study	
Pray frequently	How often do you pray?
Misfortune = God punishment	Does God send misfortunes as punishment for sins?
Afterlife belief	Do you believe in life after death?
Good Americans believe in God	Can someone who does not believe in God be a good American?
Cumulative General Social Surveys	
Church attendance	How often do you attend religious services?
Affiliation strength	Would you call yourself a strong Protestant, Catholic, Jewish, or of some other religion?
Gallup Poll Study	
Faith healing	Are you involved in or do you practice faith healing?
Religious belief	How important to you are your religious beliefs?
Bible feelings	Which one of these statements comes closest to describing your feelings about the Bible?
	A. The Bible is the actual word of God and is to be taken literally, word for word.
	B. The Bible is the inspired word of God but not everything in it should be taken literally, word for word.
	C. The Bible is an ancient book of fables, legends, history, and moral precepts recorded by men.
Religious experience	Would you say that you have ever had a "religious or mystical experience"—that is, a moment of sudden religious insight or awakening?
Born again	Would you say that you have been "born again" or have had a "born again" experience—that is, a turning point in your life when you committed yourself to Christ?
Statuses and Status Inconsistency	
E	Education
O	Occupational prestige
I	Income
X_4	High education and lower occupational prestige
X_5	Low education and higher occupational prestige
X_6	High education and low income
X_7	Low education and high income
X_8	Higher occupational prestige and low income
X_9	Lower occupational prestige and high income

of the three status components per se, the status inconsistency components per se, or a combination of both components, are modest for all religious commitment items in all models.

Table 6.3 shows the results from the Cumulative General Social Survey. In

TABLE 6.2 Regression Coefficients: Models 1, 2, and 3 for CPS National Election Study (N = 690)[a]

Model	Multiple R²	Y	Main effects			Inconsistency effects					
			E	O	I	X₄	X₅	X₆	X₇	X₈	X₉
1	.05**	Pray frequently	.496 (.008)	-.502** (-.116)	-.392** (-.149)						
	.07**	Misfortune = God punishment	-.370** (-.095)	-.670** (-.223)	-.732 (-.040)						
	.02**	Afterlife belief	.706** (.177)	-.189 (-.062)	-.771 (-.041)						
	.13**	Good Americans believe in God	.101** (.220)	.367** (.104)	.235** (.111)						
2	.06**	Pray frequently	.542 (.095)	-.754** (-.175)	-.462** (-.175)	.483 (.056)	-.115 (-.063)	.421 (.085)	.108 (.022)	-.340 (-.046)	-.745 (-.033)
	.08**	Misfortune = God punishment	-.945 (-.024)	-.650** (-.216)	-.620 (-.034)	-.268 (-.004)	.160 (.013)	.201 (.058)	-.318** (-.107)	-.176 (-.034)	-.256 (-.017)
	.02**	Afterlife belief	.741** (.186)	-.309 (-.102)	-.204 (-.010)	.361 (.060)	.499 (.041)	.706 (.020)	.467 (.015)	-.332 (-.065)	-.572 (-.003)
	.13**	Good Americans believe in God	.107** (.234)	.199 (.056)	.315** (.148)	-.250 (-.036)	-.501 (-.036)	-.946 (-.023)	-.194 (-.051)	-.188 (-.031)	.967 (.058)
3	.01	Pray frequently				.480 (.005)	-.515 (-.028)	.164 (.033)	.304 (.063)	-.356 (-.049)	-.724 (-.032)
	.03**	Misfortune = God punishment				-.224 (-.036)	.456 (.039)	.221 (.064)	-.321** (-.108)	-.390 (-.007)	-.845 (-.058)
	.01	Afterlife belief				.110 (.018)	.972* (.081)	-.858 (-.024)	.178 (.060)	-.237 (-.046)	-.353 (-.023)
	.01	Good Americans believe in God				-.361 (-.053)	-.389 (-.002)	-.209 (-.051)	-.923 (-.024)	-.442 (-.001)	.761 (.046)

[a] Standardized coefficients appear in parentheses.

** $p < .05$

* $p < .10$

TABLE 6.3 Regression Coefficients: Models 1, 2, and 3 for Cumulative General Social Surveys ($N = 2413$)[a]

Model	Multiple R²	Y	Main effects			Inconsistency effects					
			E	O	I	X_4	X_5	X_6	X_7	X_8	X_9
1	.009**	Church attendance	−.786 (−.008)	.203** (.107)	−.299 (−.032)						
	.004**	Affiliation strength	−.231 (−.007)	.434** (.064)	−.187** (−.056)						
2	.015**	Church attendance	−.478 (−.054)	.277** (.147)	−.251 (−.027)	.287 (.000)	.360** (.062)	−.862 (−.013)	.313 (.019)	−.375 (−.023)	−.220* (−.049)
	.008**	Affiliation strength	−.170 (−.053)	.685** (.101)	−.157 (−.047)	−.736** (−.055)	.945* (.046)	−.199 (−.000)	−.214 (−.003)	−.852 (−.014)	.576 (.003)
3	.007**	Church attendance				.100 (.027)	.241* (.041)	−.329 (−.005)	.138 (.008)	−.106** (−.066)	−.406 (−.009)
	.004	Affiliation strength				−.492 (−.036)	.619 (.030)	.116 (.005)	−.545 (−.008)	−.292* (−.051)	.620 (.036)

[a] Standardized coefficients appear in parentheses.

** $p < .05$

* $p < .10$

145

Model 1, for CHURCH ATTENDANCE, only occupational prestige is positively related. This finding supports that of Dynes (1955)—that occupational prestige has a strong positive relationship to church–sect religiosity. This finding also partially supports Demerath's finding that churchlike religiosity is positively related to individual status, although Demerath combines the three statuses into an overall status index for his analysis.

For AFFILIATION STRENGTH, occupational prestige and income have positive and negative relationships, respectively. From this finding, we might speculate that inconsistency between these statuses might have a significant relationship to AFFILIATION STRENGTH. However, in Model 2 only occupation and the high education–lower occupational prestige inconsistency (X_4) have positive relationships to AFFILIATION STRENGTH, whereas low education–higher occupational prestige (X_5) has a negative relationship to this item. Also, in this model, occupational prestige and the low education–higher occupational prestige inconsistency (X_5) and the lower occupational prestige–higher income inconsistency (X_9) have negative and positive relationships, respectively, to CHURCH ATTENDANCE. This finding is the same as Demerath's so far as a status inconsistency type for church attendance is concerned, but the sign of the relationship is opposite to that found by Demerath. In other words, Demerath found that only high inconsistency between higher occupational prestige and low education has a positive relationship to CHURCH ATTENDANCE. In addition to the lower occupational prestige–higher income inconsistency (X_9), in this study, the same inconsistency type was seen to have a negative relationship to CHURCH ATTENDANCE.

In Model 3, status inconsistency components have impact only on CHURCH ATTENDANCE. As in the CPS National Election Study results, the three status components still explain CHURCH ATTENDANCE better than the status inconsistency components.

From this table, we can conclude that, even though status inconsistency effects add substantially to the percentage of variation in the dependent variables, the total explanatory powers for both dependent variables are modest, similar to the findings from the CPS National Election Study shown in Table 6.2.

Table 6.4 presents the results based on the Gallup poll data. In Model 1, of the five religious items, the three status components have the strongest impact on BIBLE FEELINGS.

For FAITH HEALING, only income has a significant negative relationship. Therefore, this finding that lower income people are somewhat more involved in faith healing than the average partially supports the general speculation that faith healing is a lower-class phenomenon. For RELIGIOUS BELIEF and BIBLE FEELINGS, only education has a negative relationship; in particular, its relationship to the latter dependent variable is strong. For RELIGIOUS EXPERIENCE,

TABLE 6.4 Regression Coefficients: Models 1, 2, and 3 for Gallup Poll Study ($N = 816$)[a]

Model	Multiple R^2	Y	Main effects			Inconsistency effects					
			E	O	I	X_4	X_5	X_6	X_7	X_8	X_9
1	.008*	Faith healing	-.264 (-.018)	-.290 (-.025)	-.496* (-.069)						
	.016**	Religious belief	-.562** (-.125)	.128 (.034)	.887 (-.038)						
	.135**	Bible feelings	-.141** (-.371)	.510 (.016)	-.293 (-.015)						
	.008	Religious experience	-.106 (-.039)	-.418 (-.018)	-.823 (-.059)						
	.036**	Born again	-.390** (-.139)	-.558 (-.024)	-.103** (-.073)						
2	.027**	Faith healing	.144 (.010)	-.907 (-.079)	-.289 (-.040)	-.342 (-.015)	-.476* (-.153)	-.836 (-.089)	.287 (.016)	.571 (.069)	.363 (.033)
	.028**	Religious belief	-.182 (-.040)	.491 (.013)	-.250* (-.109)	-.124 (-.017)	-.184 (-.018)	.365** (.122)	-.290 (-.051)	.101 (.003)	.190 (.055)
	.138**	Bible feelings	-.128** (-.338)	.875 (.028)	-.119 (-.061)	-.252 (-.004)	-.377 (-.044)	.115 (.004)	-.641 (-.012)	.140 (.063)	-.864 (-.002)
	.021**	Religious experience	-.572 (-.021)	-.273 (-.012)	-.989 (-.071)	-.349** (-.082)	-.305 (-.050)	.149 (.082)	.151 (.004)	-.107 (-.067)	-.441 (-.021)
	.042**	Born again	-.334* (-.119)	-.278 (-.012)	-.136 (-.095)	-.125 (-.029)	-.142 (-.002)	.141 (.076)	-.308 (-.008)	-.119 (-.073)	-.108 (-.050)
3	.020**	Faith healing				-.722 (-.033)	-.450** (-.144)	-.942** (-.101)	.471 (.026)	.659 (.079)	.164 (.015)
	.016**	Religious belief				-.939 (-.013)	-.303 (-.030)	.344** (.115)	-.240 (-.042)	-.961 (-.036)	.266* (.077)
	.042**	Bible feelings				.299 (.051)	-.953** (-.112)	.241* (.096)	-.396* (-.077)	.244 (.011)	-.980 (-.003)
	.015*	Religious experience				-.356** (-.084)	-.333 (-.055)	.137 (.076)	.401 (.011)	-.139* (-.088)	-.278 (-.013)
	.012	Born again				-.706 (-.016)	-.162 (-.025)	.174* (.093)	-.698 (-.019)	-.175** (-.106)	-.946 (-.044)

[a] Standardized coefficients appear in parentheses.
** $p < .05$
* $p < .10$

147

contrary to the general expectation that this phenomenon is prevalent among lower-class persons, status components per se do not have an impact on religious experience. This finding supports those of Greeley (1975) and Wuthnow (1978).

For BORN AGAIN, both education and income have significant negative relationships. This finding contradicts the suggestion of Quebedeaux (1978) that ''born again'' is a middle-class phenomenon.

From Model 1 we can conclude that education is the single strongest predictor for these five religious commitment items, and, in general, it can be stated that sectlike religiosity is more prevalent among lower-class persons. In Model 2, one inconsistency, low education with higher occupational prestige (X_5), is positively related to FAITH HEALING. Income and high education–lower income are negatively related to RELIGIOUS BELIEF. Also, the high education–lower occupational prestige inconsistency is positively related to RELIGIOUS EXPERIENCE.

An interesting finding is that, among all three status dimensions and the six status inconsistencies, only one inconsistency (X_5) is positively associated with FAITH HEALING and only one (X_4) is positively associated with RELIGIOUS EXPERIENCE. Also, Model 2 finds status inconsistency adding substantially to the percentage of variation in some of the dependent variables, specifically, FAITH HEALING, RELIGIOUS BELIEF, and RELIGIOUS EXPERIENCE. However, the total percentages of variation in these three religious commitment items are still modest.

In Model 3, the status inconsistencies per se have impact on all religious commitment items except BORN AGAIN. However, all of their explanatory powers are quite modest. Although it has been speculated that RELIGIOUS EXPERIENCE and BORN AGAIN are consequences of status inconsistency, the Gallup poll data supports only the former case.

Another striking finding is that, in comparing Models 1 and 3, FAITH HEALING and RELIGIOUS EXPERIENCE can be better explained by status inconsistency components rather than the three status components. Also, both the status inconsistency components and the three status components have the same degree of impact on RELIGIOUS BELIEF.

Comparing the three data sets, we can conclude that, from all Model 1's, in general all three status dimensions are somewhat related to ten different aspects of religious commitment. GOOD AMERICANS BELIEVE IN GOD is the only item to which all three statuses are significantly related, and RELIGIOUS EXPERIENCE is the only item to which none of the three statuses is related. The Model 1's from all three data sources generally support Demerath's finding that sectlike religiosity is prevalent among lower-class persons.

From the Model 2's among the three data sets, we can conclude that, in general, the addition of status inconsistency components to status components does not significantly increase the total variation in religious commitment.

Also, we can see that in almost all cases the greatest effect is that of a status component rather than that of status inconsistency. The only exceptions are the cases of FAITH HEALING, RELIGIOUS EXPERIENCE, and RELIGIOUS BELIEF.

So far as the types and directions of the status inconsistencies are concerned, education–occupational prestige inconsistencies (X_4 and X_5), the low education–higher income inconsistency (X_7), and the lower occupational prestige–higher income inconsistency (X_9) have positive relationships to various religious commitment items. The low education–higher occupational prestige inconsistency (X_5) and the high education–lower income inconsistency (X_6) both have negative relationships to various religious commitment items. The higher occupational prestige–lower income inconsistency (X_8) is the only one that does not affect any religious commitment item. We also can see that besides the low education–higher income inconsistency type, which has both positive and negative relationships to religious commitment items, all four other status inconsistency patterns have either positive or negative relationships to religious commitment. Also, the findings of this study show that status inconsistencies have more significant positive relationships than negative relationships to religious commitment. In other words, in general, status inconsistents are more involved or more active in some aspects of religious commitment than they are less involved or less active.

Another significant finding is that the inconsistency between low education and higher occupational prestige (X_5), which is the only status inconsistency type meaningfully associated with church attendance in Demerath's analysis, in this study is also meaningfully associated with other aspects of religious commitment, specifically AFFILIATION STRENGTH and FAITH HEALING.

From Model 3, we can conclude that only on half of the 11 different religious commitment items do status inconsistency components provide impact, and these impacts are greater than those of status components for two religious commitment items (i.e., FAITH HEALING and RELIGIOUS EXPERIENCE). With respect to significant relationships between status inconsistency and religious commitment, the low education–higher occupational prestige inconsistency and the high education–lower income inconsistency have positive effects on FAITH HEALING. The high education–lower occupational prestige inconsistency and the higher occupational prestige–lower income inconsistency also have positive effects on RELIGIOUS EXPERIENCE.

Overall, these results show that neither the three status components per se, the status inconsistency components per se, nor a combination of both has significant explanatory powers for all 11 aspects of religious commitment. Hence, we might speculate that other auxiliary statuses, such as age, sex, race, and religious preference, might increase the explanatory powers of the various religious commitment items. To test this speculation, further analyses were performed. The results are summarized in Tables 6.5, 6.6, and 6.7.

From the CPS National Election Survey (Table 6.5), we can see that each of

TABLE 6.5 Regression Coefficients with Auxiliary Statuses: CPS National Election Study[a]

Multiple R²	Y	E	O	I	Age	Race	Sex	Religious preference
.11**	Pray frequently	.449 (.079)	−.500** (−.116)	−.194 (−.073)	.167** (.252)	.239* (.071)	.251** (.104)	.972 (.038)
.09**	Misfortune = God punishment	−.314 (−.080)	−.563** (−.188)	.562 (.031)	.112 (.024)	.297** (.119)	−.113* (−.066)	−.100 (−.057)
.04**	Afterlife belief	.688** (.173)	−.183 (−.060)	−.438 (−.002)	.491 (.010)	.290 (.011)	.133* (.077)	−.195** (−.108)
.15**	Good Americans believe in God	.105** (.230)	.265 (.075)	.195** (.092)	.123 (.023)	−.372** (−.127)	.361 (.001)	.155* (.074)
						0 = white 1 = black	0 = male 1 = female	0 = Protestant 1 = Catholic

[a] Standardized coefficients appear in parentheses.

** $p < .05$

* $p < .10$

150

the seven statuses is somewhat significantly related to religious commitment. However, the inclusion of auxiliary statuses does not increase the explanatory power to any significant degree.

Comparing Tables 6.2 and 6.5—even if age, race, sex, and religious preference do relate somewhat to religious commitment—the explanatory power for PRAY FREQUENTLY increases by only 6%, MISFORTUNE = GOD PUNISHMENT by 3%, AFTERLIFE BELIEF by 1%, and GOOD AMERICANS BELIEVE IN GOD by 2%.

From Table 6.6, the Cumulative General Social Survey, we can see that religious preference, age, and race are among the auxiliary statuses related to CHURCH ATTENDANCE and AFFILIATION STRENGTH. Compared with the increases in explanatory power seen for the National Election data (Tables 6.3 and 6.6), explanatory powers are significantly increased for the General Social Survey by adding the auxiliary statuses. Nonetheless, the total amounts of explanatory powers are still quite modest.

In Table 6.7, the Gallup poll data, we can see that, among the auxiliary statuses, race and sex are significantly related to all items except FAITH HEALING. Thus, the explanatory power in this case, like that of the Cumulative General Social Survey data, significantly increases by adding the auxiliary statuses. However, the magnitudes of the explanatory powers for all religious commitment items are still modest. Even after adding the auxiliary statuses, the multiple R for FAITH HEALING is still not significant.

In summary, the addition of the auxiliary statuses does not significantly increase explanatory power in any of the three data sets.

VI. Conclusions

The present analysis, based on three data sets—CPS National Election Study, Cumulative General Social Survey, and Gallup poll—parallels the conclusions reached with regard to previous studies of status inconsistency and its effects. Whereas the various methodological problems of the previous analyses have been addressed and a method suitable for the theoretical assumptions of status inconsistency analysis has been introduced to resolve these problems, the modest results obtained in this analysis may be a consequence of other considerations, perhaps of the subject matter itself—religious commitment.

So far as the relationships of the three statuses (i.e., education, occupational prestige, and income) to different aspects of religious commitment are concerned, the findings are not entirely consistent but do suggest that social status is associated with religious commitment; in particular, that sectlike religiosity is more prevalent among lower-social-status persons.

So far as the relationships of both statuses and status inconsistencies to

TABLE 6.6 Regression Coefficients with Auxiliary Statuses: Cumulative General Social Surveys[a]

Multiple R²	Y	E	O	I	Age	Race	Sex	Protestant	Catholic	Jewish
.175**	Church attendance	.859**	.151**	-.645**	.341**	.733**	-.151	2.839**	3.450**	.994**
		(.098)	(.080)	(-.070)	(.168)	(.080)	(-.027)	(.520)	(.572)	(.050)
.033**	Affiliation strength	.120	.315	-.229**	.106**	.170**	-.792	-.666**	-.666**	-.818**
		(.038)	(.046)	(-.069)	(.148)	(.053)	(-.041)	(-.330)	(-.320)	(-.123)

0 = white	0 = female
1 = black	1 = male

[a] Standardized coefficients appear in parentheses.

** $p < .05$

* $p < .10$

TABLE 6.7 Regression Coefficients with Auxiliary Statuses: Gallup Poll Study[a]

	Multiple R²	E	O	I	Age	Race	Sex	Protestant	Catholic	Jewish	Eastern Orthodox
Faith healing	.01	-.357 (-.025)	-.307 (-.026)	-.262 (-.036)	-.133 (-.008)	.774 (.010)	-.305 (-.063)	.442 (.009)	-.124 (-.024)	-.558 (-.035)	-.840 (-.012)
Bible feelings	.20**	-.126** (-.332)	.108 (.034)	.326 (.016)	.140 (.031)	-.216** (-.099)	-.892** (-.068)	.672** (.505)	.514** (.375)	.180 (.042)	-.780 (-.043)
Religious belief	.12**	-.214 (-.048)	.709 (.019)	.389 (.017)	-.891** (-.171)	-.232** (-.093)	-.285** (-.185)	.759** (.481)	.826** (.509)	.117 (.022)	-.809 (-.037)
Religious experience	.05**	-.763 (-.028)	-.923 (-.004)	-.138 (-.010)	-.282 (-.009)	-.120** (-.080)	-.712** (-.076)	.116 (.122)	-.325 (-.033)	-.130 (-.042)	-.281 (-.021)
Born again	.14**	-.340** (-.121)	-.102 (-.004)	.320 (.002)	.366 (.011)	-.138** (-.089)	-.118** (-.124)	.165 (.168)	-.982 (-.097)	-.244* (-.077)	-.342 (-.025)

[a] Standardized coefficients appear in parentheses.

** $p < .05$

* $p < .10$

1 = white   1 = male
0 = black   0 = female

153

religious commitment are concerned, the findings of the present study do lend some support to the general speculation that both statuses and status inconsistencies are related to some aspects of religious commitment, especially Demerath's speculation that sectlike religiosity is related to low status and high status inconsistency.

In his analysis of status inconsistency and religious commitment, Demerath found that high status inconsistency is only meaningfully related to church attendance when other factors are controlled. Moreover, he found that high status inconsistency does lead to high church attendance when it involves high occupational prestige and low education. In the present study, this finding is reversed. The present study also shows that this specific status inconsistency type is also meaningfully associated with other aspects of religious commitment (i.e., FAITH HEALING, BIBLE FEELINGS, and AFFILIATION STRENGTH).

The findings of the present analysis show that, in general, status-inconsistent persons are more involved or more active in their different religious commitments rather than less involved or less active.

An interesting finding was that FAITH HEALING and RELIGIOUS EXPERIENCE are the only 2, out of the 11 religious commitment items, that can be better explained or predicted by status inconsistencies than by the three statuses. This finding supports the speculation that religious experience is due to status inconsistency. Moreover, people who have inconsistency between low education and higher occupational prestige and/or people who have inconsistency between high education and lower income are somewhat more involved in or practice faith healing. And people who have high education and lower occupational prestige and/or people who have higher occupational prestige and lower income have had a religious or mystical experience more often than the general population average. However, the total amounts of variation in these two religious commitment items are modest. The greatest amount of variation explained by status inconsistencies was, for example, .042. This is also true of both statuses and auxiliary statuses. Therefore, contrary to previous findings and general speculation, none of the statuses, auxiliary statuses, or status inconsistencies are particularly useful for predicting or explaining the various aspects of religious commitment. The implication is that future analyses will require that different independent variables be assessed in order to achieve higher degrees of explanatory power for religious commitment and its various forms.

Acknowledgments

The author gratefully acknowledges the helpful comments made by James Beniger, Kent Smith, Howard Taylor, and Robert Wuthnow.

References

Althauser, R. P.
　1971 "Multicollinearity and non-additive regression models." In H. M. Blalock, Jr. (ed.), *Causal Models in the Social Sciences.* Chicago: Aldine-Atherton.

Bauman, K. E.
　1968 "Status inconsistency, unsatisfactory social interaction, and community satisfaction in an area of rapid growth." *Social Forces* 47 (September):45–52.

Blalock, Hubert M, Jr.
　1963 "Correlated independent variables: The problem of multicollinearity." *Social Forces* 42 (December):233–237.
　1965 "Theory building and the statistical concept of interaction." *American Sociological Review* 30 (June):374–380.
　1966a "Comment: Status inconsistency and the identification problem." *Public Opinion Quarterly* 30 (Spring):130–132.
　1966b "The identification problem and theory building: The case of status inconsistency." *American Sociological Review* 31 (February):52–61.
　1967a "Status inconsistency and interaction: Some alternative models." *American Journal of Sociology* 73 (November):305–315.
　1967b "Status inconsistency, social mobility, status interaction and structural effects." *American Sociological Review* 32 (October):780–801.
　1967c "Test of status inconsistency theory: A note of caution." *Pacific Sociological Review* 10 (Fall):69–74.

Demerath, N. J. III
　1965 *Social Class in American Protestantism.* Chicago: Rand McNally.

Doreian, Patrick, and Norman Stockman
　1969 "A critique of the multidimensional approach to stratification." *The Sociological Review* 17 (March):47–65.

Dynes, Russell R.
　1955 "The church–sect typology and socio–economic status." *American Sociological Review* 20 (1955):555–560.

Gordon, R. A.
　1968 "Issues in multiple regression." *American Journal of Sociology* 73 (March):592–616.

Greeley, Andrew M.
　1975 *The Sociology of the Paranormal: A Reconnaissance.* Berkeley, California: Sage Publications.

Hornung, C. A.
　1972 *Status Consistency: A Method of Measurement and Empirical Examination.* Doctoral dissertation, Syracuse University.
　1977 "Social status, status inconsistency and psychological stress." *American Sociological Review* 42 (August): 623–638.

Kasl, Stanislav V.
　1976 "Status inconsistency: Some conceptual and methodological considerations." In John P. Robinson *et al.* (eds.), *Measures of Occupational Attitudes and Occupational Characteristics.* Ann Arbor, Michigan: Institute for Social Research.

Lenski, Gerhard E.
　1954 "Status crystallization: A non-vertical dimension of social status." *American Sociological Review* 19 (August):405–413.
　1964 "Comment." *Public Opinion Quarterly* 28 (Summer):326–330.

Olsen, Marvin E., and Judy C. Tully

    1972 "Socioeconomic–ethnic status inconsistency and preference for political change." *American Sociological Review* 37 (October):560–574.

Quebedeaux, Richard

    1978 *The Worldly Evangelicals.* San Francisco: Harper & Row.

Smith, Kent, and M. S. Sasaki

    1979 "A method for decreasing multicollinearity in models with multiplicative functions." *Sociological Methods and Research* (forthcoming).

Southwood, K. E.

    1978 "Substantive theory and statistical interaction: Five models." *American Journal of Sociology* 83 (March):1154–1203.

Taylor, Howard

    1973 "Linear models of consistency: Some extension of Blalock's strategy." *American Journal of Sociology* 78 (March):1192–1215.

Treiman, Donald

    1966 "Status discrepancy and prejudice." *American Journal of Sociology* 77 (May): 651–664.

Wuthnow, Robert

    1978 *Experimentation in American Religion: The New Mysticisms and Their Implications for the Churches.* Berkeley, California: University of California Press.

Chapter 7

The Religious Factor and Delinquency: Another Look at the Hellfire Hypotheses[1]

GARY F. JENSEN and MAYNARD L. ERICKSON

I. Introduction

Whether as an opiate for the masses (Marx), a basic integrative mechanism (Durkheim), or a source of other social and cultural patterns (Weber), religion has been viewed by grand theoreticians as playing some role in shaping society and human behavior. However, the importance of "organized religion" as a control mechanism in modern America has been increasingly questioned. Glock and Stark (1965:184) state that "Looking at American society as a whole. . . organized religion at present is neither a prominent witness to its own value system nor a major focal point around which ultimate commitments to norms, values, and beliefs are formed." Schuman (1971), in his replication of Lenski's (1961) study of the religious

[1] Parts of this chapter were presented under the title "Delinquency and Damnation: Another Look at the Hellfire Hypothesis" at the 1977 convention of the Pacific Sociological Association. The data were gathered as part of a larger study of "Community Tolerance and Measures of Delinquency" supported by a grant from the National Institute of Mental Health (MH 22350).

157

factor in Detroit, questions also the current applicability of earlier conclusions concerning the relationship between religion and economics.

Similarly, whereas early criminological research[2] accorded a role to the church as a mechanism of social control, most contemporary criminologists seem to have come to a tacit understanding that the religious factor is either an irrelevant explanation for crime and delinquency or, at least, one that can be safely ignored. Contemporary criminological theory and research have come to concentrate on other institutions thought to be more important for understanding such phenomena (e.g., the family, school, and the law). Contemporary criminology textbooks rarely deal with the religious factor, and when it is mentioned the overall impression is that its effects are trivial or irrelevant.[3]

Such skepticism does have some empirical support. With the publication of Hirschi and Stark's (1969) "Hellfire and Delinquency" in the late 1960s, many criminologists believed that the religious factor had finally been laid to rest. Using survey data from several thousand adolescents, they found that denomination, church attendance, and belief in supernatural sanctions were not significantly related to delinquency. The inconsistency between their results and earlier research was handled by noting that prior correlations were small and possibly spurious. Thus, their findings appeared to provide further support for the view that religious institutions had become irrelevant to yet another dimension of modern life.

However, more recent research has suggested that certain measures of religiosity are, in fact, relevant to predicting some kinds of criminal or delinquent activities. Burkett and White (1974:455) argue that, where secular values do not clearly define certain criminal activities as bad or immoral, religious participation or church-linked beliefs can be important deterrents to delinquency. They suggest, for instance, that such offenses as marijuana and alcohol use run counter to religious traditions of "asceticism" and hypothesize that a variable such as church attendance should be more relevant to "victimless" offenses than to more serious conventional crimes. Using procedures similar to those of Hirschi and Stark, they did find certain measures of the religious factor to be more predictive of alcohol and marijuana use than a delinquency index based on property crime and violent offenses. Consistent with Hirschi and Stark's data, they could find no significant variations between Catholics and Protestants.

---

[2] For a review of some of that research, see Joseph P. Fitzpatrick, "The Role of Religion in Programs for the Prevention and Correction of Crime and Delinquency." Task Force Report: Juvenile Delinquency and Youth Crime. Washington, D.C.: U.S. Government Printing Office, 1967.

[3] Most texts do not even touch on the topic, and those that do relegate religion to chapters on "Questionable Crime Theories" (Schur, 1969:82–83) or merely note that its relevance has not been demonstrated (Sutherland and Cressey, 1974:234).

Two subsequent studies have yielded similar results. Higgins and Albrecht (1977) report "modest to moderately strong" negative relationships between frequency of church attendance and 17 types of self-reported delinquency. The strongest associations tend to involve drinking and drug use. Higgins and Albrecht suggest that their findings may have diverged from those in Hirschi and Stark's research because of differences in research setting. Their sample consisted of tenth graders in the South (Atlanta, Georgia), whereas Hirschi and Stark's sample was drawn from junior and senior high schools in the San Francisco Bay area. The second study, by Albrecht, Chadwick, and Alcorn (1977), reports that among Mormon teenagers measures of religiosity were significantly related to measures of delinquency and more strongly related to victimless delinquent offenses than to delinquent offenses with victims.

At present, all we can safely conclude is that church attendance is related to delinquency (and especially to drinking and drug use) in some samples and settings but not in others. Although variations in findings are currently interpreted as products of region and/or of the types of offenses studied, these and other possibilities have yet to be adequately explored. For example, Burkett and White (1974:461) predict that "future research should reveal a clear relationship between religion and the commission of other victimless crimes by adolescents." They cite several characteristics of offenses that might account for variations by offense. They note that the offenses they studied are (*a*) "victimless" offenses that are (*b*) viewed by an increasing number of influential people as less serious than property or interpersonal crimes and that (*c*) such offenses run counter to "the long tradition of Christian support for a morality of personal asceticism." By considering a wider range of offenses, it would be possible to assess whether their argument applies to victimless offenses in general, to offenses that involve the use of drugs alone, or to all "minor" offenses, victimless or not.

If their argument about asceticism is correct, it is surprising that they found no denominational differences. However, denominational differences have received very little attention in the four studies just discussed. In fact, none of the studies actually presents any data for denominations. Higgins and Albrecht note only that controlling for religious affiliation does not affect observed relationships. They do not specify their denominational breakdowns nor do they consider the possibility of interaction between religious affiliation and church attendance. Hirschi and Stark (1969), and Burkett and White (1974) found a "Catholic–Protestant–Other" breakdown to be unrelated to self-reported delinquency, but they ignore the possibility that church attendance may be more relevant to understanding some forms of delinquency in some denominations than in others. Finally, Albrecht, Chadwick, and Alcorn include only one religious denomination in their study.

It should also be noted that the three studies that considered denominational differences report on no denominations with clear religious proscriptions concerning activities such as drinking or drug use. Yet, variation in associations observed from one study to another may reflect the denominations encompassed by the samples studied. For example, Higgins and Albrecht's sample may have included a large proportion of Southern Baptists, and church attendance could be more relevant to delinquency in such relatively fundamentalistic churches than in some other denominations. Moreover, there are some faiths that clearly prohibit certain forms of "victimless" offenses directly and vociferously rather than indirectly, through emphasis on "maintaining self-control" or "asceticism." For example, the Church of Jesus Christ of Latter Day Saints (Mormons) clearly defines certain common adolescent activities as violations of religious precepts. Participation in such a religion may be far more relevant to differentiating among adolescents than participation as a "Catholic" or a "Protestant." Some Mormons actually apply a deviant label, "Jack Mormon," to Mormons who are not faithful to their religion in terms of either their behavior or their religious observance or both. We know of no comparable labels for nonpracticing Protestants or Catholics. Thus, not only should we consider a wider range of denominations, but we should also assess possible interactions between denomination and religious participation in efforts to predict delinquent behavior. Since Albrecht, Chadwick, and Alcorn consider the relationship between religiosity and delinquency in a totally Mormon sample, they can only speculate that their findings are unique to certain denominations.

A final issue raised in prior research—but which has not been empirically resolved—is the "importance" or relative predictive power of the religious factor as a determinant or correlate of delinquent behavior. The issue is comparable to the "fully-only" controversy raised by Lenski in his analysis of the religious factor in Detroit. Burkett and White report gamma coefficients of $-.36$ and $-.32$ relating church attendance to beer use and marijuana use and $-.15$ when relating church attendance to the delinquency index. The comparable coefficients for belief in supernatural sanctions were $-.21$, $-.12$, and $-.19$, respectively. Using these results, they suggest that such variables "effectively deter" and that there are "moderately strong" relationships between religion and the use of alcohol and marijuana. Whether these relationships are "strong" is open to debate. One way to approach the issue is to establish a basis for comparison. Rather than merely declaring that relationships are strong or weak (on the basis of what many statisticians would view as small gamma coefficients), research should compare relationships involving religious variables with relationships involving other purported deterrents. In an absolute sense, religious variables might explain only a small amount of variance. Yet, in a comparative context they may be more consequential than other variables thought to deter delinquency.

II. Research Design

Research Issues

This investigation attempts to build upon the research discussed previously. First, we assess the relationship between similar measures of religiosity and self-reported delinquent offenses that vary along the three dimensions suggested by Burkett and White. Second, we compare not only Catholics and Protestants but Mormons as well, and we consider the possibility of interaction between religious participation and denomination. Third, we examine such relationships among youths in both metropolitan and small-town settings. And, finally, we examine the issue of relative importance by comparing the contribution of religious variables to explained variance with the relative contribution of other social control variables—participation in conventional secular activities, adolescent relationships with parents and teachers, and attitudes toward the law.

Samples and Setting

These issues are examined using questionnaire data gathered from 3268 high school students in 1975. The sample from which data were obtained included (*a*) 80% of the students in attendance at high schools in three small towns in Southern Arizona and (*b*) 63% of the students in attendance at three metropolitan high schools in Tucson, Arizona (one parochial and two public).

Two of the small-town schools allowed the questionnaire to be administered to all students (unless a student's parents objected), which resulted in samples of about 85% of the available population (974 cases). One small-town school required written parental consent, yielding a sample of 52% of the in-school population (110 cases). The two public high schools allowed the questionnaire in Social Studies and English classes unless a student's parents objected (fewer than 5% withheld permission), yielding an additional 1601 cases, or about 61% of the students in attendance. The one parochial school required participation in Social Studies and English classes that encompassed about 72% of the available population (583 cases). Overall, then, the sample encompassed around 70% of the students in attendance at the six schools.

The metropolitan area of Tucson has a population of over 400,000 and ranks in the top 10 in terms of crime rates for standard metropolitan areas. The three small towns are in the adjacent county and include a mining town of about 7500, a farm town of about 2500, and a tourist town of about 1200 population. Each of the small-town high schools draws on the surrounding hinterland and on other small communities in the area.

Measures

The questionnaire included items relevant to religious affiliation, church attendance, participation in church activities for young people, belief in supernatural sanctions, and delinquency. Since the survey was carried out in the southwestern United States and included one parochial school, 48% of the sample is Catholic. Thirty-two percent identified themselves as Protestant, 3% as Mormon, 1% as Jewish, and 15% as "other" or "none." However, the study was not originally designed to deal with the religious factor in detail, and, hence, we do not have further breakdowns among Protestants and Catholics. We are able to compare Anglo Catholics, Chicano Catholics, Anglo Protestants, and Mormons.

Church attendance was determined by asking "How many times during the last year have you attended church?" Participation in church activities was based on the question "During the last month, how many times would you guess you have taken part in a church activity for young people?" We also used both Hirschi and Stark's and Burkett and White's items concerning supernatural beliefs: "Do you believe there is a life after death?" and "Do you believe the devil actually exists?" (Response categories for these latter two items were "definitely yes," "yes," "uncertain," "no," and "definitely not.") Since there are divergent findings using these items, we used the same wording and response categories as the two prior studies.

To assess involvement in delinquency, students were asked how many times in the last year they had committed each of 18 different acts. The questionnaire was administered anonymously, and extensive procedures were utilized to assure students of the anonymity of their responses.[4] Subjects were informed that such data were vital to the project, since conflict with the law might make a difference in how people feel about important issues. Since previous research calls for a specification by type of offense, we carried out our initial analysis on all 18 offense categories.

We also asked students to assign "magnitude estimation"[5] scores to delinquent acts, indicating how "serious" they considered each to be (with petty theft as the standard or basis for comparison). As expected, those offenses most serious in the "eyes of the law" were given high scores, and offenses such as drinking and "status offenses" scored low. Marijuana use ranked number 11 and drinking number 16 out of the 18 offenses.[6]

---

[4] The questionnaire was administered by project staff in classrooms. Students were allowed to exchange questionnaires before they began and could place them in a box in any order they chose.

[5] Special instructions using illnesses or classroom behavior were used to familiarize students with the technique. They were presented with petty theft ("stealing something worth less than $100") as a standard equal to 100 and were asked to assign a seriousness score to each of the other offenses. In the analysis, offenses are ranked in terms of median magnitude estimates of seriousness.

[6] The rank order of the offenses is summarized in the tables to follow, where they are listed in order from least to most serious.

III. Findings

Participation and Belief Items

Table 7.1 presents the gamma coefficients and the results of chi-square tests of significance relating participation and belief in the supernatural to each of the 18 offenses. Church attendance is most consistently related to self-reported delinquency, with chi-square values statistically significant at the .01 level for 13 of 18 offenses. Participation in church youth activities is significantly related to 7 of 18 offense types, and belief in a life after death is related to 7. Belief in the devil is significantly related to only 4. In terms of the magnitude of the gamma coefficients, church attendance tends to have the greatest inverse relationship to delinquency, followed by youth activities, belief in a life after death, and belief in the devil.

Only 3 offenses produce significant inverse relationships with all four religious items: drinking, drunkenness, and marijuana use. Thus, consistent with Burkett and White's study, measures of religiosity are more predictive of drinking and marijuana use than any of the other offenses that comprise the Hirschi and Stark delinquency index. Drinking and marijuana use are more strongly related to church attendance than 11 of 13 nondrug offenses and more

TABLE 7.1 Delinquency by Religious Participation and Belief Items

Offense[a]	Item							
	Attendance		Activities		Hereafter		Devil	
Smoking	−.11[b]	(s)[c]	−.14	(s)	−.01		−.01	
Truancy	−.29	(s)	−.14	(s)	−.09		−.07	
Drinking	−.26	(s)	−.26	(s)	−.18	(s)	−.17	(s)
Defiance	−.02		−.00		−.03		−.01	
Drunkenness	−.21	(s)	−.20	(s)	−.11	(s)	−.11	(s)
Fighting	−.11	(s)	−.12	(s)	−.06		−.07	
Runaway	−.11		+.00		−.03		−.06	
Marijuana	−.23	(s)	−.19	(s)	−.08	(s)	−.09	(s)
Shoplifting	−.13		−.10		−.06	(s)	−.07	
Petty theft	−.16	(s)	−.12		−.08	(s)	−.07	
Vandalism	−.16	(s)	−.10		−.05		−.07	
Drugs	−.25	(s)	−.28	(s)	−.00		−.07	
Assault	−.13	(s)	−.11		−.07		−.08	
Breaking/entering	−.21	(s)	−.13		−.12	(s)	−.13	(s)
Robbery	−.14	(s)	−.14		−.05		−.10	
Auto/joyriding	−.09		+.12		+.00		−.00	
Grand theft	−.31	(s)	−.20		−.16	(s)	−.14	
Armed robbery	−.04		+.10		−.12		−.06	

[a] Offenses are ordered below from least (smoking) to most (armed robbery) serious as determined by median magnitude estimate by the total sample.

[b] Coefficients reported are gamma coefficients.

[c] Chi-square values with probabilities of $\leq$ .01 are indicated by ''(s).''

strongly related to church youth activities than 12 of 13. The only other offenses that are significantly related to church attendance are truancy and grand theft. Grand theft is significantly related to youth activities as well. Grand theft was included in the Hirschi and Stark index but accounted for a very small proportion of offenses in their index.

The order of the 18 offenses in terms of seriousness is summarized in Table 7.1—offenses are listed from least to most serious as determined by median magnitude estimates for the sample as a whole. There does not appear to be much correspondence between seriousness of offenses and the degree of association between religious variables and delinquency. The rank order correlation between offense seriousness and degree of association is −.04 using gamma coefficients for church attendance and −.09 using the coefficients for church youth activities.[7] Comparable coefficients involving belief in a life after death and in the devil are +.02 and +.11. Limiting our analysis to only those associations in which chi-square values are significant does not alter this interpretation, since, even for drug offenses, seriousness does not coincide with the magnitude of associations between measures of religiosity and of self-reported delinquency. In summary, for the full range of offenses considered, seriousness alone does not account for variability in the associations observed.

Although we have not included all "victimless" offenses in our study, we can consider the relevance of measures of religiosity to four adolescent status offenses: running away from home, defiance of parents, truancy, and smoking. Neither of the first two offenses are significantly related to any of the religious measures, but smoking and truancy are both significantly related to the participation items. Gamma coefficients for these four offenses are comparable to those found for drinking and marijuana use in only one instance (truancy in relation to church attendance). The gamma coefficients between church attendance and smoking, runaway, and defiance are smaller than those found for 7 of 10 "crimes with victims" (robbery, grand theft, petty theft, shoplifting, vandalism, assault, and breaking and entering). Thus, within the limits of the offenses studied, our findings fail to support the notion that it is the victimless quality of drinking and marijuana use that accounts for their more persistent and relatively stronger association with measures of religiosity than most other offenses. Alternative possibilities will be considered later, when participation is examined within denominational categories.

Denomination

We reported earlier that neither Hirschi and Stark nor Burkett and White found significant differences in delinquency by denomination. Hirschi and

---

[7] The same conclusions are supported using "odds–ratios" as a measure of association as well. In fact, the rank order of offenses in terms of odds–ratios was nearly identical to the rank order using gamma coefficients.

Stark give no indication of the categories they compared, and Burkett and White indicate only that a "Catholic–Protestant–Other" breakdown was unrelated to delinquency. In Table 7.2 the proportions of self-identified Catholics, Protestants, and Mormons who indicate having committed delinquent offense(s) are summarized. Statistically significant relationships (chisquare values at the .01 level) are found between denomination and seven offenses (breaking and entering, shoplifting, truancy, robbery, drinking, drunkenness, and marijuana use). Comparing Catholic students with Protestant students, the former have a significantly higher proportion reporting breaking and entering, shoplifting, vandalism, robbery, drinking, and drunkenness, whereas the latter have significantly higher proprotionate involvement in truancy. Mormon youths are significantly less likely than Protestant and Catholic youths combined to report smoking, drinking, and drunkenness. Thus, in contrast to earlier research, we do find some significant differences by religious affiliation.

The differences between Catholics and Protestants and between Mormons and both these categories combined do not appear attributable to differences in father's educational status. Gamma coefficients relating the Catholic–Protestant dichotomy to the seven offenses in which differences were statisti-

TABLE 7.2 Proportion Reporting Delinquent Offenses by Denomination

	Denomination		
Offenses	Catholic[a]	Protestant[b]	Mormon[c]
Smoking	52.0	49.6	38.0
Truancy	49.2	58.7	55.4
Drinking	77.3	70.9	51.5
Defiance	66.1	65.8	64.0
Drunkenness	64.3	55.3	38.6
Fighting	32.5	29.1	28.0
Runaway	11.2	12.2	14.0
Marijuana	45.8	42.2	32.7
Shoplifting	40.6	33.0	34.0
Petty theft	22.3	19.5	27.0
Vandalism	25.7	20.5	18.0
Drugs	14.6	17.2	12.9
Assault	18.4	15.1	17.0
Breaking/entering	15.2	11.0	11.1
Robbery	8.3	4.5	5.0
Auto/joyriding	11.3	11.1	9.9
Grand theft	7.5	5.7	8.0
Armed robbery	2.9	2.1	4.0

[a] Based upon which percentage is computed, ranged between 1509 and 1530. Variations are due to missing data.

[b] Base varies between 991 and 999.

[c] Base varies between 99 and 101.

cally significant ranged from + .31 (with Catholics ordered first) for robbery to + .15 for vandalism. Net partial gamma coefficients holding father's educational status constant (by subdivision—less than high school, high school graduate, more than high school) were nearly identical with the zero order coefficients.[8] Similarly, a non-Mormon–Mormon dichotomy yielded gamma coefficients of –.26 for smoking, –.47 for drinking, and –.42 for drunkenness. Net partials with father's educational status held constant were –.24, –.51, and –.43. Thus, the patterns observed persist despite controls for father's educational status.

Since the study was carried out in a southwestern state, we also considered the possible impact of ethnic status on denominational differences. However, not all comparisons were possible, since there were no Chicano Mormons and only 25 Chicano Protestants. In all instances, the original differences persist, with Catholic students, Anglo or Chicano, highest for breaking and entering, shoplifting, vandalism, robbery, drinking, and drunkenness.[9] Both Anglo and Chicano Catholics are lower on truancy. Finally, Mormons rank lower than either Anglo Protestants or Anglo Catholics. Chi-square tests relating denomination to these eight offenses *for Anglos alone* were significant at the .01 level for five offenses and were significant at the .05 level for two others. The only exception was robbery, in which case the high Catholic rate seems to have reflected higher Chicano involvement.

Since a sizable proportion of our sample (33%) was drawn from small towns, as compared with earlier studies based on metropolitan populations, we also examined the relationships between rates of offending and denomination within the small-town and metropolitan subsamples separately. Depending on the level of significance chosen, the data suggest that disparate findings concerning denomination might be attributed to the types of population that have been studied (see Table 7.3). In the metropolitan sample, 4 of 18 offenses (truancy, robbery, drinking, and drunkenness) are significantly related to denomination at the .05 level, as compared with 10 of 18 in the small-town

---

[8] The original gamma coefficients and net partials when father's educational status is held constant are as follows (zero order first and net partial second): burglary (+ .18, + .18); shoplifting (+ .16, + .15); vandalism (+ .15, + .16); truancy (–.21, –.19); robbery (+ .31, + .31); drinking (+ .17, + .17); and drunkenness (+ .18, + .19). Comparing non-Mormons (Catholics and Protestants combined) with Mormons, the coefficients are as follows: smoking (–.21, –.24); drinking (–.47, –.51); and drunkenness (–.42, –.43).

[9] The proportion self-reporting those offenses that differed significantly between Catholics and Protestants or between Mormons and non-Mormons are as follows (with the rates for Chicano Catholics listed first, followed by Anglo Catholics, Anglo Protestants, and Anglo Mormons): burglary (17%, 14%, 10%, 11%); shoplifting (46%, 38%, 33%, 33%); vandalism (26%, 26%, 19%, 19%); smoking (48%, 53%, 50%, 36%); truancy (51%, 47%, 58%, 55%); robbery (11%, 6%, 4%, 5%); drinking (76%, 79%, 71%, 50%); drunkenness (64%, 64%, 55%, 37%); and marijuana use (46%, 46%, 42%, 32%).

TABLE 7.3 Proportion Reporting Delinquent Offenses by Denomination and Community Setting

Offense	Small town (N = 864)			Metropolitan (N = 1740)		
	Catholic	Protestant	Mormon	Catholic	Protestant	Mormon
Smoking	55.0	49.7	35.6[a]	50.6	49.6	40.0
Truancy	57.6	48.6	37.8[b]	45.1	63.7	69.6[b]
Drinking	78.7	70.0	44.4[b]	76.7	71.3	57.1[b]
Defiance	66.4	64.7	64.4	66.0	66.3	63.6
Drunkenness	69.7	53.7	31.1[b]	61.6	56.1	44.6[b]
Fighting	37.7	31.6	20.5[a]	30.0	27.8	33.9
Runaway	13.7	15.6	17.8	4.4	10.6	10.9
Marijuana	45.8	38.0	22.2[b]	45.7	44.2	41.1
Shoplifting	48.9	35.8	27.3[b]	36.6	31.6	39.3
Petty theft	27.0	20.1	22.7	19.9	19.2	30.4
Vandalism	24.6	18.2	15.9	26.3	21.6	19.6
Drugs	15.1	19.8	6.7[a]	14.4	15.9	17.9
Assault	20.6	16.3	15.9	11.2	14.6	17.9
Breaking/entering	18.2	12.3	7.0[a]	13.8	10.4	14.3
Robbery	10.6	4.9	6.7[a]	7.3	4.3	3.6[a]
Auto/joyriding	10.5	12.0	13.3	11.7	10.7	7.1
Grand theft	9.2	4.9	4.5	6.1	6.1	10.7
Armed robbery	3.2	2.8	4.4	2.7	1.8	3.6

[a] Chi-square relating offense to denomination significant at .05 level.
[b] Chi-square significant at .01 level.

sample. At the .01 level, the contrast is not as striking; 5 offenses are statistically related at that level in the small-town sample and 3 in the metropolitan sample. Of the 7 offenses that were significantly related at the .01 level in the entire sample, only 3 are significant at the .05 level in the metropolitan sample, whereas all 7 are so related in the small-town sample. Moreover, considering all forms of drug use, the differences are, without exception, more prominent in the small-town sample. For small-town youth, 20% more Catholics than Mormons report smoking, as compared with a 10% difference in the metropolitan sample. Marijuana use varies little by denomination in the metropolitan sample but considerably in the small-town sample. In conclusion, had our study included only metropolitan students, our observations concerning denominational differences would have been quite comparable to previous studies, all of which were based on metropolitan populations.

Participation and Denomination

Just as the relevance of religious denomination may vary from one community setting to another, denomination and participation may interact to produce more striking differences than either variable alone. One hypothesis is that participation in a religion that strongly emphasizes asceticism and clearly proscribes drug use should be particularly consequential for these forms of activity. The coefficients summarized in Table 7.4 tend to support that hypothesis. The weak association between church attendance and smoking observed earlier is limited to Catholics and Protestants. The coefficients for Catholics and Protestants are −.12 and −.16, respectively, as compared with −.54 for Mormons. For drinking, the comparable coefficients are −.25 for Catholics, −.37 for Protestants, and −.77 for Mormons. For drunkenness, the gamma coefficients for Catholics, Protestants, and Mormons are −.31, −.62, and −.65, respectively. For marijuana use, they are −.36, −.40, and −.45. And finally, for other illicit drug use, the coefficients are −.43, −.16, and −.49. Thus, in every instance, church attendance is more strongly related to drug use among Mormon youth than among Catholics or Protestants. The variation is less prominent for more serious drug use.

The bivariate analysis revealed relationships between offenses and participation in church youth activities to be somewhat weaker than relationships involving church attendance per se. Yet, a similar pattern of interaction by af-

TABLE 7.4 Proportion Reporting Delinquent Offenses by Church Attendance by Denomination

	Denomination								
	Catholic			Protestant			Mormon		
Offense	Low[a]	High	(γ)[b]	Low	High	(γ)[b]	Low	High	(γ)[b]
Smoking	55%	49%	(−.12)	54%	46%	(−.16)	48%	22%	(−.54)
Truancy	64%	32%	(−.57)	64%	54%	(−.19)	64%	47%	(−.35)
Drinking	82%	73%	(−.25)	80%	64%	(−.37)	73%	26%	(−.77)
Defiance	68%	63%	(−.11)	66%	65%	(−.01)	65%	61%	(−.08)
Drunkenness	72%	57%	(−.31)	70%	35%	(−.62)	56%	21%	(−.65)
Fighting	37%	27%	(−.21)	33%	26%	(−.17)	33%	24%	(−.23)
Runaway	14%	7%	(−.32)	13%	12%	(−.04)	8%	17%	(+.38)
Marijuana	55%	37%	(−.36)	50%	30%	(−.40)	42%	21%	(−.45)
Shoplifting	45%	35%	(−.21)	38%	28%	(−.21)	44%	24%	(−.42)
Petty theft	24%	20%	(−.12)	25%	14%	(−.35)	27%	24%	(−.08)
Vandalism	30%	20%	(−.25)	24%	17%	(−.22)	25%	11%	(−.46)
Drugs	20%	9%	(−.43)	20%	15%	(−.16)	17%	6%	(−.49)
Assault	21%	15%	(−.19)	17%	13%	(−.13)	21%	13%	(−.27)
Breaking/entering	18%	12%	(−.21)	15%	7%	(−.44)	15%	6%	(−.36)
Robbery	11%	5%	(−.39)	4%	4%	(+.02)	4%	4%	(−.01)
Auto/joyriding	13%	8%	(−.19)	10%	12%	(+.10)	8%	11%	(+.13)
Grand theft	10%	4%	(−.41)	8%	3%	(−.30)	11%	4%	(−.48)
Armed robbery	4%	2%	(−.19)	1%	2%	(+.22)	4%	2%	(−.35)

[a] Attendance (Low or High) was dichotomized at the median for each denomination. Delinquency was dichotomized into zero and one or more.

[b] Measures in parentheses are gamma coefficients.

filiation appears in the data. There is no relationship between participation in youth activities and smoking (gamma = + .01) and only a slight association for drinking, drunkenness, and marijuana use among Catholics (gamma coefficients are − .05 in each case). In contrast, the coefficients for Protestants were − .21, − .27, − .25, and − .29 for these offenses. For Mormon youths, the comparable coefficients were − .55, − .69, − .38, and − .23. For the use of other illicit drugs, the coefficients for Catholics, Protestants, and Mormons were − .22, − .25, and − .26, respectively.

Among drug use offenses, the interaction appears most prominent for the common adolescent activities of smoking and drinking. In general, the more serious the drug use, the less prominent the interaction. This pattern makes sense if we consider that all three churches may be quite comparable in their stands on "serious" drug use. The most distinctive characteristics of the Mormon church may be the prohibition of the less serious form of substance use (tobacco and alcohol).

These findings suggest one possible explanation for the variable associations observed earlier in this chapter and in Burkett and White's analysis. Rather than focusing on characteristics of offenses (seriousness, victimization, and drug use), consideration ought to be given to the types of moral messages presented by specific denominations or churches. Burkett and White search for the source of variation in religiosity–delinquency relationships in the nature of the offenses and ignore denomination because they could find no consistent bivariate relationships involving denomination. One interpretation of our findings is that religious messages concerning different forms of behavior differ by denomination for some activities but are quite similar for others. If religious participation reflects exposure to such messages, then churches may be conveying similar messages concerning certain "serious" yet victimless offenses like narcotics use. Offenses such as smoking may be of little concern to some denominations but of great concern to others. In short, variations by offense may represent a complex blend both of properties of offenses and of the variable moral concerns of different denominations.

Predictive Efficiency

We noted earlier that it is difficult to judge the "importance" of the relationships involving the religious factor without some basis for comparison. In Table 7.5, we have summarized the increment in explained variance for a drug use index (squared "part correlations") attributable to the religious items[10] when introduced along with blocks of items measuring other common dimen-

---

[10] The church attendance and church youth-activities items were entered into the analysis as interval scales. The two belief items were entered with values ranging from zero to four.

sions of the social bond.[11] The analysis was carried out both by introducing social-bond variables into a stepwise regression analysis prior to measures of religiosity as well as subsequent to the religiosity items. We present the findings for the entire sample first and then consider the same issues for Catholics, Protestants, and Mormons separately.

When added to the analysis after the blocks of social control variables have been entered, we find that the religious items increase R^2 by about 3.5% over

TABLE 7.5   Increments[a] in R^2 Relating a Drug Use Index[b] to Blocks of Religious and Secular Items

	Total Sample	Catholics	Protestants	Mormons
I. Increment in R^2 due to religious block (C) when added to:				
a. Secular activities (A)	.035	.027	.048	.215
b. Law items (L)	.008	.008	.010	.136
c. School items (S)	.019	.013	.028	.176
d. Parent items (P)	.029	.023	.041	.169
(C + A + L + S + P)[c]	(.225)	(.222)	(.269)	(.490)
II. Increment in R^2 due to A, L, S, or P when added to the religious block:				
a. Secular activities	.004	.033	.013	.074
b. Law items	.174	.201	.202	.195
c. School items	.064	.097	.076	.099
d. Parent items	.031	.069	.043	.082

[a] The increments shown are also referred to as squared "part correlations."

[b] Figures in parentheses are the squared multiple correlation coefficients when all five blocks of items are introduced.

[c] The drug use index is a score ranging from zero through four, created by adding reports of tobacco use (0, 1), drinking (0, 1), marijuana use (0, 1), and the use of other illicit drugs (0, 1).

[11] *Attitudes toward the law* were based on responses to the items "It's OK to break the law if you can get away with it," "To get what you want in this world, you have to do some things that are against the law," "Most things that get teenagers in trouble with the law don't really hurt anyone," and "I have a lot of respect for the police in my town." *Relationships with parents* were based on the following items asked separately for mother and father: "I feel very close to my father (mother)," "I don't get along with my father (mother)." *Attachment to school* was based on responses to the items "I care what my teachers think of me," "Going to school is making me a better person," "Getting good grades is important to me," and "Would you like to be the kind of person your teachers are?" The responses were in the form of Likert scales and were assigned values of zero to four. *Conventional secular activities* included participation in interscholastic sports (0, 1), number of school club memberships (0–4), participation in outside clubs (0, 1), and participation in scouts (0, 1). All of these are central to dimensions of the social bond as delineated by social control theorists (see especially Hirschi, 1969).

conventional secular activities, 2.9% over relationships with parents, 1.9% over attachment to school items, and less than 1% over acceptance of the law as morally binding (see Table 7.5). Reversing the order in which the variables are introduced into the stepwise regression analysis yielded increments of only .4% for conventional secular activities over the proportion of variance accounted for by the religious items, 3.1% for relationships with parents over the religious variables, and 6.4% for attachment to school. Finally, the law items account for 17.4% explained variance over what is accounted for by the religious items. In summary, when the results of both types of analysis are considered, the measures of religious involvement are (*a*) more predictive of delinquency than secular activities; (*b*) about the same as items dealing with parents; and (*c*) less important (in a predictive sense) than attitudes toward the law. Thus, in terms of predictive efficiency, measures of religious involvement are not irrelevant, but neither are they the most "important" variables for understanding rates of juvenile delinquency.

In Table 7.5, we also present the results of the analysis applied to Catholics, Protestants, and Mormons separately. For the sample as a whole, the importance of the religious items (as judged by the increment in R^2) varies depending on what block is included in the regression analysis. However, the relative importance of the religious items is much greater among Mormons than for the other two groups. Among Catholics, the increment in explained variance ranges from .8% to 2.7%. For Protestants, it ranges between 1.0% and 4.8%. For Mormons, however, it ranges between 13.6% and 21.5%. Furthermore, whereas variable attitudes towards the law lead to comparable increments in each denomination (.201, .202, and .195 among Catholics, Protestants, and Mormons, respectively), only among Mormons do we find the religious items making anywhere near the same contribution to explained variance. Among Mormons, the two blocks dealing with religion and the law explain 41% of the variance as compared with only 20% among Catholics and 25% among Protestants. In these latter two groups, all but a small proportion of the total explained variance is attributable to the law items.

By examining standardized regression coefficients (so-called "path coefficients") involving individual items in the block of religious items, it is possible to identify the source of denominational variation in explained variance. Among Mormons, it is measures of belief in a life after death and church attendance that yield the strongest correlations and the strongest path coefficients. For example, the direct path between church attendance and drug use is − .37, and the coefficient between a belief in a life after death and drug use is also − .37. When the religious items and the law items are introduced together, the direct path is − .20 for church attendance and − .36 for belief in a life after death. The strongest path for any law item was − .34.

In contrast, among Catholics and Protestants the only religious item

significantly related to drug use is church attendance, with a path coefficient of
$-.17$ among Catholics and $-.17$ among Protestants. These coefficients are
reduced to $-.083$ and $-.058$ when introduced together with the law items.
Thus, for all three denominations, some of the covariance between church attendance and drug use is indirect, through the relationship between church attendance and attitudes toward the law. However, even when all items in all
blocks are introduced simultaneously, the path coefficients for church attendance are significant in all three categories ($-.07$ for Catholics, $-.05$ for
Protestants, and $-.26$ for Mormons). Among Mormons, the coefficient
relating a belief in a life after death to drug use is $-.27$ when all items are introduced simultaneously. In summary, church attendance makes a difference
that cannot be totally eliminated by introducing additional social control
variables. Moreover, the explained variance attributable to the religious items
among Mormons reflects a persistent relationship between drug use and attendance and belief in a life after death.

IV. A Final Note: Reanalyzing the Richmond Data

Together with the studies by Burkett and White, Higgins and Albrecht, and
Albrecht, Chadwick, and Alcorn, the results reported in this chapter are seemingly inconsistent with the original findings of Hirschi and Stark concerning
the religious factor and delinquency. The inconsistencies have been "explained" by noting the possibilities of variation by offense and variation by
regional setting. Our analysis—together with the Albrecht, Chadwick, and
Alcorn study—has suggested the possibility of variation by denominational
composition of the samples as well.

Possible specifications by offense can be tested using Hirschi and Stark's
original data base—the Richmond Youth Study.[12] Their questionnaire included items dealing with two drug activities (drinking and smoking).[13] To be
consistent with other research, we expected that the Richmond Youth data
would yield stronger relationships between drinking, smoking, and church attendance than for the offenses in Hirschi and Stark's delinquency index.

The findings are, in fact, consistent with this expectation. Church attendance is significantly related to three offenses in the Richmond sample: drink-

---

[12] For details on the Richmond Youth Study, see Wilson, Hirschi, and Elder (1965). Since
Hirschi and Stark found no evidence of interaction involving race, sex, church attendance, and
delinquency, this supplementary analysis is based on the white male sample from that study (N =
1588).

[13] The specific items dealing with drinking and smoking were as follows: "Do you drink beer,
wine, or liquor away from home?" and "Do you smoke cigarettes?" The analysis is based on a
simple yes–no dichotomy.

ing, smoking, and truancy (with gamma coefficients of $-.18$, $-.28$, and $-.30$, respectively). The coefficient relating church attendance to drinking is quite close both to that obtained by Burkett and White for beer use and to our own data on drinking. Moreover, church attendance was not significantly related to any of the measures of theft (less than \$2, \$2-\$50, and more than \$50), vandalism, fighting, or joyriding.

Although there were no direct measures of denominational positions or messages concerning delinquent activities, the Richmond data did include student perceptions of their priest's or minister's disapproval of gambling.[14] There was considerable variation among denominations in perceived disapproval. Categories in which a majority perceived disapproval were Baptists (63%), a variety of small Protestant sects (60%),[15] and Methodists (54%). Fifty percent of Catholics perceived disapproval, as did 41% of Lutherans, 36% of Presbyterians, and 19% of Episcopalians.

For simplicity, we combined the Baptists, Methodists, and other Protestant sects into a ''high disapproval'' category and the Lutherans, Presbyterians, and Episcopalians into a ''low disapproval'' category. Such combinations were necessitated by (*a*) the limited number of cases in many Protestant denominations and (*b*) the low frequency of many delinquent offenses. However, since a sizeable proportion of Higgins and Albrecht's sample may have been Baptist, we did consider the relationships among Baptists separately in some of the analysis. In Table 7.6, we have summarized the relationships between church attendance and nine delinquent activities for Baptists and Catholics and for the high and low disapproval denominations.

These findings appear to be quite consistent with the other findings presented in this chapter. There are *no* significant relationships between church attendance and delinquency in the category of Protestant denominations with low perceived pastoral disapproval of gambling, and the average gamma coefficient is $-.06$. However, six of nine coefficients were negative. For Protestant denominations ''high'' in disapproval, all coefficients are negative and chi-squares were significant in five instances. The average gamma coefficient was $-.37$. For Baptists alone, there were three statistically significant relationships and an average gamma of $-.41$, with all associations in the expected direction. Finally, for Catholics, eight of nine coefficients were negative, with an average gamma of $-.19$. In sum, if we accept disapproval of gambling as a crude indicator of asceticism, it appears that church attendance is most likely to be relevant to delinquency in ascetic denominations.

---

[14] The item was ''How does your pastor (minister, priest, rabbi) feel about gambling?'' Response categories were ''He approves,'' ''He disapproves,'' ''He doesn't care,'' and ''I don't know.''

[15] These small denominations were Pentacostal, Church of Christ, Assembly of God, and Church of God in Christ. The percentages indicating perceived disapproval ranged from 52 to 78%.

TABLE 7.6 Proportion Reporting One or More Offenses by Church Attendance and Denominational Classifications

	Classification							
	High disapproval				Low disapproval			
	Baptist		Protestant		Protestant		Catholic	
	Low[a]	High	Low	High	Low	High	Low	High
Drinking	27%*	14%	31%*	13%	30%	22%	44%*	27%
	(−.41)**		(−.52)		(−.21)		(−.35)	
Smoking	38%*	19%	33%*	17%	24%	16%	44%*	25%
	(−.44)		(−.42)		(−.24)		(−.42)	
Fighting	26%	17%	24%	20%	24%	23%	29%	27%
	(−.26)		(−.14)		(−.01)		(−.05)	
Vandalism	13%	9%	13%	9%	9%	14%	19%	17%
	(−.20)		(−.20)		(+.26)		(−.06)	
Joyriding	10%	3%	10%*	3%	10%	6%	16%	9%
	(−.60)		(−.62)		(−.23)		(−.30)	
Truancy	44%	29%	39%*	29%	37%	29%	49%	38%
	(−.31)		(−.22)		(−.22)		(−.20)	
Theft (< $2.)	20%	19%	21%	18%	21%	30%	35%	26%
	(−.02)		(−.12)		(+.24)		(−.22)	
Theft ($2.–$50.)	20%*	5%	16%*	3%	6%	9%	12%	12%
	(−.66)		(−.68)		(+.21)		(+.01)	
Theft (< $50.)	7%	1%	5%	2%	3%	1%	5%	7%
	(−.76)		(−.39)		(−.41)		(+.17)	
Average gamma	(−.41)		(−.37)		(−.06)		(−.19)	

[a] Low and high refer to attendance.

* Chi-square test statistic significant at the .05 level.

** Coefficients in parentheses are gamma coefficients for the 2 × 2 tables.

Six of the offenses in Table 7.6 overlapped with the Higgins and Albrecht study, and the average gamma based on those six is very similar in the two bodies of data. The average in Higgins and Albrecht's study was −.37 as compared with −.41 for Baptists and −.40 for the high disapproval category. In contrast, the average was only −.03 for those six offenses in the low disapproval category and −.16 for Catholics. Thus, had the Richmond data been limited to certain denominations that may predominate in other samples, the results would not be strikingly different from those observed in subsequent research.

V. Summary and Implications

We began this chapter by noting the view that organized religion is ineffective or irrelevant as a source of institutional control in modern America. The research reported in this chapter both supports and refutes this view, depending on the particular findings one chooses to highlight. Paraphrasing Glock and Stark, "on the whole," organized religion does not appear to be "a major focal point" for the formation of commitments to conventional norms, values, and beliefs for most Americans. Moreover, consistent with dominant orientations in criminological theory, bonds to some other institutions appear to be more relevant to understanding delinquency. On the other hand, our findings suggest that we should move beyond considerations of "the whole" and begin to specify the variable conditions affecting the relevance of the religious factor.

Our analysis suggests several issues for further inquiry. For one, religious variables appear more likely to be significantly related to drug use than to the types of offenses that have previously been used in "general delinquency indices." This observation was the major contribution of Burkett and White's study and is generally reconfirmed by our findings as well. Second, it does not appear to be offense seriousness alone or necessarily, the "victimless" nature of some offenses that accounts for variable associations with measures of religiosity. As an alternative, we suggest that the moral messages of particular churches or denominations must be considered.

In contrast to earlier research, we did find differences in delinquency by denomination and considerable evidence of interaction between denomination and religious participation. Our findings concerning Mormons suggest that denominational differences may be obvious when considering denominations that take clear and distinguishing stands concerning specific forms of delinquent behavior. Moreover, denominational differences are most prominent for those who regularly participate in church. These findings suggest that both religious affiliation and religious participation should be considered in research on the relationship between religion and delinquency. Denominational differences are most prominent among participants, and participation is most relevant to drug use in denominations that clearly prohibit it. The reanalysis of the Richmond data lends further support to this observation and points toward a reconciliation of seemingly divergent findings.

The findings involving denomination and delinquency in small towns as compared with metropolitan areas suggest another basis for reconciling divergent research results. Had our study been limited to the metropolitan sample and to a Catholic–Protestant comparison, the findings would have been almost identical to those reported in two earlier studies. Delinquency is more likely to be related to denomination in the small-town sample. It may be that religious affiliation is more likely to be a basis for social differentiation in small towns than in large urban settings. Furthermore, religious affiliation may be more visible and more consequential for social interaction and social relationships in settings where people are likely to know one another's background.

Finally, concerning the issue of importance or predictive efficiency, the data show that religious beliefs and participation explain as much or more variance in drug use than participation in many other types of secular activities, and they explain as much variation as familial relations. On the other hand, measures of attachment to school and to the law are better predictors of delinquency than church participation. However, there is evidence that the importance of religion varies by denomination, both absolutely and relative to other variables. Thus, for example, among Mormons the religious items were second only to attitudes toward the law in their contribution to explained variance. Using the Richmond data, it appears that church attendance has the greatest effect in controlling delinquency in those denominations with the greatest emphasis on asceticism.

Overall, our findings suggest that past inconsistencies in research results concerning the religious factor and delinquency may be understandable in terms of the samples studied. There is considerable similarity in research results for similar offenses in similar groups and settings. Most delinquency research, however, has been carried out in large metropolitan settings, and most recent research has concentrated on testing general theories of delinquency that are presumed to apply to a wide range of settings. For example, tests of social control theories have focused on the most obvious control mechanisms that are likely to operate "generally"—regardless of sample and setting (e.g., Hepburn, 1976; Hindelang, 1973; Hirschi, 1969; Jensen and Eve, 1976). However, we are beginning to accumulate evidence that some variables are more relevant for some types of behavior than others in some settings. There are groups for whom religious involvement and belief are significant correlates of delinquency. In addition, there are social settings where denomination makes a difference for delinquency involvement. General theories are typically mute on such interaction. Future research should consider auxiliary arguments and hypotheses that focus on the institutional control mechanisms of specific groups.

References

Albrecht, S. L., B. A. Chadwick, and D. S. Alcorn
   1977 "Religiosity and deviance: Application of an attitude–behavior contingent consistency model." *Journal for the Scientific Study of Religion* 16: 263–274.
Burkett, S. R., and M. White
   1974 "Hellfire and delinquency: Another look." *Journal for the Scientific Study of Religion* 13: 455–462.
Fitzpatrick, P.
   1967 "The role of religion in programs for the prevention and correction of crime and delinquency." President's Commission on Law Enforcement and Administration of

Justice, Task Force Report: Juvenile Delinquency and Youth Crime. Washington, D.C.: U.S. Government Printing Office.

Glock, C. Y., and R. Stark
1965 *Religion and Society in Tension.* Chicago: Rand McNally.

Hepburn, J. R.
1976 "Testing alternative models of delinquency causation." *The Journal of Criminal and Criminology* 67: 450–460.

Higgins, P. C., and G. L. Albrecht
1977 "Hellfire and delinquency revisited." *Social Forces* 55: 962–958.

Hindelang, M. J.
1973 "Causes of delinquency: A partial replication and extension." *Social Problems* 21: 471–487.

Hirschi, T.
1969 *Causes of Delinquency.* Berkeley and Los Angeles: University of California Press.

Hirschi, T., and R. Stark
1969 "Hellfire and delinquency." *Social Problems* 17: 202–213.

Jensen, G. F., and R. Eve
1976 "Sex differences in delinquency." *Criminology* 13: 427–448.

Lenski, G.
1961 *The Religious Factor.* New York: Doubleday.

Schur, E.
1969 *Our Criminal Society.* Englewood Cliffs, New Jersey: Prentice-Hall.

Schuman, H.
1971 "The religious factor in Detroit: Review, replication, and reanalysis." *American Sociological Review* 36: 30–47.

Sutherland, E. H., and D. R. Cressey
1974 *Criminology.* New York: J. B. Lippincott Company.

Wilson, A. B., T. Hirschi, and G. Elder
1965 "Technical report no. 1: Secondary school survey." Survey Research Center, University of California, Berkeley (mimeo).

Chapter 8

Religious Commitment, Affiliation, and Marriage Dissolution

JAMES McCARTHY

I. Introduction

The crude divorce rate in the United States in 1975 was 4.8 per thousand, compared with a rate of 2.2 per thousand in 1960. According to results from the 1975 Current Population Survey, projections based on period divorce rates imply that about one-third of the married persons between 25 and 35 years old in 1975 may eventually end their first marriage in divorce (U.S. Census Bureau, 1976:6). Although any crude rate provides only limited information about the incidence of an event in a population, the more than doubling of the crude divorce rate in recent years clearly indicates that there have been substantial changes in marriage and divorce behavior during this period.

Previous Research on Religion and Marriage Dissolution

One regular focus of more detailed studies of divorce has been the difference in rates of divorce by religion. Several early studies specifically examined

The Religious Dimension:
New Directions in Quantitative Research

Catholic–non-Catholic differences on divorce and consistently found Catholics to be considerably less likely to divorce than non-Catholics (Burchinal and Chancellor, 1963; Landis, 1949; Monahan and Kephart, 1954; Weeks, 1943). Unfortunately, each of these studies is based on a severely limited sample from which no useable generalization can be made. The first data source adequate for a study of social differentials in marriage dissolution was the 1970 National Fertility Study, which was based on a national sample of ever-married women from whom complete marriage histories were collected.[1] The information from this study on marriage dissolution, including separation as well as divorce, has been published in two articles (Bumpass and Sweet, 1972; Sweet and Bumpass, 1974), and these results confirm the general pattern of religious differences reported by earlier studies, although this study reports smaller religious differences than were reported earlier. As a whole, Protestants differ from Catholics by only three percentage points in the likelihood of dissolving their marriages. There is, however, considerable variation among Protestant denominations. Episcopalians, Baptists, and fundamentalist Protestants have the highest likelihood of divorce (controlling for other relevant variables), and Roman Catholics, Lutherans, and other Protestants are similar, with a level of dissolution slightly below the mean. Jews have the lowest level of dissolution, and those with no religion are only slightly above the mean level, at a level lower than Episcopalians, Baptists, and fundamentalist Protestants (Bumpass and Sweet, 1972:758).

Convergence of Religious Differences

Although the results of these studies might lead one to conclude that the religious variations in marriage dissolution in the United States are becoming smaller, the problems associated with the data bases of the early studies are too serious to allow any such conclusion, as plausible as that conclusion may seem.

There exists in the literature, however, related evidence that can be used to formulate a series of hypotheses about current religious differences in marriage dissolution and about the possible recent convergence of these differences.

McRae (1977) has examined differences in attitudes toward divorce by religion using data from the 1958 and 1971 Detroit Area Studies. His results conclusively show a convergence of religious differences. All religious groups

---

[1] Although the 1967 Survey of Economic Opportunity and more recent Current Population Surveys also asked questions on marriage and marriage dissolution, these surveys did not gather complete marriage histories but, rather, asked questions only on first and current or most recent marriage. As a result, the second marriage of those married more than twice are not included, and information, based on these surveys, on remarriage and dissolution of second marriages would be potentially misleading. Sweet (1973:5–7), in discussing the survey of Economic Opportunity, concluded that the data could only be used to study first marriages.

became more tolerant of divorce, but Catholics demonstrated the greatest amount of change, with the result that Catholic attitudes are much closer to those of non-Catholics in 1971 than they were in 1958. When the analysis was extended to examine Catholics for whom religion was more salient, as measured by several attitudinal questions, the results indicated that the change in this group was as great as the change among less-religious Catholics.

This change in Catholics' attitudes toward divorce and their divorce behavior, to be examined in this chapter, are best understood in the broader context of general changes in both the structure of the Catholic Church and the behavior and beliefs of the Catholic population.

The decline in the religious participation of U.S. Catholics in the last 10 years has been widely discussed and documented. According to Greeley, McCready, and McCourt (1976), weekly Mass attendance has declined by 30% in the last decade and monthly confession has declined by 54%. Greeley *et al.* (1976) present several models used to explain this decline in religious participation and conclude that the factors most responsible for the decline are a lack of acceptance of the authority of the Pope and a lack of acceptance of the Church's sexual ethic. Opposition to the Church's position on birth control accounts for 48% of the decline in church attendance and opposition to the Church's position on divorce and opposition to Papal authority each explains 26% of the decline. Views on birth control and divorce have an additional indirect effect, since they explain a significant portion of the nonacceptance of Papal authority, with the birth control factor explaining 25% and the divorce factor 11%.

Westoff and Jones (1977) and Westoff and Bumpass (1973) present evidence on the birth control practice of U.S. Catholic women and on trends in that practice over the period 1955–1975. Both reports conclude that there is a substantial convergence of Catholic and non-Catholic contraceptive practice, and Westoff and Jones (1977:207) predict that by 1980 the two groups will be indistinguishable in terms of contraceptive practice. According to Westoff and Bumpass (1973:42), for the period from 1965 to 1970 the increase in nonconformity of Catholics with the Church's position on birth control is not just associated with a decline in religious practice. Those women who continue to practice their religion are apparently ignoring the Church's teaching on birth control. These researchers found that nonconformity to the birth control teaching increased by 16% between 1965 and 1970. With no change in the proportion receiving communion monthly, the increase would have been 14%.

Change in Catholic Attitudes and Behavior, and the Church's Response

The results cited clearly demonstrate substantial changes in recent years in Catholic attitudes and behavior concerning issues related to sexual and family matters. There has been a significant decline in the religious participation of Catholics, but the changes reported cannot be explained simply by a general decline in religious participation. Even those Catholics who continue to practice regularly have changed considerably in their use of birth control and in their attitudes toward divorce.

Whereas the Church has not changed its official position on either birth control or divorce, there has apparently been more flexibility introduced in the administration of the Church's position toward divorce. Technically, divorce itself has never been forbidden by the Catholic Church, although it certainly has been discouraged and certainly has not been approved of. Remarriage following a divorce, however, has never been sanctioned.

The Church has always recognized that annulments are possible in situations in which evidence suggests that a valid marriage never existed. One example of an invalid marriage would be one that was never consummated; another would result from an individual entering marriage with invalid conditions attached, either a desire not to have children or a belief that the union would not last until death.

A committee of the Catholic Theological Society of America (1972:258–260) was formed to study the problem of second marriages and recommended that, in light of the documents of the Second Vatican Council, several of the traditional grounds for annulment be redefined and extended. For example, the committee suggested that psychological as well as physical impotence be considered as grounds for invalidity of marriage. The grounds would be not only the inability to perform a particular act of consummation but also the inability to participate in a "total community of life and love." Furthermore, the committee, considering the general American attitude toward marriage and divorce, suggested that even in Catholic marriages the intention of indissolubility required for entering marriage may be implicitly conditioned. However, the committee stopped short of a completely teleological explanation for marriage dissolution by stating that it could not be assumed that every first marriage that failed was invalid from the beginning.

At every level, the Church hierarchy has recently attempted to extend its efforts on behalf of divorced and remarried Catholics. A fact sheet, prepared by the Ministry to Divorced Catholics of the Archdiocese of Newark, refers to statements by the Prefect of the Sacred Congregation of Doctrine of the Faith in Rome, by the National Conference of Catholic Bishops in Washington, D.C., and by the local Archbishop, each encouraging the Church to concern itself with the problems of divorced and remarried Catholics.

Most recently, in May 1977, as reported in the *New York Times,* the U.S. National Council of Catholic Bishops ended the practice of automatically excommunicating any divorced and remarried Catholic.

Research Design and Hypotheses

The literature on divorce and other family and sexual matters just reviewed suggests several clear lines for research on religious differences in marriage dissolution in the United States. These lines can best be expressed by a series of hypotheses about the relationship between religious affiliation, religious commitment, and marriage dissolution.

1. Catholics are less likely to dissolve marriages than are non-Catholics.
2. The differences in marriage dissolution between Catholics and non-Catholics are less for more recent marriage cohorts than for earlier marriage cohorts.
3. The convergence of Catholic and non-Catholic differences results from relatively greater increases in dissolution among Catholics.
4. The predicted increase in Catholic marriage dissolution is distributed across all categories of religious commitment. Dissolution will increase for both active and nominal Catholics.

II. Data and Methods

The 1973 National Survey of Family Growth (NSFG) conducted by the National Center for Health Statistics is a data set that is well-suited for an analysis of religious differences in marriage behavior. Like the 1970 National Fertility Survey (NFS) used by Bumpass and Sweet (1972), the NSFG is based on a national sample of ever-married women, with a sample size of 9797. The NSFG asked detailed questions on all marriages, including dates of the beginning and termination of marriages. The date of final separation, defined as the date the couple last lived together, as well as the date of divorce or widowhood, were obtained. Women were also asked their religious affiliation and their level of religious commitment, as indicated by the frequency of their religious activity. Non-Catholic women were asked how often they attended religious services, whereas Catholic women were asked how often they received communion.

Bias

The NSFG is a cross-sectional survey and, therefore, requires a specific kind of analysis of marital status, since the survey cannot collect complete marital histories from every woman. Marital histories from cross-sectional surveys are inadequate in several regards because the interview both selects and censors the information available for analysis.

First, the sample is designed so that the mortality of married women is undetectable. A woman had to have been alive to answer the questions. Second, and more important, the marriage histories obtained may be incomplete. If a woman is married at the time of the survey, she may subsequently divorce, separate, or be widowed. If a woman is not married at the time of the survey or her marriage dissolves after the survey, she may remarry and start the cycle again.

Life Table Techniques

The ideal data set would be one that included complete life-time histories. Since such a set is not available, the analysis must rely on techniques that allow the calculation of life-time rates using information from a one-time, cross-sectional survey. The synthetic life table is a standard demographic technique that can produce life-time calculations from information covering a much shorter time-span. Although life tables are typically calculated from annual mortality data, they have been applied to other demographic events and to data sets other than vital statistics series. Potter (1966) and Vaughn *et al.* (1977) used life-table techniques to measure contraceptive effectiveness, whereas McCarthy (1978) applied life tables to the study of marriage behavior. Each of these studies used data from fertility surveys.

Essentially, a synthetic life table considers all available information and fits it together to produce an estimate of the life-time distribution of a particular event or set of events in a population. Several standard life table terms should be defined at the beginning of this discussion. First, a life table calculation assumes an interest in the distribution of an event or set of events in a population over some time frame. The population under consideration is referred to as the population at risk, and the time frame is precisely defined as the duration of exposure to risk. In the case of marriage dissolution, the population at risk is the group of ever-married women in the survey. The duration of exposure to risk is marriage duration, and the events of interest are separation, divorce, and widowhood.

A life table calculated from survey data must, however, consider the incomplete histories contained in such data. This is accomplished by considering all individuals that had actually been exposed to risk of any duration, regardless of whether they had yet experienced any of the events of interest. Taking two examples from this study, a woman who at the time of interview had been married for 5 years would be included as exposed to the risk of dissolution at each duration from 0 to 5. A woman whose marriage dissolved after 3 years would be included as exposed to the risk of dissolution at each duration from 0 to 3, and the event of the dissolution of her marriage would be included at duration 3.

A life table is based on calculating the rate of occurrence of each event at each duration. This is done simply by dividing the number of events at each duration by the number of individuals exposed to risk at the same duration.[2] The duration-specific rates can be cumulated to give a total probability of experiencing an event up to any duration. In considering the religious differences in marriage dissolution in the United States, this chapter will report the last measure described, the cumulative probability of dissolving a marriage at certain marriage durations.

Competing Risks

When marriage dissolution is the event of interest, the population is actually at risk of two general types of events, death of one spouse and voluntary dissolution. The latter includes annulment, separation, and divorce. The two general sources of dissolution are in competition in the sense that a woman, for the purpose of this analysis, can only experience one. Even though a separated or divorced woman's former husband could, obviously, die, the event of the voluntary dissolution would have already removed her from the population at risk. Because the life table calculations are based on discrete time-intervals, the

---

[2] The description of life table calculations presented in the text is purposely simple to avoid needlessly confusing the nondemographers among the readers. The calculations reported make one major simplifying assumption that does warrant both mention and justification. The dissolution tables calculate q_x directly, as follows:

$$_nq_x = \frac{l_x - l_{x+n}}{l_x}$$

for the single risk case, and

$$q_x'^k = 1 - (P_x T)^{d_x^k/d_x^T}$$

for the competing risk situations, with k representing the particular risk of interest and T representing all risks. The q_x, p_x, d_x, and l_x symbols are all defined in standard life table terms. A general discussion of the application of life table techniques to marriage dissolution can be found in McCarthy (1977).

These q_x calculations assume that the curve between l_x and l_{x+n} is a straight line, that the event in question is evenly distributed throughout the time interval x to $x + n$. Since the interval used in the calculations is 1 year, one could question whether this assumption might influence the rates produced. As a verification of the legitimacy of making such an assumption, the interval was reduced from one year to one month, and the cumulative probabilities that were produced by the monthly calculation differed from the yearly ones only in the third decimal place. These monthly calculations were made for several groups, and the small differences persisted. As a result, the assumption of equal distribution of events in the interval can be supported reasonably, and tables based on single-year intervals are reported.

probability of each event's occurring at a particular duration is not independent of the probability associated with a competing event at the same duration. If time were treated, as it theoretically should be, in a continuous manner, this lack of independence would not be a problem. For this reason, it is possible to approximate independence mathematically. In the case of competing risks, one can calculate associated single decrement life tables that will isolate a single event and exhibit the characteristics of that event in an independent form. Chaing (1968) and Jordan (1952) present general discussions on the calculation of these tables, whereas McCarthy (1977) describes the application of these techniques when marriage dissolution is the event of interest.

Marriage Dissolution: Social and Legal Measures

Voluntary marriage dissolution, however, is really a process rather than an event, and this process usually occurs in at least two distinct stages. One could define the end of a marriage, from a social perspective, as the time at which a couple finally stop living together. In a legal sense, the date of a divorce decree defines the end of a marriage. In some cases, couples separate but never obtain divorces.

So, the process of marriage dissolution can be defined by one of two duration measures, the duration from marriage to separation or the duration from marriage to divorce. One can also consider the intermediate duration that results from the difference of these two, namely, the duration from separation to divorce.

III. Results

Table 8.1 contains a complete series of marriage dissolution tables, based on the first marriages of black and white respondents. The results in this table are not directly relevant to the hypotheses being tested, but they do demonstrate factors that are important to the substantive analysis that follows. Table 8.1 (A) presents the cumulative probability of separating by duration of marriage and by race.[3] Blacks are considerably more likely to separate than whites.

---

[3] All probabilities are based on weighted frequencies, but unweighted frequencies are reported in all tables. Following normal Census Bureau procedures, the National Center for Health Statistics attaches a weight to each respondent to inflate the size of the sample to the size of the corresponding part of the U.S. population. This procedure is used to make national estimates of events reported in U.S. Government surveys. In order to insure that the results in this study are comparable to other uses of the National Survey of Family Growth, the weighted frequencies were used for all calculations. However, the use of weighted frequencies clearly creates problems in the estimation of standard errors. A discussion of standard errors of cumulative probabilities, and several examples of such standard errors, are contained in the Appendix.

TABLE 8.1 First Marriage Dissolution Tables: By Race

A. Cumulative probability of separating after marriage: By duration of marriage and race

Duration	Blacks	Whites
1	.061	.024
2	.119	.047
3	.171	.069
4	.215	.090
5	.243	.108
10	.404	.180
15	.482	.226

B. Cumulative probability of divorcing after separation: By duration of separation and race

Duration	Blacks	Whites
1	.184	.514
2	.295	.759
3	.374	.829
4	.428	.883
5	.467	.912

C. Cumulative probability of divorcing after marriage: By duration of marriage and race

Duration	Blacks	Whites
1	.017	.010
2	.044	.025
3	.069	.045
4	.094	.062
5	.109	.084
10	.207	.156
15	.276	.208
(N)	(3252)	(5823)

Within 5 years after marriage, the probability of separating is .243 for blacks and .108 for whites. The ratio of black to white probabilities persists until the end of the table at duration 15 when blacks have a separation probability of .482 compared to one of .226 for whites. The magnitude of these differences clearly indicates that race must be considered in any analysis of differentials in marriage dissolution by religion.

Parts B and C of Table 8.1 provide an additional guide for the presentation of subsequent results. Table 8.1 (B) shows the cumulative probability of obtaining a legal divorce after a separation has already taken place. Duration of exposure, in this case, is defined as the interval from date of separation to date of divorce or to date of interview if no divorce takes place. According to the results in Table 8.1 (B), whites are much more likely actually to obtain a legal divorce than blacks. Within 5 years the probability of divorcing for whites is approximately .9, whereas for blacks it is less than .5. Extending the analysis to as long as 10 years from separation does not produce substantial increases in the probability of obtaining a divorce for blacks.

Using divorce as the operational definition of dissolution presents results that are interesting, more because of the information they conceal than for their face value. These results are shown in Table 8.1 (C). Because of the relatively low probability of black separations leading to divorces, the racial differences in dissolution probabilities are substantially smaller when divorce is used as a measure of dissolution than when separation is used.

The differences between separation rates and divorce rates for whites are small and can be explained by the need for a legal waiting time between separation and divorce. Simply assuming that the interval from separation to divorce takes 2 years for whites, on the average, one can accurately estimate duration patterns of separation from knowledge of patterns of divorce, or patterns of divorce from knowledge of separation. For blacks, however, because of the relatively low probability of obtaining a divorce after separation, divorce as a measure of marriage dissolution seriously underestimates the true level of dissolution.

Since the interest in this chapter focuses on social differences in marriage and divorce behavior, and not on variations in access to legal forms of marriage dissolution, separation date, the date the couple last lived together, appears to be the more appropriate definition of the end of a marriage. Accordingly, the substantive comparisons to follow will be based on differences in the cumulative probability of separating by duration from date of marriage to date of separation.

Religious Affiliation and Marriage Dissolution

Table 8.2 presents the cumulative probability of separating at various marriage durations for groups defined by race and religion. The results for all religious and racial groups are presented, but the discussion will focus on the differences between Catholics and Protestants, since the number of Jews and the number of blacks with no religion are too small to produce reliable results. The results partially support the first hypothesis, which stated that Catholics would be less likely to dissolve marriages. For whites, the results are in line with the prediction, with Catholics having .184 probability of separating by duration 15 and Protestants having a probability of .236 at the same duration. The differences between the two groups, however, are quite small; approximately .03 at duration 5, .04 at duration 10, and .05 at duration 15. For

TABLE 8.2 Probability of Separating after First Marriage; by
Race, Religion, and Marriage Duration

Religion	Duration	Black's	White's
Protestant	5	.240	.111
	10	.406	.187
	15	.477	.236
	(N)	(2869)	(3717)
Catholic	5	.236	.083
	10	.397	.142
	15	.570	.184
	(N)	(270)	(1740)
Jewish[a]	5		.105
	10		.149
	15		.202
	(N)		(104)
None	5	.292	.275
	10	.328	.416
	15	.390	.493
	(N)	(81)	(187)

[a] Of the 104 Jews, 101 are white and 3 are nonwhite.

blacks, one sees the opposite results, with black Catholics being more likely to
separate than black Protestants. Although the absolute religious difference is
greater for blacks, the size of the sample of black Catholics and the approximate standard errors from Table A.1 (see Appendix) suggest a cautious interpretation of this difference. Although the Catholic–Protestant difference for
whites is smaller than that for blacks, the size of the sample of white Catholics
is substantially larger than that of black Catholics, and the results for whites
are less likely to be due to sampling errors.

Religious Commitment and Marriage Dissolution

To assess the effect of religious commitment on marriage dissolution, the
measure of religious participation described earlier has been used to define
three groups, those who participate at least monthly, those who participate less
than monthly but at least yearly, and those who participate less than yearly.
Because the total number of black Catholics is so small, this more detailed part
of the analysis will be limited to black Protestants, white Protestants, and
white Catholics. Each of these groups has a sample that is sufficiently large to
allow further subclassification. Results are presented in Table 8.3.

For all three groups, the level of religious commitment has an important effect on the probability of separating. For both black and white Protestants, the
probability of separating increases substantially as religious commitment

TABLE 8.3 Probability of Separating after First Marriage, by Race, Religion, Religious Commitment, and Marriage Duration

Religious commitment	Duration	Black Protestants	White Protestants	White Catholics
Monthly participation	5	.208	.081	.035
	10	.359	.125	.060
	15	.423	.166	.088
	(*N*)	(1994)	(2001)	(655)
Yearly participation	5	.266	.128	.050
	10	.478	.214	.088
	15	.566	.287	.099
	(*N*)	(579)	(950)	(497)
Less than yearly participation	5	.418	.172	.168
	10	.606	.331	.288
	15	.690	.372	.375
	(*N*)	(296)	(766)	(577)

decreases. However, for Catholics there is effectively no difference between those who participate monthly and those who participate yearly, with separation probabilities of .088 and .099, respectively. The white Catholics who participate monthly or yearly are also much less likely to separate than are the corresponding categories of either white or black Protestants.

The category including those who participate less than yearly is a particularly interesting one. Whereas blacks in this category are considerably more likely to separate than whites, there is no difference whatsoever between white Protestants and white Catholics whose religious participation is less than once a year. These results suggest that the relatively small overall Catholic–Protestant differences reported for whites in Table 8.2 is actually due to the combination of a greater Catholic–Protestant difference for the actively religious and no difference between nominal Protestants and nominal Catholics. The difference between white Protestants and white Catholics who participate less than monthly but at least yearly is particularly striking.

Time Trends in Separation,
and the Convergence of Religious Differences

The results presented in Table 8.3 for whites can be further disaggregated in an attempt to measure any time trends in the pattern of Catholic–Protestant differences in the probability of separating. Table 8.4 shows the results

TABLE 8.4   Probability of Separating after First Marriage, by Religion, Religious Commitment, Marriage Cohort, and Marriage Duration (Whites)[a]

Religious commitment	Marriage date	Duration	Protestants	Catholics		
Monthly participation	Pre-1960	5	.066	.029		
		10	.102	.041		
		(N)	(880)	(276)		
					r = 1.48	r = 2.10
	Post-1960	5	.094	.039		
		10	.151	.086		
		(N)	(1121)	(389)		
Yearly participation	Pre-1960	5	.111	.034		
		10	.209	.060		
		(N)	(361)	(160)		
					r = 1.00	r = 1.80
	Post-1960	5	.140	.061		
		10	.210	.108		
		(N)	(589)	(337)		
Less than yearly participation	Pre-1960	5	.139	.155		
		10	.281	.262		
		(N)	(280)	(188)		
					r = 1.34	r = 1.16
	Post-1960	5	.192	.175		
		10	.378	.305		
		(N)	(486)	(389)		

[a] r = ratio of post-1960 probabilities to pre-1960 probabilities.

specified by religion, religious commitment, and marriage date. Because of the limits of sample size, women of only two time periods are considered, those married before 1960 and those married during 1960 or later. Since the survey was conducted in late 1973, the more recent cohort can only have a maximum marriage duration of 14 years. Accordingly, duration-specific comparisons in this table will be limited to the first 10 years of marriage.

Active Catholics, those whose religious participation is at least yearly, show the greatest relative change over time, although their absolute level of dissolution is still low even in the more recent cohort. Protestants who participate yearly show no change, whereas the remaining categories, those with less than yearly participation and Protestants who participate monthly, show somewhat less relative change than active Catholics. The rates of change in separation probabilities do show some support for the presence of converging Catholic–Protestant divorce behavior, even though active Catholics are still much less likely to separate than are their Protestant counterpart. In addition, the distribution of both Protestants and Catholics across commitment categories shifts in the direction of a smaller proportion highly committed in the post-1960 cohort than was the case in the pre-1960 cohort. In the later group, 51% of the Protestants and 35% of the Catholics participated at least monthly. The corresponding figures for the earlier group are 58% and 44%. These figures would result in increased overall separation rates even if there were no change at all in separation rates within categories of religious commitment.

Remarriage and the Dissolution of Second Marriages

It is not the action of a separation or divorce that places a Catholic woman in a position not approved by the Church, but it is, rather, the event of a remarriage. Although the automatic excommunication of couples in second marriages has been eliminated, remarrying without a Church annulment of the first marriage is not validly possible. The results in Table 8.5 show that white Catholics are less likely to remarry than white Protestants but substantially more likely to remarry than black Protestants. The number of Catholics ex-

TABLE 8.5 Probability of Remarriage after Separation by Race, Religion, and Duration from Separation

Duration	Black Protestants	White Protestants	White Catholics
1	.043	.103	.044
2	.090	.294	.151
3	.128	.465	.305
4	.179	.590	.406
5	.252	.683	.493
10	.378	.865	.692
(N)	(1090)	(719)	(242)

TABLE 8.6 Probability of Separating after a Second Marriage by Race, Religion, and Marriage Duration

Duration	Black Protestants	White Protestants	White Catholics
1	.042	.041	.042
2	.108	.088	.072
3	.145	.112	.114
4	.172	.154	.132
5	.191	.204	.165
10	.291	.274	.264
(N)	(405)	(554)	(139)

posed to the risk of remarriage after separation is too small to justify examining remarriage probabilities by level of religious commitment.

According to the results in Table 8.6, those Catholic women who do remarry are just as likely to separate from their second husbands as are either black or white Protestants. There are no substantial racial or religious differences in the probability of separating after a second marriage. Comparing Table 8.6 with Table 8.2, white Catholics who remarry do have a higher probability of dissolving a second marriage than a first marriage.

IV. Summary and Conclusion

Several hypotheses about the relationship between religion and marriage dissolution were presented in the introduction, and the evidence just reported provides a base for evaluating these hypotheses. First, Catholics are less likely to dissolve marriages than are non-Catholics. In addition, the increase in separation rates for those married more recently was greater for Catholics than for Protestants. Although the direction of this change supports the idea of a convergence in religious differences in marriage dissolution, the magnitude of the change is not particularly great. The result is that Catholics are still, even in a more recent cohort, less likely to separate than Protestants.

The increases in dissolution rates among active Catholics were relatively greater than the increases among Protestants and among nominal Catholics. There were no differences in separation probabilities between Catholics and Protestants whose commitment to their religion was only nominal. Catholics are slightly less likely to remarry than are Protestants, but those who do are equally likely to end a second marriage by separation.

These results suggest several interesting possibilities about the future of religious differences in marriage dissolution in the United States. Perhaps the most important point refers to the substantial differences in separation probabilities between active and nominal Catholics and the persistence of these differences in the more recent marriage cohorts. When previous researchers considered religious differences in attitudes toward divorce and toward contraceptive practices, they showed evidence of considerable convergence between Catholics and non-Catholics (McRae, 1977; Westoff and Bumpass, 1973; Westoff and Jones, 1977). This convergence was based on substantial changes in attitudes or behavior among all Catholics, including those who participate actively in their religion. Both the degree of change and its presence among active as well as nominal Catholics led these authors to suggest that complete convergence was very likely. In fact, Westoff and Jones (1977:207) predict that by 1980 there will be little to differentiate between the contraceptive practices of Catholics and of non-Catholics.

In the case of marriage dissolution, predictions about the future are much more difficult to make. First, one must distinguish between the actively and the nominally religious. The actively religious continue to have low rates of separation, even though these rates are increasing. Active Catholics have consistently very low rates of separation, lower than those of active Protestants. If convergence is to come about as a result of increases in separation probabilities among active Catholics, then it is probably not likely to occur very soon.

However, convergence could also result from a shift in the distribution of Catholics among categories of religious commitment. If many more Catholics were to move into the nominal category, assuming constant separation rates within categories, then overall Catholic–Protestant rates would move closer together. This possibility can be questioned for two reasons: First, one can question whether the decline of Catholic religious participation will continue or whether it will level off; second, one can question whether the high separation rate of nominal Catholics will continue. The second question is perhaps the more confusing.

It is quite clear that there is an association between being a nominal Catholic and ending a first marriage by separating. It is not at all clear that one or the other is the causal factor. One could make a plausible case for either. It is likely that a nominal Catholic would feel little pressure to conform to Church regulations on marriage and divorce and would not be closely integrated into a dominant Catholic social network. Such people might simply be more willing to end an unsatisfactory marriage. In this situation, the lack of commitment would be the prior condition and, presumably, have an influence on marital status.

However, the event of a separation or divorce, and particularly the event of a remarriage, could just as well be the prior condition influencing the religious commitment of Catholics. Although the Church has never condemned divorce and has recently removed the punishment of excommunication for the remarried, the acceptance of divorced Catholics by the Church has in the past been limited. It could well be that an atmosphere of nonacceptance of separation, divorce, and remarriage had a negative effect on the religious commitment of separated Catholics. But this atmosphere has certainly changed in the recent past and is likely to continue to change. Organized national groups within the Catholic Church, including the North American Conference of Separated and Divorced Catholics, are attempting to direct Church activity and programs to Catholics whose marriages have dissolved. Although these activities are not likely to reduce marriage dissolution among Catholics, they are likely to reduce the numbers of Catholics who are only nominally religious because they have dissolved a marriage. If these programs are very effective, they may well increase the separation rate among active Catholics, not for any intrinsic reason but because separated and divorced Catholics will be more able to maintain an active role in the Church and will not be forced into nominal status simply as a result of marriage dissolution. This hypothetical sequence of events would also increase the convergence of Catholic–Protestant separation rates.

Using related evidence on changes in Catholic attitudes and behavior in other areas of family life and the evidence reported in this investigation on changes in Catholic separation probabilities, the final conclusion is that one can expect movement in the direction of convergence of Catholic–Protestant differences in marriage dissolution. There are, however, many institutional and individual actions that would affect the pace of this convergence, and even its continuation. One can predict the consequences for separation among Catholics of an increase in the Church's acceptance of and ministry to divorced Catholics, of a change in the overall separation rate in the total population, or of a general decline in the religious commitment of the Catholic population. The overall association between religion and marriage dissolution, however, is dependent on the relative dominance of one or more of these situations and is, therefore, difficult to predict.

Appendix: Calculation of Standard Errors for Marriage Table Probabilities

The sample for the 1973 NSFG was drawn by a multistage cluster design, and a weight was added to each respondent to inflate the sample to the size of the United States population. All the values reported in marriage tables are based on the weighted sample. Since the weighted sample has been inflated to the population size, the usual procedures for calculating the variance and standard error of life-table values are not appropriate. Mosteller and Tukey (1977) provide a description of a technique, called the jackknife, that makes estimates of variance and standard error when usual procedures cannot be applied. Although the major application of this approach has been in situations of small samples, the particular characteristics of the weighting process used in the 1973 NSFG indicate that the jackknife is appropriate in this situation.

The jackknife is essentially a rather simple procedure and can be described in very general terms. The first step is simply making the desired calculation for all the data. In this case, this involves computing a set of marriage tables. For reasons apparent from the text, only the separation tables will be considered here, and the calculation produces a set of separation probabilities, p_i, where i is duration of marriage. The first step is noted as p_{iALL}, the set of separation probabilities computed from all the data.

The data are then randomly divided into 10 groups, and the separation probabilities are calculated "for each of the slightly reduced bodies of data obtained by leaving out just one of the groups" (Mosteller and Tukey,

1977:135), resulting in sets of separation probabilities p_{ij}, where i is duration of marriage and j indicates which group was left out of a particular calculation. The value of j has a range from 1 to 10. Mosteller and Tukey then define pseudo-values, $p_{i \cdot j}$, as

$$P_{i \cdot j} = 10 p_{iALL} - 9 p_{ij}, \qquad j = 1, 2, \ldots 10.$$

The variance, S^2, is then calculated by

$$S^2_i = \frac{\Sigma p^2_{i \cdot j} - \frac{1}{10}(\Sigma p_{i \cdot j})^2}{9}, \qquad S^2_{i \cdot} = \frac{S^2_i}{10},$$

and the standard error, S.E.$_{i \cdot}$, is defined as S.E.$_{i \cdot}$ = S^2_i.

Although the jackknife is conceptually simple, the calculation is time-consuming and expensive in terms of computer costs, and it would be difficult to perform even on all separation tables. Table A–1 presents standard errors for two separation tables for subsamples of blacks and whites. The two tables chosen for each racial group were selected to cover the range of frequencies on which tables in the text have been based. Since frequencies are reported with each of the tables in the text, an estimate of standard errors can be made by using the results for whatever group from Table A–1 is approximately the same size as the group of interest.

TABLE A–1 Standard Errors of Cumulative Probabilities of Separating

Duration	Blacks		Whites	
5	.008	.052	.005	.003
10	.018	.050	.005	.045
15	.016	.058	.007	.089
N	3249	188	5828	178

References

Archdiocese of Newark
    n.d. "Ministry to Divorced Catholics," Fact Sheet.
Bumpass, L. L., and J. A. Sweet
    1972 "Differentials in marital instability: 1970." *American Sociological Review* 37: 754–766.
Burchinal, L. B., and L. E. Chancellor
    1963 "Survival rates among religiously homogamous and interreligious marriages." *Social Forces* 41:353–362.
Catholic Theological Society of America
    1972 "Statement of the committee to study the problems of second marriages." *America* 127:258–260.

Chiang, C. L.
1968 *Introduction to Stochastic Processes in Biostatistics.* New York: John Wiley and Sons, Inc.

Greeley, A, M., W. C. McGready, and K. McCourt
1976 *Catholic Schools in a Declining Church.* Kansas City: Sheed and Ward, Inc.

Jordan, C. W.
1952 *Life Contingencies.* Chicago: The Society of Actuaries.

Landis, J. T.
1949 "Marriages of mixed and non-mixed religious faith." *American Sociological Review* 14:401–407.

McCarthy, J. F.
1977 *Patterns of Marriage Dissolution in the United States.* Unpublished Doctoral Thesis, Princeton University.

McCarthy, J. F.
1978 "A comparison of the dissolution of first and second marriages." *Demography 15:* 345–359.

McRae, J. A.
1977 *"The secularization of divorce."* University of Arizona (mimeo).

Monahan, T. P., and W. M. Kephart
1954 "Divorces and desertion by religious and mixed-religious groups." *American Journal of Sociology* 59:454–465.

Potter, R. G.
1966 "Application of life table techniques to measurement of contraceptive effectiveness." *Demography* 3:297–304.

Sweet, J. A., and L. L. Bumpass
1974 "Differentials in marital instability of the black population." *Phylon* 35:323–331.

Thornton, A.
1977 "Decomposing the re-marriage process." *Population Studies* 31:383–392.

U.S. Bureau of the Census
1976 Current Population Reports, Series P-20, No. 297. Number, timing and duration of marriages and divorces in the United States: June, 1975. Washington, D.C.: United States Government Printing Office

Vaughan, B., J. Trussell, J. Menken, and E. F. Jones
1977 "Contraceptive failure among married women in the United States, 1970–1973." *Family Planning Perspectives* 9:251–258.

Weeks, H. A.
1943 "Differential divorce rates by occupation." *Social Forces* 21:334–337.

Westoff, C. F., and L. L. Bumpass
1973 "The revolution in birth control practices of U.S. Roman Catholics." *Science* 179: 41–44.

Westoff, C. F. and E. F. Jones
1977 "The secularization of U.S. Catholic birth control practices. *Family Planning Perspectives* 9:203–207.

Chapter 9

Religious Affiliation and Socioeconomic Achievement

JAMES A. RICCIO

I. Introduction

Today, as in the past, it is common to find that different religious groups in multifaith societies often vary markedly in terms of their average levels of socioeconomic achievement. The reasons for these differences have never been quite as obvious as the fact of their existence, and a number of social scientists have devoted considerable amounts of energy to a search for appropriate explanations. The results of these efforts, as they apply to the American case, are the concern of this chapter. Here the major empirical studies attempting to assess the ways in which an individual's religious affiliation influences his or her socioeconomic achievement will be summarized and critiqued. The issue remains a controversial one, as the number of contradictory findings will indicate. Yet, as the weaknesses of these studies are revealed, the opportunity for more conclusive research in the future is correspondingly improved.

The Religious Dimension:
New Directions in Quantitative Research

199

II. Max Weber and the Protestant Ethic

The preoccupation of many contemporary social scientists with religion and achievement can, of course, be traced to Max Weber's prominent work, *The Protestant Ethic and the Spirit of Capitalism* (1958). Weber's central intention in that work was not to formulate an explanation for differential achievement among religious groups but, rather, to account for the emergence of a set of norms and values conducive to the rise of capitalism. He labeled this set of norms and values the "capitalist spirit." It consisted essentially of three components: (*a*) an expectation that economic behavior would be "rational," that is, based on the calculated pursuit of profit; (*b*) a high evaluation of work as an end in itself; and (*c*) a high evaluation of an ascetic style of life. Weber argued that the capitalist spirit was actually embodied in the religious doctrines of certain Protestant denominations, particularly Calvinism and Puritanism. In contrast, he believed that Catholicism placed little value on rational economic behavior. It seemed, in fact, to offer its followers consolation for economic failure.

Though primarily concerned with the religious origins of the capitalist spirit prior to the development of capitalism itself, Weber claimed that, even within the European capitalist societies of his time, religious affiliation was associated with attitudes toward economic behavior. This, he thought, explained the differential socioeconomic achievement that existed among certain religious groups. For example, he observed a greater tendency for Protestants, as compared with Catholics, to be owners of capital, business leaders, and more highly skilled laborers (1958:39). Yet, Weber also suggested that religious differences in economic behavior might decline.

III. Summary of Studies

In order to present conveniently the general findings of the studies that have been done on religion and socioeconomic achievement, each study will be summarized according to the dimensions of socioeconomic achievement it investigated. These fall into the following categories: (*a*) occupational and income achievement; (*b*) educational attainment; and (*c*) achievement motivation, values, and aspirations.

Occupational and Income Achievement

The flurry of research on the Protestant ethic hypothesis that has been witnessed over the last two decades was greatly inspired by Lenski's study, *The Religious Factor* (1963). This was a study of the male respondents of a probability sample survey of the Detroit metropolitan area. Lenski found significant variation in occupational achievement among several socioreligious groups. Dividing the sample into four social classes—upper middle, lower middle, upper working, lower working—on the basis of collapsed census occupational categories and matching respondents for class origins, he discovered that more white Protestant men than Catholic men rose into the upper middle class or retained that status; Catholic men were more likely to move into or remain in the lower half of the working class. There was little mobility out of the working class for black Protestants. Jews were excluded from the analysis because of the small size of the group (1963:84–85).

Another study of the Detroit area was conducted by Mayer and Sharp (1962) and yielded results consistent with those of Lenski. Utilizing combined data from probability surveys conducted between 1954 and 1959, Mayer and Sharp were able to construct a rank ordering of 12 religious denominations in terms of five measures of socioeconomic achievement: (*a*) family income; (*b*) percentage of self-employed; (*c*) percentage in professional, managerial, proprietary, or official occupational positions; (*d*) median school year completed; and (*e*) percentage in three or more formal social groups. Using a weighting scheme to control for ethnicity, generation, region in which reared, size of community in which reared, and length of time in Detroit, Mayer and Sharp found most Protestant denominations to exceed Roman Catholics significantly in social and economic standing, and Jews and members of the Eastern Orthodox faith were found to have the highest levels of achievement.

The obvious hazards of making societal inferences on the basis of community studies encouraged many researchers to utilize national samples. One of the earliest of such efforts was carried out by Mack, Murphy, and Yellin (1956). Using a nonprobability sample of white males drawn from three white collar occupational categories—salesmen, engineers, and bankers—they compared Protestant and Catholic mobility patterns, both between and within generations. Census occupational categories were used to index socioeconomic position. With controls for father's occupation and respondent's age, the analysis revealed no significant Protestant—Catholic differences in either pattern of occupational achievement.

These conclusions were contested by Lenski, however, in a reanalysis of the same set of data. He claimed that Mack, Murphy, and Yellin used an inappropriate procedure to test for significance and that Protestants were, in fact, more upwardly mobile than Catholics (Lenski, 1963:83).

A study by Jackson, Fox, and Crockett, Jr. (1970) of a national cluster-probability sample of white males found significant differences between Protestants and Catholics with regard to occupational achievement and mobility. Five occupational categories were distinguished: (*a*) professional or business; (*b*) lower white collar (clerical, technical, sales); (*c*) skilled manual; (*d*) semiskilled or unskilled manual; and (*e*) farmer. When father's occupation was held constant, Protestants were found to have higher rates of entrance into the professional and business occupations, whereas Catholics were more likely than Protestants to enter lower white-collar occupations. The *range* of mobility of each group was also found to differ: When starting from the same social origins (in terms of father's occupation), Protestants were more sharply upwardly mobile whereas Catholics were more sharply downwardly mobile. All of these differences remained significant when controls for ethnicity, region in which reared, age, generation of American residence, and size of community in which reared were introduced.

A study by Gockel (1969) analyzed religious differences in male income attainment on a national probability sample of Jews, Catholics, 10 Protestant denominations, and men with no religious preference. Using a regression analysis and controlling for respondent's occupational status (Duncan's SEI), race, education, region of current residence (North versus South), and size of community of current residence, no important Protestant–Catholic differences were found. However, when the Protestant denominations, Jews, and those with no preference were considered, some significant differences among the groups were revealed. With the previously mentioned controls in effect, Congregationalists, Episcopalians, and Jews were found to have somewhat higher incomes, on the average, than the other groups.

Like Gockel, Goldstein (1969) discovered little difference between Catholics and Protestants in general with regard to income in a tabular analysis of 1957 census data (the only census to include a question on religious affiliation). Jews had higher income achievement than either of these groups, but this advantage was sharply reduced when a control for respondent's occupation was introduced. Looking at the relative percentage of men in white-collar occupations, Jews ranked highest, followed by white Protestants, then Catholics, and, finally, nonwhite Protestants. The differences among these groups were reduced but not eliminated when education was controlled and when the analysis was limited to urban residents only.

Warren (1970), using multiple-classification analysis on two national probability samples of American males, found that initial religious affiliation had no important net effect on occupational achievement (Duncan's SEI); almost all of the variation could be accounted for by differences in social origin and educational attainment. Such was not the case with income, however. With controls for father's occupational status and respondent's occupational and educational attainment, there were still significant, though attenuated, differences among some of the religious groups. Jews, Episcopalians, Congregationalists, and Presbyterians tended to have the highest incomes, Baptists and unspecified Protestants tended to have the lowest incomes, and other religious groups were found to occupy the intermediate levels.

Most of the studies investigating religion and achievement have been static analyses that ignore changes over time. A major study that departs from this tradition was prepared by Glenn and Hyland (1967), who used 18 national surveys conducted between 1943 and 1965 to summarize trends in Catholic–Protestant achievement differentials. Although comparability among samples was hindered by differences in the scales used to measure key variables, it appeared that, among white males, Protestants ranked well above Catholics in income and occupational status in the 1940s but that Catholics had achieved comparatively higher standing by the mid-1960s. Glenn and Hyland concluded that "An important reason for the more rapid advancement of Catholics is their heavy concentration in the larger non-Southern metropolitan areas, where earnings, occupational distributions, educational opportunities, and rates of upward mobility are more favorable than in the typical home communities of Protestants [1967:85]." This was suggested by the fact that, in the more recent studies they reviewed, an introduction of controls for current region of the country, current community size, and respondent's age showed Protestants to rank slightly above Catholics. Although they were primarily interested in Protestant–Catholic differentials, they did note that Jews ranked above both of these groups in terms of income and occupational achievement for the entire period.

In another review, Lipset and Bendix (1959) examined two national probability studies of male occupational achievement to estimate the impact of being Catholic or Protestant. One study classified occupations into nonmanual, manual, and farm categories, and the other employed the census 11-category scale. Both studies included controls for race and generation of American residence, and the former included an additional control for father's occupation. The first study revealed no significant differences between Protestants and Catholics. In the second study, comparisons between first and second generations showed Protestants to be of higher occupational status; by the third generation, however, this difference had disappeared.

Other than the investigation by Mack, Murphy, and Yellin, none of the previously mentioned studies could estimate the effects that religion might have on intragenerational changes of occupational and income achievement, for they all used cross-sectional data that did not provide career histories. In contrast, Featherman (1971) attempted to estimate such within-generation effects of religion by using longitudinal data for the decade 1957–1967. His sample was a subsample drawn from the Princeton Fertility Study's larger stratified random sample. It consisted of white males who were fathers with two young children and who resided in seven of the largest Standard Metropolitan Areas. Six religioethnic subgroups (Jews, Anglo-Saxon Protestants, other Protestants, Italian and Mexican Roman Catholics, other Roman Catholics, and other or no religion) were included in a multiple regression analysis that sought to explain respondent's occupation (1947 NORC prestige scale) and income at both the beginning and end of the time period. To remove the influence of social background factors, controls were introduced for father's occupation, size of family in which reared, and extent of farm or rural residence. With respondent's education also controlled, religioethnic group status was found to have no net impact on income or occupation at the beginning of the time period. There was also no independent influence of group affiliation on respondent's occupation and income at the end of the decade when controls for the first income and occupation measures were used in addition to controls for education and father's occupation. He concluded, therefore, that no important differences in occupational or income achievement exist among religious and ethnic groups, either within generations or between them, that cannot be accounted for by other social status characteristics of the groups.

Two other studies concerned with religion and achievement considered the possibility that the religious context of one's formal education might affect one's later socioeconomic achievement. In one inquiry, Bressler and Westoff (1963) noted that a difference might be expected between Catholics educated in Catholic schools and Catholics educated in public schools, for Catholic schools might more effectively inculcate religious values that conflict with values emphasizing high socioeconomic achievement. If Catholicism is not oriented toward "this-worldly" achievement and if Catholic schools give greater stress to such teachings, then Catholics educated in Catholic schools might have weaker achievement values and, hence, lower actual achievement than Catholics educated in public schools.

Like Featherman, Bressler and Westoff drew their respondents from the Princeton Fertility Study. Five measures of economic achievement were constructed: (*a*) respondent's occupation (1947 NORC prestige scale); (*b*) total earnings in the year prior to the interview; (*c*) the change in earnings since marriage; (*d*) intergenerational mobility; and (*e*) intragenerational mobility since marriage. With educational attainment controlled, no substantial differences on any of these measures were discovered among the two groups of Catholics.

Greeley and Rossi (1966) also investigated this issue. They analyzed a national probability sample and introduced controls for parents' socioeconomic status and for a crude measure of respondent's "knowledge." They discovered that Catholics educated in Catholic schools had slightly higher educational and occupational attainment (Duncan's SEI). However, these differences were not large enough to contradict the inferences drawn by Bressler and Westoff. Rather, as the researchers state, their findings imply that "there is no evidence that Catholic education interferes with occupational or educational achievement [1966:146]."

Educational Attainment

Educational attainment, in and of itself, can be considered an aspect of socioeconomic achievement. Yet, it has also been shown to be a key determinant of occupational and income achievement in American society (Blau and Duncan, 1967). According to the studies previously summarized, differences in educational attainment seem to be an important source of the differences in occupational and income achievement that were observed among religious groups. Considering the general importance of education, then, a closer look at educational patterns among religious groups is warranted. The findings of the studies already discussed (to the extent that they bear on this issue), as well as the findings of other pertinent inquiries, will be addressed in this section.

Lenski (1963:262) found that educational differences were not large among the white Protestants, Catholics, and Jews in his sample. However, members of these groups were considerably more likely than black Protestants to receive some college training.

Lenski also made some comparisons among the religious groups in terms of educational persistence—the tendency to complete a given level of schooling once it is begun. Catholics were found to have lower persistence rates than Protestants, and this could not be explained by differences in social-class origins of the groups. Lenski argued that different persistence rates, like attainment differences, might be indicative of different success values or motivational patterns between religious groups (1963:263–266).

Fox and Jackson (1973) researched both the educational attainment and the persistence differentials between Protestants and Catholics, using a national cluster sample of white males. Controlling for ethnicity, region of birth, age, generation, father's occupation, and size of current community, they found Protestants to be slightly more likely than Catholics to have a college degree and substantially more likely to complete college once enrolled. However, the very small number of cases in their sample prevented them from establishing that these differences were statistically significant. There were no consistent religious differences in persistence rates at the high-school level.

Another study of educational attainment was conducted by Goldstein (1969). His analysis of census data revealed substantial differences among several religious groups for both males and females. Especially pronounced were the differences between Jews and Gentiles with regard to college education: A substantially higher proportion of Jews had achieved at least some college education or had earned a college degree. In terms of overall educational attainment, the groups could be ranked just as he found them to rank in terms of occupational achievement: Jews at the top, followed by white Protestants, then Catholics, then nonwhite Protestants. This was without controls other than for sex, however.

Glenn and Hyland (1967) found that the educational differences between Catholics and Protestants had largely disappeared over the 22-year period they studied. Controlling for region and community size, little difference in educational attainment or in persistence in school was revealed. Only in terms of the percentage starting college did Protestants maintain a statistically significant advantage. Yet, the authors contend that even this difference may not be religiously based; it is more likely, they suggest, to be a consequence of differences in parental status, a variable that could not be controlled in their analysis. Jews substantially exceeded both Protestants and Catholics for the entire period in terms of the proportion starting and completing college. However, this, too, may be a consequence of parental status.

Featherman's (1971) study used more controls and a greater differentiation of religious denominations than did the four preceding studies. He discovered that there was, indeed, a net religioethnic group influence on educational attainment that could not be accounted for by his three social background measures. In terms of the average number of years of schooling completed, the following rank–order of the religioethnic groups emerged: Jews were first, followed by Anglo-Saxon Protestants, other Protestants, Roman Catholics of other than Italian or Mexican extraction, Italian and Mexican Roman Catholics, and, finally, those with no or other religious preference.

Similarly, Warren (1970) found independent religious influences on educational attainment. Controls for race, father's occupational status, and region of origin reduced but did not eliminate the higher educational achievement of some groups over others. As with income, Jews, Episcopalians, Congregationalists, and Presbyterians had the most education, and Baptists and unspecified Protestants had the least.

Achievement Motivation, Values, and Aspirations

Several studies have sought to determine whether orientations toward achievement, in the form of motivations, values, and aspirations, vary substantially among religious groups and whether they are important for explaining actual differentials in socioeconomic achievement.

An early attempt at this was undertaken by Rosen (1969) with a non-probability sample of French-Canadians, Southern Italians, Greeks, Eastern European Jews, blacks, and white Protestants in four Northeastern states. The respondents consisted of boys aged 8–14 and their mothers. On the basis of Hollingshead's Index of Social Position, which is a weighted combination of occupational position and education, it was apparent that these groups had different levels of socioeconomic achievement, which Rosen predicted would be associated with differences in orientations toward achievement.

Rosen thought it fruitful to distinguish among the following three components of this "achievement syndrome": a psychological motivation to achieve, achievement values, and achievement aspirations. Each was believed to be relevant to socioeconomic achievement in distinct but complementary ways. The achievement motive, a concept developed by McClellan *et al.* (1953), is a psychological disposition impelling an individual to excel in situations involving standards of excellence. Achievement values define as more or less desirable the individual's acceptance of types of behavior that are conducive to high achievement. Three sets of values were identified by Rosen as elements of the achievement syndrome: (*a*) an activistic–passivistic orientation, which concerns the belief that one has the capacity to change one's life situation; (*b*) an individualistic–collectivistic orientation, which refers to the importance attached to individual needs and wishes relative to those of the group; and (*c*) present–future orientation, which refers to the comparative evaluation of immediate gratification of impulses versus deferment of gratification in expectation of future gain. Achievement aspirations, the third component of the achievement syndrome, orient the individual toward specifically socioeconomic goals.

Rosen ascertained the levels of achievement motivation among the boys in his sample by means of a Thematic Apperception Test (TAT), and he made an assessment of achievement values and of educational and occupation aspirations through interviews with the mothers. His analysis revealed statistically significant mean differences among some of the groups with respect to each aspect of the achievement syndrome. To assess the influence of religious group affiliation, Greeks were treated as Greek Orthodox, and Italians and French-Canadians were treated as Roman Catholics. In terms of achievement motivation as well as achievement values and aspirations, Jews, Greeks, and white Protestants ranked significantly above Italians and French-Canadians. These differences were reduced but not eliminated when social class was controlled.

Other studies that investigated the influence of religion on an individual's orientation toward achievement focused on one or several of the components of Rosen's achievement syndrome. Veroff and his associates (1962), for example, further investigated the association between religious affiliation and achievement motivation. They administered thematic apperceptive measures to white male adults drawn from a national probability sample. With no variables controlled, the researchers found that Jewish men had the highest need-achievement scores, followed by Catholics and then by Protestants. The higher scores of Catholics as compared with Protestants contrasted with results reported by Rosen, as well as with theoretical expectations. This encouraged Veroff and his associates to explore their findings further by introducing several statistical controls. With controls for age, region, place of residence, and generation, the difference between Catholics and Protestants persisted, but it was restricted to the middle age-group. They could not, therefore, corroborate the findings of Rosen's analysis. However, they interpreted this inconsistency as stemming from the fact that Rosen's nonprobability sample was limited to Northeastern residents who were likely to have high incomes. Within their own sample, Veroff *et al.* found that within this particular group—upper-income Northeasterners—Protestants did have higher need-achievement scores than Catholics.

Lenski's inquiry into the relationship between religion and achievement orientation focused on work-related values, attitudes toward work, and childrearing practices. To assess the impact of religion on work values, he asked respondents to rate the following five characteristics of a job in order of importance: (*a*) high income; (*b*) no danger of being fired; (*c*) short working hours; (*d*) good chances for advancement; and (*e*) interesting work, giving a feeling of satisfaction. Lenski suggested that the first and fourth items expressed the "Protestant ethic" and would, therefore, be differentially ranked by Jews, Catholics, and white Protestants. Yet, this did not turn out to be the case: A quite similar evaluation of all the work characteristics was expressed by each group (1963:89–92).

The religious groups did differ, however, in terms of their members' attitudes toward work. Three separate attitudes were examined: (*a*) positive attitudes, expressing a high evaluation of work for its own sake; (*b*) neutral attitudes, stressing an attraction to work for its extrinsic rewards or for a lack of more attractive alternatives; and (*c*) negative attitudes, suggesting a desire to quit working if it were possible to do so. Jewish males were found most likely to express positive attitudes and least likely to express negative attitudes. Also, white Protestants were somewhat more likely to express positive attitudes than were Catholics or black Protestants. For white Protestants and Catholics, the differences were not reduced when controls were introduced for region of birth, generation, and social class (1963:96–97).

Lenski's final effort to assess differences in orientations toward achievement focused on childrearing values. He sought to determine the relative importance that the members of each religious group attributed to obedience over intellectual autonomy as values they hoped to instill in their children. Using a five-item scale and controlling for respondent's social-class origin, education, and current class position, Lenski concluded that white Protestants were significantly more likely than Catholics to value autonomy over obedience.

Kohn (1969) also addressed the issue of autonomy versus obedience—or, in his terminology, self-direction versus conformity—using data from a national probability sample of fathers and employing much more detailed attitudinal scales to ascertain parental values. Like Lenski, he assumed (although he did not attempt to demonstrate) that self-direction is an important prerequisite for high levels of socioeconomic achievement. In contrast to Lenski, however, Kohn found that religious background had no significant influence on the valuation of self-direction or conformity. With controls for social class (Hollingshead's Index), it appeared that Protestant, Catholic, and Jewish fathers did not, on the average, differ in the emphasis they gave to conformity or self-direction (1969:61). Rather, the most important influence was by far the social class position of the father: The higher the social class, the more highly was self-direction valued over conformity. This was true regardless of religion, sex, order of birth of the child, race, national background, region of the country, and size of the community of current residence (1969:72).

Several other studies have approached the question of religious influence on achievement orientation by asking if religious background and nonsecular education have consequences for occupational values and aspirations. In a study of 4000 college graduates in June, 1961, using a stratified probability sample, Greeley (1963) investigated religious differences in career plans and occupational values. Controlling for sex, hometown size, and SES rank (upper or lower half, based on father's occupation, income, and education), some small differences were found among Catholics, Protestants, and Jews. In general, it appeared that Catholics were more favorably disposed to careers in business, Protestants were more likely to choose education, and Jews were more likely to choose law and medicine. These differences were especially pronounced at the low SES level.

With the same controls in effect, it also appeared that monetary reward was consistently more important to Jews as an occupational value than it was to Catholics, and more important to Catholics than to Protestants (1963:66). When Catholics were compared with Protestant denominations, although without any background variables controlled, Catholics still ranked higher both in terms of the importance of money as an occupational value and in terms of the likelihood of choosing a business career (1963:67–71).

Greeley's inquiry into the possibility that a parochial formal education would alter Catholic values demonstrated that such was not the case. Comparing Catholics who went to Catholic schools—at both the secondary and the college levels—with Catholics who went to non-Catholic schools, there was little indication of major differences in career plans or occupational values (1963:73–85).

That a Catholic education has no important consequences for orientations toward socioeconomic achievement was further supported by Bressler and Westoff (1963). In the same study that was referred to earlier, they included 30 attitude items attempting to tap the relative valuation of achievement. These items fell under three general headings: (*a*) commitment to work; (*b*) drive to get ahead; and (*c*) importance of getting ahead. The analysis revealed, however, that no important differences in achievement values existed between Catholics educated in parochial or in secular schools.

Finally, Featherman (1971) attempted, at the first stage of his longitudinal study, to estimate the importance of motivational variables for explaining group differences in occupational and income achievement. He constructed three motivational scales from questionnaire items and used factor analysis to demonstrate the internal consistency of each. The first index, "Primary Work Orientation," was intended to assess the extent to which work was regarded as an intrinsically satisfying activity. The second scale, "Materialistic Orientation," was used to tap the importance attached to material goals in life. The third index, "Subjective Achievement Orientation," was a measure of the level of an individual's satisfaction with his socioeconomic achievement. Using multiple regression techniques, Featherman discovered that the religioethnic groups could be distinguished in terms of these motivations but that these motivations did not act as intervening variables between group affiliation and occupational and income achievement when social origins and educational background were controlled. It should be recalled that Featherman found religioethnic group affiliation to have a net impact on educational attainment, but, unfortunately, he did not attempt to measure the association between the motivational indexes and this dimension of achievement. Thus, he did not address the issue of whether or not religious affiliation influences educational achievement through an influence on motivations.

Table 9.1 provides a schematic summary of the studies we have reviewed. Before attempting to draw any general conclusions, it will be useful to consider first some of the limitations of these studies.

IV. The Operationalization of Key Concepts

Serious limitations may be imposed on any sociological study by an improper operationalization of concepts. This problem plagues many of the studies of religious affiliation and socioeconomic achievement. In this section, a critical examination will be made of the ways in which several key concepts in these studies have been operationalized. Specifically, this review will focus on the indicators of religious affiliation, of occupational and financial achievement, and of achievement motivation, values, and aspirations.

Religious Affiliation

When measuring religious affiliation, all of the studies reviewed here (except Warren's) fail to distinguish clearly between current and previous religious affiliations of the respondents. This obscures the extent to which religious affiliation is a determinant of the level of socioeconomic achievement or a consequence of it. Warren (1970:143) points out that over 17% of American men change their religious affiliations sometime during their life

TABLE 9.1 Summary of Studies of Religious Affiliation and Socioeconomic Achievement

Study	Sample	Achievement dimensions	Dimension indicators	Religious groups	Control variables	Findings
Lenski (1963)	Detroit, probability	occupation	four categories	Protestants, Catholics	father's occupation, sex	Males only. Upward mobility and status was highest for white Protestants and lowest for black Protestants.
		education	level of schooling, persistence rates	Protestants, Catholics, Jews	father's occupation (for persistence only), sex	Males only. In general, small attainment differences. Catholics had lower persistence rates than Protestants.
		achievement orientation	work values	(same)	none	Similar evaluations of work characteristics by each group.
			attitudes toward work	(same)	(Protestant–Catholic comparison only): social class, region born, generation, sex	Males only. Jews were most positive, followed by white Protestants, then Catholics and black Protestants.
			childrearing values	Protestants, Catholics	race, father's occupation, social class, education	Whites only. Protestants were more likely than Catholics to value autonomy over obedience.
Mayer and Sharp (1962)	Detroit, several probability samples	occupation, income, education	five socioeconomic measures	nine Protestant denominations, Roman Catholics, Eastern Orthodox, Jews	ethnicity, generation, region where reared, community size where reared, time in Detroit	Rank-order of groups in terms of socioeconomic standing: Jews and Eastern Orthodox, Protestant denominations, Roman Catholics.

(continued)

TABLE 9.1, cont.

Study	Sample	Achievement dimensions	Dimension indicators	Religious groups	Control variables	Findings
Mack, Murphy, and Yellin (1956)	national, nonprobability, white male salesmen, bankers, and engineers	occupation	census scale	Protestants, Catholics	father's occupation, age	No significant differences in terms of mobility between and within generations.
Jackson, Fox, and Crockett, Jr. (1970)	national, probability, white males only	occupation	five categories	Protestants, Catholics	father's occupation, region where reared, community size where reared, ethnicity, age, generation	Protestants were more likely to enter professional and business occupations and were more sharply upwardly mobile. Catholics were more likely to enter lower white-collar occupations and were more sharply downwardly mobile.
Gockel (1969)	national, probability, males only	income	respondent's income	10 Protestant denominations, Catholics, Jews, no religion	occupation, race, education, region of current residence, size of current community	No important Protestant–Catholic differences. With other groups included, Congregationalists, Episcopalians, and Jews had somewhat higher incomes than others.
Goldstein (1969)	national (1957 census)	income	respondent's income	Protestants, Catholics, Jews	occupation	Slight Jewish advantage
		occupation	percentage in white-collar occupations	(same)	education, urban residence	Rank-order revealed: Jews, white Protestants, Catholics, nonwhite Protestants.
		education	level of schooling	(same)	sex	(same)

212

Study	Sample	SES variable	Measure	Religious groups	Controls	Findings
Warren 1970	national, probability, males only	occupation	Duncan's SEI	Protestant denominations, Catholics, Jews	father's occupation, education	No net influence of religion on SEI.
		income	respondent's income	(same)	father's occupation, education, occupation	Some net influence of religion: Jews, Episcopalians, Congregationalists, and Presbyterians ranked highest, and Baptists and unspecified Protestants ranked lowest.
		education	years of schooling	(same)	father's occupation, race, region where reared	(same)
Glenn and Hyland (1967)	18 national samples (1943–1965), white males only	income and occupation	(varied by survey)	Protestants, Catholics, Jews	current region, age, current community size	Before controls, Protestants ranked above Catholics in the 1940s but below them in the 1960s. After controls (1960s only), a slight Protestant advantage. In both cases, Jews ranked highest.
		education	years or level of schooling, persistence rates	(same)	region, current community size	Significant Jewish advantage. Minimal Protestant–Catholic differences by the 1960s.
Lipset and Bendix (1959)	2 national probability samples, males only	occupation	first sample: nonmanual, manual, farm; second sample: census scale	Protestant, Catholic	race, generation, and (for first sample only) father's occupation	First sample: No significant differences. Second sample: Protestants had higher status for first and second generations but not for third.
Featherman (1971)	seven of largest SMAs, probability,	occupation and income	NORC scale respondent's income	Anglo-Saxon Protestants, other Protestants, Italian and	father's occupation, size of family of origin, extent of farm or rural residence,	No net influence of religio-ethnic affiliation.

(continued)

213

TABLE 9.1, cont.

Study	Sample	Achievement dimensions	Dimension indicators	Religious groups	Control variables	Findings
	fathers of two children, whites only	education	years of schooling	Mexican Roman Catholics, other Roman Catholics, Jews, no/other religion	education	Some net influence of religio-ethnic affiliation. Rank-order: Jews, Anglo-Saxon Protestants, other Protestants, other Roman Catholics, Italian and Mexican Roman Catholics, no/other religion.
				(same)	(same, minus education)	
		achievement orientation	three motivation scales	(same)	father's occupation, education	The groups were distinguished in terms of motivations, but these motivations had no net influence on later achievement.
Bressler and Westoff (1963)	same as Featherman's	occupation and income	five occupation and income measures	Catholics only	years of schooling	No substantial differences between Catholics educated in parochial schools and Catholics educated in public schools.
		achievement orientation	commitment to work; drive for and importance of getting ahead	(same)	(same)	(same)
Greeley and Rossi (1966)	national, probability	occupation and education	Duncan's SEI, years of schooling	Catholics only	Parents' SES, respondent's knowledge	Slight advantage of Catholics educated in parochial schools over Catholics educated in public schools

Study	Sample		Measure	Groups compared	Controls	Findings
Fox and Jackson (1973)	national, probability, white males only	education	level of schooling, persistence rates	Protestants, Catholics	father's occupation, region of birth, age, ethnicity, current community size, generation	Protestants were somewhat more likely to have a college degree and had substantially higher college persistence rates. Not statistically significant.
Rosen (1969)	four Northeastern states, non-probability	achievement orientation	TAT, achievement values and aspirations	Greek Orthodox, Jews, white Protestants, Roman Catholics	social class	Jews, Greek Orthodox, and white Protestants ranked above the Roman Catholics.
Veroff et al. (1962)	national, probability, white males only	achievement orientation	TAT	Protestants, Catholics, Jews	age, current region, current residence, generation	A net Protestant advantage was found for middle-aged respondents.
Kohn (1969)	national, probability, fathers only	achievement orientation	childrearing values	Protestants, Catholics, Jews	social class	No significant differences among the fathers in terms of their relative valuation of self-direction and conformity.
Greeley (1963)	national, probability, college graduates	achievement orientation	career plans	Protestants, Catholics, Jews	father's SES, hometown size, sex	Protestants were more favorable toward careers in education, Catholics toward business, and Jews toward law and medicine.
			importance of money	(same)	(same)	Rank-order revealed: Jews, Catholics, Protestants
			(same)	Protestant denominations, Catholics	none	Catholics ranked first.
			occupational plans and values	Catholics only	none	No difference between Catholics educated in parochial schools and Catholics educated in public schools

215

cycles, often *in response to* changes in their socioeconomic positions. He reasoned that

> if a person rises substantially above the norm for his religious group or falls substantially below it, he may find that his religious preference no longer reflects his values nor meets his needs; as a result, he may seek a new preference that will reinforce his new socioeconomic position [1970:149].

One obvious way to circumvent this "chicken–egg" dilemma would be to separate those individuals who have changed their religious preferences from those who have not and then to analyze the two groups separately. It is, perhaps, surprising that no research has yet done this.

Some of the studies of religion and achievement confront a second limitation by failing to distinguish among the various denominations of Protestantism. This is problematic, for, as Glock and Stark (1965:121) have suggested, the differences in many religious beliefs among Protestants are greater than the differences in beliefs between Protestants and Catholics. It is quite possible that among the religious beliefs that vary within Protestantism are ones that are conducive to socioeconomic achievement. This would be consistent with Weber's contention that only some of the Protestant denominations embody the spirit of capitalism within their doctrines. Similarly, there may be greater differences among Protestants than between Protestants and Catholics in terms of the various background characteristics that are associated with achievement. Thus, the influence of religious affiliation on socioeconomic achievement may be seriously obscured by lumping all Protestant denominations together. Gockel's study of male income attainment offers one illustration of this. It will be recalled that, whereas he found no significant Catholic–Protestant differences, some significant differences were indeed revealed when the analysis was broadened to examine the Protestant denominations separately.

Occupational Status and Income

The use of occupational status to estimate socioeconomic achievement rests on the assumption that one's share of highly valued material and nonmaterial rewards in society is largely determined by one's occupation. However, the association between such rewards and measures of occupational status may be rather loose. This is certainly the case for income. Jencks (1972:226) observed, for example, that the earnings of individuals in the same occupational categories are almost as unequal as the earnings of individuals taken randomly. Thurow (1975:10) adds that a large dispersion of income within occupations is found even if one examines a more detailed list of occupational titles than the 11-category census scale. It appears, then, that occupational differences among religious groups cannot be used to estimate income differences accurately.

Consequently, those studies that include a separate measure for income give a clearer sense of the way in which religious groups compare in terms of socioeconomic achievement, for it is entirely possible that income and occupational differences will not always be in the same direction (e.g., Warren, 1970).

The strength of the association between occupational status and rewards other than income is not quite as obvious. Parkin (1971:25) argues that there is a fairly strong relationship between occupation and such advantages as long-term income prospects, security of employment, promotion opportunities, better working conditions, and other built-in fringe benefits. This is in accord with common impressions, but empirical support for such a conclusion is not yet extensive. If it is true, however, it encourages confidence that the previous studies that use occupational status as a dependent variable are indeed measuring relative differences in socioeconomic achievement among religious groups. But if it is not true—that is, if these nonincome rewards are as unequally distributed within occupational categories as between them—then there would be little justification for using occupational status as an indicator of socioeconomic achievement.

Assuming for the moment that occupational status is an adequate measure for socioeconomic achievement, it is still necessary to decide upon the relative merits of scales of varying degrees of refinement. On the whole, it would seem that the more occupations included, the better the scale. As the number of occupational categories to be included in a scale increases, however, it becomes less obvious how to rank them. One solution to this problem is the 1947 NORC (North–Hatt) prestige scale. This scale, which was used in several studies of religion and achievement, ranks 90 occupational positions in terms of their relative social evaluation at the national level. It was derived from a national survey that asked respondents to rank the "general standing," in their own opinion, of each of the 90 occupations. They were allowed to choose from six responses, ranging from "excellent standing" to "poor standing," and including a "don't know" category. These occupations were then rank-ordered in terms of the percentage of "excellent" or "good" responses they received.

Although this scale has been widely used, there are several problems that make questionable its utility as a measure of occupational achievement. First, it is doubtful that the respondents offered their evaluation of the prestige or "honor" of each occupation. The question in the NORC study was worded as follows: "For each job mentioned, please pick out the statement that best gives your own personal opinion of the general standing that such a job has [Reiss, Jr., 1961:19]." This does not even seem to solicit from the respondents their evaluation of occupations in terms of honor or prestige. It is, thus, not surprising that Reiss, in an analysis of this study, found that other factors were indeed more important:

The respondents in the NORC study, when asked to rate the "general standing" of occupations, do not appear to have made their evaluation in terms of a conscious awareness of the social prestige attached to the occupation. They are more likely, in fact, to emphasize the relevance of indicators sociologists use to measure socioeconomic status, particularly the *income* of the occupational position and the *education and training needed* [1961:37, emphasis in original].

If respondents ranked occupations in terms of their *perceptions* of other rewards and certain prerequisites rather than in terms of prestige, it is not clear that these perceptions accurately describe the differentials that exist in fact. As with the less-refined scales, it is possible that differences in material and non-material rewards are greater within the 90 occupational categories than between them. If so, the use of the NORC scale may not represent much of an improvement over the other kinds of occupational scales used to index socioeconomic achievement. These limitations also apply to Duncan's Socioeconomic Index (SEI), which is a prestige scale for all occupations but which is based on the prestige scores of the 1947 NORC scale (Reiss, Jr., 1961:109–138). Perhaps a more enlightening approach to measuring the impact of religion on socioeconomic achievement would be to consider the various dimensions of achievement separately, rather than to use occupational scales that blend all of these dimensions together.

Several of the previous studies attempted to estimate the differences in income existing among the members of various religious groups. This focus on income no doubt represents an interest in the general financial situations of these individuals. However, the use of income measures may not be an adequate way of estimating the financial resources of individuals. It may also be necessary to consider their "wealth." Thurow (1975:14) argues that "no assessment of the distribution of economic prizes is complete if it examines either income or wealth alone." He drew this conclusion from an examination of a 1962 Federal Reserve Board study of income and wealth in the United States that showed that individuals earning similar amounts of income owned very different amounts of physical wealth (1975:13).

This finding is significant because it implies that the way in which religious groups differ in terms of income may not be the same as the way in which they differ in terms of total wealth. Because none of the studies reviewed here has considered wealth as a dependent variable, no conclusions can be drawn with regard to the impact of religious affiliation on the financial dimension of socioeconomic achievement.

The use of income as an index of financial status also presents problems for models of achievement when it is employed as a control variable to remove the influence of differential financial resources. First, by ignoring wealth differences, a control for income may not adequately control for substantial financial advantages that some religious groups might enjoy over others.

Failure to control for such advantages might then distort the real net influence of religious affiliation on achievement. A related problem is that a control for income—and/or wealth—does not take into consideration the fact that the level of financial resources available *per person* may differ significantly among religious groups. For example, Catholics at a given level of income and wealth may have a lower level of resources available per person than other religious groups because of their tendency to have larger families (Ryder and Westoff, 1971:68–71). With a lower level of financial resources available to them, children from Catholic families may confront greater obstacles to higher socioeconomic achievement. Thus, controlling for income and wealth without considering average family size fails to eliminate the influence of economic advantage.

Since the studies of religion and achievement previously summarized have included neither controls for wealth nor controls for financial resources available per person, the estimates they provide for the net influence of religious affiliation on socioeconomic achievement must be treated cautiously.

Caution is further warranted by the fact that most of the studies controlled for the influence of social status origins by controlling only father's of head's occupational status, based on the manual–nonmanual dichotomy, the census categories, or the 1947 NORC prestige scale. However, this may be a source of misleading estimates of the true influence of social origins, for, as mentioned, there is only a loose association between occupational status and income and wealth.

It may be noted, finally, that the studies of religion and achievement, using these measures of occupational status and income, do not offer any clear insight into the way in which religion might influence achievement at the *highest* levels of the socioeconomic structure. The measures of achievement were too crude to isolate "elites" from "nonelites," and the samples were too small to capture any significant number of elites suitable for statistical analysis. Yet, it is entirely possible that the process of achievement at the elite level is substantially different from the process of achievement among nonelite positions, with religion playing an important role at the former level and not at the latter.

In a study of strategic elites, Keller (1963) found most of such elites to be Protestant (especially Presbyterian and Episcopalian), suggesting that religious affiliation is indeed associated with achievement at the elite level. She also found that Protestant, Catholic, and Jewish elites had experienced different paths of upward mobility. Among business elites, for example, Jews rose primarily from middle and upper-middle class business families, whereas Catholic business leaders rose to those statuses from lower-class origins and through expanding business bureaucracies (1963:208–209). These comments should illustrate the point that it may not be accurate to draw inferences about the influence of religious affiliation on the attainment of elite positions from studies that do not pay attention to elites.

Orientations toward Achievement

Just as the measures of occupational status cast some doubt on the findings of studies reviewed here, so too are the various measures of achievement orientation a source of skepticism. Several of the studies previously summarized attempted to assess the extent to which members of some religious groups, on the average, have a greater psychological "need for achievement" than do the members of other religious groups. The technique used to measure need-achievement was the Thematic Apperception Test. The theoretical rationale behind this instrument is the Freudian hypothesis that motivations are revealed in fantasy (McClelland *et al.,* 1953:107). Thus, it was expected that an individual motivated to achieve would fantasize about achievement, and the TAT was considered to be a means for tapping such an achievement predisposition. According to this procedure, respondents are presented with a series of pictures that show individuals engaged in some ambiguous action and are then asked to write or to tell an imaginative story about each picture. These stories are coded for their achievement imagery, which is then taken to be an index of an individual's psychological need for achievement. An essential criterion for accepting a respondent's story as indicative of achievement motivation is the inclusion in the story of references to an achievement goal.

This attempt to assess a predisposition toward achievement by means of the Thematic Apperception Test is open to various criticisms. Important among these is the doubt that the stories that subjects provide in response to pictorial cues can actually be used to discriminate need-achievement from other concerns and interests of the subjects. Turner has suggested, for example, that the test might reveal what the subjects have been anxious about or simply what they have experienced in day-to-day situations (see Crockett, Jr., 1966:295).

Although there may be measurement difficulties associated with the concept of need-achievement, there is another, perhaps more crucial, limitation. This concerns the actual appropriateness of the concept for models of socioeconomic achievement. The measurement of need-achievement does not indicate specific types of achievement activity. Thus, knowing that members of some groups have higher need-achievement scores than the members of other groups tells nothing about their degree of commitment to high *socioeconomic* achievement. Recognizing this, Rosen suggested that it is also necessary to know their socioeconomic achievement values and aspirations. This implies, however, that the three variables may not always vary in the same directions, at least theoretically. For example, it implies that strong socioeconomic achievement values and aspirations may coexist with low need-achievement. Yet, if need-achievement is defined as "concern over competition with a standard of excellence,'' individuals with strong socioeconomic achievement values and aspirations also have, by definition, high need-achievement. On the other hand, it does not follow that individuals with weak socioeconomic achievement values and aspirations have low need-achievement; socioeconomic achievement is not the only achievement goal that the need-achievement score depends on. It is unlikely, however, that high need-achievement, in the context of weak socioeconomic achievement values and aspirations, will be conducive to high socioeconomic achievement. What all of this seems to suggest is that knowing the need-achievement scores of individuals, if it were possible, would provide little understanding of their predispositions toward actual socioeconomic achievement. It would be more fruitful to focus exclusively on socioeconomic achievement values and aspirations.

It is interesting to note that, among the studies of religion and socioeconomic achievement that did focus on values and aspirations, there is a marked similarity in the types of survey questions used to measure them. Unfortunately, however, there appear to be some rather severe limitations imposed by the form and wording of these questions. Space limitations make it impossible to reproduce and criticize here each question from every survey; only a handful of items will be subjected to scrutiny. But this should be sufficient to make the point that these studies have not satisfactorily measured achievement values. The questions used may be categorized under four general headings: (*a*) the importance of "getting ahead"; (*b*) orientations toward work; (*c*) the relative importance of various job characteristics; and (*d*) childrearing values.

Table 9.2 presents several representative questions from each category and in-

TABLE 9.2 Sample of Items Used to Measure Achievement Values

Item	Response options	Study
A. Importance of getting ahead		
1) I spend a lot of time thinking about how to improve my chances of getting ahead.	yes–no	Bressler and Westoff, 1963; Featherman, 1971
2) Getting ahead is one of the most important things in life to me.	yes–no	(same)
3) Would you be willing to leave your friends (or parents) in order to get ahead?	yes–no	Bressler and Westoff, 1963; Rosen, 1969
B. Work orientation		
1) If I inherited so much money that I didn't have to work, I'd still work at the same thing I am now doing.	yes–no	Bressler and Westoff, 1963; Featherman, 1971
2) I would much rather relax around the house all day than go to work.	yes–no	(same)

(continued)

TABLE 9.2, cont.

Item	Response options	Study
3) Some people tell us that they could not really be happy unless they were working at some job. But others say that they would be a lot happier if they didn't have to work. How do you feel about this?	open-ended	Lenski, 1963
C. Job characteristics		
1) All a man should want out of life in the way of a career is a secure, not-too-difficult job with enough pay to afford a nice car and, eventually, a home of his own.	agree–disagree	Rosen, 1969
2) Which of the following things would you most prefer in a job? Which comes next? Which comes third? -high income -no danger of being fired -short working hours -good chance for advancement -the work is interesting and gives a sense of accomplishment	forced ranking	Lenski, 1963
3) Which of these characteristics would be very important to you in picking a job or career?[a] -making a lot of money -opportunities to be helpful to others or useful to society -living and working in the world of ideas	pick as many as apply	Greeley, 1963
D. Childrearing values		
Which of the following qualities would you pick as the most important for a child to have? Which comes next? Which comes third? -to be obedient -to be well-liked or popular -to think for himself -to help others when they need help	forced ranking	Lenski, 1963; Kohn[b] 1969

[a] NOTE: This is a partial list only.
[b] NOTE: Kohn's scale includes additional characteristics.

dicates the studies employing them, either exactly as stated or in slightly modified form.

One criticism that applies to several of the items is that they do not distinguish between what an individual values "in general" and what an individual values *given his or her particular situation* at the time of the interview. They do not force respondents to ignore their own situations in stating the importance they attach to certain values. For example, items B–1 and B–2 do not refer to just *any* job in the labor force; rather, the respondents are asked about the importance and desirability of their *own* jobs. Thus, it is possible that those who say they would prefer to work are individuals who have interesting jobs, and perhaps they would have chosen the other alternative—that is, not to work—had they been employed in different jobs. Moreover, it may be that respondents, when asked about working in general (B–3), could not answer that question honestly, for they may know little about jobs other than those that they have held. Items C–2 and C–3 ignore the current employment and financial situations of the respondents. Those who do not place prime importance on making a lot of money may be individuals who already have a comfortable financial background that they take for granted when answering the questions, and they may, as a result, be more concerned with other job characteristics. This would not indicate, however, that such individuals value money less than they value those other characteristics or that they value making money less than do other individuals who state that it is their most important concern in a job.

A second criticism of many of the questions about values is the vagueness of the central ideas. For example, "to get ahead" (A–1,2,3) may mean different things to different people. For some people it may refer to higher income, whereas for others it may refer to a more intrinsically satisfying job or to breaking into more prestigious social circles. These do not necessarily go together, and the sacrifices one may be willing to make on their behalf may vary considerably. Yet, the phrase "to get ahead" can be construed to refer to any of them. Hence, it does not discriminate clearly among different kinds of success values. These questions also ignore the fact that some people who would like very much to "get ahead" may not contemplate it seriously if they believe that their prospects are dim. And those who have already made great strides in their careers may believe that they have already "gotten ahead" and may not aspire to still further advancement. It would be misleading, however, to conclude that "getting ahead" is not an important value for such people.

There is also a problem inherent in questions that force respondents to rank certain preferences in order of importance (e.g., items C–2, D). It is quite possible that many respondents find the choices difficult to rank in any particular order. They may, for example, attach equal or similar importance to *several* of the choices. If so, the rank orders they provide will be arbitrary,

Similarly, forcing respondents to answer categorically "yes–no" or "agree–disagree" may exaggerate the degree of conviction with which they hold such values.

For each of these reasons, the studies that have investigated the relationship between religion and socioeconomic achievement values fail to clarify the nature of this relationship.

V. Problems in Interpreting the Role of Religious Doctrines

Given the various problems that afflict studies of religion and socioeconomic achievement, the precise nature of this relationship is still in question. Even if it could be shown that religious affiliation does have some net impact on achievement, though, the existing studies offer no support for the proposition that such differences can ultimately be traced to the influence of variant religious doctrines. This stems from the fact that no attempts were made—with the exception of Lenski's effort—to measure the actual religious beliefs of respondents and then to relate these beliefs to levels of socioeconomic achievement. Even if different orientations toward worldly activity are emphasized by the teachings of different religious groups, knowing an individual's religious affiliation does not necessarily indicate the extent to which the individual has internalized or is committed to the teachings of his or her denomination.

Only Lenski (1963) made an effort to tap religious beliefs and to relate them to achievement. He constructed a measure of "doctrinal orthodoxy" to assess the degree of acceptance of the prescribed doctrines of one's church. However, the particular *content* of the religious beliefs adhered to by members of various churches was ignored. He only asked, for example, such questions as whether one believes in God and how much time one spends praying (1963:25, 56).

In addition to the inadequacy of much of the empirical data, there are several potent theoretical reasons for expecting religious doctrines and, hence, religious values and beliefs to be of no consequence at all for achievement. One such reason lies with contradictory interpretations of the various doctrines as they relate to achievement values. In contrast to Weber, several scholars claim that, historically, Catholic dogma was no less conducive to a "capitalist ethos" than were Calvinist and Protestant teachings. Robertson (1965) argues, for example, that the Roman Catholic Churches stressed the same economic precepts in the sixteenth and seventeenth centuries. A similar interpretation is offered by Greeley (1964), who notes that

> Within the Church of Rome there is and has been room for all kinds of divergent and paradoxical emphases to such an extent that simple statements about its position are

extremely risky. . . . Indeed, the rationalization of human striving attributed to the Calvinists can with equal justice be attributed to the Jesuits [1964:31].

A similar debate between Weber and Sombart concerning the influence of Judaism on the rise of capitalism also raised conflicting interpretations of Judaic dogma (Lenski, 1963:113).

In general, if similar inducements for socioeconomic achievement can be found within the teachings of different religious traditions, it is questionable whether or not such teachings are an important source of actual achievement differentials among religious groups.

Another reason for doubting the importance of religious doctrines is that achievement norms and values seem to be more clearly the domain of social institutions other than religious bodies. Glock and Stark (1965) suggest that this is part of a more general characteristic of modern societies in which the norms and values for secular behavior are not significantly informed by religious teachings. They make the following assertion:

> Confronted on the one hand by the abstract prescriptions of religion and on the other by the concrete norms and values made explicit by law, by the context in which they labor, and by secular groups, men are almost inexorably led to follow the latter— partly because these sanctioning systems are more salient, but also because the nature of a religiously inspired choice is not clear [1965:183].

It has also been suggested that if religious groups are characterized by distinctive normative and value patterns, it is quite plausible that these patterns are a consequence of the historical and cultural experiences or traditions of the groups (Greeley, 1963, Herberg, 1956, Winter, 1962). Greeley's contention offers an illustration of this point of view:

> We would certainly hold with Lenski that religious groups are primary groups which form segregated communication networks limited to the adherents of the same faith and facilitating the development and transmission of distinctive political and economic norms, or, alternatively, distinctive role images. We would merely affirm that these differences do not flow from religious ideology but from cultural experience [1963:129].

It appears, then, that the argument for religiously inspired socioeconomic behavior is less than compelling.

VI. Conclusions

The foregoing review of the major studies investigating the relationship between religious affiliation and socioeconomic achievement has found these studies to be plagued by serious conceptual and methodological deficiencies. Among these are the failure of many studies to treat Protestant denominations independently, the use of problematic occupational scales to estimate social status origins as well as socioeconomic achievement, the use of income as the sole index of financial rewards, the inappropriate concern with need-achievement measures, the focus on current religious preference, and the failure to measure religious beliefs and commitment directly.

Research strategies were also found to be deficient. For example, some of the studies relied on nonprobability samples. Also, in most of the studies, several important controls were not simultaneously included, with the result that any net difference observed between religious groups might easily be attributed to the noncontrolled variables.

For all of these reasons, whether or not religious affiliation is an important attribute to consider in the process of socioeconomic achievement in American society is still an open empirical question. However, it may be said on behalf of these studies that, despite the differences in their samples, research designs, and measurements of variables, they generally point to the same conclusion, which is that *religious affiliation does not explain much of the variance in socioeconomic achievement.* The debate actually seems to concern whether religious affiliation has *any* net impact at all that cannot be accounted for by other important variables and that may be attributed to religious values and beliefs. This is not surprising when one considers the aforementioned ambiguities in the various religious doctrines and the minimal role played by churches in informing achievement norms and values.

Acknowledgments

I would like to thank Melvin Tumin, Suzanne Keller, and JoAnn Shotwell for commenting on an earlier draft of this paper.

References

Blau, Peter M., and Otis Dudley Duncan
    1967 *The American Occupational Structure.* New York: Wiley.
Bressler, Marvin, and Charles F. Westoff
    1963 "Catholic education, economic values and achievement." *American Journal of Sociology* 69:225–233.
Crockett, Harry J. Jr.
    1966 "Psychological origins of mobility." Pp. 270–309 in N. J. Smelser and S. M. Lipset (eds.), *Social Structure and Mobility in Economic Development.* Chicago: Aldine.

Featherman, David L.
  1971 "The socioeconomic achievement of white religio-ethnic subgroups: Social and psychological explanations." *American Sociological Review* 31:207–222.

Fox, William S., and Elton F. Jackson
  1973 "Protestant–Catholic differences in educational achievement and persistence in school." *Journal for the Scientific Study of Religion* 12:65–84.

Glenn, Norval D., and Ruth Hyland
  1967 "Religious preference and worldly success: Some evidence from national surveys." *American Sociological Review* 32:73–85.

Glock, Charles Y., and Rodney Stark
  1965 *Religion and Society in Tension.* Chicago: Rand McNally.

Gockel, Galen
  1969 "Income and religious affiliation: A regression analysis." *American Journal of Sociology* 74:632–647.

Goldstein, Sidney
  1969 "Socioeconomic differentials among religious groups in the United States." *American Journal of Sociology* 74:348–355.

Greeley, Andrew M.
  1963 *Religion and Career; A Study of College Graduates.* New York: Sheed and Ward.
  1964 "The Protestant ethnic: Time for a moratorium." *Sociological Analysis* 25:20–33.

Greeley, Andrew M., and Peter H. Rossi
  1966 *The Education Of Catholic Americans.* Chicago: Aldine.

Herberg, Will
  1956 *Protestant, Catholic, Jew.* Garden City: Doubleday.

Jackson, Elton F., William S. Fox, and Harry Crockett, Jr.
  1970 "Religion and occupational achievement." *American Sociological Review* 35:48–63.

Jencks, C., M. Smith, H. Ackland, M. Jo Bane, D. Cohen, H. Gintis, B. Heyns, and S. Michelson
  1972 *Inequality: A Reassessment of the Effects of Family and Schooling in America.* New York: Basic Books.

Keller, Suzanne I.
  1963 *Beyond the Ruling Class; Strategic Elites in Modern Society.* New York: Random House.

Kohn, Melvin L.
  1969 *Class and Conformity; A Study in Values.* Homewood, Illinois: Dorsey.

Lenski, Gehard
  1963 *The Religious Factor.* New York: Doubleday.

Lipset, Seymour M., and Reinhard Bendix
  1959 *Social Mobility in Industrial Society.* Berkeley: University of California Press.

Mack, Raymond, Raymond J. Murphy, and Seymour Yellin
  1956 "The Protestant ethic, level of aspiration and social mobility: An empirical test." *American Sociological Review* 21:295–300.

McClelland, D. C., J. Atkinson, R. Clark, and E. Lowell
  1953 *The Achievement Motive.* New York: Appleton-Century-Crofts.

Mayer, Albert, and Harry Sharp
  1962 "Religious preference and worldly success." *American Sociological Review* 27:218–227.

Parkin, Frank
    1971   *Class Inequality and Political Order.* New York: Praeger.
Reiss, Albert J. Jr.
    1961   *Occupations and Social Status.* New York: Free Press.
Robertson, H. M.
    1965   "A criticism of Max Weber and his school." Pp. 65–86 in Robert W. Green (ed.), *Protestantism and Capitalism; The Weber Thesis and Its Critics.* Boston: D. C. Heath.
Rosen, Bernard C.
    [1959] "Race, ethnicity, and the achievement syndrome." Reprinted as pp. 131–153 in B. C.
    1969   Rosen, H. J. Crockett, and C. Z. Nunn (eds.), *Achievement in American Society.* Cambridge, Massachusetts: Schenkman.
Thurow, Lester C.
    1975   *Generating Inequality; Mechanisms of Distribution in the U.S. Economy.* New York: Basic Books.
Veroff, Joseph, Gerald Gurin, and Sheila Feld
    1962   "Achievement motivation and religious background." *American Sociological Review* 27:205–218.
Warren, Bruce
    1970   "Socioeconomic achievement and religion." Pp. 130–155 in E. O. Laumann (ed.), *Social Stratification: Research and Theory for the 1970s.* New York: Bobbs-Merrill.
Weber, Max
    1958   *The Protestant Ethic and the Spirit of Capitalism* (translated by Talcott Parsons). New York: Charles Scribner's Sons.
Ryder, Norman B., and Charles F. Westoff
    1971   *Reproduction in the United States: 1965.* Princeton, New Jersey: Princeton University Press.
Winter, Gibson
    1962   "Methodological reflections on *The Religious Factor.*" *Journal for the Scientfic Study of Religion* 2:53–63.

Part III

NEW DIRECTIONS IN RESEARCH ON RELIGION AND SOCIAL CHANGE

Chapter 10

The Blending of Catholic
Reproductive Behavior

CHARLES F. WESTOFF

I. Introduction

The demographic study of religious groups in the United States is seriously impeded by the lack of any official statistics on religion. With the one exception of a question on religion included by the Bureau of the Census in the March 1957 Current Population Survey (U.S. Bureau of the Census)—an adventure that was quickly frustrated by the objections of several religious organizations—there has been no effort by federal agencies to collect such information. In fact, there is resistance to such proposals. The result of this lack of data is that our knowledge of the demographic and of other characteristics of religious groups is derived from special surveys, most of which have been conducted by university research organizations.

The particular focus of this review is to summarize the most salient features of such survey findings on the trend of religious differentials in reproductive behavior. The primary focus is on the Catholic–non-Catholic differential, which has carried special significance for contraception, for abortion, and for

The Religious Dimension:
New Directions in Quantitative Research

fertility itself. The time frame is 1951 to 1975, with emphasis on the last 10 years of this period. The data are from national probability sample surveys of currently married women of reproductive age; these were conducted every 5 years between 1955 and 1975 (Freedman, Whelpton, and Campbell, 1959; Ryder and Westoff, 1971; Westoff and Ryder, 1977; Whelpton, Cambell, and Patterson, 1966). Because of additional limitations on the 1975 study, the data presented here are confined to currently married, white women who have been married only once, married less than 25 years, and married before the age of 25.

II. Contraceptive Behavior

The traditional and still official stance of the Roman Catholic Church has been to ban any use of contraceptive methods other than periodic continence (the rhythm method). In Table 10.1 we have assembled data from the five fertility surveys on the trend in the conformity of Catholics to this Church position on birth control. "Conformity" is defined as having never used any method of contraception or having used only the rhythm method. The table is organized by marriage cohort and by duration of marriage. The change over time is dramatic: The cohort married in 1931–1935 (by 20–24 years of marriage) showed 73.3% of Catholics conforming, in contrast with 30.0% after that length of marriage for the cohort of 1951–1955. Sharp declines in confor-

TABLE 10.1 Percentage of Catholic Women Aged 18-39 Who Conformed with Church Teaching on Birth Control by Never Using any Form of Contraception or by Using the Rhythm Method Only

| Marriage cohort | Duration of marriage | | | | |
	< 5	5–9	10–14	15–19	20–24
1931–1935					73.3
1936–1940				66.6	63.3
1941–1945			60.4	50.0	47.0
1946–1950		58.0	60.2	46.2	37.0
1951–1955	80.3	50.6	48.7	42.9	30.0
1956–1960	67.5	45.8	40.5	16.4	
1961–1965	52.6	26.6	19.3		
1966–1970	21.2	4.5			
1971–1975	9.5				

Sources: Estimates on the first diagonal are from the 1955 Growth of American Family Study; those on the second diagonal are from the 1960 Growth of American Family Study. Estimates on the third, fourth, and fifth diagonals are from the 1965, 1970, and 1975 National Fertility Studies, respectively.

This table is reproduced from Charles F. Westoff, "The Secularization of U.S. Catholic Birth Control Practices," *Family Planning Perspectives* 9, September/October 1977, p. 203.

mity are evident in all of the earlier marriage duration categories as well. By 1975, among those married less than five years, only 9.5% were in conformity with Church teaching on birth control. Considering the number of years of marriage remaining to this cohort, only a very small fraction can be expected to be in conformity by the end of their reproductive lives.

A similar analysis (not shown here) was conducted for Catholic women who, as indexed by the frequency they report receiving Communion, are active participants in their church's religious obligations. Among those receiving Communion at least once a month, the pattern of change was very similar to that in Table 10.1 for all Catholic women (Westoff and Jones, 1977: 204).

A detailed comparison of the actual methods of contraception currently used by Catholics and non-Catholics is presented in Table 10.2. It is of interest whether certain methods are adopted by Catholics that might be regarded as less of a deviation from Church teaching than others. A pattern of convergence

TABLE 10.2 Current Contraceptive Exposure, 1965–1975, for non-Catholic and Catholic Women less than Forty-five Years of Age (Distributions in 1965 and 1975 Standardized by 1970 Marriage Duration Composition)

	Non-Catholic			Catholic		
Type of exposure	1975	1970	1965	1975	1970	1965
Total number	2434	2780	1975	895	1004	851
Percentage of total	100.0	100.0	100.0	100.0	100.0	100.0
Using contraception	79.9	69.2	70.0	76.4	63.2	58.5
Not using contraception	20.1	30.8	30.0	23.6	36.8	41.5
Pregnant, postpartum trying to get pregnant	11.6	14.0	14.2	13.2	17.6	21.2
Sterile and other nonuse	8.5	16.8	15.8	10.4	19.2	20.3
Number of users	1938	1923	1396	679	635	505
Percentage of total users	100.0	100.0	100.0	100.0	100.0	100.0
Wife sterilized	17.5	7.5	5.5	12.9	4.6	2.5
Husband sterilized	15.6	8.3	5.1	13.1	3.6	1.3
Pill	34.3	36.2	30.7	34.2	33.1	21.8
IUD	9.0	7.1	1.2	7.6	8.8	0.8
Diaphragm	4.1	6.5	12.8	3.5	3.5	4.2
Condom	9.6	15.3	23.4	14.9	13.2	18.3
Withdrawal	1.8	2.0	3.4	2.4	3.5	5.7
Foam	3.9	6.7	3.4	2.6	6.3	2.2
Rhythm	1.7	3.6	4.2	5.9	17.8	31.8
Douche	0.5	2.5	3.5	0.3	1.6	3.2
Other	2.0	4.4	6.7	2.6	4.1	8.1

Source: This table is adapted from Table 3 in Charles F. Westoff, "The Secularization of U.S. Catholic Birth Control Practices," *Family Planning Perspectives* 9, September/October 1977, p. 203.

between 1965 and 1975 is clearly discernible. The only method for which there are appreciably fewer Catholic users is for sterilization. By 1975, a total of 33.1% of non-Catholic users had been sterilized, as compared with 26.0% of Catholics. However, judging from the growth in the popularity of these procedures among Catholics over the decade (only 3.8% of users had been sterilized by 1965), it appears that Catholics are clearly participating in the large-scale trend toward surgical sterilization observed in the general population.

The inescapable conclusion from this evidence is that Catholic contraceptive behavior has lost almost all of its distinctiveness; by 1980, there will be nothing to differentiate Catholics from non-Catholics in this area. Since the U.S. Conference of Catholic Bishops only recently reaffirmed the traditional stance on birth control, the impasse between the official position and the behavior of U.S. Catholic married couples can only grow worse. A crisis of authority within the Church has been an obvious result of this impasse, and it seems likely that some relaxation of the official position will occur sometime in the future.

III. Attitudes toward Abortion

Although some softening of the position of the Vatican or of the clergy is a likely outcome of the impasse between teaching and practice on contraception, there is no evidence of any such development in connection with abortion. The Catholic Church has aligned itself very clearly on the side of the Right to Life lobby and similar antiabortion groups. Although the most interesting questions concern the extent of Catholic women's reliance on abortion and the trend over time in Catholic abortion rates, no data on such subjects exist, and we must be content with assessing the attitudes of Catholics toward abortion and the extent to which they seem to be converging over time with the attitudes of non-Catholics.

A series of seven questions was asked in the 1965, 1970, and 1975 surveys. The wording and order of the questions was the same in each year. The format reads as follows:

"I'm going to read you a list of seven possible reasons why a woman might have a pregnancy interrupted. Would you tell me whether you think it would be all right for a woman to do this:

1. If the pregnancy seriously endangered the woman's health?
2. If the woman was not married?
3. If the couple could not afford another child?
4. If they didn't want any more children?
5. If the woman had good reason to believe the child might be deformed?

6. If the woman had been raped?
7. If the woman wanted it for any reason?''
   (Question 7 was asked only in 1970 and in 1975.)

As the distributions of the responses to these questions suggest in Table 10.3, the items form two clusters—the "hard" reasons (health, rape, and deformity), on which the majority of both Catholics and non-Catholics approved abortion in 1975, and the "soft" reasons (unmarried, money, no more, and any reason), on which the majority still disapprove of abortion. Although there has been an almost completely consistent increase between 1965 and 1970 and between 1970 and 1975 in approval of abortion for every reason cited for both Catholics and non-Catholics, there is evidence of convergence between the two groups only for the "hard" reasons. Catholics and non-Catholics have diverged across the decade in their approval of abortion for all of the "soft" reasons as a result of greater absolute increases in approval by non-Catholics.

The six items common to all three surveys are summarized in an index (a simple summation of the number of items approved) in Table 10.4, where the mean index score is shown for Catholics and for non-Catholics by marriage cohort and marriage duration. The strong effect of the trend between 1965 and 1975 is seen for both Catholics and non-Catholics: The attitude toward abortion becomes more favorable at all durations with each new cohort (the vertical comparison in Table 10.4) as well as with increasing duration within a cohort (the horizontal comparison). The bottom panel shows a mixed picture of the trend in the religious differential, no doubt because of the combination in this index of the "soft" and "hard" items on which the trend is different for Catholics and for non-Catholics.

To summarize: There is clear evidence of a sharp increase in favorable at-

TABLE 10.3 The Percentage of Catholic and non-Catholic Women under Forty-five Years of Age Who approve[a] of Abortion under Various Circumstances: 1965, 1970, 1975

	Catholic			Non-Catholic			Percentage difference (NC–C)		
Circumstance	1975	1970	1965	1975	1970	1965	1975	1970	1965
Health	88.6	81.8	76.7	96.1	92.9	93.4	7.5	11.1	16.7
Rape	72.4	61.6	42.5	82.5	76.1	57.1	10.1	14.5	14.6
Deformity	67.8	58.8	40.8	81.0	74.8	57.6	13.2	16.0	16.8
Unmarried	31.2	20.7	8.6	48.3	35.4	13.3	17.1	14.7	4.7
Money	27.2	15.6	7.9	41.6	28.4	11.8	14.4	12.8	3.9
No more	26.2	13.6	5.0	40.7	23.7	7.9	14.5	10.1	2.9
Any reason	22.5	9.8	NA	34.4	18.3	NA	11.9	8.5	NA

[a] Responses other than "yes" or "no" and no answers, which collectively ranged from 1–6%, were excluded from the calculation of the percentage approving.

TABLE 10.4 Mean Index Score on Attitudes toward Abortion for Catholic and non-Catholic Women under Forty-five Years of Age, by Marriage Cohort and Duration of Marriage: 1965, 1970, 1975

Marriage cohort	< 5	5–9	10–14	15–19	20–24
Catholics					
1941–1945					1.77
1946–1950				2.00	2.59
1951–1955			1.89	2.34	2.82
1956–1960		1.67	2.48	2.89	
1961–1965	1.74	2.65	2.97		
1966–1970	2.54	2.94			
1971–1975	3.57				
Non-Catholics					
1941–1945					2.55
1946–1950				2.60	3.21
1951–1955			2.36	3.36	3.78
1956–1960		2.31	3.32	3.76	
1961–1965	2.34	3.37	3.84		
1966–1970	3.37	3.84			
1971–1975	4.08				
Difference (NC – C)					
1941–1945					.78
1946–1950				.60	.62
1951–1955			.47	1.02	.96
1956–1960		.64	.84	.87	
1961–1965	.60	.72	.87		
1966–1970	.83	.90			
1971–1975	.51				

titudes toward abortion between 1965 and 1975 among both Catholics and non-Catholics. Because this change in attitude has increased at approximately the same rate in both groups (although differentially for hard and soft items), no convergence has yet occurred. The average Catholic attitude in 1975 was about at the level that non-Catholic attitudes were between 1965 and 1970, although there is some evidence that newly married Catholic women (duration less than 5 years) are closing the distance from non-Catholics more rapidly.

IV. Fertility

As far as can be determined from fragmentary and indirect evidence, Catholic fertility in the early decades of the twentieth century was significantly higher than non-Catholic fertility (Barnett, 1965; Robinson, 1936; and Stouffer, 1935). Between the 1920s and 1940s, some convergence seemed to be occurring, perhaps connected with the increasing proportion of native-born

Catholic Americans (Jaffe, 1939). Just prior to the baby boom, there was, evidently, considerable convergence in the making (Freedman, Whelpton, and Campbell, 1959). This trend was sharply reversed during the baby boom of the 1950s.

In this section, we reconstruct marital fertility rates (from birth record data) for marriage cohorts, beginning with the cohort of 1936–1940, up to the 1971–1975 cohort. In order to increase the reliability of observations, we have merged the early survey data, in effect treating the surveys as a single sample. Two measures of marital fertility are employed: Cumulative births by marriage cohort and duration (Table 10.5) and a period rate, the total marital fertility rate (TMFR), which is a summation of duration-specific rates and can be interpreted as the number of births a married woman would have by the end of a specified number of years of marriage if she reproduced at the then current rates of women at each duration of marriage. These TMFR's are plotted in 2-year averages in Figure 10.1 for the period 1951–1975, a period that shows

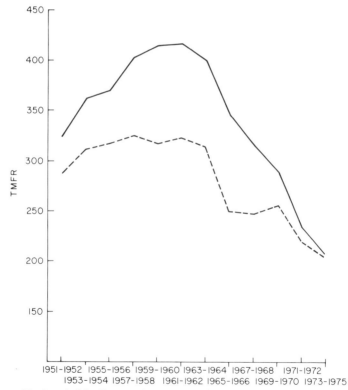

Figure 10.1 Total marital fertility rates for Catholics and non-Catholics from survey data: 1951–1975. [From Charles F. Westoff and Elise F. Jones, "The End of Catholic Fertility," *Demography* 16 (2).]

TABLE 10.5 Cumulative Number of Births by Duration of Marriage for Catholic and non-Catholic Marriage Cohorts, Based on Merged Survey Data

Marriage cohort	Cumulative births by average duration (years)				Number of women			
	2.5	7.5	12.5	17.5	2.5	7.5	12.5	17.5
Catholics								
1936–1940	.61	1.92	2.78	3.26	150	150	150	150
1941–1945	.72	1.99	2.76	3.13	346	346	346	206·
1946–1950	.87	2.28	3.18	3.74	671	671	463	318
1951–1955	.89	2.67	3.62	3.97	656	501	348	167
1956–1960	1.15	2.82	3.36	3.57	512	392	213	155
1961–1965	1.06	2.32	2.86		427	226	162	
1966–1970	.92	2.00			277	200		
1971–1975	.62				282			
Non-Catholics								
1936–1940	.55	1.66	2.34	2.72	440	440	440	440
1941–1945	.68	1.89	2.55	2.91	992	992	992	616
1946–1950	.77	2.04	2.72	3.03	1694	1694	1240	882
1951–1955	.84	2.20	2.80	2.92	1529	1170	853	463
1956–1960	.87	2.24	2.72	2.88	1233	956	521	390
1961–1965	.83	1.93	2.36		1027	628	476	
1966–1970	.73	1.70			733	505		
1971–1975	.57				760			
Ratio non-Catholic–Catholic								
1936–1940	.90	.86	.84	.83				
1941–1945	.94	.95	.92	.93				
1946–1950	.89	.89	.86	.81				
1951–1955	.94	.82	.77	.74				
1956–1960	.76	.79	.81	.81				
1961–1965	.78	.83	.83					
1966–1970	.79	.85						
1971–1975	.92							

Source: Charles F. Westoff and Elise F. Jones, ''The End of 'Catholic' Fertility,'' *Demography* 16 (2).

the baby boom as well as the rapid decline in marital fertility beginning in the early 1960s.

The real cohort data (Table 10.5) show the historical record of change. At each duration, there is an indication of the early movement toward convergence of Catholic and non-Catholic fertility, followed by sharp reversal and divergence for the cohorts whose early childbearing occurred during the baby boom, and then a return to convergence after the baby boom.

The period, or synthetic cohort, TMFR provides a more current view of the religious reproductive differential. The series that is plotted in Figure 10.1 was checked against a similar marital fertility rate for white women in the U.S. Vital Statistics data, and a very close fit was observed for the 25 years, a finding that increases confidence in the validity of this reconstruction.

The trend of the differential is clearly revealed in Figure 10.1, with the disproportionate increase in Catholic fertility during the baby boom causing the divergence, and then the more precipitous decline in Catholic fertility resulting in a sharp convergence by 1973-1975. The rates for this latest period are only slightly over two births per woman.

V. Summary and Conclusions

The recent changes in American Catholic reproductive behavior seem to be very clear: There has been a dramatic move toward convergence of Catholic with non-Catholic contraceptive behavior and fertility. Attitudes toward abortion reveal a strong trend among Catholics toward a greater acceptance, but the rate of change among non-Catholics has been about the same, so that convergence has not occurred except for the strongest reasons (health, rape, deformity of the fetus). But this is an observation only about the trend in *attitude* toward abortion; we know nothing about religious differences in abortion rates per se. However, with respect to behavior, we do know that Catholics can no longer be characterized as a distinctive group in terms of contraception or of fertility.

This convergence, which had been evident for several decades before World War II, was, undoubtedly, a response to the broad processes of assimilation that were rapidly minimizing the differences between Catholics and other Americans. However, the trend toward convergence was reversed during the baby boom as Catholic fertility increased much more sharply than non-Catholic fertility. There is no really satisfactory explanation of this divergence between 1955-1956 and 1961-1962. This dramatic increase was followed by an equally dramatic decline that was undoubtedly accelerated by the growing popularity of the pill during the period of moral ambiguity of the mid-sixties preceding the Papal Encyclical of 1968 that reaffirmed the traditional teaching of the Church on birth control. It is possible, of course, that the fertility of the two groups will diverge again in the future, but, in view of the almost universal adoption of the whole range of modern contraceptive methods by contemporary Catholics and the blending of Catholics into the mainstream of American life, any such divergence seems very unlikely.

References

Barnett, Larry D.
1965   "Religious differentials in fertility planning and fertility in the United States." *Family Life Coordinator* 14:161–170.

Freedman, R., P. K. Whelpton, and A. A. Campbell
1959   *Family Planning, Sterility and Population Growth.* New York: McGraw-Hill.

Jaffe, A. J.
1939   "Religious differential in the net reproduction rate." *Journal of the American Statistical Association* 34:335–342.

Jones, Elise F. and Charles F. Westoff
1978   "How attitudes toward abortion are changing." *Population: Behavioral, Social and Environmental Issues* 1:5–21.

Robinson, Gilbert K.
1936   "The Catholic birth rate: Further facts and implications." *American Journal of Sociology* 31:757–766.

Ryder, N. B. and C. F. Westoff
1971   *Reproduction in the United States: 1965.* Princeton: Princeton University Press.

Stouffer, Samuel A.
1935   "Trends in the fertility of Catholics and non-Catholics." *American Journal of Sociology* 41:143–166.

U.S. Bureau of the Census
1957   Religion Reported by the Civilian Population of the United States: March 1957. *Current Population Reports,* Series P-20, No. 79.

Westoff, Charles F. and Larry Bumpass
1973   "The revolution in birth control practices of U.S. Roman Catholics." *Science* 179: 41–44.

Westoff, Charles and Elise F. Jones
1977   "The secularization of U.S. Catholic birth control practices." *Family Planning Perspectives* 9:203–207.

Westoff, Charles F. and Elise F. Jones
1978   "The end of "Catholic" fertility." *Demography* 16 (2).

Westoff, Charles F. and N. B. Ryder
1977   *The Contraceptive Revolution.* Princeton: Princeton University Press.

Whelpton, P. K., A. A. Campbell, and J. E. Patterson
1966   *Fertility and Family Planning in the United States.* Princeton: Princeton University Press.

Chapter 11

Social Change and Commitment to the Work Ethic

LARRY BLACKWOOD

I. Introduction

In his classic work, Weber (1958) posited that the work ethic, or the emphasis on the intrinsic value of one's occupation, had its beginnings in the doctrines of religion, particularly Protestantism. Although some research findings on contemporary religiously based differences in commitment to the work ethic lend support to Weber's hypotheses (e.g., Lenski, 1963), it has been suggested by others (e.g., Samuelsson, 1961) that a religious basis for the work ethic does not exist. Weber himself concluded that religion was of no importance after the establishment of the capitalist economic order (1958:70). In addition, it has been speculated that, because of the erosion of its religious basis or other reasons, commitment to the work ethic has been declining over time.

The purpose of this chapter is to address some of these issues by testing for a possible decline in commitment to the work ethic over time and by assessing the role of religion in effecting any such changes. Religion may or may not be related to the work ethic and its stability or decline. And if the work ethic has no basis in religion, the nature of the other factors will be explored.

II. Methods

Data

Data collected in the 1958 and, again, in the 1971 Detroit Area Studies were utilized in the present analysis. (For a description of the sampling and data collection procedures, see Duncan *et al.,* 1973.) The 1958 baseline study contained a number of items relevant to religion and to attitudes toward work. The original set of items was developed and reported by Lenski (1963). Some of these items were repeated in the 1971 survey, including one considered, by Lenski, as indicative of the work ethic. Respondents were asked to rank five work-related values in order of importance. The five values were (*a*) high income; (*b*) no danger of being fired; (*c*) working hours short, lots of free time; (*d*) chances for advancement; and (*e*) the work is important and gives a feeling of accomplishment. Although male respondents were asked to respond in accordance with values preferred for their own job, married females were asked to rank the values in relation to their husbands' jobs. Hence, females were essentially responding to a different question. For this reason, the present analysis is restricted to male respondents.

A dichotomous variable was constructed that measured the relative order in which the respondent ranked the values "work important" and "short hours." The other values were not used because preliminary examination of the data indicated that their rankings were highly dependent on economic or on other material needs. (It can be argued that it is hard to be concerned with moral or ethical job values unless one is relatively secure economically.) Using relative rankings of the "work important" and "short hours" responses ostensibly allowed a respondent to express such a need (for example, by choosing money as being most important) and still express commitment to the work ethic by his ranking of "work important" with respect to "short hours." As Lenski (1963:89) designed the question, the "work important" value was intended to be closest to Weber's original conception of the work ethic, and "short hours" was meant to express a directly opposite idea. The variable as constructed then is considered to be a measure of commitment or noncommitment to the work ethic.

Technique of Analysis

The techniques of log-linear contingency table analysis developed by Goodman were used. These techniques allow the multivariate analysis of nominal data and provide a systematic strategy for testing the significance of relationships and establishing estimates of effects. Also, they may be adapted (Duncan, 1975) to test for differences between categories of polytomous variables, and the related technique of logit regression (Theil, 1970; Wuthnow and Blackwood, 1977) affords specific tests for linearity.

The outcome of the use of these techniques is the selection of a preferred model, the expected frequencies of which are used to calculate estimates of population effects. Three basic criteria were used in the present analysis for selecting a model: (*a*) the *p*-value of the model is .10 or larger; (*b*) adding any additional effect to the model does not significantly improve its fit at the .05 level of significance; and (*c*) the model contains no effects that, if dropped out of the model, do not significantly decrease the fit at the .05 level. Ambiguity as to the importance of certain effects sometimes occurs, in which case other means of selection must be employed. Deviations from these three criteria in selecting preferred models are noted in the text.

Procedure

After first establishing the general temporal trend in commitment to the work ethic, the basic logic of the analysis was to evaluate the religious or secular basis for the work ethic within the context of the change over time. This method, in addition to affording an evaluation of the importance of each variable as a basis for the work ethic during the 13-year time period, also provided an indication of their contributions to effecting changes over time. Temporal variations in commitment to the work ethic could result from changes in population composition with regard to a variable and/or to changes in the magnitude of the effect of the variable on the work ethic over time. The importance of any such variables in explaining changes over time is gauged by the degree of attenuation of the "year" or temporal effect in the models.

III. Analysis and Results

Net Change in Commitment to the Work Ethic

In 1958, 87% of the 284 male respondents preferred "work important" to "short hours." In 1971, the figure had dropped to 70% of the 799 respondents. Thus, although commitment to work remained the dominant value, some decline is apparent. Although available evidence does not disclose whether or not this change is indicative of a long-term trend, it does show that the change did not occur to the exception of shifts in other values. During this same period in Detroit, there was also a decrease in faith in the government, a decrease in favorable attitudes toward other public institutions, and what most would consider to be liberalization of attitudes regarding foreign policy, racial questions, freedom of speech, abortion, divorce, and religion (Duncan *et al.*,

1973). Thus, the present findings should be interpreted as applying to a period of apparently significant broad-scale change (although the reasons for change in each case surely vary), whether or not that change is peculiar to the 13-year period studied.

Religion and the Work Ethic

Religious Affiliation

According to Weber, the work ethic is derived from Protestant religious beliefs; therefore, one might expect commitment to the work ethic to vary by religious affiliation. If commitment does vary by affiliation, then the decline over time might be due to changes within certain religious groups. For example, if Protestants display a high degree of commitment whereas other groups are low, the decline over time might be restricted to changes within that group. Alternatively, the degree of commitment among Protestants might remain the same, with the decline being due to a shift in the number of Protestants in the population over time. The first type of effect would be demonstrated statistically by the appearance of a significant affiliation–year interaction term in the preferred model, whereas the latter effect would imply a lack of significance or a reduction in magnitude of the independent year effect (as compared with the bivariate case). Table 11.1 presents the response distribution of commitment to the work ethic by five major religious groups in the Detroit area by year.

The preferred model from the analysis of Table 11.1 indicates that the only significant difference in commitment to the work ethic among the five religion categories is between black Protestants and all white groups, including those

TABLE 11.1 Work Ethic by Major Socioreligious Group[a]

	1958		1971		
Socioreligious group	Short hours	Work important	Short hours	Work important	Total
Black Protestant	12	33	51	68	164
White Protestant	10	96	52	233	391
White Catholic	13	92	53	221	379
White Jew	0	11	2	12	25
White no preference	1	10	15	36	62

[a] Preferred model = {1234567} {12} {17}, df = 7, $\chi^2 = 6.39$, $p > .25$, where:

1 = Job value
2 = Year
3 = White no preference
4 = White Jew
5 = White Catholic
6 = White Protestant
7 = Black Protestant

with no religious preference. Once the black Protestant effect was in the model, adding effects representing the contrasts between the other categories did not significantly improve the fit. The expected odds on preferring "work important" are 3.1 times as high for all whites as for black Protestants. Lacking sufficient cases of black Catholics, black Jews, and blacks with no preference, we cannot specifically tell whether the black–white difference is because of something different about black Protestants in particular or because of the color difference alone. However, some information on the black–white difference can be obtained by controlling for social class as an alternative explanation to a black–white religious difference. This was tested for by using a three-category education variable (0–8 years of school, 9–12 years, and 13 or more years) as a proxy for social class. The log of the odds on choosing "work important" were regressed on dummy variable scores for religion, year, and scaled scores for education using logit regression techniques. Figure 11.1 shows the graph of the expected log-odds on choosing "work important" using three categories of education.

It was found that education has a positive linear relationship to commitment to the work ethic and that controlling for the effects of education reduced but did not eliminate the black–white difference. In addition, the analysis revealed a marginally significant difference between whites with no preference and

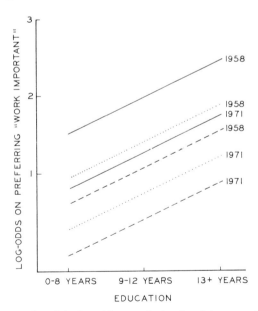

Figure 11.1 Regression of the log-odds on preferring "work important" on year, education, and socioreligious category. Key:—White Protestant, Catholic, or Jew; – – Black Protestant; • • • White, no preference.

other white groups, which did not occur previously. As before, however, there were no differences among white Protestants, Catholics, and Jews. The expected odds on preferring "work important" for members of the four major white religious groups are 1.6 and 1.9 times as high as for whites with no preference and for black Protestants, respectively.

These findings seem to indicate, with the possible exceptions of black Protestants and whites with no religious preference, that there are no contemporary differences in commitment to the work ethic due to religious affiliation. That the black–white difference persists when education is controlled suggests that the tendency for blacks to be less committed to the work ethic is not due entirely to overrepresentation of blacks in the lower classes. It may be that commitment to the work ethic is characteristic of all white religious groups. Blacks, and white with no religious preference, may then be generally less committed to the doctrine of "the calling" and, because they are outside all white religious groups, to the work ethic. This idea is partially supported by the fact that a model constraining black Protestants and whites with no preference to have identical odds provides a closer fit to the data than the model represented by Figure 11.1. This finding is somewhat tenuous, however, because the small number of cases in the two groups makes it difficult to detect statistically significant differences between them.

The analysis of religious affiliation not only provides no more than minimal evidence in support of the hypothesis of a religious basis for the work ethic but also does little to explain the decline in commitment to the work ethic over time. There were no significant affiliation–year interaction terms in the preferred models, and the independent year effects remained significant when controlling for both affiliation and education. It appears, then, that an explanation of both the basis for the work ethic and its decline over time lies elsewhere.

Religious Commitment

Although there appears to be little or no basis for the work ethic in religious affiliation, there may be a more important general religious basis present in which case commitment to the work ethic would be expected to covary with degree of religiosity or extent of beliefs, as opposed to denominational differences. In that case, changes in devotionalism and doctrinal orthodoxy within all religious groups over time might then explain the general drop in commitment to the work ethic in cases in which affiliation did not. Church attendance has been widely used as a measure of religiosity or devotionalism, and it is examined first here.

Using logit regression, log-odds on preferring "work important" were regressed on ranked scores for frequency of church attendance and dummy scores for year and religion categories. The preferred regression model provided a good fit (χ^2 = 20.87, df = 27) and showed attendance to have a positive linear relationship to the log-odds on preferring "work important," indicating perhaps some general religious basis for the work ethic. No difference between white Protestants and Catholics was found in the effect of church attendance. The effect of church attendance was relatively pronounced (the slope of the regression line was .17) across five categories ranging from "never attend" to "once a week or more." No interaction effects were significant, indicating the absence of a changing relationship between religiosity and the work ethic that could account for the decline in commitment over time. Also, although attendance dropped over time, this could at best only partially explain the overall erosion of commitment to the work ethic, since the year effect was still clearly significant and since even those who attended most often lost commitment over time and at the same rate as those who never attended.

Similar findings were obtained with a dichotomous item indicating participation in church activities, other than attending services, as the measure of religious involvement. As with church attendance, the preferred model (χ^2 = 7.09, df = 8) showed independent effects of year and religious affiliation, with no Protestant–Catholic difference. The expected odds on choosing "work important" for those involved in other church activities were 1.9 times as high as for others. Although this may indicate some basis for the work ethic in religiosity, the lack of interactions or of other attenuations of the year effect indicates, as was true with church attendance, that this measure of religiosity provides no understanding of the decline in commitment over time.

A third method used to assess the general religious basis for the work ethic involved analyzing personal religious belief using four different items. The items were (*a*) belief in God; (*b*) belief in life after death; (*c*) agreement with the idea that one has the right to question what his church teaches; and (*d*) agreement with the idea that the right of free speech includes the right to make speeches criticizing religion. Table 11.2 summarizes results for the analysis of these four items in relation to the work ethic (controlling for year and for religious affiliation).

Belief in God is not related at all to commitment to the work ethic, and, but for two exceptions, the other items show the opposite of what would be expected if commitment to the work ethic had a religious basis. Respondents with the least orthodox beliefs and the most tolerance of criticism of religion are the most likely to be committed to the work ethic.

The case of black Protestants and belief in life after death is an interesting exception to the above generalization. Up to this point, blacks have consistently shown less commitment to the work ethic. However, blacks who believe in life after death begin to approach whites in degree of commitment. Weber's explanation of the development of the work ethic in connection with the doctrine of the "calling" involved the Protestants' concern with salvation in the

TABLE 11.2   Summary of Analysis of Work Ethic by Personal Religious Belief Items

Religious belief item	Year	Black Protestant Yes[a]	No	White Protestant Yes	No	White Catholic Yes	No	p-value for preferred model
Believe in God	1958	2.7	2.7	8.3	8.3	8.3	8.3	> .50
	1971	1.4	1.4	4.3	4.3	4.3	4.3	
Speeches against religion	1958	3.8	2.0	12.3	6.3	7.5	10.0	> .75
	1971	1.9	.97	6.0	3.1	3.7	4.9	
Believe in life after death	1958	4.5	1.4	8.4	8.8	8.4	8.8	> .50
	1971	2.3	.74	4.3	4.5	4.3	4.5	
Right to question church	1958	3.5	1.1	9.7	7.7	9.7	7.7	> .90
	1971	1.7	.50	4.5	3.6	4.5	3.6	

The header spans: "Expected Odds on "Work Important"" covers Black Protestant, White Protestant, White Catholic columns.

[a] Yes refers to agreement with or belief in the item. Unsure responses were combined with the "no" responses.

afterlife. It appears that, although this connection does not now hold for whites, it has a strong influence in the black Protestant groups. This is consistent with Lenski's findings using the more extensive 1958 data on measures of the spirit of capitalism. Lenski found that the difference in commitment to the spirit of capitalism between marginal and active black Protestant church members was much greater than for the white Protestant group (1963:122). It seems, then, that the strongest case we have for a contemporary religious base for the work ethic is limited to the black Protestant group. If there was historically a religious basis for the work ethic for both blacks and whites, it appears that religious values among blacks have not yet been secularized to the same extent as among whites.

Taken at face value, the findings on church attendance and participation in other church activities suggest at least some basis in religion for the work ethic (even though they do not account for the change over time), whereas the data on personal religious beliefs suggest the opposite. This apparent contradiction in findings may be attributable to the inherent limitations that measures of participation have as indicators of religiosity. Demerath (1965:14) suggests that attendance and other involvement measures are indicators only of the "doing" aspect of religiosity rather than of the more important "feeling" aspects. Goode (1966) further advances this argument by concluding that church attendance is only a specific instance of general voluntary organizational participation and should not be used as an indicator of religiosity at all. Applied to the present data, this idea suggests that both church attendance and participation in other church activities are associated with commitment to the work ethic only to the extent that they reflect participation in any type of voluntary organization activity and not at all because they are measures of religiosity. Some support for this interpretation derives from the fact that participation in other church activities was found to have a positive rather than a negative relationship both to belief in the right to question the church and to belief that the right of free speech includes the right to criticize religion.

Discussion of Findings on Religion

This analysis of religion generally indicates little religious basis for the work ethic and a corresponding insignificant role for religion in effecting change in commitment to the work ethic over time. Weber posited that a relationship between religion and positive attitudes toward work was necessary for the emergence of capitalism as an economic order. Once the order was established, however, it was a different matter: "Any [present day] relationship between religious beliefs and conduct [in regard to the spirit of capitalism] is generally absent, and where it exists. . .it tends to be of the negative sort. The people filled with the spirit of capitalism today tend to be indifferent, if not hostile, to the Church [Weber, 1958:70]." Furthermore, he stated that "the essential elements of the spirit of capitalism although still in existence, had lost their religious basis even by the time of Benjamin Franklin [181]." Although the work ethic may never have been related to religious beliefs, it can be argued that the absence of a base in religion shown in our analysis at least supports Weber's conception that, in an established capitalistic society, the work ethic belongs to the secular rather than to the religious realm of ideas. Church attendance and participation in other church activities, interpreted as indicators of general participation in voluntary organizations devoid of any religious connotations, further support this idea. That is, they indicate that the greater the involvement in the dominant secular system, the greater the likelihood of expressing its values, in this case, the spirit of capitalism of which the work ethic is part. If true, this would explain why blacks (who are more marginal than whites in terms of involvement in the general secular order) and those whites with no religious preference (if it can be assumed that nonchurch members are more marginal to the system even in a generally secular society) are less committed to the work ethic. The next sections explore further the hypothesis that commitment to the work ethic varies with extent of identification with the dominant secular value-system.

Secular Involvement and the Work Ethic

If the work ethic is more likely a part of the secular rather than of the religious realm of ideas, then that part of the secular value system with which the work ethic is probably most closely associated, and which dominates over others, is the capitalist economic order. Furthermore, if the work ethic is closely associated with the prevailing economic order, then changes in the relationship between them might be responsible for the erosion of the work ethic.

In the present data, several variables were used to test for the relationship between involvement in the capitalist economic order and commitment to the work ethic. As with the analysis of religion, we will be looking for strong relationships between these variables and commitment to the work ethic in order to derive a secular basis both for the work ethic and for compositional changes within the population or interaction effects with "year" to explain the erosion of the work ethic over time.

Social class was considered as a measure of involvement, with the idea that those in the upper classes would have more at stake in the capitalist system and would thus be more likely to express its values. Union membership was also considered, since it can be regarded as a characteristicly in "opposition" to the basic ideas of capitalism.

A third group of variables analyzed consisted of measures of anomie. Merton (1957) suggests that a disjunction between universally held goals and the means to obtain those goals on a societal level leads to feelings of anomie on the part of some individuals. Part of several modes of adaptations to these feelings of anomie involves the rejection of the societal goals by the individual. In a capitalist society, where one of the dominant goals is to have an intrinsically interesting job, the existence of feelings of anomie in individuals (perhaps partly due to a lack of availability of interesting jobs) may result, then, in the rejection of the work ethic as a part of a mode of adaptation.

The last variable considered was occupation, with the assumption being that those in higher-ranking occupations are more deeply entrenched in the economic system and are thus more likely to espouse its values. Of all the indicators of degree of identification with the capitalist economic order, occupation can perhaps be expected to vary most closely with commitment to the work ethic, as it is within the occupational context that the work ethic is evaluated by the individual worker. Furthermore, the changing character of occupations over time has been implicated theoretically as a factor that has increased conditions conducive to the decline of the work ethic.

For example, Schumpeter (1950) proposed that the increasing rationalization and specialization of work over time, as witnessed by the increasing bureaucratization of even higher levels of business, destroys the importance and, thus, the initiative and interest, of the individual worker. Schumpeter states that "innovation itself is being reduced to routine. Technological progress is increasingly becoming the business of trained specialists who turn out what is required and make it work in predictable ways. The romance of earlier commercial adventure is rapidly wearing away, because so many more things can be strictly calculated that had of old to be visualized in a flash of genius [1950:133]."

Individual interest in work is further destroyed by what Schumpeter refers to as the vanishing of the proprietary interest, or interest generated in the worker by the fact that he owns and therefore has a stake in the business (1950:141). Many salaried executives and all salaried managers and submanagers, according to Schumpeter, tend to acquire employee attitudes because of lack of specific benefits to be gained from furthering the company's interests.

Data from the federal government's census of business support some of Schumpeter's ideas regarding increasing bureaucratization. The proportion of retail and wholesale trade establishments that employed over 100 persons, although small, increased by 50% between 1958 and 1967. Also, whereas the total number of wholesale and retail trade establishments was slightly greater in 1967 than in 1958, the number of these that were proprietary or partnership businesses in 1967 was less than 10% of the number in 1958 (U.S. Department of Commerce, 1958, 1967).

Mills (1953) expresses similar ideas in connection with the increasing alienation of white-collar workers. The process of bureaucratization, according to Mills, has extended to the managerial and professional levels, where work that previously involved imagination and initiative is becoming more like factory production. Mills states: "There are few, if any, features of wage work (except heavy toil which is decreasingly a factor in wage work) that do not also characterize at least some white collar work. For here, too, the human traits of the individual, from his physique to his psychic disposition, become units in the functionally rational calculation of managers [1953:227]."

Applying the ideas of Schumpeter and Mills to the present data, we can expect that, because of increased alienation, white-collar workers as a group in Detroit will be forced to seek elsewhere for meaning in their lives and will in the process also become less committed to the work ethic. Implicit in our hypothesis is the assumption that those in higher-status jobs can be expected to abandon the work ethic faster than those in lower-status jobs because the lower-status workers, typified by the auto assembly-line worker, occupy positions that were bureaucratized and specialized much earlier in the development of capitalism. They should, therefore, already exhibit a relatively constant, low level of commitment to the work ethic. That is, just as the advent of capitalism alienated the craftsman from his work by forcing him from his shop to the factory (where the end product as the meaning in his work was removed physically and legally from him), the continued success of capitalism is now subjecting the white-collar worker to the same processes.

Social Class and Union Membership

It was shown earlier that education was positively related to commitment to the work ethic. Assuming that education is a reasonable proxy for social class,

TABLE 11.3 Expected Odds on Preferring "Work Important" by Subjective Class Identification

Class identification	1958		1971	
	Blacks	Whites	Blacks	Whites
Middle	4.9	11.2	2.3	5.3
Working	3.0	6.8	1.4	3.2

then some evidence that the work ethic has a secular basis in a capitalist society is provided. This idea was further supported when subjective class identification was examined with regard to the work ethic. The results of that analysis are presented in Table 11.3. Identifying with the working class reduced the expected odds on choosing "work important" by a factor of .63. Union membership also reduced the odds on choosing "work important." (See Table 11.4.)

These data are encouraging in that they suggest a relationship between commitment to the work ethic and identification with the capitalist economic system. However, they do not account for the erosion of the work ethic over time, as the year effect remained unaltered in all cases.

Anomie

Five items from the Srole scale were used to measure anomie. They were agreement or disagreement with the following statements: (*a*) Most people don't really care what happens to the next fellow; (*b*) Children born today have a wonderful future to look forward to; (*c*) Nowadays a person has to live pretty much for today and let tomorrow take care of itself; (*d*) These days a person doesn't really know whom he can count on; and (*e*) It's hardly fair to bring children into the world the way things look for the future.

Four of the five items were found to be negatively related to commitment to the work ethic. The second item was unrelated to it. Table 11.5 shows the expected odds for the four items. Controlling for education as a measure of social class reduced the effects somewhat but did not eliminate them. These findings dealing with anomie further support the hypothesis that commitment to the work ethic depends upon one's orientation to the secular capitalistic society, but they do not explain the changes over time in that the erosion appears to be occurring even among those who are most strongly involved in the system.

TABLE 11.4 Expected Odds on Preferring "Work Important" by Labor Union Membership

Union membership	1958		1971	
	Blacks	Whites	Blacks	Whites
United Auto Workers	2.2	4.8	1.1	2.3
Other union	2.9	6.4	1.4	3.1
None	5.8	12.6	2.9	6.2

TABLE 11.5   Summary of Analysis of Work Ethic by Four Anomie Items

| Anomie item | Year | Blacks | | Whites | | p-value for preferred model |
		Yes[a]	No	Yes	No	
Live for today	1958	2.3	4.2	5.4	9.6	> .26
	1971	1.2	2.2	2.9	5.1	
Don't know who can count on	1958	2.8	7.0	6.1	15.4	> .94
	1971	1.3	3.4	2.9	7.4	
People don't care about next guy	1958	2.4	4.2	5.9	10.3	> .41
	1971	1.3	2.2	3.1	5.4	
Hardly fair to bring children	1958	2.2	3.5	5.5	8.6	> .80
	1971	1.2	1.9	3.1	4.8	

The Expected Odds on "Work Important" span the Blacks and Whites columns.

[a] Yes refers to agreement with the item. Unsure responses were combined with the "no" responses.

Occupation

An extensive list of occupational groups was recoded into the following four categories for the present analysis: (*a*) professionals and managers; (*b*) clerical and sales persons; (*c*) craftsmen and foremen; and (*d*) operatives, service workers, and non-farm laborers. Figure 11.2 presents a graph of the expected odds from the preferred model resulting from the analysis of the occupational data.[1] The preferred model showed no statistical difference between the middle two occupation categories, but significant interactions of professional and managerial occupations with year and choice of job values clearly supports our hypothesis and accounts for much of the change over time. Although even the lower-status workers became somewhat less committed to the work ethic over time, the professional and managerial workers were found to be abandoning the work ethic approximately four times faster than the middle two occupation groups and eight times faster than those with operative or service jobs. Tests for linearity of effects, using logit regression, failed to provide an adequate model, further indicating that the non-linearity in the graph is not due to sampling error. Further analysis (data not shown) revealed no significant age or birth-cohort effects, suggesting that it is not just the newer cohorts of white-collar workers who are less committed to the work ethic.

---

[1] Preferred model: {234567} {13} {124} {127}, df = 25, χ^2 = 8.41, p > .99, 1 = work ethic; 2 = year; 3 = color; 4 = operatives, service, nonfarm workers; 5 = craftsmen, foremen; 6 = clerical, sales workers; 7 = professionals, managerials. Eliminating any one of the three-way interactions from this model did not significantly decrease the fit of the model, whereas eliminating both effects did. This represents a situation not covered by the criteria developed for the choice of a preferred model. Both effects were obviously important, therefore both were included in the preferred model. In any case, the {127} effect, the most substantively critical, also appeared to be the most statistically important.

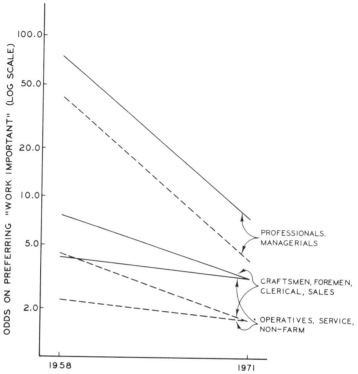

Figure 11.2 Expected odds on preferring "work important" by occupation, year, and color. Key:—Whites; – – Blacks.

These findings, with one qualification, seem to be consistent with the theories of Schumpeter and Mills. It is obvious that the white-collar shift away from valuing work is not complete but only at an early stage, at least in Detroit, since our data showed commitment to work to be by far the dominant work value in almost all subpopulations studied. Mills and Schumpeter, however, writing before the baseline year (1958), concluded that most of the change had already occurred. Certainly, the bureaucratization of white-collar jobs was in full swing at the time of their writings. Perhaps it takes time for workers, even in the face of decreased meaning in their jobs, to abandon the moral commitment to work. This idea has been infused in American culture probably since its founding, and it seems to be only recently that leisure-time activities could be considered a viable alternative to work as the central meaning for most people's lives.

Although the theories of Mills and Schumpeter suggest that job dissatisfaction may be an intervening variable between bureaucratization and abandonment of the work ethic, comparison of trends found in the present analysis with trends in job satisfaction should be made cautiously, if at all. It is entirely possible that the shift away from the work ethic could be occurring concurrently with constant or even increasing levels of job satisfaction (e.g., a decrease in satisfaction because of a loss of intrinsic meaningfulness of work might be prevented by shifting away from valuing the work ethic). It should also be noted that other research, particularly that of Kohn (1969, 1976), suggests an alternative explanation of the findings. Based on his analysis involving measures of bureaucratization, Kohn (1969:168, 194) concluded that bureaucracy was conducive to valuing intrinsic aspects of work. Kohn's findings applied to the present analysis would suggest that the shift away from the work ethic is occurring despite increasing opportunities for meaningfulness in occupational pursuits. Further study is needed to verify both the trend and its interpretation.

Assuming the validity of our findings, we can ask what implications a trend away from the work ethic has for a capitalist society. Many of the popular authors see the "downfall of the American way of life." Schumpeter predicts that capitalism is fated to be replaced by socialism. Perhaps, however, there may not be that great a change. Analysis of first choices of job values (data not reported), using all five values mentioned in the introduction, shows that, for whites at least, the pursuit of the dollar, like the desire for shorter hours, is gaining importance. The increasing importance of money and the desire for material goods may be enough to keep people at their jobs, working hard even if they find no intrinsic fulfillment in their work.

Acknowledgments

I wish to thank Otis Dudley Duncan and Mark Warr for helpful comments on an earlier draft of this paper.

References

Demerath, N. J.
  1965 *Social Class in American Protestantism.* Chicago:Rand McNally and Company.
Duncan, Otis Dudley
  1975 "Partitioning polytomous variables in multiway contingency analysis." *Social Science Research* 4:167–182.
Duncan, Otis Dudley, Howard Schuman, and Beverly Duncan
  1973 *Social Change in a Metropolitan Community.* New York:Russell Sage Foundation.
Goode, Erich
  1966 "Social class and church participation." *American Journal of Sociology* 72:102–111.

Goodman, Leo A.
  1972 "A modified multiple regression approach to the analysis of dichotomous variables."
        American Sociological Review 37(February):28–46.

Kohn, Melvin L.
  1969 *Class and Conformity: A Study in Values.* Homewood, Illinois:The Dorsey Press.

Kohn, Melvin L.
  1976 "Occupational structure and alienation." *American Journal of Sociology*
        82(July):111–130.

Lenski, Gerhard
  1963 *The Religious Factor.* Garden City, New York:Anchor Books.

Merton, Robert K.
  1957 "Social structure and anomie." In Donald R. Cressey and David A. Ward (eds.),
        Delinquency, Crime, and Social Process, 1969. New York:Harper and Row.

Mills, C. Wright
  1953 *White Collar, The American Middle Classes.* New York:Oxford University Press.

Samuelsson, Kurt
  1961 *Religion and Economic Action: A Critique of Max Weber.* New York:Harper
        and Row.

Schumpeter, Joseph A.
  1950 *Capitalism, Socialism, and Democracy (third edition).* New York:Harper and
        Brothers.

Srole, Leo
  1956 "Social integration and certain corollaries: An exploratory study." *American
        Sociological Review* 21(December):709–716.

Theil, Henri
  1970 "On the estimation of relationships involving qualitative variables." *American
        Journal of Sociology* 76(July):103–154.

United States Department of Commerce
  1958 Census of Business, Vols. I, III.
  1967 Census of Business, Vols. I, III.

Weber, Max
  1958 *The Protestant Ethic and the Spirit of Capitalism.* New York:Charles Scribner's Sons.

Wuthnow, Robert and Larry Blackwood
  1977 "Logit regression techniques in the study of religion." *The Review of Religious
        Research* 19(Fall):83–90.

Chapter 12

The Effects of Residential Migration on Church Attendance in the United States

ROBERT WUTHNOW and KEVIN CHRISTIANO

I. Introduction

The effect of migration on religious commitment has not been a topic of particular interest among American sociologists of religion in recent years. It is curious that it has not been, for there are theoretical reasons to suspect that the effect might be great. Even the American theologian Harvey Cox, who noted approvingly the modern trend toward geographical mobility in the "technopolis" of his *The Secular City* (1966), was moved to concede mobility's presumably negative effect on religious commitment. "Let us admit at once," he wrote, "that high mobility does play havoc with traditional religion. It separates people from the holy places. It mixes them with neighbors whose gods have different names and who worship them in different ways [Cox, 1966:47]."

To the degree that religious behavior is rooted in a spectrum of localisms—from the simple comfort one may feel in the company of familiar fellow worshippers to the sometimes unique consensus on issues of theological

The Religious Dimension:
New Directions in Quantitative Research

import that a church group nurtures—we might expect religious participation to diminish in the face of social processes, such as migration, that are naturally destructive of localism. Ancient religions drew abundantly upon their immediate environments for symbolizations of the sacred, and, although, this tendency may not appear to be as obvious in the modern case, we cannot easily dismiss the idea that much in an individual's religious behavior is at least sustained by experiences with specific places, persons, and contexts. Migration, then, figures importantly in this discussion as a force potentially disruptive of the smaller patterns upon which religious attachments are based.

As another example of the theoretical importance of migration, Will Herberg's (1960) well-known theory of ethnic assimilation, sometimes called the "three-generations hypothesis," suggests that religious participation is likely to vary in relation to the length of time that has elapsed since one's family first emigrated to America. This theory is, in fact, an adaptation from the work of immigration historian Marcus Lee Hansen, who, 40 years ago, claimed to have discovered "the almost universal phenomenon that what the son wishes to forget, the grandson wishes to remember [Hansen, 1952:495]." First-generation (immigrant) Americans are presumed to adhere quite fervently to their religious faith, often organized around distinctively ethnic institutions such as the national parish, as a source of security in an alien land. Second-generation Americans, in contrast, are thought to abandon their faith in an attempt to assimilate into the mainstream of American culture; "the second generation," says Hansen (1952:495), "is not interested in and does not write any history." But third-generation Americans, secure now in both their legal and their cultural citizenship, presumably return to the faith of their fathers to find their roots and identity while at the same time sealing the process of Americanization (Bender and Kagiwada, 1968:360–362; Nelsen and Allen, 1974:907–910; Simpson, 1975:1, 9). Only a little research has been done to test this theory or to extend it to subsequent generations (Abramson, 1973; Lazerwitz and Rowitz, 1964; Lenski, 1961; Nelsen and Allen, 1974; Simpson, 1975).

As yet another example, there has been much debate over the effects of urbanization on religious commitment. Some have argued that urbanization leads to secularization (e.g., Cox, 1966). Others have suggested that urbanization may have facilitated religious participation by making it easier to attend church (Zimmer and Hawley, 1959). Some research has compared the religious commitments of rural and urban dwellers. But hardly any attempts have been made to examine the religious styles or commitments of people who have actually migrated from rural areas to the city (exceptions are Dynes, 1956; Lenski, 1953, 1961; and Schwarzweller *et al.*, 1971) or, as perhaps is becoming increasingly important, from the city to the suburbs (Gans, 1967).

Some of the research on religious participation also suggests that it varies directly with the degree to which people feel integrated into other organizations and aspects of community life. Yet, hardly any research has been done to see if the sheer fact of moving from one community to another, as seems to be increasingly characteristic of the American population, has had any negative effect on religious participation. Nor has research been done to determine whether the region of the country to which people migrate has any effect on their religious participation.

In the absence of more extensive research on the relationship between these various sorts of migration and religious commitment, it seems useful to examine some of the available data that afford evidence on these relationships as they exist currently. This chapter explores the relationship between church attendance in the United States and the following kinds of residential migration: (*a*) immigration; (*b*) residential mobility; (*c*) regional migration; and (*d*) rural–urban–suburban migration.

II. Method

Data

The data on which this chapter is based were collected between September, 1976 and January, 1977 as part of the American National Election Study conducted by the Center for Political Studies at the University of Michigan. Interviews were conducted with 2248 randomly selected respondents. The sample was designed to represent all persons aged 18 and over residing in the United States. Because of other aspects of the research design, a weighting factor has to be applied to make the data representative of the American population. Since our interest in the present chapter is with actual respondents rather than with descriptive generalizations pertaining to the total population, unweighted data have been used. For futher information on the sample and on the study design, see Miller and Miller (1977).

Measures

Frequency of church attendance was the only measure of religious participation available in the data. It was assessed by means of a question that asked "Would you say you go to (church/synagogue) every week, almost every week, once or twice a month, a few times a year, or never?" Analysis of the relationship between migration and the various categories of church attendance indicated that the main differences occurred between those attending "every week" and those attending less frequently. Accordingly, the percentages shown in all of the following tables pertain to those who attend church every week. Twenty-five percent of the respondents said they attended every week.

Since other research has generally shown that the correlates of religious commitment are likely to differ between Catholics and Protestants, the analysis was conducted separately for these two groups. Data are shown only for white Catholics and white Protestants, since there were too few nonwhites, Jews, and persons of other religious affiliations to conduct parallel analyses on these groups.

The results are presented separately for each of the four kinds of migration listed earlier. The variables used to measure each of these kinds of migration are described in the following sections.

III. Results

Immigration

The present data afford only a crude examination of the effects of immigration on church attendance. We are limited to comparing the church attendance of "first-generation Americans" who said they were born outside the United States, "second-generation Americans" who said that either mother or father was born outside the United States, and "third (or more)-generation Americans" whose parents were both born in the United States. These comparisons, despite their limitations, seem worth presenting, since other research has largely been based only upon local samples (e.g., Lenski, 1961), rather than showing what the overall effect of immigration has been on church attendance nationally.

As shown in Table 12.1, 39% of the first generation white Catholics attend church every week. Among second-generation white Catholics, the percentage, contrary to what has been suggested in some theories, is considerably higher: 50%. And, among third-generation white Catholics, again contrary to some theories, the percentage is again smaller: 38%. Among white Protestants,

TABLE 12.1 Church Attendance by Generation American

	Generation American		
	First	Second	Third (or more)
Percentage who attend church every week among			
White Catholics	39%	50%	38%
	(37)	(115)	(317)
White Protestants	23%	24%	24%
	(31)	(84)	(1089)

there are virtually no differences among the three categories: Between 23 and 24% attend within each category.

These results are at some variance with previous work on this subject. Protestants and Catholics (but not Jews) in Lenski's Detroit area sample (1961:40–43) exhibited a trend of consistently increasing church attendance across the three generations. In a later (1964) study, Bernard Lazerwitz and Louis Rowitz reported that "the Lenski pattern" of steady increases in church attendance most accurately described comparisons among Protestant generations, with Catholics tending to reproduce the "Herberg pattern" of slumping second-generation participation (1964:532, 537).

Other research has shown that religious participation among second-generation Catholic immigrants varies depending on their country of origin—participation increasing among western Europeans but decreasing among southern Europeans (Nelson and Allen, 1974). This finding was based on a sample of residents in New York City. Unfortunately, there are too few cases in the national data to examine this possibility. What the national data suggest, however, is that the western European pattern seems to be more characteristic in general than the southern European pattern. At minimum, the national data seem not to support the Herberg theory, which suggests that second-generation immigrants abandon religion as a way of becoming American. Rather, the data tend to support other theories that have argued that church attendance is quite compatible with becoming an American and should, therefore, increase among second-generation immigrants.

If church attendance is part of the Americanization process, however, third-generation Americans should be the most likely to attend church regularly, rather than, as the data indicate, the least likely. The figures we have produced hardly constitute evidence of the "spontaneous and almost irrestistible impulse" of interest Hansen (1952:497) predicted among members of the third generation. One reason why they attend less may be that the secularization that has taken place among Catholics since Vatican II has affected more "Americanized" Catholics than more recent immigrants. Westoff (this volume), for example, has suggested that the convergence in birth control practices among Catholics and Protestants is a sign that Catholics are being assimilated into values espoused more generally in American culture. If changing birth control attitudes are one of the main reasons for Catholic defectons from church activities (as Greeley, 1976, 1977, has suggested), then assimilation may be associated with declining church attendance. We can only speculate.

It is also important, of course, that these generational differences prevail only among Catholics. This finding seems consistent with that of other research that has shown that ethnic variations in church attendance are considerably stronger among Catholics than among Protestants (Greeley, this volume). Both findings suggest that religious participation has more to do with ethnic roots among Catholics than it does among Protestants.

On the whole, these findings suggest that recency of immigration may have an effect on church attendance among Catholics, although in ways that might not have been expected and that require further exploration in order to be fully explained. As time goes on, however, it also seems likely that immigration will become less important for understanding religious participation than will various forms of internal migration, if only because the rate of immigration among younger cohorts has been reduced to a mere trickle (1.9 per 1000 population between 1971 and 1976).[1]

Residential Mobility

The second kind of migration the effects of which we sought to determine was residential mobility. We thought residential mobility might have an effect on church attendance, since other research has suggested (*a*) that people who move more or who have only recently moved into a community are less likely to be integrated into community organizations; and (*b*) that people who participate less in community organizations are also less likely to attend church (Zimmer and Hawley, 1959:353–354).

It is widely believed that Americans are a highly mobile population, and data from the Census Bureau indicate, in fact, that this is the case. Between 1970 and 1975 alone, 41.3% of the population changed residences. Seventeen percent moved to a different county, and 8.6% moved to a different state. Thus, residential mobility could affect the religious participation of millions of Americans.

Two items in the data afforded measures of residential mobility. One ascertained how many years respondents had lived in their present community. The other asked how many years respondents had lived in their present house or apartment. Like the Census figures, the responses to these questions also indicate the extent to which residential mobility is characteristic of Americans. Thirty-two percent of the white Catholics and 36% of the white Protestants had lived in their present community less than 10 years; 17% and 19%, respectively, had lived there less than 5 years. Mobility between houses, as might be expected, was even more pronounced. Sixty-two percent of the white Catholics and 63% of the white Protestants had lived in their present house less than 10 years; 38% and 40%, respectively, had lived there less than 5 years.[2]

---

[1] These and all other census figures cited are from U.S. Bureau of the Census (1977).

[2] These figures are likely to be on the low side, since the data were collected in such a way as to overrepresent residents who had not moved between 1972 and 1976.

Table 12.2 shows the percentages who attend church every week among those who have lived in their present community different lengths of time. Among white Catholics, only 20% of those who have lived in the community 1 year or less attend church every week. The figure for those who have lived in the community 2–4 years is only slightly higher (23%). Among those who have lived in the community from 5 to 10 years, however, the figure is substantially higher (39%). It is somewhat higher again for those who have lived in the community 11–20 years (43%) and still higher for those who have lived in the community more than 20 years (46%). Among white Protestants, the pattern is similar, although the differences are less pronounced. Nineteen percent of those having lived in the community a year or less attend church every week. The figures for those having lived in the community 2–4 years and 5–10 years are only slightly higher (20% in both cases). However, a higher precentage attends church every week among those having lived in the community 11–20 years (27%) or more than 20 years (26%).

Table 12.3 is similar to Table 12.2 except that it reports the relationship between church attendance and the length of time that respondents have lived in their present house or apartment. The data for white Catholics show that 30% of those who have lived in their present house 1 year or less attend church every week. The percentage among those who have lived in their house 2–4 years is slightly smaller (27%). But, among those who have lived in their house 5–10

TABLE 12.2   Church Attendance by Years in Present Community

	Years in present community				
	0–1	2–4	5–10	11–20	Over 20
Percentage who attend church every week among					
White Catholics	20%	23%	39%	43%	46%
	(39)	(44)	(72)	(104)	(229)
White Protestants	19%	20%	20%	27%	26%
	(83)	(146)	(198)	(221)	(532)

TABLE 12.3   Church Attendance by Years in Present House or Apartment

	Years in present house (apt.)				
	0–1	2–4	5–10	11–20	Over 20
Percentage who attend church every week among					
White Catholics	30%	27%	41%	48%	56%
	(86)	(101)	(114)	(108)	(78)
White Protestants	17%	21%	24%	30%	26%
	(209)	(267)	(272)	(240)	(204)

years, 41% attend church every week. The figure is higher again among those who have lived in their house 11–20 years (48%) and still higher among those who have lived there more than 20 years (56%). Among white Protestants, the data also suggest that the mobile are less likely to attend church than are the nonmobile, although again, as in Table 12.2, the differences for Protestants are not as strong as they are among Catholics. Only 17% of the Protestants who have lived in their house 1 year or less attend church every week. This figure climbs slightly (to 21%) among those having lived in their house 2–4 years. It increases slightly again (to 24%) among those having lived there 5–10 years. The highest percentage is among those who have lived in their house 11–20 years (30%), and the next highest percentage is among those having lived in their house more than 20 years (26%).

These results tend to support our initial expectations: Residential mobility appears to have a dampening effect on church attendance. The data indicate not only that newcomers are less likely to attend church than established residents but also that the longer one lives in one's community or house, the more likely one is to attend church regularly. The problem with this inference, of course, is that people who have lived at their present residence a long time are also likely to be older than people who have lived there a shorter time (a newly married couple would find it impossible to have lived in their present dwelling for 20 years, no matter how stable they might expect to be). What we have observed, therefore, may be an artifact of differences in church attendance between the young and the old.

In Table 12.4 we have controlled for the possible contaminating effect of age by showing the relationship between church attendance and years in present community separately for persons under the age of 30 and for persons aged

TABLE 12.4 Church Attendance by Years in Present Community by Age

	Years in present community				
	0–1	2–4	5–10	11–20	Over 20
Percentage who attend church every week among					
White Catholics					
Under the age of 30	21%	15%	39%	46%	37%
	(24)	(20)	(26)	(26)	(38)
Aged 30 and over	20%	29%	40%	42%	48%
	(15)	(24)	(45)	(78)	(190)
White Protestants					
Under the age of 30	16%	18%	10%	30%	14%
	(43)	(54)	(40)	(53)	(65)
Aged 30 and over	22%	21%	22%	26%	27%
	(40)	(91)	(158)	(166)	(464)

30 and over. Among white Catholics, there is still a tendency in both age groups for the more mobile to attend church less often than the less mobile. In the "30 and over" category, the percentages rise consistently, from 20% among those having lived in the community a year or less to 48% among those having lived there over 20 years. In the "under 30" category, the pattern is less consistent but shows generally the same tendency. Among white Protestants, the relationships are less clear, since the overall effect of mobility on church attendance was not as strong as among Catholics. In the "30 and over" category, there still appears to be a slightly lesser tendency for the more mobile to be regular church attenders than the less mobile: Those who have lived in their present community more than 10 years are about 5 percentage points more likely to attend church every week than those who have lived there less than 10 years. In the "under 30" category, there appears to be no relationship between church attendance and mobility that would meet statistical criteria of significance. Still, the pattern does not wholly violate that shown in the other categories. Thus, the highest percentage of church attendance is among those who have lived in a community between 11 and 20 years. Those who have lived in a community longer than 20 years are less likely to attend church. But, given that they are under the age of 30, the people in this category would, undoubtedly, be largely those still living with their parents. Thus, it is difficult to make strict comparisons between them and the other categories. Among those who have lived in the community less than 10 years, the percentages are all smaller than among those who have lived there 11–20 years.

Table 12.5 reports the relationship between church attendance and years in present house (or apartment), controlling for age. The patterns are basically

TABLE 12.5   Church Attendance by Years in Present House by Age[a]

	Years in present house (or apartment)				
	0–1	2–4	5–10	11–20	Over 20
Percentage who attend church every week among					
White Catholics					
Under the age of 30	31%	23%	41%	62%	*
	(52)	(44)	(22)	(13)	(2)
Aged 30 and over	29%	30%	41%	46%	59%
	(34)	(56)	(92)	(95)	(75)
White Protestants					
Under the age of 30	16%	22%	12%	25%	8%
	(116)	(81)	(26)	(20)	(12)
Aged 30 and over	18%	21%	26%	30%	27%
	(91)	(184)	(245)	(220)	(190)

[a] Asterisk indicates too few cases for stable percentaging.

the same as those seen in Table 12.4. Among white Catholics aged 30 and over, the percentages attending church every week rise consistently, from 29% among those having lived in their present house a year or less to 59% among those having lived in their present house more than 20 years. Among white Catholics under the age of 30, the relationship is less consistent, but the data show that the more mobile are generally less likely to be regular churchgoers than are the less mobile. The differences range from 23% among those having lived in their present house between 2 and 4 years to 62% among those having lived in their present house between 11 and 20 years. Among white Protestants aged 30 and over, there is also a general tendency for the more mobile to be less likely to attend church regularly than the less mobile. Among those having lived in their present house a year or less, only 18% attend weekly; by comparison, 30% of those having lived in their present house between 11 and 20 years attend weekly. Among Protestants under the age of 30, the pattern is virtually the same as among younger Catholics.

To summarize: More carefully designed questions would be necessary to say for sure what the relationship between church attendance and residential mobility is. But, on the basis of this evidence, it appears that there is indeed a tendency for residential mobility to dampen church attendance. Nor do the differences seem to be limited strictly to those between newcomers and more established residents. If lack of church attendance were merely a matter of newcomers' not being integrated into the community, we would have expected the greatest differences to have been between the "1 year or less" category and the other categories. As it turned out, the greatest differences were more often between those who had lived in their present community or house less than about 5 years and those who had lived there longer. Although it is impossible to say for sure, this pattern suggests that people may take a considerable time to put down roots—as far as church is concerned—and, given that many people never stay in any community longer than 5 years, some people may never establish such roots.

The evidence here indicates that church attendance is affected more by residential mobility among Catholics than it is among Protestants. It might have been expected that just the opposite would have been the case, since Catholicism tends to be more universal whereas Protestant churches might vary more from one community to another, making it more difficult for Protestants to find a satisfactory church upon moving to a new community. The more likely explanation given the present findings, however, is that Catholics take the communal aspect of their religion more seriously than do Protestants (as Lenski, 1961; Greeley, 1977, and others have argued); thus, moving to a new community becomes more disruptive of religious practice among Catholics than it does among Protestants.

Regional Migration

In this section, we consider more explicitly the effects of changes in region. Migration within the United States, especially from the Northeast and the Midwest to the South and West, has come to be far more significant numerically than foreign immigration. Between 1960 and 1976, for example, the South experienced a net increase in population due to migration of 3.5 million people. This increase represented a 6.4% gain relative to its 1960 population of 55.2 million. The West experienced an even larger gain from migration. Between 1960 and 1976, 4.7 million more people moved to than away from the West, representing a 16.6% increase relative to the West's 1960 population of 23.3 million.

Regional migration might be expected to affect church attendance in two ways. First, moving from one region to another means pulling up roots from one's community. We have just seen that residential mobility is negatively related to church attendance. Thus, we would expect regional mobility also to be negatively related to church attendance. This is, in fact, what the data show. In Table 12.6, persons presently living in a different region from that in which they were raised are compared with persons still living in the same region.[3] Among both white Catholics and white Protestants, regional migrants are less likely to attend church every week than are those who have not migrated.

The other way in which regional migration may affect church attendance is by exposing people to a new religious milieu. The West generally displays

TABLE 12.6 Church Attendance by Regional Mobility

	Living in region raised in?	
	Yes	No
Percentage who attend church every week among		
White Catholics	42%	33%
	(380)	(58)
White Protestants	25%	19%
	(880)	(236)

[3] Eight regions are used: New England (Connecticut, Maine, Massachusetts, New Hampshire, Rhode Island, Vermont), Middle Atlantic (Delaware, New Jersey, New York, Pennsylvania), East North Central (Illinois, Indiana, Michigan, Ohio, Wisconsin), West North Central (Iowa, Kansas, Minnesota, Missouri, Nebraska, North Dakota, South Dakota), Solid South (Virginia, Alabama, Arkansas, Florida, Georgia, Louisiana, Mississippi, North Carolina, South Carolina, Texas), Border States (Kentucky, Maryland, Oklahoma, Tennessee, Washington, D.C., West Virginia), Mountain States (Arizona, Colorado, Idaho, Montana, Nevada, New Mexico, Utah, Wyoming), and Pacific States (California, Oregon, Washington).

lower rates of religious commitment than other parts of the country in comparisons made possible by national polls (these are reviewed in Wuthnow, 1978). For example, in the 1977 Gallup poll only 30% of the West had been to church in the past week, as compared with 41% of the East, 45% of the Midwest, and 46% of the South (Gallup, 1978). The South, as these figures indicate, has usually shown the highest rates of religious participation in the United States. If there is any tendency for regional migrants to conform to their new surroundings, people moving to the West, therefore, might be expected to show decreased levels of church attendance, whereas people moving to the South might show increased levels. That people do conform to their new surroundings with respect to religion has been widely suggested in the literature on foreign migration, such that, for example, immigrants to the United States, where church attendance is more common, seem to increase their levels of participation, whereas immigrants to other countries where church attendance is less common appear to decrease their religious participation (Mol, 1965, 1971).

Since we do not have information on levels of church attendance *before* people migrated to a new region, we cannot examine directly whether migration is associated with increases or with decreases in church attendance. We can, however, compare people who have migrated to certain regions with those who have stayed behind or have migrated to other regions. We can do so in greater detail for white Protestants than for white Catholics, since there are more of the former than of the latter in the sample.

Table 12.7 reports the relationship between church attendance and regional migration among white Protestants. It affords comparisons between persons still living in the region in which they were raised (Northeast, Midwest, South, or West) and persons who have migrated from each of these regions to any of the other regions.[4] The bulk of this migration is from the Northeast and Midwest to the South and West. Among Protestants raised in the Northeast, 20% of those still living in the Northeast attend church every week. By comparison, among Protestants raised in the Northeast but now living in the South, only 16% attend church weekly, and none of those who are now living in the West attend weekly. Among those raised in the Midwest, the same percentages attend church regularly whether they still live in the Midwest or have migrated to the South (24% in each case). However, 9 percentage points fewer attend church weekly among those who have migrated to the West. For Protestants who were raised in the South, enough have migrated to both the Midwest and the West to make comparisons possible. In both instances, fewer

---

[4] The initial eight regions were collapsed as follows: Northeast (New England, Middle Atlantic), Midwest (East North Central, West North Central), South (Solid South, Border States), and West (Mountain States, Pacific States). See Footnote 3 for the states included in each of these regions.

TABLE 12.7   Church Attendance by Regional Migration among White Protestants[a]

	Region living now			
	Northeast	Midwest	South	West
Percentage who attend church every week among those raised in				
Northeast	20%	*	16%	0%
	(143)	(6)	(25)	(8)
Midwest	*	24%	24%	15%
	(3)	(348)	(41)	(40)
South	*	21%	30%	19%
	(4)	(28)	(356)	(16)
West	*	*	*	14%
	(0)	(2)	(5)	(92)

[a] Asterisk indicates too few cases for stable percentaging.

of the migrants attend church weekly than of those still living in the South. (Too few of those raised in the West have migrated to make comparisons possible.)

These data uniformly indicate, again, that church attendance is negatively related to residential migration. With both migration to the South (where church attendance is higher than the average) and migration to the West (where it is lower), the data indicate that migrants to both regions have lower church attendance rates than the nonmigrants. The only exception to this pattern is among Midwesterners who migrated to the South. The data also indicate that migration to the West seems to have more of a negative impact on church attendance than does migration to the South.

Among white Catholics, the results are less clear, partly because there are fewer Catholics in the sample and fewer migrants among Catholics (for comparison, see Table 12.8). It appears that migrants from either the Northeast or the Midwest to the West are less likely to attend church regularly than persons who remain in the Northeast or the Midwest. However, unlike Protestants, it appears that Catholics who migrate to the South are *more* likely to attend church regularly than are those who remain in the Northeast or the Midwest. Unfortunately, the data afford no further comparisons.

It is risky to infer very much from these findings, since the data were collected for only one time period. Perhaps, it may be that migration to a new region reduces church attendance because people fail to become integrated into new communities. It is also possible, however, that those who migrated were less frequent churchgoers even before they migrated. At any rate, the data suggest that migration to the West from parts of the country where church attendance is higher is not likely to increase church attendance rates in the West. The data also suggest, at least for Protestants, that migrants to the

TABLE 12.8   Church Attendance by Regional Migration among White Catholics[a]

	Region living now		
	Northeast/Midwest	South	West
Percentage who attend church every week among those raised in			
Northeast/Midwest	41%	61%	20%
	(309)	(18)	(15)
South	*	54%	*
	(7)	(36)	(3)
West	*	*	29%
	(0)	(1)	(34)

[a] Asterisk indicates too few cases for stable percentaging.

South are not conforming to the high rates of church attendance characteristic of the South, where the belief that "regular church attendance is prerequisite for being a good Christian [Reed, 1972:66]" is notably strong. Clearly, the effects of regional migration warrant further investigation.

Rural-Urban-Suburban Migration

The final type of migration we are able to examine is that from rural to urban areas and from urban to suburban areas. The urbanization process, although by no means new, is recent enough to have affected the lives of many persons in the sample. For example, 62% of the Catholics and 52% of the Protestants who were raised in small towns or in the country now live in cities or in suburbs. According to census figures, the proportion of people in the United States living in rural areas declined from 36% in 1950 to 26% in 1970. And, between 1960 and 1970, metropolitan areas grew by 17.1% while nonmetropolitan areas grew by only 2.4%. Migration from cities to suburban areas is a more recent phenomenon than urbanization, but one of comparable importance in the data. For example, 49% of the Catholics and 38% of the Protestants in the sample who had been raised in cities now live in the suburbs (another 13 and 31%, respectively, live in small towns or in rural areas). Nationally, the shift to the suburbs is also evidenced by the fact that central cities declined between 1960 and 1970 from 30.0% to 27.9% of the U.S. population while the so-called "urban fringe" grew from 22.8% to 28.9% of the total population.

There has been a long tradition of speculation about the effect of urbanization on religious commitment. Most of it has suggested that urbanization has a negative impact on religious commitment. One reason is that urban people may have more things to do with their leisure time. Another is that the urban world, being "man-made," limits speculation about the supernatural. Still another is that it is difficult in cities to cultivate intimate ties of the kind conducive to a deep-felt religious community. The only counterargument has been that churches may be easier to get to in the city than in the country—a difference that presumably has been reversed since the widespread diffusion of the automobile.

As far as suburbanization is concerned, arguments about its effects on religion have been less clear-cut. Gibson Winter (1962), for example, has suggested that churches have too readily fled to the suburbs, the inference being that church attendance might be higher in the suburbs than in the cities. Yet, many suburbs have grown faster than churches could be built. Recent migrants to the suburbs, therefore, might attend church less frequently simply because they lack facilities. Beyond this, of course, migrants both to the cities and to the suburbs may be affected by the sheer act of having pulled up community roots, as we have seen in the foregoing sections.

Questions were included in the survey both about the size of the community in which respondents had been raised and about the size of the community in which they were presently living. Although the questions were not worded exactly the same, they provide a means of comparing people who have migrated in one direction or another—from rural areas to the cities or from the cities to suburban areas—with people who have not migrated.

Table 12.9 reports the data for white Protestants. A look first at the bottom row reveals that people raised in the country and still living either in the country or in small towns are more likely to attend church every week (31% and 30%, respectively) than those who have migrated either to the suburbs or to the city (24% and 22%, respectively). Persons raised in small towns and still living there are also more likely to attend church every week than are those who have migrated away from small towns. Indeed, those who have migrated from small towns to the city are less likely to attend church regularly than are

TABLE 12.9   Church Attendance by Residential Area among White Protestants

	Kind of area living now			
	City	Suburbs	Town	Country
Percentage who attend church every week among those raised in				
City	21%	17%	16%	28%
	(102)	(124)	(70)	(32)
Town	16%	15%	34%	15%
	(49)	(108)	(93)	(39)
Country	22%	24%	30%	31%
	(64)	(129)	(62)	(134)

city dwellers who grew up in the city. Thus, the data seem to support the idea that urban migration has a negative effect on religious participation. The data also tend to suggest that migration to the suburbs is negatively associated with religious participation. People raised in the city are less likely to attend church every week after they have moved to the suburbs. But, since they are also less likely to attend if they have moved to small towns, the effect may not be unique to the suburbs.

The data for white Catholics are shown in Table 12.10. As among Protestants, migrants from rural areas and small towns to cities and suburbs are less likely to attend church every week than are those who remain behind. Distinguishing between city dwellers and migrants to the suburbs, however, the pattern is different from that among Protestants: There are virtually no differences in church attendance. The data, therefore, suggest that rural-to-urban migration may have a negative effect on church attendance but that, among Catholics, the shift to the suburbs from the cities may be inconsequential as far as church attendance is concerned. This finding is in disagreement with Zimmer and Hawley's (1959:351–352) discovery that movement to the city's "fringe" decreased church participation for Catholics; however, it supports the more recent findings of Gans (1967:264–265, 298n).

What these data do not tell is whether the differences between migrants to the cities and suburbs and nonmigrants are due to selective migration, the character of city and suburban life, or the act of migration itself. More extensive analysis and more refined data would be needed to sift out these possibilities. But, whatever the reasons, the data clearly indicate that the migration of the U.S. population from rural areas to urban areas and from urban areas to suburban areas (at least among Protestants) has been importantly associated with changing rates of religious participation.

TABLE 12.10   Church Attendance by Residential Area among White Catholics[a]

	Kind of area living now			
	City	Suburbs	Town	Country
Percentage who attend church every week among those raised in				
City	38%	37%	40%	*
	(93)	(122)	(30)	(3)
Town	32%	36%	40%	*
	(34)	(66)	(35)	(5)
Country	54%	41%	58%	67%
	(13)	(32)	(38)	(9)

[a] Asterisk indicates too few cases for reliable percentaging.

IV. Discussion

The foregoing has necessarily been exploratory and tentative, based as it was on secondary analysis of data originally collected for other purposes. We have not been able to examine the reasons *why* residential migration affects church attendance. Nor have we been able to specify whether migration has a causal effect on church attendance or whether there are only correlative differences in church attendance between migrants and nonmigrants. Since speculation has abounded in the absence of scarcely any systematic evidence on these relationships, it seemed useful to examine what the relationships are, however, before worrying too much about questions of a more theoretical nature. Such questions are meaningful only if there are, in fact, systematic differences between migrants and nonmigrants. To investigate the presence or absence of such differences, we analyzed church attendance patterns, using data from a recent national sample of the American population.

What we have found is that all four of the kinds of migration investigated—immigration, residential mobility, regional migration, and rural–urban–suburban migration—were associated with differences in levels of church attendance. First-generation Catholic immigrants were less likely than were second-generation immigrants (but equally likely as third-generation immigrants) to attend church regularly; Protestants showed no differences. Residential mobility was negatively associated with church attendance, especially among Catholics. Regional migration was negatively associated with church attendance, especially when it involved migration to the West. Migration from rural areas and small towns to urban and suburban places was negatively associated with church attendance, and, among Protestants, migration from urban to suburban areas was also negatively associated with church attendance.

On the basis of these findings, it may be useful to suggest several of the research questions that now seem to warrant further investigation. First, it appears that internal migration will become increasingly more important than foreign immigration as an influence on religious participation, at least in the American case, given the prevailing economic and environmental pressures acting to stimulate the former and to retard the latter. In particular, migration to the West and South and to the suburbs appears likely to have an important aggregate impact on American church attendance in the foreseeable future. Research to specify why these impacts are likely to be felt seems particularly warranted. Second, we have seen that differences in church attendance manifest themselves not only between immediate newcomers and longer-term residents but also between residents of 5–10 years' standing in a community and residents of longer duration as well. These differences suggest that migration may be characterized best not as an ephemeral disruption of community (including church) ties, but as a more prevailing dimension in the lives of certain classes of people—a dimension that deters them from sinking deep roots into their immediate community. The situation may resemble that of societies in which family ties are maintained with a wide set of kin but on a less-than-intimate level as a protection against the likely death of any single member. In American society, it may be that certain segments of the population for whom geographical mobility at frequent and often unpredictable intervals (e.g., among young people, executives, academicians, salesmen) is a requisite for the achievement of other values protect themselves from the grief of leaving friends behind simply by avoiding deep participation in community organizations in the first place. Further research, of course, is needed to determine if such is the case and, if so, for whom. Third, research is also needed to establish the causal connection between migration and church attendance. It has been readily assumed that Americans seldom let church ties stand in the way of economic opportunities that may require residential mobility. It may be, however, that religious participation is but one aspect of family-localism that does indeed deter migration. What we have witnessed as a negative relationship between migration and church attendance may be as much a matter of selective migration as of migration effects. Finally, the relationship between migration and other indicators of religious commitment, both behavioral and attitudinal, would appear to warrant investigation, since the present inquiry has been restricted to looking only at church attendance.

It might be added, in conclusion, that these remarks are restricted to the American situation. Both the meaning of migration and its effects on religious participation are likely to vary from society to society.

References

Abramson, Harold J.
  1973 *Ethnic Diversity in Catholic America.* New York:Wiley.
Bender, Eugene I. and George Kagiwada
  1968 ''Hansen's law of 'Third Generation Return' and the study of American religio-ethnic groups.'' *Phylon* 29(Winter):360–370.
Cox, Harvey
  1966 *The Secular City: Secularization and Urbanization in Theological Perspective.* New York:Macmillan.

Dynes, Russell R.
  1956 "Rurality, migration and sectarianism." *Rural Sociology* 21(March):25–28.
Gallup, George Jr.
  1978 *Religion in America, 1977–78.* Princeton:The Gallup Organization.
Gans, Herbert J.
  1967 *The Levittowners. Ways of Life and Politics in a New Suburban Community.* New York:Vintage Books.
Greeley, Andrew M.
  1976 "Council or encyclical?" *Review of Religious Research* 18(Fall):3–24.
  1977 *The American Catholic: A Social Portrait.* New York:Basic Books.
Hansen, Marcus Lee
  1952 "The third generation in America." *Commentary* 14(November):492–500.
Herberg, Will
  1960 *Protestant-Catholic-Jew.* Garden City, New York: Doubleday.
Lazerwitz, Bernard and Louis Rowitz
  1964 "The Three Generations hypothesis." *American Journal of Sociology* 69(March): 529–538.
Lenski, Gerhard E.
  1953 "Social correlates of religious interest." *American Sociological Review* 18(October): 533–544.
  1961 *The Religious Factor.* Garden City, New York: Doubleday.
Miller, Warren E. and Arthur H. Miller
  1977 *The CPS 1976 American National Election Study.* Ann Arbor, Michigan: Inter-University Consortium for Political and Social Research.
Mol, J. J.
  1965 "The decline in religious participation of migrants." *International Migration* 3(Summer):137–142.
  1971 "Immigration absorption and religion." *International Migration Review* 5(Spring): 62–71.
Nelson, Hart M. and H. David Allen
  1974 "Ethnicity, Americanization, and religious attendance." *American Journal of Sociology* 79(January):906–922.
Reed, John Shelton
  1972 *The Enduring South: Subcultural Persistence in Mass Society.* Chapel Hill, North Carolina: The University of North Carolina Press.
Schwarzweller, Harry K., James S. Brown, and J. J. Mangalam
  1971 *Mountain Families in Transition: A Case Study of Appalachian Migration.* University Park:The Pennsylvania State University Press.
Simpson, John H.
  1975 "Ethnic groups in Canada and the Herberg thesis." Paper presented at the annual meetings of the Society for the Scientific Study of Religion, Milwaukee, Wisconsin, October 24–26.
U.S. Bureau of the Census
  1977 Statistical Abstract of the U.S.: 1977. Washington, D.C.
Winter, Gibson
  1962 *The Suburban Captivity of the Churches.* New York:Macmillan.

Wuthnow, Robert
  1978 *Experimentation in American Religion: The New Mysticisms and Their Implications for the Churches.* Berkeley and Los Angeles:University of California Press.
Zimmer, Basil G. and Amos H. Hawley
  1959 "Suburbanization and church participation." *Social Forces* 37(May):348–354.

Chapter 13

A Crisis in the Moral Order:
The Effects of Watergate upon
Confidence in Social Institutions

ALBERT BERGESEN and MARK WARR

I. Introduction

We are only vaguely aware of the specifics of the modern religious life, in the Durkheimian understanding of that idea. We seem most aware that some sort of "civil religion" constitutes the set of collective representations and public rituals for the modern corporate society. And although there is no unanimity as to the institutional location of the "sacred" in modern times, the modern political community, the nation, seems to be the embodiment of sacred purposes and transcendent goals for most of the world's national societies. Totemic documents legitimating political power and authority, like constitutions, have been identified as sacred objects (Bergesen, 1977; Lerner, 1937). Presidential inaugurations (Bellah, 1970, 1975) and national holidays (Warner, 1961), along with purges, trials, and political witch-hunts in general (Bergesen, 1977, 1978a,b), have been identified as ritualistic mechanisms engaged in the renewal of common moral sentiments.

Our understanding of the interrelationship of the corporateness of society,

The Religious Dimension:
New Directions in Quantitative Research

its symbolization through a variety of distinctly modern collective representations (images of The people, The Nation, political ideologies, and so on), and the public rituals employed in the rejuvenation of these representations remains poor. One formulation that attempts to link many of the separate components we all feel central to the idea of civil religion is Kai Erikson's notion of a boundary crisis and the resultant moral reaffirmation of collective sentiments. The scheme was first applied to the Salem witch hunts (Erikson, 1966) and has since been applied to such areas as deviance in small groups (Lauderdale, 1976), lynching in Louisiana (Inverarity, 1976), and the Chinese Cultural Revolution (Bergesen, 1978b).

In this chapter we want to critically examine this idea and to apply it to a specific historical event: Watergate. Our understanding of the specific ways in which the Durkheimian elements of our civil religion operate will be expanded through the introduction of new analytical devices, like the boundary crisis idea, and the continued application of these general schemes to particular historical events, like Watergate. Only in this way will the ambiguity and inconsistency of these formulations be removed and our understanding of the modern religious situation be extended.

The Boundary Crisis Idea

Erikson's idea begins with Durkheim's discussion of the functions of crime for the solidarity of the community. For Durkheim, crime represents acts that violate the collective conscience and thereby elicit the wrath of the larger community. The punitive reactions resulting from that wrath reaffirm the moral order. Erikson argued that a society need not wait for someone to cross its normative order before attaining the desired effect of mobilizing the community in a ritualistic frenzy. The effect could be obtained another way. The society could move its boundaries, rather than waiting for the individuals to move across the boundaries, thus creating or manufacturing the needed deviance. You can, in effect, be on the wrong side of the moral order in two ways. Durkheim's position centers on individuals violating the moral order; they take certain actions that are offensive to the collective conscience. According to Erikson, a society alters its definitions of good and evil and thereby creates or manufactures deviance by labeling individuals as outside the normative boundaries. The result is the same: individuals or groups are on the wrong side of the moral order.

Erikson's thesis raises an important question. Why does the community suddenly act to create or to manufacture deviance? Erikson reasons that the community may be responding to external threats. When collective existence is endangered by some external threat, the community responds by creating deviants (moving its moral order) for the purpose of ritually reaffirming the threatened, blurred, weakened, or insecure collective social boundaries. There are, then, three stages to the process: (*a*) a threat (*b*) that causes a boundary crisis (*c*) that in turn generates the creation of some kind of moral outsiders (deviants, subversives, criminals, etc.) as a means of repairing the threatened boundaries. There are many problems with this formulation, and we will consider some of them.

Stage I: The Threat

The most general problem here is that we just do not always know what exactly constitutes a threat to collective existence. There are many obvious possibilites: threats of war, war itself, diplomatic humiliation, political incorporation by a larger collectivity, and so on. In fact, the whole range of problems and crises that might threaten the corporate existence of any collectivity would seem to qualify. Often we do not know whether or nor there has been an external threat until we see the outpouring of ritual persecution. We usually begin with an outburst of ritual persecution and then look for the possible causes. A good part of this problem lies in the possibility that there are different magnitudes of threat and different strengths to social boundaries. There may be threats of the same magnitude, but in one society the boundaries are more vulnerable, so the result is a ritual effort at boundary repair. Conversely, some societies may have particularly resilient boundaries so that a threat of the same magnitude will have no effect or only a minor one.

Although we are still groping to understand the exact nature of these threats to collective existence, we can identify at least three general types.

External Threats to Collective Existence

The first kind of threat involves threats or acts of war, political incorporation by a larger unit, and so on—anything, in effect, that alters or threatens the nature of the collectivity in question. Examples would include: the King of England's revoking the charter under which the Massachusetts Bay Colony was established, which preceded the witch hunting in Salem; the presence of foreign armies marching on Paris and threatening the existence of the new revolutionary regime which occurred prior to the Reign of Terror during the French Revolution; or the perceived threat by the Chinese in 1965 of war with America, just before the outbreak of the Chinese Cultural Revolution in 1966 (see Bergesen, 1978b, for a further discussion of the Chinese Cultural Revolution). It appears that the ritual persecution can occur before a conflict, as with the Stalinist Purges of the late 1930s, which occurred just prior to war with Germany, wherein the collectivity seemed to be morally revitalizing itself just before taking collective action. Or the moral persecution may come after a collective crisis, as with the Palmer Raids after World War I or the McCarthy period after the Korean War. Here the collectivity seems to be revitalizing itself after a collective crisis.

Contextual Pressures

McCarthyism can be seen as a simple response to an external threat—Communism, the Soviet Union, etc. It can also be seen as a reflection of a sort of strain in collective existence that was created when new obligations were placed on the collectivity as a corporate actor, as seen in the global obligations of the United States as the hegemonic world power following World War II. This was Parson's (1962) analysis of McCarthyism: The demands to act as a corporate entity, plus the absence of a foreign policy elite, created ambiguities and strains as to how to fulfill the nation's collective obligations. The ritual persecution of subversives is one way to reaffirm a faltering national identity. Similar crises in national identity may also be generated by a contextual change, even if the collectivity has a well-developed structural apparatus for corporate decision making.

Internal Developmental Pressures

Here there may be neither an external threat nor a change in political context. The source of strain comes from the very process of developing as a corporate actor. In the case of Erikson's Puritans, they were establishing a new social order, and the process of creating institutions and, more importantly, a common collective identity, entailed ritual persecutions of enemies of the regime as a means of defining the central meaning of national existence. If a firmly established social community does not exist, it may be difficult to have crises in social boundaries that are scarcely formed. But ritual persecution may, nonetheless, still occur as a means of initially establishing a common identity, rather than as a response to some external or contextual pressures. Much of the xenophobia of new nations, and their search for enemies, may be attributable to Durkheimian elements of national development, a phase that new polities pass through as a means of establishing a national identity.

Stage II: The Boundary Crisis

The idea is simple enough: Some aspect of a collectivity's sense of itself as a corporate entity is weakened, blurred, threatened, dissolving, or becoming otherwise problematical and uncertain. There seem to be at least two parts.

Collective Identity Problems

First there are the more factual, definitional, or cognitive aspects of collective existence—the question of a collective identity. Here the crisis takes the form of not knowing what it means to be, for example, an American, a revolutionary, or a Christian. The means to reestablish this identity involve the discovery of those who oppose the common identity, for in that way it can be dramatically shown (trials, purges, confessions, inquisitions, etc.) just what it means to be a loyal American, a dedicated revolutionary, or a good Christian.

Moral Problems

A second problem focuses upon questions of good and evil, of the common morality, and of just what a country stands for. The response here is the discovery of pollutors, deviants, subversives, and anyone or anything (e.g., literature and art) that is seen as corrupting the common morality. Although we can analytically separate the definitional from the moral aspect of a boundary crisis, it is probable that they are found together during any particular outburst of ritual persecution.

Crises in collective existence are the hardest to measure or, for that matter, of which to find good examples. Although we as yet do not measure threats, we can at least provide plausible examples, and we can, and do, measure outbreaks of ritual persecutions. The second part of this chapter, dealing with Watergate and confidence in our social institutions, suggests a possible empirical way of looking at what we consider a possible boundary crisis.

Stage III: Ritual Persecution

This is the final stage: the creation of deviants as a means of reaffirming the nature of collective reality. This is the area in which we have done the most work and have had the most success in obtaining empirical data. Data have been gathered on arrests in Salem (Erikson, 1966); political trials, purges, and confessions (Bergesen, 1977); lynchings (Inverarity, 1976); and the persecution of deviants in small groups (Lauderdale, 1976). This is where we always seem to begin, with some outbreak of persecution. The identification of a possible threat to the community and the boundaries that might have been endangered are, unfortunately, almost always matters of conjecture.

II. A Specific Example: Watergate

In the rest of this chapter we want to examine a specific event, Watergate, as an example of these general Durkheimian processes of moral revitalization following collective crises. We will also focus specifically upon Stage II, the crisis in collective existence, or Erikson's boundary crisis, in part because of its elusive nature and in part because we have some data that bear on this issue.

Data and Method

We are going to examine five consecutive annual surveys conducted by the National Opinion Research Center (NORC) from 1973 through 1977 that included questions about confidence in 12 social institutions: the executive branch of the federal government, the press, the Supreme Court, organized religion, Congress, major companies, education, medicine, organized labor, television, the scientific community, and the military.

Each year's sample is purportedly representative of the noninstitutionalized adult (18 years of age and older) population of the continental United States. Block quota sampling was employed in the 1972–1974 surveys and in half of the 1975 and 1976 surveys. Full probability sampling was used in half of the 1975 and 1976 surveys and in the entire 1977 survey. This "split" sampling design was incorporated in the 1975 and 1976 surveys in order to assess differences in the sampling procedures. In this analysis, we will assume that the divergent sampling procedures do not affect the comparability of the surveys (for support of this assumption, see Turner, 1978).

In each survey year, respondents were asked to indicate the degree of confidence they felt toward the "people running" 12 different social institutions. The specific question was:

I am going to name some institutions in this country. As far as the people running these institutions are concerned, would you say you have a great deal of confidence, only some confidence, or hardly any confidence at all in them?

The order of presentation of the institutions was the same in the five surveys, with the exception that "banks and financial institutions" was added as the first institution in the last three survey years. Since a question on banks was asked in only three survey years, we will exclude that institution from this analysis. The order in which we present the institutions is not the same as that used by NORC, and can be obtained from the NORC codebooks (NORC, 1973–1977).

Of the three possible responses (a great deal, only some, and hardly any), the first two were combined to give us a dichotomous measure of "skepticism" in social institutions. The odds on skepticism (the ratio of "hardly any" responses to the other two categories combined) were computed for each institution in each survey year. The odds on lack of confidence (skepticism) in each of 12 social institutions from 1973 through 1977 are plotted in Figure 13.1. (The specific odds are presented in the Appendix.) To measure changes in skepticism from one year to the next, we computed odds ratios by dividing the odds on skepticism for each year by the odds on skepticism for the previous year. These odds ratios appear under the heading "adjacent years" in Table 13.1. In order to compute changes over a longer period, we also computed odds ratios for nonadjacent years by dividing each year's odds by the odds for

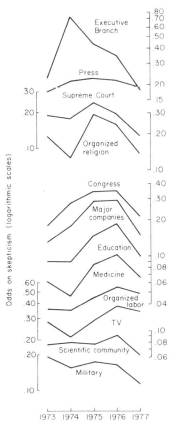

Figure 13.1 Observed odds on skepticism for twelve institutions: 1973–1977. Appropriate scales (designated as "right" or "left") for each institution are, in order: Executive branch, Press—right scale; Supreme Court—left scale; Organized religion through Medicine—right scale; Organized labor, TV—left scale; Scientific community—right scale; Military—left scale.

the period 2 years earlier. These odds ratios are presented under the heading "nonadjacent years" in Table 13.1. Each odds ratio, then, indicates the direction and magnitude of change in skepticism for a given institution and given time period. Sine the odds ratios are always computed using the later year as the numerator, an odds ratio greater than 1.0 indicates an increase in skepticism, whereas an odds ratio of less than 1.0 indicates a decrease in skepticism. In order to take into account sampling fluctuations in our estimates of changes in skepticism, a 2 × 2 table (skepticism by year) was constructed for each institution for adjacent and nonadjacent years. Chi-square was computed for each table, and in those cases where we failed to reject the null hypothesis of independence between year and skepticism (at the .05 level) an asterisk was placed beside the appropriate odds ratio (see Table 13.1).

TABLE 13.1   Odds Ratios(between Years) for Twelve Institutions[a]

Institutions	Adjacent years				Nonadjacent years		
	1973–1974	1974–1975	1975–1976	1976–1977	1973–1975	1974–1976	1975–1977
Executive branch of the federal government	3.225	.584	.801	.506	1.885	.468	.405
Press	1.229	1.047*	.973*	.857*	1.286	1.019*	.834
U.S. Supreme Court	.933*	1.360	.806	.655	1.269	1.097*	.529
Organized religion	.631	2.832	.822	.561	1.502	1.958	.461
Congress	1.518	1.275	1.015*	.604	1.936	1.294	.613
Major companies	1.352	1.632	1.027*	.496	2.207	1.677	.510
Education	.933*	1.653	1.246	.526	1.641	2.060	.656
Medicine	.769*	1.833	1.192*	.642	1.409	2.184	.765
Organized labor	.969*	1.284	1.225	.881*	1.244	1.574	1.079*
TV	.747	1.405	1.288	.892*	1.050*	1.811	1.149*
Scientific community	1.046*	.964*	1.195*	.675	1.008*	1.153*	.806*
Military	.806	1.106*	.938*	.717	.892*	1.037*	.672

[a] Asterisks indicate change in skepticism is not statistically significant. See text for discussion of tests of significance.

The odds on skepticism should be interpreted cautiously for a number of reasons. The reliability of the NORC data has been called into question because of differences in responses to the confidence items between the NORC surveys and the Harris surveys (which have also included some of those same items). Many of these differences cannot be attributed to simple sampling fluctuations (Turner, 1978). Also, we were not able to fit any models specifying, for example, equivalent slopes for particular institutions. Although minimum logit chi-square regression (Theil, 1970) is an appropriate technique for our analysis, that method requires cross-classification of the data. With longitudinal data on 12 institutions, a 13-way table is required, and the NORC sample size is too small to prevent large numbers of cells with zero frequencies. Also, since the odds on skepticism for each institution were computed using the entire sample for a particular year, the odds for each institution within a given year are not independent. Hence, similarities in the level of skepticism among institutions in the same year may be partially attributable to a "response set" on the part of some respondents. Finally, the rise in skepticism in most institutions following Watergate does not necessarily establish a causal relationship between skepticism toward the executive branch and skepticism toward other institutions. The most we can say is that the present data are consistent with such an interpretation.

III. Findings

Looking at Figure 13.1, we can see a dramatic increase in skepticism toward the executive branch in 1973–1974, followed by a rise in skepticism in eight other institutions in 1974–1975. The rise and then decline of skepticism following the dramatic increase in skepticism in the executive branch was not observed for three institutions: the press, the scientific community, and the military. The press showed a statistically significant increase for 1973–1974 (the same year as the executive branch) but failed to change significantly through the remaining years. Confidence in the scientific community showed no statistically significant changes up until 1976. Then there was a significant decrease in skepticism from 1976 to 1977. As Figure 13.1 shows, there was an increase in skepticism in the 1975–1976 period, but it was not a statistically significant change. The military shows a general decline from 1973 through 1977. (A statistically significant decline in 1973–1976 was followed by two periods of nonsignificant decline, 1974–1975 and 1973–1976, which was then followed by a period of significant decline, 1976–1977.) The following discussion of changes in skepticism will be limited to those remaining eight institutions that exhibit the general pattern of a rise in skepticism following Watergate.

Skepticism toward the Executive Branch

The first graph in Figure 13.1 depicts the odds on lack of confidence in the "people running" the executive branch of the federal government. As the focus of the Watergate scandal was the presidency itself, we expect the level of skepticism toward the executive branch to reflect the major events during Watergate. At the time of the first survey, in March and April of 1973, Watergate had not yet become a major political issue. Although the *Washington Post* had implicated White House officials in the Watergate break-in, those allegations had been vociferously denied by the White House. The 1973 survey period included the disclosure of the McCord letter, perhaps the first direct evidence of White House culpability, and the last day of the nominal survey period saw the departure of top White House officials, although this event could only have had a minimal effect on aggregate responses to the skepticism question. The impact of Watergate, then, was not large at this time (1973), and the odds on skepticism toward the executive branch reflect this (see Figure 13.1).

At the time of the second survey in March, 1974, Watergate had grown into a major domestic crisis. Nixon was embroiled in a battle over the presidential tapes, and calls for impeachment were common. The crisis of the presidency is reflected in the dramatic increase in lack of confidence in the executive branch that occurred from 1973 to 1974. Skepticism toward the executive branch reached its highest point in 1974. In that year, Nixon resigned and Ford became President, vowing to restore confidence in the executive branch. By the time of the 1975 survey, skepticism toward the executive branch was on the decline, a trend that continued through the 1977 survey. Whereas skepticism reached an upper limit in a 1-year period, a 3-year period was required for a return to the approximate initial (1973) level.

The Moral Ripple: Skepticism toward Other Institutions

As previously noted, the major impact of Watergate on skepticism toward the executive branch occurred between 1973 and 1974. Table 13.1 shows that the odds on skepticism increased by a factor of 3.2 during this period, which is quite a large increase. In absolute terms, 43% of the respondents (excluding those who gave no answer or said they did not know) indicated that they had hardly any confidence in the executive branch in 1974. Skepticism toward other institutions, though, showed no consistent pattern. Although skepticism toward major companies and toward Congress also increased, skepticism toward the remaining institutions either decreased or revealed no significant change.

From 1974 to 1975, skepticism toward the executive branch declined, although the absolute level of skepticism remained high relative to the 1973 level. However, skepticism toward all eight of the other institutions increased at this time. The second column in Table 13.1 provides fairly compelling evidence that, between 1974 and 1975, a lack of confidence had diffused from the executive branch to other institutions. The evidence is somewhat stronger when we consider the fact that for several institutions skepticism was actually decreasing prior to Watergate but then began to increase. Although changes from 1973 to 1974 cannot be characterized as trends, reversals in the direction of change nonetheless suggest a Watergate impact on confidence in other institutions.

During the next period, from 1975 to 1976, skepticism increased for education, organized labor, and TV, showed no statistically significant change for Congress, major companies, or medicine, and declined for the Supreme Court and organized religion (see Table 13.1). Compared to the increases in skepticism for all eight institutions during 1974–1975, the changes for 1975–1976 suggest the beginning of a recovery. Five of the eight institutions either declined, although the declines in organized labor and TV are very small, or did not change significantly, and the three that did increase, did so at a slower rate than in the earlier period. Nonetheless, the overall evidence does suggest the beginning of a recovery in confidence in social institutions during this period.

Finally, during the 1976–1977 period, skepticism in all eight institutions showed a decline, although the declines in organized labor and in TV were not statistically significant.

Nonadjacent Years

We also looked at changes in skepticism over 2–year periods. The relevant odds ratios are presented in Table 13.1. During the first period, 1973–1975, there was an increase in skepticism for all eight institutions, except TV. This finding is not particularly surprising, since we already know that skepticism increased for all of the institutions (other than the executive branch) from 1974 to 1975. However, the longer-term increases do indicate that, for those institutions for which skepticism decreased from 1973 to 1974, the increases from 1974 to 1975 were large enough to yield a net *increase* over the entire 2-year period. In those cases, the effect of Watergate was not only to reverse the direction of change but also to induce a change of a magnitude greater than or equal to that of the previous year. The odds ratios for 1974–1976 in Table 13.1 show that skepticism is higher in 1976 than in 1974 for all institutions except the Supreme Court. These odds ratios indicate that the beginning of the recovery of 1975–1976 was not sufficient to reduce skepticism to the 1974 level. Although a recovery had apparently begun, it was far from complete.

For the last period, 1975–1977, a statistically significant decline occurred in all eight institutions, except organized labor and TV. In these cases, strong 1975–1976 increases were proportional to the decreases in 1976–1977, yielding a net lack of change.

Summary of Findings

With the exception of TV, skepticism increased from 1973 to 1975 for all institutions. In the case of TV, however, the apparent lack of change reflects only a high level of skepticism in 1973. For most of the institutions, the net increases from 1973 to 1975 are due to large increases from 1974 to 1975, the period directly following the Watergate scandal. From 1975 to 1976, a "slowdown" in skepticism occurred, although the level of skepticism remained higher than the 1974 level for all institutions except the Supreme Court. The period from 1976 to 1977 saw a decline of skepticism for all institutions, the first clear evidence of a general recovery.

In sum, the observed changes in skepticism among the eight institutions do not appear to be independent. Whatever the cause of the "ripple" in skepticism, its effect extends to very different kinds of institutions. Moreover, the data suggest that we have captured an entire process, something that we tentatively describe as a "moral ripple." We will now go on to suggest some possible explanations for these findings.

IV. Watergate and the Boundary Crisis

There are at least two Durkheimian scenarios for Watergate. The first centers upon the original Durkheimian understanding of crime and the reaction of the larger community. Nixon and his associates, in effect, really *did* things out of the ordinary, and the community reacted to morally refortify itself. In this sense, Watergate may be more like traditional scandals, such as those surrounding President Grant or the Tea Pot Dome scandal of the 1920s. Here, people are actually engaged in violating the moral order, rather than only being so-labeled by the community for its own collective purposes. A second explanation follows the boundary crisis logic. The Vietnam war—unpopular, divisive, and increasingly perceived as morally illegitimate—was an obvious instance of a collective crisis for the United States. Was Watergate, then, a collective response to the uncertainty and divisiveness of the Vietnam War, or was it a consequence of Nixon's actual wrongdoing? If, as the defendants of Nixon claim, other presidents had committed similar acts, then the source of the reaction may have been more the needs of the corporate nation for moral revitalization than a reaction to Nixon's having violated its normative rules. Or it may also be that both sorts of things are going on at once: The nation needed rites of moral solidarity after the divisive Vietnam War and used Nixon's violations of normal political conduct as the basis for a revitalization campaign—the high public drama and ritual of impeachment proceedings, the daily media "disclosures" of new evidence, and the mobilization of persons through their "forced" preoccupation with the question of what Nixon really knew and what he really did.

Regardless of what he did or did not do, or whether others before had done similar things, the events provided a national ritual of moral revitalization wherein it was shown that "the system does work." The moral lesson, explicated in editorials, in newspaper and magazine articles, and among the populace at large, was that America is a nation of law and due process, where not even a president exists above or beyond the law. The *system,* America as a set of collective social arrangements, as a functioning corporate order, *worked.* America lived up to its ideals, overcame threats to the Republic, and reaffirmed the fundamental beliefs and assumptions upon which it was founded. Watergate was one of the best examples of the reaffirmation of collective sentiments and common beliefs in modern societies that we have seen in a long while. The nation was clearly morally aroused. Questions of the integrity of our institutions and leaders and of the ability of the system to function properly dominated discussions both in the media and in private discourse. It was drama of the highest order, and it elicited the kinds of emotions that only a mobilized collectivity can bring out in its members. One need not fantasize some primitive religious rite to capture the feeling of the Durkheimian process in action; living through the trauma of Watergate provided all the collective fervor one needed.

Assuming, then, that either the divisive Vietnam War or Nixon's own actions generated a threat (Stage I), what evidence do we have for Stage II, the crisis in collective existence, or Erikson's boundary crisis? We can look at confidence in social institutions as an indicator of the relative vitality of a society's moral order. Confidence in social institutions can reflect the moral status of the social order itself, and a drop in that confidence can be seen as a crisis in collective existence, as in Erikson's idea of a boundary crisis. Although we usually ask what causes individuals to lose faith in or feel alienated from their institutions, the question posed here is why the generalized moral worth of the social order, as expressed in the confidence questions about the 12 institutions, varies over time and, particularly, why one should get the rise and fall in confidence that we have documented in Figure 13.1.

The Moral Ripple

If we look at confidence in institutions as a sort of "moral barometer," then the dip in confidence surrounding Watergate can be seen as a reflection of what Erikson refers to as a boundary crisis. The divisive Vietnam War or Nixon's actions (Stage I) provide a crisis that is manifested in the dramatic decline in confidence in the executive branch that then spreads to other institutions (Stage II). The public drama of impeachment hearings and daily media discoveries of new evidence and disclosures act to arouse and involve the citizenry in the rituals of a nation renewing itself (Stage III). Watergate becomes not only a problem for Congress, the Supreme Court, and the press but also for our private lives. The issue of Nixon's guilt or innocence, plus the never fully answered question of just what happened, dominated the lives and discussions of ordinary citizens. The ritual of Watergate, along with the presidential election in 1976, make up Stage III in the Erikson process: the discovery (or imputation) of deviance (Nixon's and his associates' actions) and the healing ritual of Jimmy Carter's presidential campaign.

Now, why did this shiver of skepticism spread from the executive branch to other social institutions? As with our earlier discussion of the possible interpretations of the Erikson model, the same problem appears. The spread of skepticism may have reflected the magnitude of the crisis; the "vibrations of skepticism" also shook neighboring institutions, creating a sort of "domino effect" as uncertainty spread from one institution to another. Following this idea, if there were a less severe threat and, thus, less of a collective crisis, then presumably the vibrations would not have spread as far across social institutions. The imagery here is the ripple effect, with the crisis of Watergate the stone thrown into a calm pond. The resultant crisis in confidence is represented by the waves or ripples the stone generates. It first appears at the center of the social system—the executive branch—and then moves in concentric circles through social space. The harder the stone is thrown (the greater the threat), the further the ripple extends (the more social institutions drop in confidence).

Another interpretation focuses upon the political organization of society. In states that are more tightly organized, more corporate in character, large political purposes become those of various other institutions (education, economy, etc.). This is what is meant by totalitarian societies, where the central political values are applied to all other areas. This notion is similar to Swanson's (1971) idea of immanence, where collective purposes are infused into the things and structures of everyday life (see Bergesen, 1978b, for a discussion of the notion of immanence in modern political terms). The more that political values penetrate other spheres of life, the more a crisis in the polity, like the drop of confidence in the executive branch, should generate crises of confidence for other institutions. Here we are varying the organization of society, not the strength of the threat. In any concrete historical incident, of course, both factors undoubtedly operate. Societies can be arranged along a corporateness continuum (Bergesen, 1978a). This continuum represents the extent to which different areas of institutional life are managed by the polity and have their purposes subordinated to the overall goals of the corporate collectivity. Given a threat of the same magnitude, the extensiveness of the moral ripple, the number of other institutions to experience a loss in confidence, will depend upon the position of that society along the corporateness continuum. The more tightly managed and organized societies should find the ripple passing through their institutional space faster, and the magnitude of that skepticism should also be greater. For the less well-organized societies, a threat of equal magnitude should travel less far. The more tightly the society is organized, the more easily the shiver is conducted and, hence, the more the ripple effect is noticed. Some support for these ideas comes from a study of political witch-hunts (Bergesen, 1977). There it was found that corporateness (as measured by type of political party system: one, two, and multiparty) was related to the extensiveness of witch hunting across different institutional areas. The more corporate the society, the more spread-out was its witch hunting; that is, subversion was discovered in more social institutions (economy, polity, military, education, etc.).

The 1976 Presidential Election: Rites of National Reunification

Skepticism toward the executive branch peaks in 1974 and then begins to drop; the Supreme Court, the military, the press, and organized religion peak in 1975 and begin to drop. The rest, Congress, major companies, education, medicine, organized labor, TV, and the scientific community, peak in 1976 and then begin to decline. Clearly, 1976 was an important turning point for skepticism toward many social institutions. This was the year of a Presidential election, though, and this complicates matters. We usually think of the boundary-crisis repair process as organic; that is, the social order repairs itself. In this case, the healing process was interrupted by a major national rite, a presidential election. Would those areas that changed direction in 1976 have continued to rise in skepticism if it were not for the revitalization effect of a presidential election? We will not know, although, for those institutions that peaked earlier, the cycle was seemingly running its own course.

The most consistent period of decreasing skepticism followed the election of 1976. The drama and ritual of Watergate may have sufficed to reaffirm faith in the nation, and the rise in skepticism may have peaked on its own without the interference of the election. Regardless, the rite of national renewal, a Presidential election, marked an increase in confidence in all social institutions and provided another element of moral revitalization to go along with the impeachment ritual of Watergate. The election of Jimmy Carter is particularly interesting in this regard. His rise from a one-term Georgia governor not possessing any well-formed ideology or "stand on the issues" and with weak attachments to the Democratic Party, labor, and other interest groups that Democrats traditionally represent, made him, as some have observed, the first elected independent president. But Carter was more than just an independent in the narrow electoral sense of that term. He did have a constituency: the nation as a whole. For Carter was the perfect Durkheimian candidate. Appearing on the heels of Watergate and the Vietnam War and coming from "nowhere," Carter did not appear as a candidate representing the values and ideologies of any clearly identifiable social group. He spoke in broad moral terms about the central values of Americans and about their goodness and moral worth. During the Democratic primaries, while other candidates focused upon particular issues or appealed to particular groups, Carter seemed to be addressing the American People as a whole, and, even more interestingly, he seemed to be speaking for them. It was as if the process of self-renewal by which the American people were healing the wounds of Vietnam and Watergate focused upon Carter as a sort of oracle for the American people, allowing them to speak to themselves, to forgive themselves, to forget the past, and to reaffirm their essential goodness by voting for the totemic representation of their collective self—the "outsider," the "non-Washingtonian," the man who was to return decency and honesty to government. In some sense, any candidate would have filled the Durkheimian void following Watergate if he had preached moral goodness and faith in America. Carter's own campaign was a rite of national reunification.

> What he conducted was a campaign of good intentions. It may have been really about all, given his scanty and perfunctory experience, he had to commend himself. But as Wooten [the book Frady is reviewing] points out, after so protracted a national season of trauma and disillusionment, the entire country seemed "desperately determined to believe affirmatively in his undefined possibilities." His campaign proceeded, actually, like nothing so much as a kind of altar call, populist in mood, for a national New Birth—an appeal for a national redemption and atonement, a "regeneration of its fouled spirit," as Wooten puts it. Through it all Wooten adds, "he had not spoken of faults but rather of possibilities." It was as if, by his simply proposing it so, all those discomforts—Vietnam, Watergate with its complex of accessory scandals—could be expiated and dispelled, no more: "It had simply happened," explains Wooten, "and it happened yesterday and it had nothing to do with today or tomorrow"—a benign and gentle amnesia . . . a disintegration of the collective national experience into successive, disconnected oblivious episodes, without any larger comprehending continuum of memory or meaning [Frady, 1978:22; material in brackets added].

This depiction of the Carter campaign could also be a classic description of the Durkheimian process of self-renewal and moral revitalization. Carter represented collective purposes, a totem, through which the revitalization process proceeded:

> "At the end of all of his public appearances, he would quietly intone, "Can we be decent, and honest, and truthful, and fair, and compassionate . . . can we be pure, and honest, and idealistic, and compassionate?" It was like an incantation with him, as if by simply sounding the words in the air, "kind, and truthful, and decent," the reality itself might, by some magic of mimesis, be conjured forth; or more, by his sheer insistent recital of those words, he might in some way assume and own and become the qualities themselves, take on purity and compassion [Frady, 1978:23].[1]

V. Conclusion

We have, from Vietnam through the election of Jimmy Carter in 1976, an episode in the moral life of a nation. It provides an example of the workings of collective life, of the role of ritual rejuvenation and persecution, and of how individual lives can become totemic carriers of larger purposes and agents of larger social mechanics beyond their control and comprehension. Certainly, Nixon remains perplexed over the outrage at his actions, defending to the end that others had done similar things. And Carter, finding his small life elevated by the needs for collective revitalization, has come to discover the other side of the social coin, that the practicalities of running a country may provide for his downfall as much as the collective need for rejuvenation propelled his rapid ascent.

There are, and will continue to be, many interpretations of this period, and they need not be mutually exclusive. Many models, in effect, can fit the same data. In this chapter we have attempted to elucidate some of the distinctly

---

[1] There is a strange Durkheimian irony in that what the collectivity required in terms of national reunification—the broad moral platitudes of Carter—are of less use when it comes to actually running the government. Once in office, the social reality changes. Here, being without a constituency, connections, friends, obligations due, and all the ways in which a politician is grounded or enmeshed in the web of deals, political influence, and so on proved to be a handicap. What was needed for moral reaffirmation was not needed to run the country. "At the least, it is beginning to seem more and more likely that the brief political romance of the stranger, the unsullied and adventuresome outsider, is over with forever . . . . What has seemed a readiness to be glibly and indiscriminately inspiriting and reassuring . . . has not exactly dissipated the increasing unease about his actual grasp of presidential power and of the difficulties of dealing with bureaucracies,lobbies, and legislators [Frady, 1978:26]." What was needed for moral revitalization was someone from another world—unsullied, pure in motive and intent, the "Washington outsider." What was needed to run the country was someone with connections, influences, and clout, and capable of making deals—someone of this world, someone profane, not sacred.

Durkheimian features of these events, with particular attention being paid to the means by which the collectivity renews and revitalizes its moral life.

APPENDIX 13.1 Observed Odds on Skepticism for Twelve Institutions: 1973–1974

Institutions	Observed odds on skepticism				
	1973	1974	1975	1976	1977
Executive branch of the federal government	.230	.743	.434	.348	.176
Press	.175	.215	.225	.219	.188
U.S. Supreme Court	.190	.177	.241	.194	.127
Organized religion	.197	.124	.295	.243	.136
Congress	.180	.274	.349	.355	.214
Major companies	.131	.177	.289	.297	.147
Education	.091	.090	.149	.186	.098
Medicine	.062	.047	.087	.103	.066
Organized labor	.366	.355	.456	.558	.492
TV	.284	.212	.298	.384	.342
Scientific community	.078	.081	.078	.093	.063
Military	.198	.160	.177	.166	.119

References

Bellah, Robert N.
  1970 *Beyond Belief.* New York:Harper and Row.
  1975 *The Broken Covenant.* New York:Seabury.
Bergesen, Albert James
  1977 "Political witch hunts: The sacred and the subversive in cross-national perspective." *American Sociological Review* 42(April):220–233.
  1978a "Rituals, symbols, and society: Explicating the mechanisms of the moral order." *American Journal of Sociology* 83(January):1012–1021.
  1978b "A Durkheimian theory of political witch hunts with the Chinese Cultural Revolution of 1966–1969 as an example." *Journal for the Scientific Study of Religion* 17(March):19–29.
Erikson, Kai T.
  1966 *The Wayward Puritans.* New York:Wiley.
Frady, Marshall
  1978 "Why he's not the best." *New York Review of Books* May 18:18–27.
Inverarity, James M.
  1976 "Populism and lynching in Louisiana, 1889–1896: A test of Erikson's theory of the relationship between boundary crises and repressive justice." *American Sociological Review* 41(April):262–280.
Lauderdale, Pat
  1976 "Deviance and moral boundaries." *American Sociological Review* 41(August):660–676.

Lerner, Max
  1937 "Constitution and courts as symbols." *Yale Law Journal* 46:1290–1319.
National Opinion Research Center
  1973– *Codebooks for the General Social Surveys.* Chicago:NORC.
  1977
Parsons, Talcott
  1962 "Social strains in America." Pp. 209–229 in Daniel Bell (ed.), *The Radical Right.*
        New York:Anchor Books.
Swanson, Guy E.
  1971 "An organizational analysis of collectivities." *American Sociological Review*
        36(August):607–623.
Theil, Henri
  1970 "On the estimation of relationships involving qualitative variables." *American Journal of Sociology* 76(July):103–154.
Turner, Charles
  1978 "Fallible indicators of the subjective state of the nation." *American Psychologist* 33(May).
Warner, Lloyd W.
  1961 *The Family of God.* New Haven:Yale University Press.

Part IV

NEW DIRECTIONS
IN COMPARATIVE
AND HISTORICAL
RESEARCH

Chapter 14

Sovereign Groups, Subsistence Activities, and the Presence of a High God in Primitive Societies

JOHN H. SIMPSON

I. Introduction

Since the Enlightenment, enquirers have sought natural, rational, or social explanations for the human experience of the supernatural. Within the body of sociological thought, one of the most prominent efforts in this regard is Emile Durkheim's (1915) *The Elementary Forms of the Religious Life.* Durkheim argued, essentially, that religious ideas and beliefs symbolize or model the social forces, structures, and relationships that constrain and compel the action of people in societies. A religious belief, then, in Durkheim's view, is a collectively held representation of some fundamental aspect of social life.

Reasoning within the Durkheimian perspective, Swanson (1960) in his monograph, *The Birth of the Gods,* adduces the following hypothesis: The belief that a high god or monotheistic deity exists will tend to occur in those societies containing three or more different types of hierarchically ordered sovereign groups. In Swanson's view, the presence of three or more types of sovereign groups in a society, with one group dominating the others, provides the social condition that a high god symbolizes or represents.

The Religious Dimension:
New Directions in Quantitative Research

Swanson argues as follows: A high god is, in some sense, the determiner of all events that occur. He is, above all, a being who brings order among diverse and powerful "others" subordinate to him. If he is to perform this activity, he must have available at least two *distinct* subordinate others in order to create a relationship between them. Subordinate others, themselves, must have the capacity for distinct purposive collective action. A deity controlling only lesser entities would not be truly sovereign. A sovereign group is a social unit that does have the capacity for purposive collective action. It has original jurisdiction over some important social functions and a continuing organizational apparatus for making choices and for taking action. In a society, then, with three or more hierarchically ordered sovereign groups, a social model exists for a high god who, like the dominant sovereign group, reviews, judges, or modifies the actions of powerful but subordinate entities and, thereby, brings unity and order to the world's diversity.

On the basis of an analysis of a sample of primitive societies drawn from Murdock's (1957) "World Ethnographic Sample," Swanson (1960) reports that his hypothesis is sustained. High gods do tend to be present in those societies containing three or more different types of sovereign groups and absent if there are fewer than three sovereign groups.

Swanson's finding and his explanation for it have not gone unchallenged. Thus, Underhill (1975), working within a Marxian perspective, concludes that *both* political and economic complexity are strongly and independently related to monotheism, with economic complexity having the stronger independent effect. Underhill maintains that his empirical results contradict the theoretical perspective of Swanson as well as Durkheim, whose thought provides a foundation for Swanson's analysis, and he argues that his results underline the ultimate importance of material production in the formation and support of religious beliefs.

Replying to Underhill, Swanson (1975) notes that the variable "political complexity," as measured by Underhill, is not the same as the number of sovereign groups in a society. Underhill used as an indicator Murdock's (1967) coding of the number of levels of "jurisdictional hierarchy" beyond the local community. Swanson points out that political complexity, therefore, differs from the number of sovereign groups in a society in two respects. First, only those levels of jurisdiction outside the local community are counted, whereas Swanson's tabulation includes all sovereign groups whether they appear within the local community or beyond it. Second, as Murdock (1962) himself suggests, levels of jurisdiction and number of sovereign groups are conceptually different, since Swanson, for example, would count a lineage and clan as two organizations, but Murdock would only tabulate a single jurisdictional level.

Having pointed out that the number of levels of jurisdictional hierarchy and the number of sovereign groups in a society are not the same, Swanson (1975) goes on to demonstrate that the relationship between the number of sovereign groups and the presence of a high god in a society persists when economic complexity is held constant.[1]

II. Active and Inert Subsistence Raw Materials

Whereas it is clearly the case that the association between the number of sovereign groups in a society and the presence of monotheism cannot be explained by economic complexity as measured by Underhill, the relationship between sovereign groups, economic activities, and the presence of a high god in a society is by no means a dead issue. In Underhill's analysis, and also, presumably, in Swanson's reply, since he follows Underhill's coding instructions, economic complexity is measured by scoring the dependence of a society upon various activities that provide the means of subsistence. Essentially, a society is classified as low on economic complexity if it is dependent upon gathering and hunting and high if it is dependent upon settled agriculture. The full array of categories is: gathering, hunting, fishing, animal husbandry, and agriculture (Murdock, 1967). Murdock provides an estimate in terms of a percentage category score of the amount of dependence of a society upon each of these subsistence activities. Underhill's measure of economic complexity is an additive index that includes, but is not limited to, the five categories as listed. The index is highly correlated with Murdock's estimates ($Q = .99$).

A major problem in Underhill's analysis is that he does not make clear why he thinks that his index orders societies in terms of economic complexity. In what way is settled agriculture, for example, more complex, as an activity, than, say, hunting?

Underhill's index is based on Murdock's categories, which are, in turn, traceable to the adaptation by Hobhouse, Wheeler, and Ginsberg (1915, reprinted 1965) of Nieboer's (1900) classification of societies in terms of economic grades. The intent of Hobhouse, Wheeler, and Ginsberg (1965) was to categorize the general level of intellectual attainment of societies measured by "the control of man over nature as reflected in the arts of life [1965:6]." Thus, their categories reflect the level of a society's practical knowledge. Underhill, however, apparently wishes to measure the degree of complexity characteristic of the social organization and control of the productive sector of a society and its subunits. Defined in that manner, economic complexity is not, necessarily, a correlate of the level of practical knowledge. Consider a modern comparison: an automatically controlled petrochemical plant versus an

---

[1] Swanson (1975) also shows that the relationship between the number of sovereign groups and the presence of a high god persists when the number of levels of jurisdictional hierarchy is held constant.

unautomated assembly line. The continuous, automatically controlled production of petrochemicals represents a higher level of practical knowledge than does the unautomated assembly line. The assembly line requires, however, the supervisory coordination of workers' activities and, thus, is socially more complex than the petrochemical plant that has a relatively small number of workers who, essentially, monitor the continuous production process. Thus, Underhill's analysis leaves us with the following question: Can subsistence activities be meaningfully ordered in terms of a *material* dimension that, unlike Underhill's measure, must be taken into account in order to explain the presence of a high god in a society?

In recent years, organization analysts have focused attention upon the properties of technologies or task activities and the raw materials (both human and nonhuman) that are transformed into organizational outputs by task activities. Drawing upon distinctions made in the literature, the raw materials of subsistence activities can be classified on an active–inert dimension (Dornbusch and Scott, 1975; Perrow, 1967, 1970). Active raw materials have one or more of the following properties: They may be relatively volatile or unstable, present unpredictable resistance to operatives performing a subsistence activity, or be highly variable in terms of those properties that must be taken into account in order to control the material. Inert materials, on the other hand, are stable, provide predictable resistance, and have relatively uniform, easily controlled features.

Along the dimension as conceived, then, I locate plants, small land fauna, and fish toward the inert end of the scale and animals at the active end, thus nominally classifying societies dependent upon gathering, settled agriculture, or fishing together in one category and those dependent upon hunting or animal husbandry in a second category.

The face validity of the active–inert distinction is not difficult to establish. Consider, for example, the cultivation of plants for food and the herding of animals. Both plants and animals are, of course, subject to natural disasters such as disease, drought, etc. Man, however, does not have to monitor plants and keep a constant watchful eye on them in the same manner that, say, sheep require. Furthermore, bulls and stallions, for example, which are, obviously, necessary to continue a herd, may be quite unpredictable in their normal behavior and require special handling. If that were not the case, there would, probably, be no steers or geldings. Plants, by comparison, are very tranquil.

III. Data Analysis

Having isolated a suitable dimension on which the subsistence raw materials of primitive societies can be classified, some analysis will now be done to determine whether or not the material dimension must be taken into account in order to explain the presence of high gods in societies. The analysis, in effect, will pit Swanson's variable—the number of sovereign groups—against the activeness—inertness of subsistence raw materials as predictors of the presence of a high god. Should subsistence raw materials have to be taken into account in order to explain the presence of a high god, an argument will be developed to support the finding.

The data, in the form of a three-way contingency table, are analyzed using Goodman's (1970, 1972a,b, 1973) log-linear technique. The technique is employed because the data are categorical. Categorical data do not satisfy the assumptions that must be met in order to use partial correlation analysis, etc. Log-linear techniques, on the other hand, were specifically developed for the multivariate analysis of nominal data and should be used whenever data do not satisfy the canons of a higher level of measurement.

Table 14.1 contains a cross-classification of the number of sovereign groups, the activeness–inertness of subsistence raw materials, and the presence or absence of a high god in a sample of primitive societies. The societies were drawn by Swanson from Murdock's (1957) "World Ethnographic Sample" and are listed in Swanson (1960:214). They are analyzed in *The Birth of the Gods* and in Swanson's (1975) reply to Underhill.[2]

The number of sovereign groups is taken directly from Swanson's coding (1960:215). The presence of a high god follows Murdock (1967, Column 34)

TABLE 14.1 **Cross-Classification of Societies with Respect to Three Dichotomized Variables: (A) Number of Sovereign Groups; (B) Subsistence Raw Materials; (C) High God**

Number of sovereign groups (A)	Subsistence raw materials (B)	High God (C)	
		Present	Absent
Three or more	Inert	15	6
Less than three	Inert	1	13
Three or more	Active	3	0
Less than three	Active	3	3

Sources: Data reprinted from *Ethnographic Atlas* by George Peter Murdock, by permission of the University of Pittsburgh Press, © 1967 by the University of Pittsburg Press; and from *The Birth of the Gods: The Origin of Primitive Beliefs* by Guy E. Swanson, by permission of the University of Michigan press, © 1960 by the University of Michigan Press.

[2] Fifty societies appear on Swanson's (1960) list. Of these, 48 can be located in Murdock (1967). Using Murdock's identification code, they are: Ie3, Id1, Sf2, Ai3, Nj2, Ac3, Ne12, Sc3, Na19, Sa1, Ig5, Cd2, Na3, Af43, Aa3, Ib1, If4, Ia3, Ng10, Cj3, Ei7, Na4, Sh9, Ee3, Ab3, Ij3, Ed4, Aj7, Nd20, Aj3, Ad6, Ie9, Nc17, Ec4, Ag4, Eh3, Sj4, Ah3, Eg4, Si2, Nf2, Se4, Sg1, Nc3, Nb4, Ab12, and Nh4. Underhill (1976) argues that this is a biased sample of both the *Ethnographic Atlas* (Murdock, 1967) and the "World Ethnographic Sample" (Murdock, 1957). Swanson (1976) in reply notes that the distributions of Underhill's economic and complexity indices in this sample are not significantly different from their distributions in a random sample drawn from the *Ethnographic Atlas*.

for all societies on Swanson's list that could be found in Murdock and are coded for the presence or absence of a high god. The variable "subsistence raw materials" is a composite of Murdock's (1967) columns 7–11, which indicate, in order, the estimated relative dependence of a society upon each of the five major types of subsistence activities: gathering, hunting, fishing, animal husbandry, and agriculture. Subsistence raw materials are coded "active" if the total for columns 8 (hunting) and 10 (animal husbandry) in Murdock (1967) is five or more. This means that, if a society is at least 45–55% dependent upon animals, the raw materials of its subsistence activities are coded "active" in Table 14.1. There is one exception to this coding; it is dealt with in the discussion section to follow.

Table 14.2 contains some unsaturated log-linear models for the three-way cross-classification in Table 14.1. Inspecting the chi-square values for the models, it can be seen that neither model H_2 nor model H_3 fits the data. However, model H_1 fits the data extremely well. Model H_1 can be interpreted as the regression of C on A and B (Goodman, 1972a). Thus, the data in Table 14.1 are consistent with the view that monotheism cannot be explained by either the direct effect of sovereign groups or subsistence raw materials alone. *Both* effects are needed to account for the presence of a high god.

As in the usual regression analysis, the AB parameter in model H_1 represents the unexplained variation between the independent variables A and B and, therefore, sheds no light on the existence of a causal linkage between those variables. However, it is possible to test whether positing a causal relationship between A and B is consistent with the data. The (null) hypothesis to be evaluated is: The AB interaction in the two-way table AB is nil. Should the hypothesis be rejected, an arrow could be directed, as in the usual causal diagram, from *either* A to B *or* B to A. However, an arrow from A to B can be ruled out on substantive grounds, since it would involve having to argue that the number of sovereign groups in a society is the cause of the degree of activeness of a society's subsistence raw materials. Rejection of the hypothesis, then, is supportive evidence for a causal link from subsistence raw materials (B) to the number of sovereign groups (A).

TABLE 14.2 Chi-Square Values for Some Unsaturated Models Pertaining to Data in Table 14.1[a]

Model	Parameters in the model	Degrees of freedom	Likelihood ratio chi-square	p
H_1	AB, AC, BC	1	0.17	> .500
H_2	AB, AC	2	6.36	.042
H_3	AB, BC	2	19.07	.000
H_4	A, B	1	2.06	.151

[a] Models H_1–H_3 pertain to the 3-way table {ABC}. Model H_4 pertains to the 2-way table {AB}.

The two-way table {AB} is obtained from the three-way table {ABC} by collapsing on {C}. Model H_4 in Table 14.2 tests the hypothesis that the AB interaction in the {AB} table is nil. As can be seen, the hypothesis is not rejected, since model H_4 fits the data. A causal linkage, then, between B and A is not supported statistically. In terms of the usual causal diagrams, the data in Table 14.1 are consistent with Figure 14.1.

Before proceeding to a discussion of the results obtained in the preceding, I wish to comment on a possible objection to the findings. Lenski (1970:134) reports that 96% of herding societies contain a belief in a high god but only 40% of hunting and gathering societies have such a belief. Thus, it could be the case that the effect of subsistence raw materials upon the presence of a high god, as reported previously, is attributable only to herding and not to the hunting–herding combination (i.e., the active–inert distinction). To test this hypothesis, I recoded the subsistence raw materials variable so that animal husbandry formed one category and the four remaining types of subsistence activities the other category. A log-linear analysis of the cross-tabulation of the number of sovereign groups by subsistence raw materials (as recoded) by the presence or absence of a high god reveals that subsistence raw materials (as recoded) are no longer needed to explain the presence of a high god. Only the number of sovereign groups in a society is needed to explain the three-way table.[3] Thus, the effect of raw materials upon the presence of a high god, as reported earlier, is not simply due to the dependence of a society upon animal husbandry for subsistence. Hunting must also be taken into consideration.

IV. Discussion

The preceding results and the procedures used to obtain them differ in important respects from both Underhill's and Swanson's efforts. Unlike Underhill, the analysis employs sovereign groups rather than jurisdictional levels, being consistent with Swanson in that regard. Unlike both Underhill and Swanson, a specific feature of subsistence raw materials is used in the investigation, rather than a diffuse measure of economic complexity. Finally, unlike economic complexity in Swanson's analysis, the raw-materials variable does make a significant contribution to explaining the presence of a high god.

The causal diagram in Figure 14.1 is consistent with the results of the analysis. Since the relationship between the independent variables was shown to be noncausal, only the AC and BC arrows need further substantive elaboration. As far as the AC arrow is concerned, there would appear to be no reason not to adopt Swanson's explanation for the presence of a high god in societies

---

[3] Likelihood ratio chi-square values are as follows (models correspond to those in Table 14.2): H_1—2.14, $p < 0.143$; H_2—2.16, $p < 0.340$.

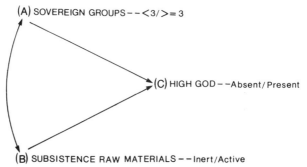

Figure 14.1   A causal diagram consistent with the data in Table 14.1.

with three or more sovereign groups. The number of sovereign groups is, then, one independent factor explaining monotheism.

What about the BC arrow in Figure 14.1? Why should active raw materials provide independent support for the presence of a high god? The answer to that question begins with the following observation: Active raw materials may provide contingencies that are best dealt with by the skilled and, sometimes, necessarily swift action of individuals and/or the concerted action of highly motivated individuals. Hence, active raw materials support and encourage pragmatic and autonomous role definitions and provide a milieu in which extraordinary accomplishment in work is societally adaptive and the motivation to achieve is socially reinforced. A bit of evidence culled from some data presented by Swanson supports this view.

Chart 2 in Swanson (1971) lists a number of primitive societies classified in terms of the degree to which the theme of need achievement is present in a society's folktales. Cross-classifying the need-achievement scores of these societies with their dependence upon active versus inert raw materials produces the following results: Of the three societies that depend upon active raw materials, all (100%) have high need-achievement scores. Twenty-five remaining societies depend upon inert materials for subsistence. Of these, 32% (8) have high need-achievement scores and 68% (17) have middle or low need-achievement scores. Thus, although the evidence is not strong because of the small number of societies in the sample coded "active," it is clearly in a direction that supports the contention that active raw materials are found in conjunction with a societal emphasis upon individual prowess, autonomy, and achievement.

Additional evidence in support of the contention that active raw materials are associated with efficacious individual performance comes from a reanalysis of data reported by Barry, Child, and Bacon (1959). Table 14.3 contains a cross-classification of societies with a strong emphasis upon either compliance or assertion training and dependence upon inert or active subsistence raw materials. The null hypothesis that the AB interaction in Table 14.3 is nil is rejected (likelihood ration chi-square = 5.78, $p < .016$). Hence, the nature of

TABLE 14.3 Cross-Classification of Societies
with Respect to Two Dichotomous
Variables: (A) Socialization
Emphasis; (B) Subsistence Raw
Materials[a]

Socialization emphasis (A)	Subsistence raw materials (B)	
	Inert	Active
Compliance	8	4
Assertion	2	9

[a] The societies classified in this table are found in Barry, Child, and Bacon in the column labeled "Extremes in accumulation" (reproduced by permission of the American Anthropological Association from the *American Anthropologist* 61:60, 1959). Within each accumulation category, societies are ranked in terms of the preponderance of compliance and assertion. In order to obtain societies that unambiguously socialize for assertion or for compliance, I dichotomized the high-and low-accumulation societies, taking those societies at the median or above in compliance and assertion, respectively. Societies are classified as active if they are at least 40% dependent upon animals or very large sea mammals for subsistence.

subsistence raw materials affects the degree of assertion versus compliance training in a society. Why is that the case? Individual assertion is socially adaptive, I submit, in the face of contingencies that might occur because a society depends upon active raw materials for subsistence (e.g., domestic animals stampeding during transhumance, or buffalo avoiding a "pound" were it not for the quick action of some individual [Ross, 1970:78–79]).

A high god, then, can be viewed not only as the symbolic arbiter and judge of the world's events but also as the symbolic representation of the efficacious, pragmatic worker. A high god, therefore, can be expected to emerge in societies with three or more sovereign groups *and* in societies in which highly motivated, pragmatic individual action is a valued type. This type of action will be valued in societies in which the means of subsistence may require, from time to time, swift, efficacious responses as a necessary condition for appropriating those means. In such circumstances, the work done is usually performed on behalf of the entire society or of some significant sovereign unit within the society (e.g., the family). Thus, the worker as an adaptive agent for a sovereign unit provides the means of life through extraordinary action. The quality of action exhibited by the worker as an adaptive agent is, then, a model for a high god who through his acts sustains the life of a people.

One final empirical point provides additional support for the argument. The active–inert classification of subsistence raw materials solves the problem of the deviant cases in *The Birth of the Gods*. As Swanson (1960) points out, five societies in his sample are inconsistent with the prediction of the presence of a high god when a society has three or more sovereign groups. Of the five societies, three have at least three sovereign groups but do not have a monotheistic deity. They are the Orokaiva, the Timbira, and the Yokuts. According to my coding, all of these societies depend upon inert raw materials for subsistence. The two remaining societies are the Lengua and the Yahgan. Each has fewer than three sovereign groups, but a high god is present. According to my coding, the Lengua depend upon active raw materials for subsistence. That leaves the Yahgan.

The Yahgan are the one exception to the coding scheme mentioned earlier in the chapter. This exception arose in connection with the consideration of whether to code fishing as a subsistence activity dealing with active or with inert raw materials. Clearly, fishing includes considerable variation in the degree of activeness of raw materials. Thus, fish harvested from streams or rivers are more akin to the small fauna of gathering than, say, to whales pursued in an ocean hunt. In coding fishing, therefore, the following procedure was adopted, and it was adopted *before* the deviant cases in *The Birth of the Gods* were examined. A sublist was made of all societies in the sample for which the sum of hunting plus fishing plus animal husbandry, according to Murdock's codes (1967, columns 8, 9, 10), was five or more. For those societies on the sublist that fish in freshwater (a substantial majority), fishing was coded inert. Fishing was also coded inert for those societies located near salt water that do not fish from boats or pursue fish and relatively small aquatic animals from water craft. The remaining category consists of societies that pursue very large aquatic animals (e.g., whales) in boats. For these societies, the decision was made to code fishing as active. In fact, only one society in the sample falls into this category, the Yahgan of Tierra del Fuego. They possess one sovereign group, yet they have a high god. The Yahgan hunt whales in bark canoes.

V. Conclusions

As noted earlier, Underhill (1975) says that his results contradict the theoretical perspective of Swanson and Durkheim. Thus, his analysis shows that "the effects of economic complexity on monotheism are not explained through the intervening mechanism of political organization. The economic system has effects on monotheism that have nothing to do with political organization [p. 859]." According to Underhill, his results are consistent with the central importance Marx and Engels assign to the effect of economic and technological arrangements upon religion.

In his rejoinder, Swanson (1975) points out that "variation in the number of sovereign groups in hierarchy explains a significant amount of the variance in monotheism when either economic complexity or number of jurisdictional levels is controlled [p. 869]." Swanson's findings, then, support a Durkheimian perspective.

The results reported in this chapter indicate that both the organization of the pursuit of collective purposes and subsistence raw materials have significant independent effects upon monotheism. Furthermore, subsistence raw materials are not causally related to the number of sovereign groups in a society. Are the findings reported in this chapter consistent with Underhill's Marxian interpretation or with Swanson's Durkheimian position? I conclude that they qualify Swanson and provide no test of the Marxian position.

An assessment of the Marxian position using the results obtained in this chapter depends upon being able to argue that the properties of subsistence raw materials are valid indicators of the general economic organization of a society. Such an argument is, I believe, precarious. In a recent article, Norr and Norr (1977) code subsistence activities quite differently from the way in which they are coded in this chapter, their intent being to measure the organization and control of production techniques in primitive and in traditional societies. They show that production techniques, as they code them, are correlated with the organization and control of economies. Since my coding differs substantially from that of the Norrs', it seems unlikely that it is a good indicator of the organization and control of primitive economies. The results in this chapter, then, are effectively mute on the relationship between the organization, complexity, and control of a society's economy and monotheism.

Although the findings provide no test for conclusions derived from a Marxian perspective, they do suggest that Swanson's view needs qualification. Since a relationship remains between the nature of subsistence raw materials and the presence of a high god, when the number of sovereign groups is controlled, a material factor related to functional adaptation does play a role in determining the prevalence of monotheism in addition to the effect of social organization found by Swanson. Both factors—material and social—must be taken into consideration in order to account for the presence of a high god.

References

Barry, Herbert III, Irvin L. Child, and Margaret K. Bacon
    1959 "Relation of child training to subsistence economy." *American Anthropologist* 61:51–63.
Dornbusch, Sanford M. and W. Richard Scott
    1975 *Evaluation and the Exercise of Authority.* San Francisco: Jossey-Bass.
Durkheim, Emile
    1915 *The Elementary Forms of the Religious Life.* London:George Allen and Unwin.
Goodman, Leo A.
    1970 "The multivariate analysis of qualitative data: Interactions among multiple classifications." *Journal of the American Statistical Association* 65:226–256.
    1972a "A modified multiple regression approach to the analysis of dichotomous variables." *American Sociological Review* 37:28–46.
    1972b "A general model for the analysis of surveys." *American Journal of Sociology* 77: 1035–1086.

1973 "The analysis of multidimensional contingency tables when some variables are posterior to others: A modified path analysis approach." *Biometrika* 60:179–192.

Hobhouse, L. T., G. C. Wheeler, and M. Ginsberg
1965 *The Material Culture and Social Institutions of the Simpler Peoples.* London:Routledge and Kegan Paul. Originally published by Chapman and Hall, London, 1915.

Lenski, Gerhard
1970 *Human Societies: A Macrolevel Introduction to Sociology.* New York:McGraw-Hill.

Murdock, George P.
1957 "World Ethnographic Sample." *American Anthropologist* 59:644–687.
1962 "Ethnographic atlas." *Ethnology* 1:265–286.
1967 *Ethnographic Atlas.* Pittsburg:University of Pittsburg Press.

Nieboer, H. J.
1900 *Slavery as an Industrial System.* The Hague:Nijhoff.

Norr, James L. and Kathleen L. Norr
1977 "Societal complexity or production techniques: Another look at Udy's data on the structure of work organizations." *American Journal of Sociology* 82:845–853.

Perrow, Charles
1967 "A framework for the comparative analysis of organizations." *American Sociological Review* 32:194–208.
1970 *Organizational Analysis: A Sociological View.* Belmont, California: Wadsworth.

Ross, Eric
1970 *Beyond the River and the Bay.* Toronto:University of Toronto Press.

Swanson, Guy E.
1960 *The Birth of the Gods: The Origin of Primitive Beliefs.* Ann Arbor:University of Michigan Press.
1971 "An organizational analysis of collectivities." *American Sociological Review* 36:607–624.
1975 "Monotheism, materialism, and collective purpose: An analysis of Underhill's correlations." *American Journal of Sociology* 80:862–869.
1976 "Comment on Underhill's reply." *American Journal of Sociology* 82:421–423.

Underhill, Ralph
1975 "Economic and political antecedents of monotheism: A cross-cultural study." *American Journal of Sociology* 8:841–861.
1976 "Economy, polity, and monotheism: Reply to Swanson." *American Journal of Sociology* 82:418–421.

Chapter 15

Moral Climates of Nations: Measurement and Classification[1]

PHILLIP E. HAMMOND and KIRK R. WILLIAMS

I. Prefatory Note

Moral climates differ from society to society. Furthermore, variations in moral climates are thought to be related to variations in social institutions and social behavior. An implicit continuum is thus suggested, with the crassest variables (e.g., population size, dollar income) at one end and the most ethereal notions (e.g., justice, goodness) at the other. Efforts to demonstrate relationships between variables falling at different points on this continuum require measurement, however, a task made more elusive the further removed from the "crass" end of the continuum the variables are.

Consider just three examples from the social scientific study of law, all of which argue for a relationship between concrete laws and other, more abstract moral characteristics of society. Pospisil (1958) reports that the Kapauku Pa-

[1] This chapter is part of research undertaken with Boris Kozolchyk of the University of Arizona College of Law. Entitled "Models of Fairness and Legal Systems," the project was supported by the National Science Foundation, Grant GS–38286.

The Religious Dimension:
New Directions in Quantitative Research

puans' "legal decisions" accord with their "values"; Hoebel (1954) asserts that laws reflect the "jural postulates" of peoples; and David and Brierly (1968) claim a correspondence between laws and a society's "sense of justice." Making intuitive sense, these propositions are, nevertheless, difficult to test because of measurement problems, especially those surrounding "values," "jural postulates," and "sense of justice" (i.e., moral climates). Indeed, the authors just cited offer only illustrations of their propositions.

It is the aim here to suggest a (not *the*) measurement and classification scheme to be used in such macrosocial inquiries as those just mentioned. Our units are contemporary nation-states, and we use available data to draw inferences as to some of their abstract moral characteristics. Of course, the resulting classification will not be applicable to all research questions, but, on the other hand, the virtue of abstraction is broader potential application. We will have succeeded if others find that our measures *are* systematically related to a variety of social phenomena.

II. Introduction

We begin with a conclusion reached early in this century by several scholars (e.g., Huxley, 1915; Westermarck, 1912) who noted that, despite ethnographic variety, all societies have a "Golden Rule." As Westermarck put in his *The Origin and Development of the Moral Ideas,* after amassing his "scientific" evidence: "So far, St Augustine was right in saying that 'Do as thou wouldst be done by' is a sentence which all nations under heaven are agreed upon [p. 103]." Obviously, however, the Golden Rule does not apply to everyone in all circumstances, so perhaps a more accurate rendering of this idea is to say that all societies distinguish between persons toward whom certain moral obligations are recognized and those toward whom they are not. For want of a better term, let us call relationships with the former persons "primordial ties" and then restate the Westermarck observation: All cultures distinguish some interpersonal relationships as primordial ties, and this distinction is found in their moral codes.

Once we presume the existence of primordial ties and recognize that certain moral obligations extend to those within—but not outside—the boundary, then the stage is set for revenge, retribution, feuds, etc., as well as for rewards, brotherhood, mutuality, etc. That is to say, the moral code expands to account for ever-more-complex social phenomena, and social structural apparatus (e.g., courts, police) come into existence to express it (Miller and Schwartz, 1964).

This expanded moral code may deal with an infinite variety of substantive problems; this is one clear message of cultural relativity. On the other hand, as the ubiquity of the Golden Rule suggests, these substantive problems always appear "on top of" certain basic moral distinctions. Whereas the enumeration of substantive cultural differences may be inevitably incomplete, if not, therefore, impossible, classification of the underlying moral distinctions may be relatively simple.[2] Thus, as Nelson (1972) shows, over centuries the laws and practices surrounding usury systematically changed (for reasons he specifies) as changes occurred in the definition of who was a "brother." Of course, the substance of the meaning of "brother" may be culturally very relative, but some moral distinction between brother and nonbrother would seem to be imposed in all societies. Hence, our concern is summarized in the following assertion: Every society has a notion of morality resembling the Golden Rule, but societies differ in who applies it and to whom it applies.

Two examples will be given, each reflecting the changing application of the *lex talionis* doctrine:

1. From earliest times, a wrong committed by an individual could be revenged by punishing the offender's group as well as (or instead of) the offender himself. "They visit the iniquity of the fathers and forefathers upon the children and the descendants [Westermarck, 1912:49]." As the history of numerous peoples reveals, however, this doctrine changed in a direction that, without challenging the idea of "fair" retaliation, altered the definition of who may fairly be punished. Thus, in Judaism the modified rule is promulgated first in Deuteronomy 24:16 and later in II kings, Jeremiah, and Ezekiel. Virtually identical admonitions can be found in the Roman Law, the Koran, the "law of Edmund," thirteenth century Swedish law, Slavonic law, etc. (Westermarck:70–71, 177 ff.) The idea emerges that only the offender, not his "brother," is eligible for retribution.

2. A correlative change is exemplified in the narrower doctrine of how much retaliation is fair. The famous "eye-for-an-eye" rule, laid down in the Mosaic tradition, stipulated an upper limit on punishment (Exodus 21:24), contrary to popular current opinion, which sees it as a warrant for at least equal revenge. Obviously, the prior condition had regarded as "fair" two (or more) eyes for an eye, but Moses mandates that no more than was lost can be claimed. The Christian modification, which at first glance appears so radical in its admonition to turn the other cheek (Matthew 5:38–41), can (Matthew 7:1–2) be interpreted merely as a next step in a progression away from the "feud" solution to felt injustice.

One sees in such instances, then, not so much changing standards in what is moral as change in the defintion of those toward whom one is to behave morally. The boundaries of primordial ties shift, in other words, and thus the targets of vengeance and rewards shift.

---

[2] For example, societies differ enormously in kinship systems, some primitive peoples having incredibly complex ways of reckoning lineage. The distinction between who is and is not related may be quite simple, however.

III. Two Kinds of Morality

From this rather fundamental viewpoint can be derived two kinds of morality, depending upon the presumed relationship of the involved parties:

1. Between those bound by what we have called primordial ties, morality involves A treating B as if he were A. With the kin group or other "brotherhood" serving as the type case, we can note that A is to behave toward those within the group (his "brothers") in the same manner as he would behave for himself, even if he, in some sense, "loses" in the bargain.

Because A and B are related by primordial ties, they must uphold a certain brotherhood morality. However, C and B, because unrelated by primordial ties, share no brotherhood. Morality now is best expressed by the phrase caveat emptor. Each party is legitimately expected to be on his own lookout, with no recourse to any loyalty or consideration beyond the encounter itself. Indeed, as in the case of the enemy who dares to enter another's territory, it is only proper to treat him as "fair game." The use of "primordial ties" in morally defining persons necessarily leads to a distinction between those who—as "brothers"—qualify for especially good treatment and others who—as nonbrothers—may be legitimately used, cheated, ignored, or whatever. A few examples can be cited:

a. K. L. Karst and his associates (*The Evolution of Law in the Barrios of Caracas*) point to the overwhelming importance of the kinship group in the lives of the people living in the socioeconomically undeveloped *barrios* of Venezuela. Whatever security they enjoy, whatever enforcement of agreements they achieve, is likely to result from the concerted effort of the family group.

b. A similar portrait—this one of the importance of the "neighborhood"—is drawn by Oscar Lewis (*Five Families,* p. 274) as he describes the periodic delivery by truck of water into a Mexico City *barrio.* The law stipulates a limit on the amount of water each family may receive, but neighbors routinely collaborate and connive to get more, even knowing that the consequence will be that families farther away will thus get no water at all.

c. Of a different sort is the situation in India described by David and Brierly (1968:424): "If . . . some concern is carried on by all the members of one family . . . and there are no non-family associates, the rules of Indian commercial law in the *Indian Partnership Act* will not apply. The dealings of the partners will come under Hindu law because they form part of their *statut* rather than part of a contract between them." In other words, the formal provisions of the commercial code are not invoked if the partners are believed to be yet bound by informal (primordial) ties.

What all three examples illustrate is the existence of a marked difference in moral orientation toward those who are within the primordial boundaries from those who are without.

2. The second kind of morality calls for a universal orientation from everyone toward all. This kind of morality is represented by a contract between strangers in which both parties are obliged to look out for each other's welfare as well as their own. It is unlike the first, since A is not expected to suffer (turn the other cheek) because B is a brother, nor is A expected to capitalize (get two eyes for the loss of one) because B is an "enemy" rather than a brother.[3] Instead, all participants, whatever their own outcomes, are expected to uphold the arrangements leading to those outcomes. At the extreme is the convicted murderer who is expected to go to the gallows believing in the justice of the system that condemns him. But there is no difference in kind in the case of the contractor who, despite unpredictable weather that causes him to lose money on a contract, is expected nevertheless to uphold (and "believe in") the terms of that contract. The model—though of course not necessarily the reality—is a system of cooperating units who presume nothing about each other except a mutual commitment to the sanctity of contract.

It is obvious that all societies exhibit both kinds of morality but differ in their mix. We inquire, therefore, into the distribution of the two kinds of morality. Hypothetically, in drawing a social relationship at random from a society, what is the probability of observing one or the other kind of morality at its base?

IV. Secular Change and Two Kinds of Morality: Primordial Ties

Theorists of secular social change concur in the issue we have just reviewed—that is, the redefinition of moral relationships accompanying secular change. From "tribal brotherhood" to "universal otherhood" is the capsule summary Benjamin Nelson (1972) gives it. Change tends to blunt the distinctions based on primordial ties, distinctions that characterize partners as trusted brothers or distrusted enemies, and to replace them with a general category of "other." Consider the following three sweeping formulations notable for their similarities despite divergent authorship; what they express is the standard understanding:

---

[3] Lon L. Fuller (1969) suggests three "social contexts" to be found along a "spectrum"—relations structured (*a*) by kinship; (*b*) between "friendly strangers"; and (*c*) by "repulsions of shared hostility." He suggests that, whereas enacted and contractual law are congenial to the middle category, "customary" law oftentimes regulates behavior at both extremes. Thus, he says, enacted laws may try but often fail in bringing about legally desired behavior in family life, for example. His first and third contexts parallel our first morality, his second, our second.

1. [Change] means not only the disintegration of the old kinship or family group, which is as well an economic, political and religious unity. It means the construction of a new basis for the family; new moral principles for business; a distinct political state with new means for government, new conceptions of authority and liberty; finally a national or universal religion. And the individual on this higher level takes a more voluntary attitude toward these institutions. In the presence of new conflicting ends, he sets up or adopts a standard for himself [Dewey and Tufts, 1932:80, discussing the development of "modern moral consciousness"].

2. One of the principal driving intellectual forces of the [social] revolution was . . . based on certain ideas about man's nature that find expression in the American Declaration of Independence and in the French Declaration of the Rights of Man and of the Citizen . . . . The emphasis on a man's right to conduct his own affairs and to move laterally and vertically in society was a reaction against the tendency under feudalism to fix a man in a place and status [Merryman, 1969:16, 18, discussing the rise of modern states in civil law countries].

3. Christianity teaches a universal ethic, a brotherhood of mankind. This is in contrast with the Bantu ethical system, which usually does not involve those outside the family or tribal group. Hospitality is to be shown the traveler, but Bantu ethics has a very limited notion of the worth of anyone outside the primary group. Christian ethics (in theory, although obviously not always in practice) expands the ethical community to encompass every human being. The idea that a nonrelative is an equal with whom one can plan, work and share is crucial to political development. National integration requires this widening of horizons. Effective administration means that government officials have to adopt a national perspective and not regard their positions as opportunities for providing money and jobs only for their family members. The widening of the ethical system and the idea of a universal community as professed in Christianity would seem to be inescapably linked to what we call modernization [Adelman, 1974:38, discussing several kinds of impact Christianity has had on the culture of Zaire].

This change, this "dissolving" of ties based on kinship, village, class, caste, clan, guild, language, religion, or whatever, is a notable feature of social life. Interpersonal relations—let us say of a commercial nature—are conducted more and more between "individuals," between persons known to each other *only* on the one basis. Sales are made between buyer and seller; buyer and seller are not also brothers, fellow-believers, caste peers, etc. It is not that family, religion, and caste disappear, but rather that these identities become less and less relevant for behavior outside their immediate arenas.

In summary, secular change brings with it a reduction in the role primordial ties play. With the correlative redefinition of interpersonal relationships, therefore, it is expected that the distribution of the two kinds of morality will also undergo change. The kind of morality that sees relationships between "brothers" and "enemies" will recede, we predict, and the kind of morality between "benevolent strangers" will intrude into more and more relationships.

V. Secular Change and Two Kinds of Morality: Massification or Mobilization?

What has just been reviewed is so often stated that it takes on the character of received wisdom. Of course, all ascribed group memberships recede in importance. As interaction increases across such lines, how can those lines do anything other than diminish?

However, a potential for error creeps in at this point. Granted that individuals go forth without the armor of their primordial ties, this does not mean that they necessarily go forth as individuals. To a significant degree in Western industrialized societies it is true that they have, and this has given rise to charges of "mass" society, of 200 million souls connected only by highways, of individuation to the point of identity loss, of lonely crowds, and so forth (see Nisbet, 1953, for a cogent argument along these lines). But, as scholars were somewhat later in observing, societies differ considerably in the new definition made of persons breaking away from traditional ties. This difference, we want to argue, has an impact on moral climates in addition to the impact of diminished primordial ties.

One of the ways this difference can be conceived is seen in the terms Guy E. Swanson has developed in his studies (1960, 1967, 1968) of both primitive tribes and medieval societies. Though there are middle categories, the labels of which need not concern us, the extremes of his continuum he calls "commensal" and "heterarchic," representing differences in "the *means,* if any, by which members . . . [can] legitimately shape actions by that society's social system [1968:108; emphasis added]". In commensal regimes, persons have only their identity as citizen-at-large as a basis for participation. In heterarchic regimes, by contrast, persons' participation in the regime is in turn based only on their membership in groups or organizations "that are not themselves agencies or creatures of the regime [p. 108]." In effect, then, the characterization is of regimes that, on the one hand, mediate or reconcile or coordinate the diverse, legitimate interests of people (heterarchic) or, on the other hand, regard persons as material to be mobilized in the interests of the regime (commensal). Apter (1965) uses "reconciliation" versus "mobilization" to signify this same "heterarchic–commensal" continuum.[4]

As was noted early about the United States, the regime was "federalist" not only in formal terms but also in terms of the importance of voluntary associations that channeled peoples' interests. Persons were not only citizens of the government but also legitimate members of many other groups as well. The result is what Swanson (Apter) would call a heterarchic (reconciliation) regime but which could more generally be called political pluralism.

---

[4] Apter is chiefly interested in contemporary developing nations. See also Apter (1963).

It is critical to see that the underlying difference being identified is of major importance for the way people see each other and is thus important to the way moral rules are applied. Essentially, it is the difference in the degree of centralization in a society—whether people are seen as "wards" of the state, to be loyal primarily to it, or seen as possibly loyal to many different and competing groups. In formal political terms, a "federal" system acknowledges its constituent units, a "centralized" system does not.[5]

The implication for the distribution of the two kinds of morality would seem to be this: In a politically diversified society, more relationships will be defined in terms of the second kind of morality, wherein persons are seen as individuals. In the centralized society, these relationships will more likely be expressed in terms of the brother–nonbrother kind of morality. Citizens are more likely seen as "comrades" or "brothers," with the state the "big brother." But, just as persons may be brothers or comrades, so may they lose their eligibility and become enemies instead. The moral rules apply in this case to those who qualify.

VI. The Two Dimensions Considered Together

Two observations need to be made about the relationship between these two dimensions of moral climates. First, they are conceptually distinct. On the basis of knowledge about the importance of primordial (ascribed) ties for social interaction, one cannot theoretically predict where a society will fall on the diversity–centralization dimension. The reason has to do with the second observation. We can assume that, as ascribed characteristics recede in importance, one's sense of self and social identity depends less and less on such things as race, language, religion, caste, guild, and family. But what, then, takes their place? Does the state step in, offering a sociomoral identity as "citizen"? Or are people left to make their way through a "lonely crowd," establishing meaningful relationships where they can, but largely on personal, individual terms? The former characterizes the centralized, mobilized, corporate society, the latter the diversified, reconciliatory, heterarchic society. In the former, persons who have lost their tribal identities are offered (forced to take?) membership in the new, single tribe. In the latter, such persons remain a mass of single individuals.

We exaggerate, of course. We have not yet described any real society, that being our task presently. We would point out, however, that differences along these two dimensions have implications for "who behaves morally toward

---

[5] Still other scholars refer to the degree of "corporateness" the society exhibits. By this they mean the proportion of important activities that are channeled through (incorporated into) a central state. See Meyer and Rubinson (1974) and Bergesen (1973) for this usage.

whom and why." That is, these distinctions go right to the issue of the moral and legal definitions of persons and thus intrude in such matters as contracts, inheritance, sales, and marriage. We therefore expect them to show up in diverse settings.

The task now is to determine some way of empirically representing these two conceptual dimensions. Specifically, we must determine (*a*) whether interpersonal relationships are bound predominantly in primordial ties; and (*b*) whether persons identify each other primarily as agents of the state or as representatives of competing subgroups thereof? A direct measure of these dimensions would require a survey of people living in the various countries of the world, which simply is not feasible. Consequently, some alternative technique must be used. The strategy employed here is to identify and to measure conditions of social life that, presumably, are associated with the breakdown of primordial ties and the redefinition of people's identities. Variables pertaining to the former are viewed as dimensions of so-called socioeconomic development, whereas those concerning the latter are considered attributes of national polities.

VII. Socioeconomic Development and Diminishing Primordial Ties

Social theorists often subsume discussions of historical secular change under the rubrics of "modernization" or "socioeconomic development." These terms typically refer to extensive structural changes in society. There is a recurrent theme in this literature: As societies "develop," they become structurally differentiated, and their members become increasingly interdependent. This theme may shed light on the following question: Why do people come to interact with "nonbrothers," that is, those outside ascribed groups (e.g., families, clans, or tribes), and why do they become meaningful to each other for reasons other than "brotherhood"? In short, why do primordial ties diminish?

For illustrative purposes, consider a key aspect of structural differentiation, the "division of labor." This term refers to specialization in sustenance activities, defined as any expenditure of human energy in the production of goods and services that provides a livelihood (Gibbs and Martin, 1959). Within so-called "primitive" societies, the degree of division of labor is relatively low, and interaction is based upon something other than distinctions among persons as to their sustenance activities.

Increasing specialization alters the basis of social interaction. Whatever the "causal" force, when persons devote a greater proportion of time and energy to specific tasks, the responsibility for the performance of other tasks is relegated to other persons. Consequently, individuals become dependent upon one another. Furthermore, people must engage in some form of exchange to obtain the desired goods and services they do not provide for themselves. Durkheim (1964:125) argued that "exchange always presupposes some division of labor more or less developed," and Lenski (1966:204) argues similarly: "The development of specialization necessarily implies the development of trade and commerce, since specialists must exchange the products of their labors for those of others."

If the foregoing is true, then one can expect an increase in the frequency of interaction among persons who are "impersonally meaningful" to each other. Specifically, people do not interact with one another simply because they are "brothers"; rather, persons seek out "universal others" who can provide specific goods or perform specific tasks.

Hence, socioeconomic development is associated with the diminution of primordial ties, and we measure the latter concept with four dimensions of the former: the degree of population concentration, technological development, economic development, and industrialization.[6] These dimensions are measured as follows:

Population Concentration: The number of persons living in cities of 100,000 or more per capita as of 1960.

Technological Development: Consumption of energy per capita as of 1960.

Economic Development: Gross domestic product per capita as of 1960.

Industrialization: Gross domestic product per capita originating in industrial activity as of 1960.

VIII. Political Structure and the Articulation of Interests

Recall that societies seem to differ concerning the nature of the "new" identities people take on once they break away from primordial ties. Are persons expected to act in behalf of self-interests or national interests? Are they identified as representatives of constituent subgroups or as agents of the state? It is assumed that one can learn which of these moral definitions is fostered within countries by analyzing the character of national governments, which tend toward one of two arrangements. The first is essentially the monolithic form of

---

[6] It has been argued that indicators of socioeconomic development are so highly intercorrelated that the use of one or another set of them should not markedly affect the empirical results of a given line of research (see, e.g., Moore, 1955, or Schnore, 1969). Data for these indicators were obtained from Banks (1971).

government in which collective interests are embodied in a single national agency or person. This kind of political structure allows for the official recognition and articulation of one interest, that of the nation as a whole. Thus, one's identity as citizen or "ward" of the state is most likely salient.

The contrasting structural arrangement is the diverse or federative form of government. This structure incorporates different private or special interests, representing a synthesis of many constituent groups within a country. Thus, one's identity is multidimensional, deriving from numerous group affiliations, and the salience of any specific dimension is dependent upon the context of interaction.

Given the foregoing, one can reasonably assume that, within countries with monolithic governmental structures, people view each other, at least officially, as agents of the state—the interests and goals of "The People" are the interests and goals of the nation, and vice versa. Conversely, within countries with diverse governmental machinery, people view each other as agents of their "grouped" selves—the well-being of the nation derives from the various interests of constituent units.[7]

To measure this difference in the way interests are articulated, five attributes are considered: heterogeneity of political parties, effectiveness of the legislature, competitiveness of the nominating process, legislative coalitions, and party legitimacy. All of these are conceived of as dimensions of political diversity.

The linkage between each of these dimensions and the construct "political diversity" is straightforward. Heterogeneity of political parties indicates a structural accommodation for the representation of many different interests or political views. If countries have no political parties, authority probably resides in some national figure (e.g., a monarch or a dictator who embodies the interests of the entire collectivity).

Effectiveness of the legislature indicates whether this branch of government, if it exists, has autonomous powers. If a legislative body is absent, then collective interests probably are affirmed by some national figure, who most likely is located in the executive branch of government.

Concerning the other three dimensions, the following might be said: Within countries having governmental structures that provide for political diversity, decisions are made and public policies are formulated on the basis of "compromises" and "coalitions" among the various competing groups. But this, in turn, means that competing voices, whether nominees or parties, are

---

[7] There is no assurance that "official" or governmental conceptions of "moral reality" will always correspond to those of the public at large (i.e., the "unofficial"). To assume a perfect correlation is hazardous. Nonetheless, political organization provides the opportunity, at least in principle, for the articulation of interests. The question is whether these interests are divergent and competing or uniform and pertaining to the collectivity as a whole.

accorded a right to exist. Measures of these dimensions, all as of 1960, are as follows:[8]

Heterogeneity of Political Parties: The number of seats in the lower house of the legislature divided by the total number of these seats held by the largest party. The greater the number of parties represented in the lower house, the larger the value on this variable. For example, a country with no parties gets a score of 0, a one-party system gets a score of 1.0, a nation in which the largest party controls 50 out of 100 seats gets a score of 2.0, etc.

Effectiveness of Legislature: Effective (3), partly effective (2), largely ineffective (1), and no legislature (0).

Competitiveness of the Nominating Process: Competitive (3), partially competitive (2), largely noncompetitive (1), and no competition (0).

Legislative Coalitions: More than one party, no coalitions (3); more than one party, coalition with opposition (2); more than one party, coalition without opposition (1); and no coalition, no opposition (0).

Party Legitimacy: No parties excluded (3), one of more minor or "extremist" parties excluded (2), significant exclusion of parties (or groups) (1), and no parties or all but dominant party and satellites excluded (0).

IX. Construction of Composite Indexes

Remember that the objective here is to develop two orderings of contemporary nations that capture the meaning of the two conceptual dimensions discussed earlier. We contend this can be done by employing the measures of socioeconomic development and political diversity. This requires a consolidation of the measures into two composite indexes, one for socioeconomic development and one for political diversity.[9]

Construction of the indexes involved two tasks. First, intercorrelations (Pearson's Product Moment Correlation) among each of the two sets of measures were calculated. The relationships were all direct, as expected, and moderate to strong in magnitude for both sets of variables (socioeconomic development: $r = .41$ through $r = .96$; and, political diversity: $r = .64$ through $r = .85$).

Second, given these findings, composite scores representing socioeconomic development and political diversity were calculated for all countries. These scores, two for each nation, represent a given country's position vis-a-vis all

---

[8] All data for these dimensions were obtained from Banks (1971).

[9] We began with a list of 155 nations, obtained from the 1967 *United Nations Statistical Yearbook,* but we ended up with 106 countries for analytical purposes. Data were unavailable for 49 of the original set of countries.

other countries. Thus, a composite score of political diversity is the average of a country's scores for heterogeneity of political parties, effectiveness of the legislature, competitiveness of the nominating process, legislative coalitions, and party legitimacy. The two sets of composite scores represent the socioeconomic development index (SDI) and the political diversity index (PDI).[10]

X. The Cross-Classification of Countries

Table 15.1 displays the cross-classification of contemporary countries according to the socioeconomic development and political diversity indexes. Both of the indexes are subdivided into six ordinal categories. The maximum and minimum index scores, respectively, for each category are shown in parentheses under the row (for PDI) and column (for SDI) labels of Table 15.1.

Bear in mind that the cross-classification is derived from data at one time, namely, 1960.[11] One should consider this when examining Table 15.1, because countries may experience substantial historical variability in socioeconomic development and in the structure of national government.

Socioeconomic development is usually thought of as a process occurring over a long period. Nonetheless, as the term implies, countries are viewed as changing from a low to a high degree of socioeconomic development. Moreover, it is assumed that, although countries may experience periodic and temporary "set-backs" for one reason or another, it is highly improbable that they will proceed to a relatively high degree of socioeconomic development and then recede to a relatively low one. In relation to Table 15.1, the shift is from right to left, and it is very unlikely that countries found in the left-hand column (high socioeconomic development) at one period will be found in the right-hand column (low socioeconomic development) at a later one.

Concerning the character of national governments, through-time variability

---

[10] The actual statistical procedure for calculating composite scores is as follows. First, the raw data values were transformed into standardized scores (Z-scores). This was done to ensure that the various measures could be meaningfully compared. Second, for each country the Z-scores for the set of measures pertaining to socioeconomic development were added together and the sum divided by the number of variables (N) for which data were available for a given country. The same was done for the measures of political diversity. The composite scores (CS), therefore, are simply averages of Z-scores:

$$CS_{ik} = \frac{\Sigma Z_{ij}}{N_i},$$

where i = countries, k = indexes (SDI or PDI), and j = variable elements of the indexes.

[11] Data for both indexes are available for other periods in Banks (1971).

TABLE 15.1 Cross-Classification of Countries according to the Categorized Political Diversity and Socioeconomic Development Indexes

Political Diversity → High	Socioeconomic Development High → Low						
	3.303, .935	.818, .012	-.033, -.405	-.429, -.621	-.665, -.776	-.807, -1.001	
1.580, 1.016	Norway, Switzerland, Luxemburg, Netherlands, Denmark, Sweden, Iceland, U.K., New Zealand, U.S.	Chile, Lebanon, Italy, Japan, Finland, Israel, Ireland	Peru				
	10	7	1	0	0	0	18
.732, .993	France, Belgium, West Germany, Canada, Australia, Austria	Greece, Uruguay, South Africa	Brazil, Costa Rica	Philippines, Ecuador	Ceylon, India	Nigeria, Cameroun, Madagascar	
	6	3	2	2	2	3	18
.153, .600	Venezuela	Argentina	Panama, South Korea, Mexico, Cyprus, Colombia	Bolivia, Guatemala, Gabon, Congo (Brazzaville)	Burma, Chad, Honduras, Laos, Central African Republic	Malaysia, Somalia	
	1	1	5	4	5	2	18
.078, -.878			Iran, Syria, Nicaragua	South Vietnam, Ghana, Senegal, Tunisia	Liberia, Ivory Coast, Dahomey, Indonesia, Cambodia	Upper Volta, Mali, Ethopia, Afghanistan, Guinea	
	0	0	3	4	5	5	17

	Czechoslovakia, East Germany	Bulgaria, Spain, Poland, Hungary, USSR	Portugal, Mongolia, Romania	Albania, Dominican Republic, People's Republic of China, Paraguay	North Korea	Niger, Mauritania, Togo, North Vietnam	
−.881, −.881	2	5	3	4	1	4	19
−1.001, −.312		Cuba	Jordan, Morocco, Libya, UAR, Iraq	Saudi Arabia, Turkey, El Salvador	Haiti, Pakistan, Thailand, Malawi	Nepal, Yemen, Sudan	16
	0	1	5	3	4	3	
	19	17	19	17	17	17	106

Low ⟶

325

means that countries fluctuate between diverse and centralized forms of government; hence, they manifest governmental instability. Such changes may be abrupt (e.g., revolutions or coups d'état). Consequently, classification of nations at two separate times may yield different pictures as to the political diversity of some countries. In terms of Table 15.1, countries should maintain their position vis-à-vis other countries as to their socioeconomic development status (i.e., remain in the same column) in the short run, but some may experience marked changes as to political diversity (i.e., be reclassified in different rows).

Finally, although it is reasonable to assume that countries undergo a historical shift from a low to a high degree of socioeconomic development, it is not necessarily true that their national governments shift correlatively from unitary to diverse forms, although data in Table 15.1 suggests that this does occur to some extent (Gamma = .399). It would be hazardous to assume causality in either direction here. As countries undergo socioeconomic development, they may take on either diverse or centralized forms of government, but the choice is probably dependent upon a variety of historical circumstances.

XI. Correlates of the Classification Scheme

If, as we have been arguing, the two indexes of socioeconomic development and political diversity are independent, then they should reveal different relationships with other characteristics of societies. Put another way, they should be differently reflected in the moral climates of nations. It is our task in the present section to show what some of these differences might be.

Our desire is to find characteristics significantly related to one but not both of the two indexes—and thereby learn what is distinctive rather than similar about the two measures. Of the various characteristics available in the cross-national data files, 26 met our criteria of inclusion.[12] Of these, only one (to be discussed; see Footnote 14) was similarly related to both SDI and PDI.[13] All others were more powerfully linked to SDI or to PDI. These are presented in the next two tables.

The characteristics in Table 15.2 are listed in descending order of their rela-

---

[12] Several dozen characteristics were available to us. Two criteria guided our selection of the 26 considered here. First, we arbitrarily decided that SDI and PDI together must "account" for at least 25% of the variance in a characteristic (i.e., $r^2 \geq .25$), and, second, we excluded characteristics that were similar in meaning (e.g., calories per capita versus protein grams per capita per diem).

[13] In determining the independent effect of each index (SDI and PDI) controlling for the other, we arbitrarily decided that the unstandardized regression coefficient should be at least twice the size of its standard error. Typically, this meant a Beta coefficient (i.e., standardized regression coefficient) of about .14 or larger.

TABLE 15.2   Characteristics of Nations Related to Socioeconomic Development (SDI) in
Descending Order of the Relationship

Characteristic	Source[a]	(Column 1) r^2	(Column 2) SDI (Beta)	(Column 3) PDI (Beta)[b]
Newspaper circulation (per capita)	c	.74	.79	.14
Educational expenditure (per capita)	a	.70	.84	
Literacy rate	c	.70	.81	
Secondary school enrollment (1955)	b	.70	.79	
Tertiary school enrollment (1955)	b	.62	.79	
Interest articulation by non-associational groups	c	.61	−.74	
Character of bureaucracy (degree of bureaucratic civil service)	c	.57	.62	.24
Defense expenditure (per capita)	a	.56	.82	−.17
Calories (per capita)	a	.56	.78	
Primary school enrollment (per capita)	b	.55	.63	.19
Social Insurance Program Experience (SIPE)	d	.53	.62	
Government revenue (per capita)	b	.51	.71	
Sectoral income distribution	a	.40	−.63	
Number of scientific journals published	a	.37	.62	

[a] a = Taylor and Hudson; b = John Meyer *et al.*; c = Banks and Textor; d = Cutright.
[b] A blank indicates a Beta of less than .14.

tionship with the combined SDI and PDI indexes (Column 1). The list, in other words, is made up of national features that are strongly related to the indexes. More important, however, is the information in Columns 2 and 3, which reveals—for these 14 items of Table 15.2—that the strong relationships shown in Column 1 are almost entirely owing to the influence of SDI, not PDI. In fact, the Beta coefficients for PDI meet or exceed .14 (see Footnote 14) in only four cases; however, these PDI Betas are considerably smaller than the corresponding SDI Betas. In short, Table 15.2 reveals how nations that differ socioeconomically also differ in other ways.

What does Table 15.2 show? First, several items show that per capita spending goes up with socioeconomic development—for education, defense, and government revenue. Second, a number of items are shown that reveal consequences of these expenditures: Educational enrollment at all levels (as percentages of appropriate age-groups) increases; the literacy rate goes up, as does calorie consumption; more newspapers are circulated, more scientific journals are published, and more welfare programs (Social Insurance Program Experience, SIPE) are instituted. So far, none of this is very surprising.

Third, however, are the several not-so-obvious relationships. The characteristic called "Interest Articulation by Non-Associational Groups" is strongly—and negatively—related to SDI. This is, essentially, a measure of the importance of kinship, ethnic, or other nonformalized groups in conveying and pursuing people's interests. Table 15.2 shows that, with socioeconomic development, this importance sharply declines. What replaces it is suggested by the item called "Character of Bureaucracy," a measure of the elaborateness of the civil service. Note that it is strongly—and positively—related to SDI.

Finally, there is the measure of "Sectoral Income Distribution," a gauge of the degree to which various sectors of a population share in a nation's income. Table 15.2 reveals that socioeconomic development is associated with greater income equality (the negative sign appearing because *in*equality is what the item measures).

Altogether, we might summarize the findings of Table 15.2 by noting that, as socioeconomic development increases, more people engage in more activities through impersonal agencies such as schools, newspapers, government bureaucracies, formal welfare programs, and the like.

Table 15.3 has an entirely different flavor. Observe that in a variety of ways the PDI is strongly related to the mode and ease with which individual interests can be pursued. Whether reflected in such items as press freedom and politically independent higher education or in such proximate measures as shared power among branches of government ("Horizontal Power Distribution") and multiple paths to political leadership ("Elitism"), this set of characteristics is persuasive. The more politically diverse a nation is, the more

TABLE 15.3   Characteristics of Nations Related to Political Diversity (PDI) in Descending Order of the Relationship

Characteristic	Source[a]	(Column 1) r^2	(Column 2) PDI (Beta)	(Column 3) SDI (Beta)[b]
Formal political representativeness (1961–1965)	b	.70	.61	.34
Horizontal power distribution	c	.60	.65	.22
Representative character of regime	c	.59	.63	.24
Role of police (political or merely law enforcing)	c	.56	− .64	− .19
Press and broadcast freedom	a	.52	.68	
Constitutional status of regime	c	.49	.75	
Interest articulation by political parties	c	.47	.67	
Political incorporation of higher education	b	.35	− .56	
Elitism in political leadership	c	.30	− .59	
Political participation by military	c	.29	− .54	
Political participation by citizens	a	.26	.38	.20

[a] See note *a* in Table 15.2.
[b] See note *b* in Table 15.2.

likely will a multitude of agencies be found as channels for pursuit of individual interests. In contrast, the less diverse a nation is, the more likely will the centralized government be seen as the proper agency through which individuals must go.

Strangely enough, then, socioeconomic development and political diversity have a similar effect, though in markedly different ways. Socioeconomic development weakens the effective hold that traditional agencies (family, neighborhood, church, guild, etc.) have over individuals, leading to the creation of substitute agencies that are largely bureaucratic in some sense. Political diversity, on the other hand, means the creation of many different such agencies, each a competing unit in the struggle for power. The first dimension refers to the diminished power of traditional categories; the second refers to the nature of the replacement categories. The first refers to the declining importance of any kind of "brother versus nonbrother" distinction; the second to the matter of how much of a "big brother" the government becomes. Socioeconomic development leads to increasing individualization, whereas political diversity means that individuals have multiple channels for expressing that diversity.[14]

What relationship do the indexes have with measures developed independently of this research? From an investigation published in 1974 (Cole and Hammond), we took two societal characteristics, the degree of universalism exhibited in a country's legal system and the degree of its religious pluralism. Table 15.4 shows how these two measures relate to SDI and PDI.

Legal universalism is seen to be powerfully and positively related to both SDI and PDI. (These relationships hold up, incidentally, alternately controlling for either index.) This can only mean that, with greater socioeconomic development and/or greater political diversity, persons are treated in the courts less and less according to their particular attributes and more and more in a manner like everyone else.

Religious pluralism, by contrast, is differently related to the two indexes,

TABLE 15.4 Relationship (Gammas) between the Socioeconomic Development Index and the Political Diversity Index and Two other Measures

	Legal universalism[a]	Religious pluralism[a]
With SDI	.66	−.29
With PDI	.71	.28

[a] For definition and measurement, see Cole and Hammond (1974).

[14] Both socioeconomic development and political diversity generate bureaucracy, therefore, and it was this one item out of 26 that was powerfully and simultaneously related to our two indexes.

and less strongly. With SDI, religious pluralism is negatively related, a finding commensurate with that of Cole and Hammond, who also found a small negative correlation. Their interpretation, with which we have no disagreement, is that socioeconomic development is impeded by persisting religious differences. Religious pluralism, however, is itself a kind of diversity that may be reflected in our measure. It shows a positive, though small, relationship to PDI, therefore.

In this apparent paradox, however, lies a clue of general significance. Insofar as diverse channels are political, that is, permit people and groups to pursue their interests in competition with others in that society, such diversity erodes the brother–nonbrother distinction. Maintaining the single system, and maintaining competition (plus rules governing it), cannot help weakening the moral claims persons make for special treatment. Where the brotherly consideration *is* upheld, on the other hand, and, perhaps, especially where it is expressed in religious terms as well, the diverse interests are to be seen not as competing *in* a single society but as competing *societies*. What is at issue in this case is control of the very apparatus by which moral rules and definitions are to be made. The issue, as we said at the outset, is one of *where*, if at all, the brother–nonbrother distinction applies.

XII. Conclusion

We have offered a scheme for thinking about and measuring the "moral climates" of nations. From the standpoint of an ethics capable of drawing fine lines between right and wrong, our effort is so modest as to be nonexistent. This chapter should not be read as a contribution to the field of ethics, however, for that is not its purpose. Neither should it be seen as an exercise in the reliability or validity of two indexes, for it may well be that the SDI and PDI can easily be improved as better (and more current) data become available; the moral circumstances of an entire nation are obviously not captured by two "scores," however intricately they may be derived. But it is possible that meaningful differences are revealed in such scores. Our goal here might best be described as "methodological," therefore—an endeavor to supply a method for studying the moral climates of nations and a rationale for using the method. Methodological proof thus depends upon what can be done with the method, a question only touched upon in the latter pages of this chapter. More evidence, we hope, will be forthcoming.

References

Adelman, Kenneth L.
    1974 "Christ and culture in Zaire." *Worldview* August:37–40.
Apter, David E.
    1963 "Political Religion in the New Nations." Pp. 57–105 in Clifford Geertz (ed.), *Old*

Societies and New States. New York:The Free Press.
1965   *The Politics of Modernization*. Chicago:University of Chicago Press.
Banks, Arthur S.
1971   *Cross-Polity Time-Series Data*. Cambridge:The M.I.T. Press.
Banks, Arthur S. and Robert B. Textor
1963   *A Cross-Polity Survey* Cambridge:The M.I.T. Press.
Bergesen, Albert J.
1973   "The social origins of political witch-hunts: A cross-national study of deviance." Unpublished paper.
Cole, William and P. E. Hammond
1974   "Religious pluralism, legal development, and societal complexity." *Journal for the Scientific Study of Religion* 13:177–189.
Cutright, Phillips
1965   "Political structure, economic development, and national social security programs." *American Journal of Sociology* 70(March):537–550.
David, Rene and J. E. C. Brierly
1968   *Major Legal Systems in the World Today*. New York:Free Press.
Dewey, John and James H. Tufts
1932   *Ethics (rev. ed.)*. New York:Henry Holt.
Durkheim, Emile
1964   *The Division of Labor in Society (translated by George Simpson)*. New York:The Free Press.
Fuller, Lon L.
1969   "Human interaction and the law." *American Journal of Jurisprudence* 14:1–36.
Gibbs, Jack P. and Walter T. Martin
1959   "Toward a theoretical system of human ecology." *Pacific Sociological Review* 2(Spring):29–36.
Hoebel, E. Adamson
1954   *The Law of Primitive Man*. Cambridge, Massachusetts:Harvard University Press.
Huxley, Thomas H.
1915   "Evolution and ethics." In *Collected Essays, Vol. 9*. New York:D. Appleton.
Karst, K. L., M. L. Schwartz, and A. J. Schwartz
1973   *The Evolution of Law in the Barrios of Caracas*. Los Angeles:University of California Latin American Center.
Lenski, Gerhard E.
1966   *Power and Privilege*. New York:McGraw-Hill Book Company.
Lewis, Oscar
1959   *Five Families*. New York:Basic Books.
Merryman, John Henry
1969   *The Civil Law Tradition*. Stanford, California:Stanford University Press.
Meyer, John W., Michael T. Hannon, Jr., and Richard Rubinson
1973   "National economic growth, 1950–1965: Educational and political factors." Mimeo.
Meyer, John W. and Richard Rubinson
1974   "Education and political development." Mimeo.
Miller, J. C. and R. D. Schwartz
1964   "Legal evolution and societal complexity." *American Journal of Sociology* 70:159–169.

Moore, Wilbert E.

1955 "Population and labor force in relation to economic growth." In Simon Keynets, Wilbert Moore, and Joseph J. Spengler (eds.), *Economic Growth: Brazil, India, Japan.* Durham:Duke University Press.

Nelson, Benjamin

1972 *The Idea of Usury (rev. ed.).* Chicago:University of Chicago Press.

Nisbet, Robert

1953 *The Quest for Community.* New York:Oxford.

Pospisil, Leopold

1958 *Kapauku Papuans and Their Law.* Yale University Publications in Anthropology, No. 54.

Schnore, Leo F.

1969 "The statistical measurement of urbanization and economic development." In William A. Faunce and William H. Form (eds.), *Comparative Perspectives on Industrial Society.* Boston:Little, Brown and Company.

Swanson, Guy E.

1960 *The Birth of the Gods.* Ann Arbor, Michigan:University of Michigan Press.

1967 *Religion and Regime.* Ann Arbor, Michigan:University of Michigan Press.

1968 "To live in concord with a society." In Albert J. Reiss (ed.), *Cooley and Sociological Analysis.* Ann Arbor, Michigan:University of Michigan Press.

Taylor, Charles L. and Michael C. Hudson

1972 *World Handbook of Political and Social Indicators.* New Haven:Yale University Press.

Westermarck, Edward

1912 *The Origin and Development of the Moral Ideas, Vol. 1.* London:Macmillan and Company.

Chapter 16

Spirituals, Jazz, Blues, and Soul Music: The Role of Elaborated and Restricted Codes in the Maintenance of Social Solidarity

ALBERT BERGESEN

I. Introduction

At the heart of the Durkheimian understanding of religion lies the role of ritual in the reaffirmation of collective sentiments. Since Durkheim, what we understand as ritual has been extended to many social practices not normally considered "religious" in nature. For example, Goffman (1956) has shown that the performance of interpersonal rituals of deference and demeanor act to affirm the sacredness of the self and the larger status order in which our selves are embedded. Erikson (1966) has argued that witch hunts, such as the Salem trials he studied, act to reaffirm ritually a community's collective identity, and elsewhere I have argued that modern-day political witch-hunts act to reaffirm periodically collective sentiments in national societies (Bergesen, 1977a, 1978a, b). Douglas (1966, 1970) contends that our efforts at cleaning up, brushing away dirt, and putting things in their place in general represents a ritualistic activity that functions to reaffirm the structured and categorical nature of social reality. Finally, even collective violence and social

The Religious Dimension:
New Directions in Quantitative Research

protest have been shown to have ritual significance for reaffirming threatened group identities and status positions (Bergesen, 1977b; Hofstadter, 1956; Tilly, Tilly, and Tilly, 1975).

One of the more interesting efforts at extending our understanding of ritual has been the work of Basil Bernstein (1975) and Mary Douglas (1970), who have linked elaborated and restricted linguistic codes with the solidarity of social groups. In this chapter I would like to extend this understanding of the ritual functions of language a step further by adapting the idea of elaborated and restricted codes to another language—music.

Music is a kind of language. It is a symbolic means of communicating feelings and information. Like other languages, music involves basic units (sounds or tones) and a variety of rules, or syntax, for their meaningful combination (harmony, meter, scales, orchestration, etc.). In turn, the units organize themselves into larger structures (motifs, themes, or phrases). Music, though, is somewhat more complex than our written language in that it progresses both horizontally (melody) and vertically (harmony). You can have, in effect, both a vertical musical sentence (chord structure) and a horizontal musical sentence (a melody or melodic phrase).

Elaborated and Restricted Codes

Language, and hence music, varies in form and content according to social context. Bernstein (1975) argues that there is a functional relationship between the solidarity of a group and the kind of linguistic codes that appear in it. He identifies two types of codes: elaborated and restricted. These codes differ in terms of the range of lexical and syntactical alternatives the speaker, or, in our case, the musician, has for constructing a linguistic act. The more restricted the code, the smaller the pool of lexes and syntactical alternatives. The syntax is also more complex in elaborated codes, and there is more flexibility in its use. Conversely, the syntax in restricted codes is more simple and there is more rigidity in its use. Restricted codes, like slang or specialized jargon, use more condensed symbols and phrases that only in-group members can understand. Restricted codes also use more collectively oriented words, like "we" or "us." Elaborated codes use more articulate symbols, less slang and jargon, and more emphasis upon individual feeling and intentions, as seen in more references to "I" and "me" (as opposed to "we" or "us"). Elaborated codes are not predicated upon a set of commonly held group assumptions, such that what is to be said must be spelled out in full. Elaborated codes allow the individual to communicate more personal and unique thoughts. With a greater range of linguistic material available (the larger pool of words and the more complex syntax), the individual can uniquely combine and recombine this linguistic material to represent best the particular thoughts or feelings he wishes to communicate. With a restricted code, more collective than individual sentiments are communicated, and hence the restricted code acts to reaffirm the substance of collective reality; that is, restricted codes act more like a ritual as we traditionally understand that term.

> A restricted code will arise where the form of the social relation is based upon closely shared identifications, upon an extensive range of shared expectations, upon a range of common assumptions. Thus a restricted code emerges where the culture or subculture raises the "we" above "I." . . . The use of a restricted code creates social solidarity at the cost of verbal elaboration of individual experience. The type of social solidarity realized through a restricted code points towards mechanical solidarity, whereas the type of solidarity realized through elaborated codes points toward organic solidarity. *The form of communication reinforces the form of the social relation* [Bernstein, 1975:147; emphasis added].

This last sentence emphasizes the ritualistic aspect of restricted codes. When we speak of an increase in solidarity, groupness, corporateness, or in any other terms we use to indicate that the distinctly corporate aspect of collective existence has a greater presence, we must also speak of the increased presence of ritual, whether it be large-scale religious ceremonies or restricted linguistic codes that function to support, maintain, recreate, perpetuate, and reaffirm that collective reality. Increases in ritual are easy to comprehend when we think of more conventional ceremonies. We look for more pomp, feast days, sacrifices, initiation rites, religious holidays, parades, and so on. When we consider the ritual dimensions of language, more ritual means a change in linguistic structure—the shift from elaborated to restricted codes.

Elaborated and restricted codes are opposite poles of a single continuum. Any concrete piece of speech or music will fall somewhere along that continuum. Although it is technically inaccurate to speak of these codes as if they were distinct entities, we will for purposes of convenience refer to different types of music as representing elaborated and restricted codes, realizing that we are only speaking relatively.

Social solidarity can mean a number of different things, and, accordingly, a linguistic code that reaffirms solidarity also does a lot of different things. At one level, it reinforces the social identity and relative social position of the person using the code, reminding him of his place and the place of others. This is one of the ways language regenerates the social order. Similarly, through language a person can act as a carrier of his social structure. This is the more Meadian view of the socializing function of language, focusing upon the transmission of values and culture through the linguistic realities that the individual internalizes. The presence of a restricted code can also have a direct effect upon the collective sentiments of the community independent of its effects upon the individual carrier, for language affects society not only through the individual who speaks but also directly, as with any other conventional ritual. Just as religious ceremonies of the more traditional kind—like feasts, dances, or sacrifices—have direct effects upon the solidarity of the community independent of their effects upon individual participants, so does the presence of a restricted linguistic code.

Restricted codes contribute to group solidarity by activating the common assumptions of all group members, the collective reality of the group itself. Because of its limitations in vocabulary, and in using simpler syntax, the restricted code cannot make sense on its own. It is like a gesture, or clue, or sign. To make sense, people must know what these cryptic utterances mean—what the condensed symbolism stands for. Since meaning is not spelled out within the infrastructure of the linguistic act itself (because of the limitations on vocabulary and syntax), one has to have some knowledge above and beyond what is being said in order to make the linguistic act intelligible. That extra understanding is found in the set of commonly held group assumptions, which are greater during periods of high solidarity. To speak in a restricted code is to activate these group assumptions; a restricted code brings the group to life, for without these commonly held ideas the linguistic act makes no sense at all. Each time a restricted code is employed, it is analagous to running electricity through the social wires that connect group members. Members are "lit up"; they feel close to the group; and more important for our understanding of language as ritual, the collective understandings themselves are activated and, in effect, are also "lit up." An elaborated code contains enough information to be intelligible and does not require extra group understanding and, hence, does not activate the group culture as restricted codes do.

Codes and group solidarity, therefore, are causally linked. The greater the group solidarity, the more the code is restricted; that is, the more collective information it carries and the more it acts to reaffirm group life. The lower the degree of group solidarity, the more elaborated the code becomes, as personal feelings are expressed at the expense of group understanding.

Musical Codes

What has been said about these codes and their relationship to group solidarity should also apply to music, which is but another kind of language. More restricted musical codes should have a simpler rhythmic, harmonic, and melodic structure and should employ more collective symbolism in their lyrics. They will also tend to be performed in groups and to be utilized more often for social occasions. Conversely, elaborated codes will be more complex and flexible, and will allow for greater expression of individual intent and feelings. There will be a wider range of musical sounds that can be employed, and they will be more flexibly combined. The lyrics will allow for the more articulate communication of individual feelings, and the music will tend to be performed by individual artists.

II. The Case of Black American Music

To examine more systematically the relationship between group solidarity and musical codes, we will look at the music of black Americans. This is a good case for our purposes as we can examine one group over a long period of time, from slavery through the early 1970s. In taking the long view of black history, we can identify three different periods representing higher and lower degrees of black solidarity, and, accordingly, we expect to find more restricted and more elaborated musical codes. The first general period is slavery, which, relative to other periods, represents a high degree of group identity and cohesion (generated in good part by the "total institutional" character of American slavery). The sense of group solidarity is higher under slavery than in the following period, which centers on the mass migration of blacks from the rural south to Northern cities. This involves a dissipation of the cohesiveness of blacks that had existed under slavery. This is the period between 1900 and the civil rights movement of the mid-1950s. Solidarity during this middle period is lower than in the preceding experience of slavery. The last period centers on the civil rights movement, when an increase in black solidarity is seen in the appearance of collective violence, in heightened group consciousness, in the emergence of special interest organizations designed to further collective goals (SNCC, the Black panthers, civil rights groups, etc.), and in the attention the federal government gave blacks as a corporate group from the Supreme Court decision of 1954 through the civil rights legislation and Great Society programs of the 1960s.

Each of these three periods is associated with the emergence of a different style of black music. During slavery, restricted musical codes appear: work songs, field songs, rowing songs, and spirituals. During the early twentieth century, we have a period of lower solidarity and the emergence of elaborated musical codes, such as jazz and blues. Finally, during the civil rights period of the late-1950s and 1960s, we have an increase in black solidarity and the movement to a more restricted musical code in the form of soul music. Changes in social solidarity result in changes in linguistic codes and, hence, in musical codes. This does not mean, though, that established forms of music disappear. Spirituals evolved into gospel music, and gospel, in turn, has strong effects on soul music. Similarly, the blues persists till today, and, of course, jazz did not disappear with the increased solidarity of the 1960s.

In the remainder of this chapter, I want to examine more closely spirituals, jazz, blues, and soul music as examples of elaborated and restricted codes.

Specifically, I will look at their themes—collective versus individual—and musical structure—the range of tones or sounds and the simple and rigid versus complex and flexible use of musical syntax (rhythm, harmony, etc.). Restricted codes should have more collective themes and simpler and more rigid musical syntax and should be performed more often in groups. Elaborated codes should have more individualistic themes, more complex and flexible musical syntax, and should be performed more often by soloists.

Higher Group Solidarity and Restricted Codes: Slavery and Spirituals

Spirituals represent those gospel hymns and religious songs that arose during slavery and include such well-known songs as "Go Down Moses," "Joshua Fit De Battle Ob Jerico," "Swing Low Sweet Chariot," "Deep River," "Roll Jordan, Roll," and "Steal Away To Jesus."

Themes

Spirituals rely on collective images and, particularly, on the image of a "chosen people" (Levine, 1971): "de people dat is born of God," "We are the people of God," "We are da people of de Lord." These songs are about the sorrow, rebirth, and deliverance of a people. As such, spirituals stand in direct contrast to the blues, which center on the sorrow of individuals. Although there is some sense of despair, spirituals convey more of an overwhelming sense of affirmation. Spirituals are about group problems and collective salvation. "The themes [reflect] a communal life-style, rarely at all being concerned with the passage of one's individual life. It was as if slave music of the apparently religious type [spirituals] glossed over details of the personal life of the slave in favor of expressing the common desire for freedom and human dignity [Walton, 1972:20]."

The specific images are highly condensed symbols, carrying large amounts of collective information. Encounters between masters and slaves are symbolized with the biblical figures of Moses, David, and Joshua and are encoded in commonly known biblical stories, such as the Red Sea opening to allow the Hebrews to pass and then swallowing the armies of Pharaoh; little David humbling Goliath with a small stone; or the ridiculed Noah patiently constructing the ark that would deliver him. Spirituals were codes of the most obvious sort. Their meaning was known to the community not so much because of the elaboration within the specifics of the music itself, but because of the commonly held assumptions generated by a common life-situation. Everyone knew what going to the promised land meant; it did not need to be spelled out. As Fredrick Douglass said, discussing the song "O Canaan, Sweet Canaan, I Am Bound for the Land of Canaan," "There is something more than a hope of reaching heaven. We mean to reach the North, the North was our Canaan. [quoted in Walton, 1972:25]." The restricted code of spirituals ritually reaffirms group consciousness by activating those commonly held understandings every time they were sung. The moral life of the slave community was regularly renewed with the singing of these songs.

Musical Structure

A restricted code manifests itself in the limitation placed upon the range of syntactical alternatives available to construct music. The regular, surging, pulsating rhythm of spirituals represents a more rigid use of meter than, say, the rhythmic complexities of jazz or the situation in which a bluesman can stop in the middle of a song, talk to the audience, and then proceed to sing. There is some syncopation in spirituals, but certainly less than in jazz, where hitting notes before or after they are due and stretching some while shortening others is the very essence of that musical form. Spirituals "have a striking rhythmic quality . . . the swaying of the body marks the regular beat, or better surge, for it is something stronger than a beat. . . . It is subtle and elusive because it is in perfect union with the religious ecstasy that manifests itself in the swaying bodies of the whole congregation, swaying as if responding to the baton of some extremely sensitive conductor [Johnson and Johnson, 1969:28, 29]." This description captures the sense in which a spiritual becomes the embodiment of the group spirit itself. It is as if it were the group itself, as a corporate entity, that was singing and swaying.

This idea of the individual being submerged in the group can also be seen in the central role harmony plays in spirituals. In one sense, the submerging of many different voices in one harmonic tone is analogous to the submerging of individual purposes in the collective purpose of the group. Harmony creates a new sound, the composite of all the individual sounds. This can be seen as a sort of emergent musical property, much as society is itself more than the sum of its individual group members. In some sense, harmonizing is a way for the collectivity itself—sui generis, above and beyond the capabilities of its composite singers—to produce a distinctly group sound. Music that emphasizes harmony has strong collective orientations and transmits immense amounts of collective information. In this sense, spirituals and soul music, which are generally produced in groups and emphasize harmonizing, are different from the singular jazzman and bluesman, where there is less occasion for the blending of voices into a harmonic whole.

Lower Solidarity and Elaborated Codes: The Migration North and Jazz

If the period of slavery produced a closely knit community, then the period centering on the movement north represents a lower level of group solidarity—if for no other reason than that the group is more dispersed and on the move. Accordingly, we should expect to see a change in musical code, and we do. During the early decades of the twentieth century, there appeared two distinct forms of black music that are more elaborated than the spirituals, work songs, rowing songs, and field songs of slavery; these are jazz and blues. We will turn to jazz first.

By *jazz* we mean the musical tradition that can be traced to New Orleans around 1900 and that includes the big bands of the 1930s, "be-bop" of the 1940s, "cool" jazz of the 1950s, and "free form" jazz of the 1960s. Jazz artists include such well-known names as Ferdinand "Jelly Roll" Morton, Louis Armstrong, Duke Ellington, Count Basie, Charlie "Bird" Parker, Thelonious Monk, Miles Davis, John Coltrane, and Ornett Coleman, to name but a few.

Themes

Jazz is largely music without lyrics. Lyrics, even of the most individually oriented kind found in elaborated codes, do activate some common understandings in that, even to decipher an elaborated code, one must "know the language." With no lyrics, even this minimal activation of common group membership (knowing, say, English) is avoided. Although music has cultural bases, the notion of music as the "universal language" gets at the idea that the organizatin of sound per se is not culturally bound. In effect, pure music implies no group membership. There is jazz singing, and this, of course, involves lyrics. But here we have an extremely flexible and complex usage of sounds that make up "jazz phrasing." Each jazz singer gives her or his own interpretation of words and phrases. The essence of jazz singing as a musical idiom lies in verbal improvisation. And this implies a more flexible use of one's lexical pool.

Musical Structure

Jazz, as a musical idiom, is the ultimate elaborated musical code, for improvisation is its defining characteristic (Collier, 1973; Feather, 1957; Stearns, 1956; Williams, 1970). "No music depends so much upon the individual as jazz. Indeed, jazz requires not only an individual interpretation of melody, it demands spontaneous individual invention of new melody, individual articulation of motion, and individual interpretation of musical sound [Williams, 1970:11]." Musical syntax—rules for organizing tones—like meter, harmonics, or melody, is so flexibly employed in jazz that the musician virtually creates his own musical language. Because of the infinite range of sounds and their possible combinations, the individual can precisely sculpt the exact musical expression he desires. Personal intention can be precisely articulated, which is in direct contrast to the situation of the individual singing spirituals in a choral group. With spirituals and soul music, one is more an agent of the music than its creator. The individual is regulated and controlled to meet the needs of the music: Individual voices blended in harmony, bodies swaying to the pulsating beat, and stylized gestures all act to submerge the presence of any individual. The heavy emphasis upon a regular pulsating rhythm makes it difficult for the individual to step out of line and "march to his own meter." With jazz, there is no form that must be followed; there are no rules that cannot be broken. The individual can do what he wants, when he wants. Furthermore, the very moral imperative of jazz is to invent and to improvise new musical languages—the ultimate elaborated code. As an example of this flexibility in musical syntax, consider what a critic wrote about Louis Armstrong: "He adds a note here, momentarily hurries this phrase, delays that one; he spots a cliché turn of melody and avoids it, often substituting a much superior phrase of his own invention [Williams, 1970:584]." That is a flexible use of musical syntax, and an elaborated code.

Jazz is such a personal statement, such a unique combination of musical lexes and syntax, that each performance is unique. There is always some improvisation that makes even the same song sound different each time it is played. This, to say the least, is quite different from the fixed musical forms of spirituals or soul music. Anyone, in effect, can sing "Swing Low Sweet Chariot." But only Louis Armstrong can play the trumpet like Louis Armstrong. It may seem that I am mixing up the performance of a song (Armstrong on the trumpet) with the song itself (like "Swing Low Sweet Chariot"), but that is exactly the point. The essence of jazz does not reside in the song as it is written, but in how it is played. The idea of "jazzing up" a song means being flexible with lexical elements and syntax.

Lower Solidarity and Elaborated Codes: The Migration North and Blues

The other form of elaborated musical code arising during this same general period is the blues. The first traceable example is probably the "Memphis Blues," written in 1909 and published in 1912 by W. C. Handy (Apel and Daniel, 1972:33). Blues emerged in the delta and hill country of Mississippi and rural Alabama (Keil, 1966:58) and is associated with such bluesmen as Son House, Skip James, Robert Johnson, Blind Lemon Jefferson, Bobby Bland, B. B. Kind, Muddy Waters, and Junior Wells. Whereas the essentially elaborated character of jazz resides almost entirely within the infrastructure of the music, the elaborated character of blues lies both in the structure of the music and in the content of the lyrics.

Themes

In contrast to the collective orientations of spirituals, the blues are about personal problems. They focus upon the disappointments of life: love lost or unrequited, anger, anguish, and depression. The symbolism is no longer the condensed and abstract images of Moses and Pharaoh or Hebrews and Egyptians but the very personal and literal things of everyday life. This can be seen by comparing the symbols and images from the spiritual "Go Down Moses" and the blues song "Milk Cow Blues."

"Go Down Moses"

Go Down, Moses,
'Way down in Egypt land,
Tell ole Pharaoh,
Let my people go.

"Milk Cow Blues"

I stubbed my toe against the kitchen door,
And now my hens won't lay no eggs no more.

I went to church, sat in the thirteenth row,
Next day my landlord said I had to go.

The spiritual is filled with mythical images (Moses, Egypt, Pharaoh) and a group orientation (let my *people* go), whereas the blues song is filled with very concrete and literal images (my toe, the kitchen door, hens, eggs, church, and the thirteenth row) and personal referents (*I* stubbed *my* . . . , *my* hens . . . , *I* went . . ., *I* had . . .).

During slavery, people suffered, lost friends, lovers, and family, and felt the pain and anguish of which the blues speak. Yet, the lyrics are about collective plights, not personal ones. Similarly, the origins of much of the suffering depicted in the blues,—unemployment, being down and out, and so on—have social origins, such as black–white race relations, the evils of capitalism, cataclysmic events like the depression, and so on. But, just as there were personal problems during slavery and yet collective songs, so were there collective problems during the birth of the blues and yet expression in personal terms. As Charters (1970:167, 168) notes, "A W.P.A. blues will often have as little real social consciousness as a blues of infidelity. The first verse may mention the subject,

W.P.A. done tore my baby's
playhouse down.
W.P.A. done tore my baby's
playhouse down.
Done took my baby, she's nowhere
around.

but the verses that follow usually return to a standard blues pattern

> I wonder where's my baby, I wonder
>   where could she be,
> I wonder where's my baby, I wonder
>   where could she be,
> She's gone somewheres, she's gone
>   and left poor me."

Even though there was personal suffering, the greater importance of the group during slavery generated the collective images of spirituals, and, even though there were large-scale social problems during the early decades of the twentieth century, the decline in black solidarity resulted in the literal and ego-centered images of the blues.

The blues are not highly standardized songs, like spirituals, which can be passed down through generations and sung by any choral group, but highly personal expressions of inner feelings and emotions. In fact, there are arguments as to whether younger men, who have not experienced much of the ups and downs of life, or white people, with no experiential understanding of what it means to be black in white America, can "really" sing the blues.

Musical Structure

Although the blues are not as elaborated a code as jazz, there is a great deal of flexibility in the manipulation of musical sounds (there are also more restrictions in blues than in jazz, like the 12-bar blues progression and the reliance on 4/4 time). Perhaps the most well-known source of flexibility is the so-called "blue note," "the third and seventh scale degrees which are used either natural or flatted, and which are frequently played deliberately out of tune [Apel and Daniel, 1972:33]."

In singing blues, there is a very flexible approach to musical syntax, and a very wide range of vocal devices.

> blues singers make use of a fabulous variety of unorthodox vocal devices ranging from . . . "intonation tones" (sounds that are continuously changing pitch within the compass of a tone), through "falsetto twists" and "interpolated notes" to "swoops," "glides," "wavers," "clips," and many different patterns for attacking and releasing each note . . . . Unlike classical singing where the aim is to imitate an instrument, the goal of a blues singer is to make free use of his or her voice, that is, to employ every sound of which his or her voice is capable—including the mechanics of breathing—in order to attain expressiveness, especially rhythmic expressiveness [Stearns, 1956:276].

That represents a very wide lexical pool and allows for a very precise articulation of personal intent and expressiveness; and that is what is meant by an elaborated code.

Higher Solidarity and Restricted Codes: The Civil Rights Era and Soul Music

Our final period, the civil rights era, is one of increasing black consciousness and solidarity and, accordingly, a shift to a more restricted code—soul music. Haralambos (1970) conducted a study in 1968 of radio stations in Chicago, Detroit, and New York that played popular black music. All his informants (disc jockeys) agreed that the blues were decreasing in popularity in northern cities, since they no longer reflected the mood of blacks. The disc jockeys agreed that modern soul music began about 1955, when the singer Ray Charles made a secular song from the old gospel tune "This Little Light of Mine" rearranged as "This Little Girl of Mine." What is called "soul music" is associated with the establishment of black record companies, such as Motown Records and Tamla Records, both launched by Barry Gordy after he formed Gordy Records in 1959. By 1961, they had their first million sellers with the songs "Please Mister Postman" and "Shop Around." Soul music of the 1960s is associated with singing groups such as the Marvelettes, the Supremes, the Temptations, the Miracles, Martha and the Vandellas and with individual singers such as Stevie Wonder, Mary Wells, Diana Ross, Marvin Gay, Ray Charles, James Brown, and Aretha Franklin.

Themes

Soul music is light and breezy and, like spirituals, is associated with social occasions, such as dances and concerts. The songs celebrate and rejoice in the general theme of love: new love, the wonders of love, and love found and continuing. The topics are more positive and more an affirmation of love than the articulation of anguish and suffering of love lost that make up the blues. This can be seen in some of the titles from Motown Records: "I'm Crazy 'bout My Baby," "Two Lovers," "Try It, Baby," "Baby, I Need Your Loving," "That's What Love Is Made Of," "My Guy," and "Baby Love." Soul music is less the expression of a performer's personal experience than a symbolization of the group experience in general. In this sense, soul music is like the spiritual, where the origins of the music are largely unknown and, in some sense, irrelevant, since its power comes from representing the collective concerns of the group as a whole rather than the articulated experiences of an individual.

The collective orientation of soul music appears in a number of songs of the 1960s that explicitly focus on issues of black pride, solidarity, and the struggle for civil rights. These would include songs such as "We're a Winner" and "We're Rolling On" by the Impressions; "Free at Last" by James Barnes; "Together We Shall Overcome" by the Magictones; and, perhaps the most explicit of this genre, James Brown's "Say It Loud, I'm Black and I'm Proud."

The emphasis upon group pride, consciousness, and advancement can be seen in the lyrics of the song "We're a Winner" by the Impressions (Haralambos, 1970:381).

> We're a winner,
> And never let anybody say,
> Boy, you can't make it.
>
> No more tears do we cry,
> And we have finally dried our eyes,
> And we're moving on up.
>
> We're a winner,
> And everybody knows the truth,
> We just keep on pushin'
> Like your leaders tell you to.

Musical Structure

"The format . . . is simple: The songs are all written with one obvious hook line, to be repeated and hammered home . . . the beat is kept heavy, and the individual voices stay secondary to the overall sound. The rhythm sections are invariably magnificent, the singers strong and professional. Most times, the records sound as though they have been put together by a computer . . . (Cohn, 1969:135]." There are obvious similarities with spirituals, and contrasts with both blues and jazz. There is a steady regular rhythm and an absence of the rhythmic complexity of jazz or of blues songs. Unlike the blues and jazz, there is little experimentation with scale tones. Songs are sung as written, which creates a very polished and professional sound. Harmonizing is also important and reflects the subordination of individual tones to the emergent sound of the group as a whole.

There is also a repetitive quality to soul music that, in combination with the heavy beat and importance of blending voices, generates a group sound rather than the individual sound produced by solitary performances by individual bluesmen or jazz virtuosos. The rigid organization of the music, the avoidance of the unorthodox scales, and the repetition of particular verses can be seen as a symbolization of the permanence and ongoing quality of group life over the more tenuous and short-lived existences of its individual members. Both spirituals and soul music have a repetitive and cyclic quality that can be contrasted with the blues' often very linear quality (i.e., a story line with a beginning and an end). Soul music and spirituals repeat the same verses and, in some sense, could go on forever, in unending cyclic repetitions. The absence of an ending in soul music creates a problem as to when the song should stop. Theoretically, the verses could be repeated forever, and the criteria for length seem dictated by the time requirements of pop radio stations. Since the songs have no ending in and of themselves, they are simply faded out; that is, the volume is slowly decreased until the song can no longer be heard. This constitutes the end of the song.

III. Some Data

A recent study (Walker, 1976) of the expression of black solidarity and group consciousness in popular music provides some evidence in support of our argument. Walker was interested in the rise of black solidarity after World War II and examined the lyrics of popular music for signs of increasing black consciousness. His data came from Billboard Publication's cumulative annual best-selling soul (black) music singles list from 1946 through 1972 (with the exception of 1964, when the listing was not available). This provided a sample of 1100 songs that were coded as to whether or not they expressed a collective orientation and black solidarity. Two announcers on San Francisco metropolitan area black-oriented radio stations coded the songs. Songs were coded as having a collective orientation (expressing some degree of solidarity) if they met any one or more of the following five criteria (Walker, 1975:62–64):

—Do the lyrics of this song, or the title, contain references to the black racial (or ethnic) group? (e.g., black, soul, nigguh, Afro-American)
—Do the lyrics of this song, or the title, contain references to social-class groups? (i.e., rich–poor, big shots–little people, etc.)
—Do the lyrics of this song, or the title, contain references to large, non-personal groups that are not racial–ethnic or social-class types? (non-specific references such as people, children, y'all, etc.)
—Do the lyrics of this song, or title, contain moral or ethical commentary, demands, requests, or pleas? (references to right–wrong; good–bad; is–ought to be; social problems; community problems; crime; delinquency; drugs; domestic disorganization; etc.)
—Do the lyrics of this song, or title, contain references to positive social change or social improvements (or the need for these) in the lot of some social group, or is the song a kind of protest against existing social conditions? (song refers to freedom, liberation, deliverance, reform, revolution, etc.)

The proportion of songs for each year from 1946 through 1972 (except 1964) that met any one or more of these five criteria is presented in Figure 16.1. Figure 16.1 shows an increase in collective orientations during the late 1960s and early 1970s, which is consistent with our contention that there was an in-

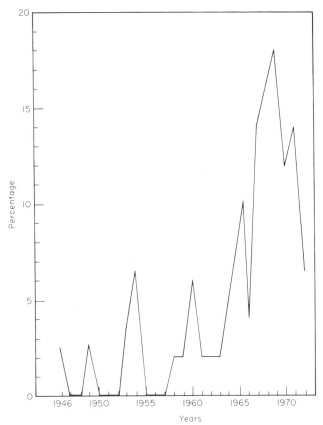

Figure 16.1 Percentage of Billboard Publication's cumulative annual bestselling soul music singles list that exhibits a collective orientation. [Adapted from Walker, 1976.]

crease in restricted codes during this period. With the passing of the civil rights era (moving into the 1970s), there appears to be a decrease in the collective orientation of black music (Figure 16.1). Although we would like to have measures of musical structure (harmonics, chords, meter, etc.), these indicators of collective orientation reflect the presence of restricted codes in that the condensed symbolism and collective orientations we do have are one of the code's defining characteristics.

Walker also coded the presence of black referents and symbols (soul, black, Afro-American, etc.) in the names of performing artists: "Is there an ethnic symbol in the name of the performing artist? (e.g., Soul Children, Jimmy Soul.)" Like the song lyrics, Figure 16.2 shows an increase in black referents and symbols in the names of performers during the late 1960s and a decline in the early 1970s. Solidarity and collective orientations in both lyrics and personal identifications of musical performers grew during the 1960s.

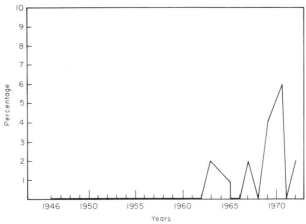

Figure 16.2 Percentage of performing artists from Billboard Publication's cumulative annual bestselling soul music singles list of those who exhibit a black ethnic referent (soul, black, Afro-American, etc.) in their name [Adapted from Walker, 1976.]

Walker also applied his coding scheme to a broader sweep of black music, and these data bear most directly on our argument. He coded a sample of 100 blues songs (taken from *The Book of Blues,* published by the Music Corporation of America [MCA]) and 30 spirituals (taken from *Thirty Negro Spirituals,* published by G. Schirmer, New York). He also divided Billboard Publication's best-selling singles into two groups, those from 1946 to 1959, which he calls "Rhythm and Blues," and those from 1960 through 1972, which he calls "Soul Music." This gives him four categories of music: Spirituals, Blues, Rhythm and Blues, and Soul. The percentage of these songs that have a collective orientation (meet one or more of his five criteria) is presented in Table 16.1. Table 16.1 shows a higher percentage of songs with collective orientations for periods of higher group solidarity: 20% of the Spirituals and 8.8% of the Soul Music. The songs of the middle period, between slavery and the civil rights movement, when group solidarity was lower, show less collective orientations: 4% of the Blues and 1.4% of the Rhythm and Blues.

TABLE 16.1 Percentage of Black Music (Songs) with a Collective Orientation

Spirituals (Slavery–1919)	Blues (1920–1945)	Rhythm and Blues (1946–1959)	Soul (1960–1972)
20.0	4.0	1.4	8.8
(N = 30)	(N = 100)	(N = 499)	(N = 601)

Source: Adapted from Walker, 1976:Table 7.

IV. Conclusion

Ritual is more than the large-scale ceremonies we are traditionally accustomed to. There is a ritual aspect to language and music; to speak, sing, or play an instrument is to participate in some ritual form, for the sounds are not random, but structured and ordered. There is a form and a pattern, and the substance of this logic constitutes the reality of linguistic and musical rituals. This is an understanding of ritual that is a step beyond observing how music accompanies ceremonies—church services, holidays, festivals, and so on—to the observation that music playing is a ritual itself. Peter Berger said that language "provides a fundamental order of relationships by the addition of syntax and grammar to vocabulary. *It is impossible to use language without participating in its order* [Berger, 1969:20; emphasis added]." To participate in its order is to use its logic and its structure and to be an agent of its code. When one speaks or makes music in a restricted code, one is contributing to the solidarity of the community, whether one is conscious of it or not. If language is ritual, then it must be true that other symbol-systems also have ritual aspects. Once we have entered the domain of symbol systems in general, almost any aspect of ordered reality qualifies. Music is one of the more obvious examples; the quest for ritual and the deciphering of symbolic forms must be extended to other less obvious areas.

Acknowledgments

I would like to thank Mark Warr for comments on an earlier draft of this paper.

References

Apel, Willi and R. T. Daniel
    1972   *The Harvard Brief Dictionary of Music.* New York:Pocket Books.
Berger, Peter L.
    1969   *The Sacred Canopy.* Garden City:Anchor.
Bergesen, Albert
    1977a "Political witch-hunts: The sacred and the subversive in cross-national perspective."
        American Sociological Review 42(April):220–233.
    1977b "Neo-ethnicity as defensive political protest." *American Sociological Review*
        42(October):823–825.
    1978a "Rituals, symbols, and society: Explicating the mechanisms of the moral order."
        American Journal of Sociology 83(January):1012–1021.
    1978b "A Durkheimian theory of political witch-hunts with the Chinese Cultural Revolution
        of 1966–1969 as an example." *Journal for the Scientific Study of Religion*
        17(March):19–29.

Bernstein, Basil
    1975 *Class, Codes and Control.* New York:Schocken Books.
Charters, Samuel
    1970 *The Poetry of Blues.* New York:Avon.
Cohn, Nick
    1969 *Rock: From the Beginning.* New York:Stein and Day.
Collier, James Lincoln
    1973 *Inside Jazz.* New York:Four Winds Press.
Douglas, Mary
    1966 *Purity and Danger.* Harmondsworth:Penguin.
    1970 *Natural Symbols.* New York:Pantheon.
Erikson, Kai T.
    1966 *The Wayward Puritans.* New York:Wiley.
Feather, Leonard
    1957 *The Book of Jazz: From Then till Now.* New York:Horizon Press.
Goffman, Erving
    1956 "The nature of deference and demeanor." *American Anthropologist* 58:473–502.
Haralambos, Michael
    1970 "Soul music and blues: Their meaning and relevance in northern United States black ghettos." In Norman E. Whitten, Jr. and John F. Szwed (eds.), *Afro-American Anthropology,* New York:The Free Press.
Hofstadter, Richard
    1956 *The Age of Reform.* New York:Knopf.
Johnson, James Weldon and J. R. Johnson
    1969 *The Books of American Negro Spirituals.* New York:The Viking Press.
Keil, Charles
    1966 *Urban Blues.* Chicago:University of Chicago Press.
Levine, Lawrence W.
    1971 "Slave songs and slave consciousness." Pp. 99–130 in Tamara K. Hareven (ed.), *Anonymous Americans: Explorations in Nineteenth-Century Social History.* Englewood Cliffs, New Jersey:Prentice-Hall.
Stearns, Marshall W.
    1956 *The Story of Jazz.* New York:Oxford University Press.
Tilly, Charles, Louise Tilly, and Richard Tilly
    1975 *The Rebellious Century, 1830–1930.* Cambridge:Harvard University Press.
Walker, Robert
    1975 *Society and Soul.* Unpublished dissertation, Stanford University.
Walton, Ortiz M.
    1972 *Music: Black, White and Blue.* New York:Morrow.
Williams, Martin
    1970 *The Jazz Tradition.* New York:Oxford University Press.

Chapter 17

Rational Exchange and Individualism: Revival Religion in the U.S., 1870–1890

GEORGE M. THOMAS

I. Introduction

This chapter examines the particular brand of revival religion that swept the United States during the nineteenth century. American life was organized around exchange and individualism in the colonial period, but, with rapid economic development early in the nineteenth century, an international market penetrated all social life, causing an expansion of rational individualism. As the central, guiding cultural myth, rational individualism made meaningful the rational organization of exchange; people used it throughout the century to restructure knowledge in the religious, political, and other social spheres. Revivalism embraced the new organization of social life. As an institutionalized system of knowledge, it articulated a unified cosmos centered on the individual. Revival religion, therefore, not only legitimated rational exchange but also supported moral reform and the development of a national polity in which each person was directly tied to the central state as a national citizen.

The Religious Dimension:
New Directions in Quantitative Research

A general contention of this chapter is that changes in organizational or cultural context or in patterns of institutionalized exchange are sufficient for effecting the rise of revivalism or for conversion from one reality to another; it is not necessary to postulate accompanying psychological or sociological crises. For example, Douglas (1966, 1970) argues that magic and ritual constitute a set of definitions and propositions used to structure and mediate reality; religious movements are carriers of new or different cosmologies.

This approach underlies the literature that examines the conflict between Christianity and society (e.g., Berger, 1967; Ellul, 1975; Niebuhr, 1951). The general interpretative structure of a society constitutes a unified cosmic order. Institutions within the society are bound to this moral order by means of specific rules that delineate legitimate meaning, activity, and organization. Christianity as an institution is positioned within this context. Discrepancies between it and the cultural environment derive from basic differences in cosmologies, and they result in a reduction of Christianity's legitimacy relative to the assumed cultural myth. Social movements and long-term trends within Christianity or within any institution are often based on the rhetorical requirements of the cultural environment: Such movements gain legitimacy by grounding institutional change in the external structure. I pursue these general ideas by first describing the intimate relationship between rational exchange and the guiding myth of individualism. I then show that a rational market expanded in the early nineteenth-century United States, creating a cultural environment radically centered on the individual. At the same time, a new revivalism burgeoned and was built, in part, from the external myth of individualism; revival religion was linked to this mythology and to an individualistic organization of exchange throughout the 1800s. In order to test this interpretation, I examine the relationship between individuation and the maintenance of revivalism in the latter part of the century.

II. The Rise and Evolution of the Rational Market

In a local small-scale market, transactions among individuals are interpreted as group exchange. The individual acts as a member of a social grouping and is restricted in exchange by rules that reaffirm the individual's place in the group and the group's position within the larger social system. Examples of this include feudalism and most tribal systems in which the interpretative structures of interaction are bonds of loyalty and kinship. When such communal systems expand into or are incorporated within a larger and more rationalized market, exhange is less regulated by these structures. Individuals become their own agents, and rational calculation comprises the new logic of social life. In short, this transformation increases the level of individuation: The degree to which the individual carries out transactions as an agent of himself or herself, independent of group memberships and of the interrelations of corporate actors (Durkheim, 1933; Marx, 1971). Highly individuated systems are ones, for example, in which small, productive family farms and small-scale entrepreneurs in business and industry engage in long-distance trade.[1]

Individuation affects all members of a population penetrated by rational exchange. Owners are motivated by private gain, unrestrained by communal commitments and definitions. Workers sell their labor in the market for wages and are not tied by custom or law to a particular position or life style, although they certainly may be constrained by particular market conditions.

Once established, the rational market evolves toward the concentration of capital and the prevalence of large corporations. This development does not affect the centrality of the individual or the fact that people are agents of themselves. However, these conditions do decrease the individual's efficacy. For both owner and laborer, success comes to depend on economic and social organizations—industrial corporations, labor unions, farmer cooperatives, or banks—rather than on the autonomous activity of the individual. Production becomes attributed to corporate entities rather than to particular people.

This study deals specifically with religious movements arising from and maintained within a system high in both individuation and efficacy of the individual, a system characterized by "effectual individuation."

III. The Construction of a Unified Cosmos: Individualism

The process of market penetration and the rise of individuation are usually interpreted in the sociological literature as an objective and phenomenological destruction of the traditional world, with social movements resulting from disorganization (see Chirot and Ragin, 1975, for a summary). This argument fails to recognize that within an individuated system persons and interactions are still linked to collective definitions. Activity is stripped of rules that maintain traditional corporate boundaries, but rational exchange entails a new interpretative system, a new cosmos, that shifts the underlying criterion of exchange from traditional structures to rational calculation (Weber, 1930). The

---

[1] Examples of noncommunal commercialized systems low in individuation are plantations, lumber camps, and mining towns. Routine long-distance trade is an important dimension in that it increases the degree to which transactions are monetarized and placed within a frame of reference exogenous to the local community. A system in which exchange is largely confined to local communities, as was that of the United States at the start of the nineteenth century, is usually much less monetarized, and transactions are interpreted and governed by a communal moral order.

logic of rational calculation levels individuals in relation to group characteristics: Everyone is a legitimate member and exchange partner within the ideologies of social equality, universality, and individual autonomy and freedom.[2] In short, transactions within an individuated system still have social meaning, but meaning centers on the individual: Individuals are not categorized according to group membership or in relation to group boundaries but are given value and related to other types of entities independent of corporate units (Durkheim, 1933; Goffman, 1956; Teggart, 1941).

The new cosmos of individualism stands in an intimate relationship with the individuation of social exchange; the two cannot be abstracted in isolation from each other. Individualism as institutional knowledge is grounded in the system of individuated activity, but it also expands the institutional preconditions under which rational exchange makes sense:

1. It is only when the general interpretative structure includes definitions of the individual as a minimally sovereign entity in the first place that rational exchange is conceivable and sensible (Weber, 1930).

2. When a rational market subsequently increases in value and penetrates all social life, each person becomes accountable as the primary unit of action. At a general level, any entity that is at the center of activity or attention becomes the focal point of institutional knowledge. Within rational exchange, the individual dominates the daily routine, and "personality" as a social concept is placed in a key position within the emergent cosmos. Furthermore, when the system of exchange is organized around effectual individuals, the person is defined as an autonomous agent oriented toward direct control over the external environment.[3]

3. Thus, with the expansion of an individuated system, the general interpretative structure becomes more radically centered on the individual, and the scope of this rational individualism is extended to all areas of life.[4]

In short, rational exchange and rational individualism go hand in hand: The

---

[2]These elements are ideals that can be qualified by rationalizations built into the knowledge system. The inequalities that inevitably arise within capitalism become interpreted in terms of individual motives, abilities, and goals, resulting in the elaboration of myths and rituals of the personality.

[3]When the system is characterized by rules that establish ineffectual individuals, the person remains the focal point of knowledge; however, "personality" and personal activity are seen to be controlled by mechanistic and often external processes. The personality is introspective and exerts control only through psychically redefining the situation by projecting internal space outward, as exemplified in modern societies by psychoanalysis, self-awareness, and self-actualization.

[4]It is, therefore, not entirely adequate to say that definitions of individuality did not exist before the rise of rational exchange; rather, the latter presupposes the existence of individual entities. For example, in the history of the West, Christianity, even the Roman Catholic forms, emphasized the authority and sacredness of each person. The "great transformation" that took place in the sixteenth and seventeenth centuries, therefore, did not introduce *de novo* conceptions of the individual. Rather, as rational exchange expanded, the interpretative structure became more ex-

greater the effectual individuation of social life, the greater the general cultural myth and institutional knowledge are characterized by effectual individualism.

Within everyday affairs, actors do not carry with them the entire picture of the cosmos. Each concrete situation is governed by particular rules and categories that make parts of the cultural system relevant, knowable, and sanctionable (Douglas, 1966; Garfinkel, 1967). The new cultural reality of rational individualism emerges at a very general level, and actors within social movements construct specific rules by applying this cosmos to all spheres of social life. In this manner, the general cosmos is specified in detailed rules within the different social spheres. It thereby constitutes a cultural environment for any given institution or institutional realm, including "economic" activity, affecting the structure of knowledge of all social spheres and causing them to become isomorphic with each other.[5] The underlying mechanism of this process is legitimacy: The general cosmos or cultural myth is a binding, external structure to which the knowledge and specific rules of each institution must conform; the greater the isomorphism between a knowledge system or an institution and the environmental myth, the more legitimate is the knowledge system.

In actuality, there are several different factions within an institutional setting, each supporting its own particular knowledge structure. That group whose system is most isomorphic to the cultural environment will be the most successful in attracting adherents; there is a movement toward the more legitimate system.[6]

As a general cultural myth, rational individualism is used to restructure religious knowledge. There are three important dimensions in the development of increasing individualism within religion. First, the religious system increasingly focuses on the personality as a unique and sacred object, and each

---

clusively centered on completely sovereign persons, and the scope of the system was extended to all realms of life.

[5] The idea of social spheres is found in several theorists (e.g., Weber, 1946), and the concept of a general myth or metaphor that integrates various life-spheres or situations is present in the work of, among others, Levi-Strauss (1962), Burke (1969), and Dooyeweerd (1969). In the creation of specific rules within the various spheres, material interest certainly plays a role, either to support or to undermine isomorphism. However, the polemics of this issue have obscured the fact that knowledge and the *organization* of activity are institutionalized and, as such, confront all members, independent of class interest (see Bendix, 1956; Meyer, 1978).

[6] If there is no knowledge structure within an institutional setting that is isomorphic to the new cultural myth, one will be created by a social movement. Factions that are illegitimate relative to the environment may resist change by tactics such as symbolic annihilation, compartmentalization, or power. When such resistance is great, additional processes become relevant: violence, solidarity, or sectarian or subcultural organization. Any empirical study must either take such tactics into account or ascertain that their use and effects are minimal, as they were in the United States of the nineteenth century.

person takes on a more active role in relation to the "Holy."[7] Second, corporate religious authority is progressively reduced, approaching the form of either an associational organization or a manager of rituals and ceremonies. For example, religious bodies in the United States are primarily voluntary associations (e.g., Lenski, 1961; cf. the analysis of Japan by Davis, 1977), whereas European churches tend to manage individual and collective rituals. The third dimension is often ignored in the analysis of religion. Although ecclesiastical authority declines, corporate reality is not negated. On the contrary, religious individualism constitutes a universalism on which is constructed the concept of a "moral community." That the individual is more directly tied to the sacred cosmos and to the moral collective reinforces the immediacy and relevance of the sovereignty of the collective.[8]

These ideas can be summarized by the following general proposition: The more social life is characterized by effectual individuation, the greater the legitimacy of a religious system that is centered on efficacious individuals, and the greater that religion's growth in adherents.[9] Nineteenth-century revivalism was just such a system, built on personal autonomy and control. The resulting implication is that revival religion was tied to rational, individualistic exchange throughout the century.

IV. Individuation and Revivalistic Piety in the United States of the Nineteenth Century

The United States was organized around petty capitalism and trade with England early in the colonial period. By the beginning of the nineteenth century, the northern states[10] were dominated by self-sufficient individuals and families organized within local, community-based capitalistic systems only loosely tied to the larger international market. Economic growth accelerated

---

[7] A system based on personal efficacy gives the individual greater control relative to the sacred. Within a system based on ineffectual individuals, personal action is passive, introspective, and internally oriented. Examples of the latter are found in the movements of the 1960s and 1970s toward drugs, meditation, astrology, and mysticism in general.

[8] This process is directly related to the concomitant emergence of individualism and the sovereignty of the nation-state: The reduction of corporate ecclesiastical authority takes place not only in the face of rising individualism but also in the context of the individual's direct link to the national collective and of the increase in the state's authority over social life (Boli-Bennett, 1978; Ellul, 1967).

[9] This discussion assumes that systems can be ordered according to their degree of individualism. For example, Arminianism, with its emphasis on free will and on personal self-determination and its deemphasis of ecclesiastical authority, is more individualistic than Calvinism. Calvinism cannot be labeled nonindividualistic in any absolute ahistorical sense, for it, in turn, marked a very dramatic increase in individualism over Catholicism.

[10] The present study is concerned with the northern United States. An extension of the analysis to several southern states is in progress.

with the technological advances of the 1820s, reaching a "take-off" in the 1840s (Bruchey, 1968; North, 1961). This constituted a breakdown of the local market and the incorporation of the local community into an international one, thus marking an increase in individuation. Individually owned and managed family farms and small-scale, self-employed capitalists made up most of the production (Moore, 1966; North, 1961). The scale and the concentration of capital and labor grew quickly in the industrial sector after the Civil War but did not emerge in force in the agrarian sector until the turn of the century (Cochran and Miller, 1961; Hays, 1957).

From the beginning, Christianity in the United States was more individualistic and pietistic than in Europe. However, as late as the mid-1700s the colonists still largely adhered to Calvinism, as is evidenced by the nature of the "First Great Awakening." A new type of revivalism emerged in the "Second Great Awakening" and swept across the country in the 1820s and 1830s. Historians of American religion have emphasized the emotional nature of this revivalism, interpreting it as an irrational reaction to social disorganization, relative deprivation, or oppression. However, emotionalism was an element built into the larger, more basic framework of individualism. Some of the elements of this structure did not differ greatly from components of European and eighteenth-century American pietism that were predominantly Calvinistic, but the revivalism was grounded in Arminianism and was more radically and comprehensively centered on the individual as an autonomous, rational creature.[11]

This dramatic break with early American pietism is manifested in four elements. First, the emphasis on the individual led to conceptions of free will or Arminianism and shades of antinomianism. Each person, ultimately, could accept or reject God; personal religious experience and authority were valued above church instruction and certified doctrine (Sweet, 1944). Second, nineteenth-century revivalism coupled radical free will with a rational unity of means and ends. It saw nothing especially miraculous in a revival, because religious behavior, as all of creation, was governed by rational laws that man was to learn and to manipulate (Finney, 1835; McLoughlin, 1959). People organized evangelism around techniques for effecting conversions; the primary criterion of the proper method was success (Cross, 1950; Weisberger, 1958).

The third element was perfect sanctification. Within Arminianism, the promise of sanctification and an abundant life meant that, if a person wills it, the Spirit will entirely sanctify the believer in this life, wiping out all effects of

---

[11]Nonconformist groups such as the Quakers and the Baptists spread after the "First Great Awakening," but on a much smaller scale—if anything, the prevailing trend was toward deism and secularization. That nineteenth-century revivalism made a distinct break with eighteenth-century religion is demonstrated in the splintering of almost all denominations over the revivalism issue (e.g., Ahlstrom, 1972). Contrasting revivals in these two periods is useful for understanding revivalism in the United States and its specific nature in the nineteenth century.

original sin and of mankind's fallen nature. "True holiness" was a second blessing from God, which brought the Christian to a "higher life." Through piety expressed in outward morality, the individual held onto salvation and either strove for or continued in a state of holiness. This gave special impetus toward moral reform (Smith, 1957). It was at this point that holiness fed into the fourth element—the quest for the millennium—for, although moral reform sprang from inward piety, it was necessary for reasons other than individual experience: The nation and the earth must be regenerated through the establishment of a reformed moral community.

There are two main views of the millennium. The first, premillennialism, emphasizes the inadequacy of even regenerate persons to establish a perfect order and asserts that things will get progressively worse until Jesus returns. Postmillennialism emerged after the Reformation and involved a dramatic departure in its view of history. Instead of the world sinking further into depravity until ultimate defeat is averted only at the last minute by Christ's return, history is an unfolding of victory. Revivalism in the nineteenth century modified this theory by shifting emphasis from the work of God to the role of the individual. Revivalism made inward piety perfectable and the millennium that much more possible; Christians did not merely prepare themselves for the new age, but, by inward growth as evidenced in a moral life-style, they helped bring it about (Tuveson, 1968).

This had special significance for the United States, in that theologians even in the 1700s singled it out to lead the advance. Its leadership was not to be based on the political coercion that characterized European states, but it would be the natural outgrowth of a nation that voluntarily chose (through the moral piety of individuals) to be perfect. Thus, the decline of the colonial theocracies was not interpreted as a setback; it was the result of God allowing America to choose freely true obedience and thereby establish a sanctified moral community. The emphasis on the nation as a moral collective did not derive solely from the postmillennial element. The building of community and nation pervaded all of the components: Inward piety did not result in introspective systems unique to the individual; each had a personal relationship to God, but all individuals were related to the same God. All were bound by the same fallen situation and the same goals of salvation, sanctification, and evangelism; the rational methods that worked in one's own church would unfailingly work in other churches throughout the nation. All were members of a chosen nation and were responsible for the construction of the moral collective (see Sizer, 1978).

The institution of revivalistic piety remained intact when translated to more urban areas in the latter part of the century. Weisberger (1958) documents the fact that revivalists applied to the city the same rational technique centered on individual choice. The millennial ideal, and moral reform in general, became increasingly focused on the nation in and of itself. Holiness was also firmly institutionalized; objections against it constituted attacks on the antinomianism that it spawned. For revivalists never accepted radical antinomianism, and the increase in formalization in the latter part of the century made them even more intolerant of it. Thus, the formalization of revivalism in the then-established evengelical churches caused a greater reliance on the organizations and creeds of the denominations, but these formal structures kept intact the core elements of Arminianism, rational evangelism, holiness, the postmillennial ideal, and the concept of a national moral collectivity.[12]

In summary, by 1800 the northern United States was characterized by small-scale local markets and an individualistic religion. Early in the century, exchange relations became more individuated within an international market. Simultaneously, there emerged a new revivalism that marked a dramatic increase in religious individualism. Both the degree of market penetration and the support of revivalism varied across the country. The new organization of exchange both supported and presupposed an institutional myth of effectual individualism, and those populations or regions that were most characterized by effectual individuation were most dominated by this myth. The specifics of this cosmology were constructed within the religious and other social spheres. Those same populations, therefore, were the most given over to the effectual individualism of revival religion. The hypothesis that is tested is: The more a population was organized within an effectually individuated market, the more that population supported revivalistic piety.[13]

V. Sample and Design

In order to test this hypothesis, I use quantitative data from the 263 counties in Maine, New York, Ohio, and Iowa from 1870 to 1890.[14] Aggregate data is

[12] Countervailing movements, such as the social gospel, liberal theology, and premillennial fundamentalism, emerged at the elite level as early as the 1870s, but they did not prevail among the ministers until the 1890s and among the laymen until after the turn of the century (Ahlstrom, 1972; McLoughlin, 1967). Clearly, revivalism as a system of knowledge remained institutionalized throughout the 1800s.

[13] The relationship of revivals to the economic sphere has not been mapped out empirically in any detail. Close readings of various histories (e.g., Cross, 1950; Weisberger, 1958) reveal impressionistic evidence that revivals occurred in areas recently undergoing economic growth.

[14] Analyzing counties by states is more parsimonious than is randomly selecting from all counties in the nation. The primary reason for selecting these four states is that they represent a variety of different levels of industrialization throughout the North and the Midwest. Interest in the spread of effectual individualism would make the ideal period of study the first half of the century, but quantitative data are scarce for this period. By examining the latter part of the 1800s, the analysis is concerned with the maintenance of effectual individualism—of revivalism—in the face of rising ineffectual individualism.

appropriate because the theoretical argument is at the institutional level: The variables are relevant to institutions that confront and shape, with phenomenological force, the experience of the entire population.

A panel design is used because it best fits the argument. Given a similar number of adherents to a particular knowledge structure across various counties at time one, the number of members at time two will vary directly with the congruence of that system with the cultural environment at time one: The greater the dominance of effectual individualism at time one, the greater the adherents to revivalism at time two (controlling for revivalism at time one). This is tested by analyzing the relationship of the distribution of revivalistic memberships at time two with indicators of effectual individuation at time one (controlling for memberships at the first time point).

Most studies examine dependent variables that are weighted (i.e., divided) by population or by total religious membership. Such equations present problems of interpretation in that effects on a ratio variable may be due to effects on the numerator, the denominator, or both (Fuiguitt and Lieberson, 1974; Schuessler, 1973). To solve this problem, I use raw variables and enter population into the equation as an explicit control; this also estimates a slope for population. The basic model is shown in Equation (1), where ''cv'' is a set of other control variables, ''a'' is the constant, and ''e'' is the error term.

$$\text{revivalistic piety } t_2 = b_1 \text{ revivalistic piety } t_1 + b_2 \text{ individuation } t_1 \quad (1)$$
$$+ b_3 \text{ population } t_2 + cv + a + e$$

Although this is a straightforward model of the theoretical argument, there are several problems. One is that any variable not scaled to population, such as the indicators of individuation and industrialization described in the following section, will have artificially small effects. This can be overcome by interacting these variables with population. Substantively, a characteristic of social organization not related to population size will affect population-related variables, partly as a function of the size of the population. There are also three estimation problems: (*a*) all variables scaled to population are extremely multicollinear; (*b*) such variables are highly skewed; and (*c*) the variance of the residuals of such analyses are correlated with some of the independent variables, most notably, population. All three of these problems can be solved by using weighted least squares: If the equation is divided by population at time two, multicollinearity, distributional irregularities, and heteroscedasticity are reduced.[15]

---

[15] In order to see if heteroscedasticity was effectively reduced, residuals for the weighted equations were calculated, and their absolute values were correlated with various independent variables. The highest correlation is .18 with revivalism at time one; the correlation with population is − .11.

VI. Concepts and Measures

Effectual Individuation

This concept is concerned with the degree to which an individual acts autonomously and efficaciously, the extent to which production is attributed to the individual. Two equations are estimated: one with an agrarian index and the other with a manufacturing one. It makes little sense to argue that the organization of manufacturing affects a population's world-view if the amount of industry in that population is minuscule; the same, of course, applies to agriculture. Therefore, in the manufacturing equations, those counties in the bottom 20% of industrialization—the ratio of manufacturing production to total production in both industry and agriculture—measured at the first point in time, 1880, are excluded; the top 20% is excluded in the agrarian equations. These cutoffs correspond to less than 18% of production in manufacturing and 31% in agriculture, respectively.

Manufacturing

A negative index of effectual individuation is used by measuring the degree to which the owner is dependent on external sources and organizations. The primary relevant factor is the amount of capital needed to maintain an establishment: The greater the requisite capital, the more dependent the individual is on external organizations and the more that successful activity, as manifested in production, is attributed to forces external to the individual. Thus, capital per manufacturing establishment is a good negative index of effectual individuation. However, concentrated capital and factors of scale dominated industry during this period, resulting in a high correlation between capital per establishment and industrialization. Other analyses show that these factors are more relevant at high levels of production (Thomas, 1978). Therefore, the relationship between capital per establishment and industrialization should be less in the less industrialized counties. The sample was split at the median of industrialization, and, for the lower half, the correlation in fact drops to .24. Therefore, analyses are reported first for the entire sample and then for counties below the median of industrialization (38.3% of production in manufacturing in 1880). Capital per manufacturing establishment is measured in 1880 and is an inverse index of effectual individuation; the hypothesis predicts that it has a negative effect on support of revivalism.[16]

---

[16] Because of the focus of this chapter, I refer to capital per manufacturing establishment as a negative index of efficacious individuation, although, given the historical situation, it also can be seen as a direct index of ineffectual individuation. At the initial stage of market penetration, this variable could indicate value within the economy and would directly measure effectual individua-

Agriculture

Unlike scale-dominated industry, agriculture was still dominated by moderate-sized family farms.[17] Consequently, we can infer that farm production was phenomenologically attributed to the individual farmer. Production per farm is measured in 1880 and is used as a direct index of effectual individuation. Because of the low relationship between production and scale, the latter can be entered into the equation. That is, we can partial out of the production variable that portion of production attributable to social organization. The best indicator available is the amount of wages per farm for 1870. Production per farm, with the amount due to hired labor partialled out, is a positive measure of effectual individuation and should positively affect revivalism; the amount of wages per farm is itself a negative indicator of this concept and, according to the hypothesis, should be negatively related to revivalism. The correlation between these two agrarian variables is .72, but, after the exclusion of cases, the multicollinearity varies around .55.

Revivalistic Piety

A denomination's membership indicates in two ways the predominance within a population of that denomination's system of knowledge. It directly measures the number of *adherents,* and it also measures the visibility or phenomenological force of the institutionalized propositions relative to *everyone* in the population. The force of a knowledge system on the individual is a function of the perceived support of the propositions, which itself is largely a function of the number of members.

The denominations varied in their ascription to revivalistic piety. If particular bodies closely adhered to it, then their memberships indicate the predominance of revivalism as a cultural institution. To this end, the denominations on which there is available data are rated on a 5-point scale (0–4) according to their ascription to revivalism, as shown in Table 17.1.[18] Two

---

tion. However, within a scale-dominated system, it is interpretable only as an index of individual inefficacy. Available measures of self-employment are not used because they are even more highly related (negatively) to industrialization, even in the less industrialized counties.

[17] This is detailed elsewhere (Thomas, 1978) and is consistent with economic history (e.g., Cochran and Miller, 1961; Hays, 1957).

[18] Several historians of religion in the United States rated the denominations on the four components previously noted: freewill, rational evangelism, perfect sanctification, and postmillennialism. Additionally, I abstracted two ratings, one from various histories and one from descriptive material found in the United States Census of 1890 (see Carroll, 1912). These were then combined into one rating. The 1880 Census information of religious bodies was never compiled; the 1890 Census includes memberships, but the 1870 enumeration contains only the seating capacity of a denomination's church buildings. The latter is a good indicator of relative memberships in that there is no great variation in the ratio of seatings to memberships across denominations, with the

TABLE 17.1 Rating of Denominations on Revivalistic Pietism (A 5-Point Scale Is Used, from 0 to 4)

Adventist	0	Methodist bodies	4
Baptist bodies in general	3	Presbyterian bodies in general	3
Northern and national convention	3	U.S.A. (Northern)	3
Southern and national convention	3	U.S. (Southern)	3
Free-will	4	Cumberland	4
Primitive	0	United	2
Christian Connection	4	Protestant Episcopal	0
Congregational	3	Reformed Church in America (Dutch)	1
Disciples of Christ	4	Reformed Church in the U.S. (German)	1
Evangelical Association	3	Unitarian	3
Friends	1	United Brethren	3
Latter Day Saints	1	Universalist	1
Lutheran bodies in general	1	Roman Catholic	0
General Synod	1	Jewish	0
General Council	2		
Synodical Conference	0		

different indices are constructed from this information. The first, the radical index, measures only the most extreme forms of revivalism; it is the sum of memberships of those denominations that are rated 4. This is a conservative index in that it does not rely heavily on the subtle differentiations present in the ratings. It is based primarily on Methodism, by far the largest of the bodies rated as four. The second indicator, the inclusive index, takes full advantage of this information and decreases the dominance of Methodism: All denominational memberships are added together, weighting each body by the appropriate rating. Substantively, this scale is interpretable as the interaction between the degree to which a denomination ascribes to revivalistic pietism and its visibility or social support. The indices are measured for 1870 and 1890; the correlations between them are .85 in 1890 and .92 in 1870 (see Table 17.2).

Control Variables

Number of Foreign-Born

Immigrants during this period were primarily members of liturgical bodies antithetical to pietism. Large groups of foreign-born within a population constitute a force away from revivalism, independent of the theoretical considerations put forth here. Therefore, the number of foreign-born in a county at time two, 1890, is controlled.

Industrialization

Industrialization is a "proxy variable" for a myriad of social dimensions. Given that the economic indicators previously described delineate the dimension of effectual individuation, industrialization is interpreted within the conventional framework that views the revival as a rural–agrarian institution. Thus, it will have a negative effect on revivalism. It is entered into the equation at time two and is measured by the ratio of manufacturing production to the sum of manufacturing and agricultural production.

Population

Because raw values are used throughout the analyses, population is entered as an explicit control.

---

exception of Catholicism, which is rated zero and does not enter the analyses. This is reflected in the high autocorrelation of the two indices (see Table 17.2). For convenience, I refer to memberships at both points in time. Finally, although use of denominational memberships may ignore possible internal dissension, different internal factions fighting over revivalism had already by this time split into distinct groups that were relatively homogeneous in relation to this dimension.

TABLE 17.2 Correlation Matrix of the Variables[a]

	1	2	3	4	5	6[b]	7[c]	8	X̄	SD
1. Inclusive index revival piety, 90	—								.59	.21
2. Inclusive index revival piety, 70	.68 (211)	—							1.34	.77
3. Radical index revival piety, 90	.85 (260)	.58 (214)	—						.08	.04
4. Radical index revival piety, 70	.66 (226)	.92 (214)	.65 (229)	—					.20	.15
5. Capital/manufacturing establishment, 80	-.20 (258)	-.16 (214)	-.25 (261)	-.11 (228)	—				6.66[d]	6.86[d]
6. Production/Farm, 80[b]	.19 (210)	-.05 (210)	.14 (210)	-.02 (210)	-.25 (210)	—			6.73[e]	2.51[e]
7. Wages/farm, 70[c]	-.28 (210)	-.05 (210)	-.27 (210)	-.08 (210)	.32 (210)	.75 (210)	—		1.03[e]	.98[e]
8. Proportion of production in manufacturing, 90	-.11 (260)	-.07 (214)	-.24 (263)	-.02 (229)	.61 (261)	-.25 (210)	.39 (210)	—	.48	.28
9. Foreign-born, 90	-.66 (260)	-.65 (214)	-.67 (263)	-.62 (229)	.21 (261)	.02 (210)	.27 (210)	.11 (263)	.13	.08

[a] Number of cases in parentheses; all variables
Scaled to population are divided by population, 1890.
[b] Controlling for wages/farm, 1870.
[c] Controlling for production/farm, 1880.
[d] In thousands.
[e] In hundreds.

365

VII. Results

The correlations among the religious, economic, and control variables are reported in Table 17.2. All are in the direction hypothesized. Additionally, there is very little multicollinearity except where already noted. The core of the results are seen in the regression equations. Table 17.3 presents the unstandardized slopes and their standard errors for the independent and control variables in relation to the inclusive index of revivalism.[19] The autoregression term is large and significant, indicating a stability of denominational memberships; but it also indicates a fair amount of change during this period. The population coefficient is also substantial. The number of foreign-born in a county dominates the analysis, with large negative effects on revivalism. These relationships hold both for the whole sample and for the less industrialized counties.[20] Equations (1) and (4) show that industrialization negatively influences revivalistic membership and support conventional lines of reasoning. The statistical significance of the coefficient is lower for the less industrialized counties, but this is most likely due to the small number of cases, in that the actual slopes are similar.

Equations (2) and (3) show that, without controlling for industrialization, the inverse index of effectual individuation—capital per establishment—has a significant negative effect on revivalism. In the less industrialized counties, this variable and industrialization are not highly correlated, permitting the inclusion of both in the model. When this is done in Equation (6), the slope of industrialization is decreased and not significant, whereas that of capital per establishment is not altered, and remains significant. It, therefore, seems safe to infer that effectual individuation, as inversely measured by the average amount of capital invested in a manufacturing establishment, is a dimension distinct from industrialization. These variables are historically and theoretically intertwined and, therefore, have closely related consequences for support of revival religion; but effectual individuation has causal effects that are independent of industrialization.

---

[19] Because there is a directional hypothesis for all of the variables, one-tailed tests of significance are used.

[20] Part of the high relationship between foreign-born populations and revivalism is due to measurement error in the latter variable among immigrant groups. For example, some Lutheran bodies are rated one because in relation to, say, Methodism, they are rather liturgical. However, in relation to mainline Lutheran bodies, they represent a move toward revivalism, possibly warranting a higher score. Ratings of immigrant bodies better taking into account the traditions from which they were formed are being constructed. If anything, this measurement error is attenuating the effects of theoretical interest: Analyses were performed that excluded counties with a large proportion of foreign-born: Whereas the coefficient of foreign-born was reduced, the other variables had identical or larger effects on the acceptance of revivalism.

TABLE 17.3 Panel Analysis of Revivalistic Piety, 1870–1890: Inclusive Index[a]

Eq.	Capital per manufacturing establishment, 1880 XPop90[b]	Production per farm, 1880 XPop90[c]	Wages per farm, 1870 XPop90[c]	Proportion production in manufacturing, 1890 XPop90	Foreign-born, 1890	Population, 1890[d]	Revival piety index, 1870	Constant	Cases
All counties									
1				−.17(.04)**	−.82(.16)**	.66	.12(.02)**	−769	211
2[e]		−.23(.14)*			−.79(.18)**	.53	.14(.02)**	−222	194
3[f]		.25(.07)**	−.52(.26)**	−.14(.06)**	−.96(.21)**	.52	.12(.02)**	−317	159
Counties in bottom half of industrialization, 1880[g]									
4				−.16(.11)*	−1.2(.26)**	.72	.10(.02)**	−425	86
5[e]	−1.8(.72)**				−1.0(.31)**	.59	.12(.03)**	1051	69
6[e]	−1.9(.79)**			.06(.15)	−1.0(.31)**	.56	.12(.03)**	1427	69
7	.21(.10)**	−.78(.33)**		−.12(.11)	−1.1(.26)**	.60	.11(.02)**	−334	86

[a] Weighted least squares estimates of slopes; standard errors in parentheses; one-tailed test of significance: * .05 < p ≤ .10; ** p ≤ .05.
[b] In hundreds of thousands of dollars.
[c] In thousands of dollars.
[d] Standard error not calculated.
[e] Counties with less than 18% production in manufacturing in 1880 excluded.
[f] Counties with more than 69% production in manufacturing in 1880 excluded.
[g] Counties with more than 38.3% of production in manufacturing excluded.

367

The coefficients of the agrarian indices are reported in Equations (3) and (7). For comparison purposes, they are estimated in the less-industrialized counties even though there is no problem of multicollinearity with industrialization. Production per farm is a positive index of effectual individuation and, as predicted, has a positive influence on the acceptance of revivalism. Wages per farm is included so as to partial out factors of scale that may be entailed in the first variable, and it is substantively interpreted as an inverse indicator of efficacy. In support of the hypothesis, it decreases the adherence to revival religion. Thus, in line with the general argument, effectual individuation within the agrarian sector, as measured by these two variables, has a positive causal relationship to the acceptance of revivalistic piety.

Table 17.4 shows identical analyses for the radical scale of revival religion. Taking into account the difference in metric of the two dependent variables, the results are substantively identical.

It could be argued that the independent variables are affecting total religious membership or religiosity, resulting in spurious relationships to pietistic memberships. This is not credible in relation to the radical index, which includes a small proportion of total members. Nevertheless, total membership was included as a control in each of the reported equations. Although it had a large positive relationship to both scales of revivalism, the other coefficients were either identical to or larger than those reported.

VIII. Summary and Discussion

The major conclusion of the analyses is that effectual individuation of exchange relations increased the acceptance and maintenance of revival religion, independent of the more general nature of industrialization and other relevant variables. Thus, both the hypothesis and the general direction of the theoretical interpretation are supported. Individual rational exchange is intimately related to individualistic knowledge-systems like nineteenth-century revivalism. This revivalism and other similar religious movements are legitimated by the external structure, and they further articulate that structure within a new unified cosmos. The present analysis, coupled with evidence that nineteenth-century revivalism tended toward moral and social reform (Hammond, 1974; Smith, 1957) and favored the nationalistic ideology of the Republican party (Ahlstrom, 1972; Jensen, 1971; Kleppner, 1970; Thomas, 1978), implies that nineteenth-century revivalism was an attempt to create a new moral and political order, one in which each person was directly linked to God as a free-willed and potentially perfect individual and to the nation-state as a national citizen.

This supports an institutional view not only of religious symbols but also of

TABLE 17.4 Panel Analysis of Revivalistic Piety, 1870–1890: Radical Index[a]

Eq.	Capital per manufacturing establishment, 1880 XPop90[b]	Production per farm, 1880 XPop90[c]	Wages per farm, 1870 XPop90[c]	Proportion production in manufacturing, 1890 XPop90	Foreign-born, 1890	Population, 1890[d]	Revival piety index, 1870	Constant	Cases
All counties									
1				−.04(.01)**	−.16(.03)**	.10	.12(.02)**	−80	229
2[e]	−.05(.03)**				−.12(.03)**	.07	.15(.02)**	111	201
3[f]		.04(.01)**	−.10(.05)**	−.04(.01)**	−.20(.04)**	.09	.11(.02)**	−46	175
Counties in bottom half of industrialization, 1880[g]									
4				−.04(.02)**	−.27(.05)**	.12	.08(.02)**	−30	102
5[e]	−.35(.16)**				−.19(.07)**	.09	.12(.03)**	272	74
6[e]	−.34(.17)**			−.01(.03)	−.19(.07)**	.09	.12(.03)**	242	74
7		.02(.02)	−.13(.06)**	−.03(.02)*	−.25(.05)**	.12	.09(.02)**	−59	102

[a] Weighted least squares estimates of slopes; standard errors in parentheses; one-tailed test of significance: * .05 ≤ p < .10; ** p ≤ .05.

[b] In hundreds of thousands of dollars.

[c] In thousands of dollars.

[d] Standard error not calculated.

[e] Counties with less than 18% production in manufacturing in 1880 excluded.

[f] Counties with more than 69% production in manufacturing in 1880 excluded.

[g] Counties with more than 38.3% of production in manufacturing excluded.

their relationship to social life and to other social spheres. Any institution must meet the rhetorical demands made by the larger cultural environment or lose legitimacy, relevance, and support. Social movements are the carriers of both the demands and the legitimacy process.

The present study uses these ideas to examine the inherent and often subtle tension between Christianity and its cultural environment: between revealed truth and human knowledge: between Christ and culture (Niebuhr, 1951). It places the church's struggle with this conflict in a social context. The nature and scope of this essay do not allow for the discussion of other important considerations. However, I do emphasize that it is ill-founded to espouse a scientific reductionism by asserting that the cultural order totally determined revivalistic piety: This is an illusion. It is also not appropriate to simplify the individual and corporate tensions involved by claiming that the revivalists simply "sold out" to sociocultural trends: A more complex and more adequate "prophetic critique" is required. Nevertheless, it is clear that nineteenth-century revival religion, as an institution was grounded in and gained legitimacy from a rational, individualistic world that itself was intimately linked to the expansion of a rational market.

Acknowledgments

The ideas in this essay owe a great debt to John Meyer. This chapter also benefited from close, critical readings by John Boli-Bennett and Phillip E. Hammond, discussions with Mel Fagan and Karen Thomas, the expertise of Eldon Ernst and Sandra S. Sizer, and the editorship of Robert Wuthnow. I thank the Inter-University Consortium for Political and Social Research for access to their data files.

References

Ahlstrom, Sydney
    1972 *A Religious History of the American People.* New Haven:Yale University Press.
Bendix, Reinhard
    1956 *Work and Authority in Industry.* Berkeley:University of California Press.
Berger, Peter
    1967 "A sociological view of the secularization of theology." *Journal for the Scientific Study of Religion* 6:3–16.
Boli-Bennett, John
    1978 "Human rights or state expansion? Cross-national definitions of constitutional rights, 1870–1970." Presented at the Conference on Global Human Rights, Denver and Boulder, Colorado.
Bruchey, Stuart
    1968 *The Roots of American Economic Growth, 1607–1861.* New York:Harper Torchbooks.

Burke, Kenneth
  1969 *A Rhetoric of Motives*. Berkeley:University of California Press.
Carroll, H. K.
  1912 *The Religious Forces of the United States*. New York:Scribner's Sons.
Chirot, Daniel and Charles Ragin
  1975 "The market, tradition, and peasant rebellions: The case of Romania in 1907."
        American Sociological Review 40:428–444.
Cochran, Thomas C. and William Miller
  1961 *The Age of Enterprise: A Social History of Industrial America*. New York:Harper
        Torchbooks.
Cross, Whitney R.
  1950 *The Burned-over District: The Social and Intellectual History of Enthusiastic Religion
        in Western New York, 1800-1850*. New York:Harper Torchbooks.
Davis, Winston Bradley
  1977 *Toward Modernity: A Developmental Typology of Popular Religious Affiliations in
        Japan*. Ithaca:Cornell University East Asia Papers.
Dooyeweerd, Herman
  1969 *A New Critique of Theoretical Thought*. Nutley, New Jersey: The Presbyterian and
        Reformed Publishing Company.
Douglas, Mary
  1966 *Purity and Danger*. London:Penguin Books.
  1970 *Natural Symbols*. New York:Vintage Books.
Durkheim, Emile
  1933 *The Division of Labor in Society*. New York:The Free Press.
Ellul, Jacques
  1967 *The Political Illusion*. New York:Alfred Knopf.
  1975 *The New Demons*. New York:The Seabury Press.
Finney, Charles Grandison
  1835/1960 *Lectures on Revivals of Religion (W. G. McLoughlin, ed.)*. Cambridge,
        Massachusetts: Harvard University Press.
Fuiguitt, G. and S. Lieberson
  1974 "Correlation of ratios or difference scores having common terms." Pp. 128–144 in
        H. Costner (ed.), *Sociological Methodology, 1973-74*. San Francisco:Jossey-Bass.
Garfinkel, Harold
  1967 *Studies in Ethnomethodology*. Englewood Cliffs, New Jersey:Prentice-Hall.
Goffman, Erving
  1956 "The nature of deference and demeanor." *American Anthropologist* 58:473–502.
Hammond, John L.
  1974 "Revival religion and antislavery politics." *American Sociological Review* 39:175–186.
Hays, Samuel P.
  1957 *The Response to Industrialism, 1885-1914*. Chicago:Chicago University Press.
Jensen, Richard J.
  1971 *The Winning of the Midwest: Social and Political Conflict, 1888-1896*. Chicago:
        University of Chicago Press.
Kleppner, Paul
  1970 *The Cross of Culture: A Social Analysis of Midwestern Politics, 1850-1890*. New York:
        The Free Press.

Lenski, Gerhard
  1961   *The Religious Factor.* Garden City, New York:Doubleday.

Levi-Strauss, Claude
  1962   *Totemism.* Boston:The Beacon Press.

McLoughlin, William G. Jr.
  1959   *Modern Revivalism: Charles Grandison Finney to Billy Graham.* New York:Ronald Press.
  1967   "Is there a third force in Christendom?" *Daedalus* 96(Winter):43–68.

Marx, Karl
  1971   *The Grundrisse (D. McLellan, ed. and trans.).* New York:Harper Torchbooks.

Meyer, John
  1978   "The effects of education as an institution." *American Journal of Sociology* 83:55–77.

Moore, Barrington Jr.
  1966   *Social Origins of Dictatorship and Democracy.* Boston:The Beacon Press.

Niebuhr, H. Richard
  1951   *Christ and Culture.* New York:Harper and Row.

North, Douglass C.
  1961   *The Economic Growth of the United States, 1790–1860.* Englewood Cliffs, New Jersey:Prentice-Hall.

Schuessler, K.
  1973   "Ratio variables and path models." In A. Goldberger and O. Duncan (eds.), *Structural Equation Models in Social Science.* New York:Seminar Press.

Sizer, Sandra S.
  1978   "Politics and apolitical religion: The great urban revivals of the late nineteenth century." In *Gospel Hymns and Social Religion.* Philadelphia, Pennsylvania:Temple University Press.

Smith, Timothy L.
  1957   *Revivalism and Social Reform in Mid-Nineteenth-Century America.* New York:Abingdon Press.

Sweet, William Warren
  1944   *Revivalism in America: Its Origin, Growth, and Decline.* New York:Charles Scribner's Sons.

Teggart, Fredrick J.
  1941   *Processes of History.* Berkeley, California:University of California Press.

Thomas, George M.
  1978   *Institutional Knowledge and Social Movements: Rational Exchange, Revival Religion, and Nation-Building in the U.S., 1870–1896.* Doctoral Dissertation, Stanford University.

Tuveson, Ernest Lee
  1968   *Redeemer Nation: The Idea of America's Millennial Role.* Chicago:University of Chicago Press.

Weber, Max
  1930   *The Protestant Ethic and the Spirit of Capitalism.* New York:Charles Scribner's Sons.
  1946   *Essays in Sociology (H. Gerth and C. W. Mills, eds.).* New York:Oxford University Press.

Weisberger, Bernard A.
  1958   *They Gathered at the River.* New York:Quadrangle.

Index

convergences among religious groups, 180–181, 190–192
crude divorce rates, 179
Marxian theory of religion, 309
Mass society, 317
Meditation, 58
Methodists, 117–119, 364
Migration, *see* Regional migration, Urbanization
Mobility, *see* Residential mobility
Monotheism, in primitive societies, 299–309
Moral climates, 311–330
Morality, 60–61, 64
Moral order, 277–294, 352
Mormons, 164–173
Musical codes, 336–337
Mysticism, 49, 124, 142–151

O

Occult beliefs, 53–54
Occupations
  and religious commitment, 142–151, 200–204
  and work ethic, 253–255
Optimism, 122–124

P

Parapsychology, 53–54
Plausibility structures, 40
Political attitudes
  as moral barometers, 277 294
  and religious orientations, 64, 76–79
Political authority, and high gods in primitive societies, 299–309
Political diversification, 317–318
Political parties, 320–322
Political witch-hunts, 277–278
Prayer, 122–123
Presbyterians, 117–119, 202
Primordial social ties, 314–316
Protestant ethic, 200, 208, *see also* Work ethic
Protestants
  church attendance among, 118–120
  and delinquency, 164–173
  ethnic backgrounds of, 115–118
  and marriage dissolution, 118–193
  mixed marriages among, 121–122

and mobility and church attendance, 260–272
and socioeconomic status, 200–206
and values of achievement, 206–210
and work ethic, 244–246

R

Racial attitudes, and images of God, 81–84
Regional migration, and church attendance, 267–270
Religion, confidence in, 282–288
  in primitive societies, 299–309
Religious affiliation
  and achievement motivation, 206–210
  and delinquency, 159–60, 164–169
  effect on images of God, 88–90
  and ethnicity, 115–118
  and marriage dissolution, 188–189
  and remarriage, 192
  in San Francisco Bay area, 48–49
  and socioeconomic status, 200–206
  and status inconsistency, 142–151
  and work ethic, 244–246
Religious commitment
  in criminological theory, 157–158
  defined, 18, 31
  and delinquency, 158–159
  dimensions of, 21, 35–37
  and ethnicity, 118–130
  and income, 142–151
  indexes of, 22–28
  and occupation, 142–151
  and status inconsistency, 136–137
  and work ethic, 246–249
Religious experiences, 56, 124, 142–151
Religious music, 337–349
Religious pluralism, index of, 329–330
Remarriage, and religious affiliation, 192
Residential mobility, and church attendance, 262–266
Revivalism, 351–373
Ritual, 277–294, 333–349

S

Satanism, 51–53
Scientology, 51–53
Sects, 93–105, 136
Secularization, 66, 120